MOON

W9-BQI-128

BELIZE CAYES

LEBAWIT LILY GIRMA

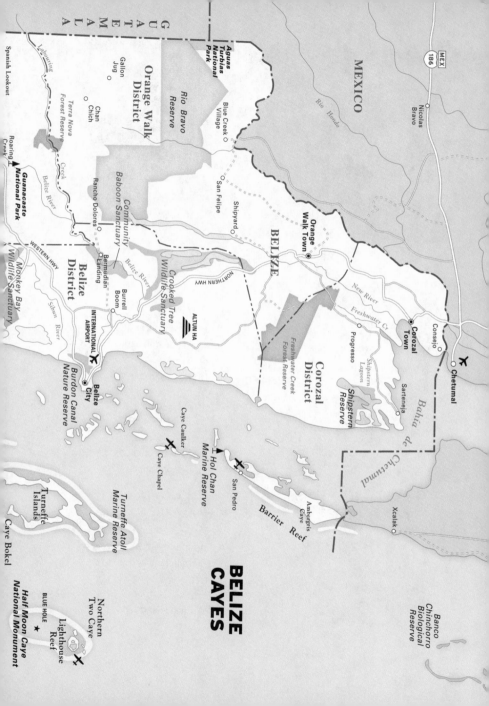

Contents

DISCOVER
the Belize Cayes

On my first trip to Belize, I immediately hopped on a connecting flight to Ambergris Caye. As fate would have it, the plane was full and I was seated next to the pilot. In a matter of minutes, the cockpit views of Belize's Caribbean coastline overshadowed my angst about flying in a puddle jumper. Surrounded by a vast expanse of sapphire and jade—sea and reef—we soared over one speck of land after another. Mangrove clumps gave way to larger plots brimming with white sand and coconut trees, beckoning from our windows. Years later, these aerial views still take my breath away.

Belize's cayes are everyone's deserted island fantasy come true. While the Belize Barrier Reef is the country's best-known asset, first-timers miss many of the islands winding along its 180 miles. More than 200 islands are scattered along the country's shoreline, north to south. They range from uninhabited plots to at least 20 coral isles offering cozy cabanas, postcard-worthy beaches, and utter seclusion. Others, like Laughingbird National Park, a World Heritage Site, are protected swoops of sand where park rangers stand ready to receive day-trippers.

The northern cayes are the most visited—Ambergris being the only caye with paved roads and cars—not least for offering a wide array of tourist amenities and

Clockwise from top left: diver hovering above coral at South Water Caye; luxury treehouse; Silk Cayes; Hopkins Beach; beach near Hopkins.

proximity to Belize City. Those who venture off the tourist trail and head south, just an additional one- to two-hour journey, are rewarded with the most spectacular Caribbean scenery. Tobacco Caye's rustic, overwater cabanas, Ranguana Caye's charming cottages, and Glover's Reef's adventure camp sites are just a handful of idyllic island getaways. Meanwhile, renting an entire caye is a distinct possibility on French Louie Caye or remote Lime Caye, among others.

A stone's throw from the cayes, a symbolic white line of surf signals the reef's entrance—a happy sight for divers and snorkelers who find their bliss in marine reserves teeming with giant corals, sponges, and colorful critters.

Regardless of your chosen island, days are spent alfresco: kayaking, sailing, fishing, feasting on fresh catch, swimming alongside rays and turtles, gazing at magnificent frigatebirds hovering in blue skies. Or mastering the art of *dolce* far niente: the sweetness of doing nothing.

Clockwise from top left: Ranguana Caye; Silk Cayes; nurse sharks at Shark Ray Alley, Hol Chan Marine Reserve; Caye Caulker's Split.

Planning Your Trip

Where to Go

Northern Cayes

This group of islands is the most visited part of Belize. **Ambergris Caye** lures with swanky **beach resorts**, endless **bars**, and plentiful **restaurants**. **Caye Caulker**, just down the reef, offers a less dizzying pace with an authentic, Caribbean vibe and opportunities for snorkeling at **The Split** or at its own **local reserve**, when you're not viewing manatees at nearby **Swallow Caye Wildlife Sanctuary**. The northern atolls of **Turneffe Islands** and **Lighthouse Reef Atoll** offer spectacular **wall diving**, beautiful beaches and bird life, and Belize's iconic, great **Blue Hole.**

Southern Coast and Southern Cayes

Those who make it south will face the quandary of selecting from a dozen or more gorgeous cayes to stay on or visit for the day, as well as deciding on mainland stopovers for extra culture, beach, and rainforest adventures. **Dangriga** is the center of Belize's **Garífuna** population, with an Afro-Caribbean beat, cultural and outdoor activities, and a strategic location on the coast for trips to nearby **South Water Caye Marine Reserve** and **Glover's Reef Atoll** for spectacular snorkeling and diving. It's also a short drive to **Billy Barquedier National Park.** Just down the coast; lazy **Hopkins** has long stretches of **beach** and plenty of dining and accommodation options, including a strong Garífuna vibe. Farther south, the **Placencia Peninsula** is the home to 16 miles of "barefoot perfect" beaches and the low-key, albeit touristy village of **Placencia.** Off the coast are marine

Caye Caulker

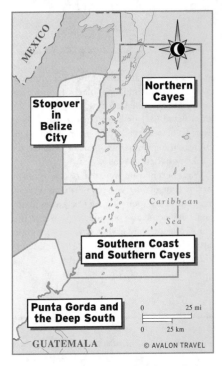

Northern Cayes

Stopover in Belize City

Caribbean

Sea

Southern Coast and Southern Cayes

Punta Gorda and the Deep South

MEXICO

GUATEMALA

0   25 mi

0   25 km

© AVALON TRAVEL

Punta Gorda and the Deep South

Few visitors get off the beaten path and into the "deep south" of Belize. But Punta Gorda and its surroundings offer all of Belize in one area: cayes and reef, ruins and caves, rainforests and rivers. A mere 30 minutes from the coast, the Snake Cayes offer top-notch snorkeling or diving in the protected Port Honduras Marine Reserve, while the remote and most uncrowded islands in Belize, the Sapodilla Cayes—considered a World Heritage Site—are home to two of Belize's most beautiful white sand coral beaches at Lime Caye and Hunting Caye, where you can stay in cabanas or pitch a tent and explore pristine, giant corals minutes offshore, a place where rays and turtles roam daily. On the mainland, hop on the cacao trail and glimpse life in a Mayan village, or take a private drumming lesson at one of the Garífuna drum schools. The archaeological site of Lubaantun begs exploring, as do the beautiful waterfalls at Río Blanco National Park and Blue Creek Cave.

Stopover in Belize City

Often skipped by travelers, Belize City is nonetheless the hub of Belizean city life and transport. Boats depart daily to the northern cayes, and domestic airlines connect to the rest of the country. The city is also the heart of Belize's colonial past and of the Creole culture. A few historic sights, such as the Museum of Belize and the Fort George area, make it worth a quick half-day visit, at a minimum. Whether or not you appreciate the city's unique grit and Caribbean texture, on your way through don't miss nearby attractions like The Belize Zoo, the Community Baboon Sanctuary, and Altun Ha.

reserves teeming with marinelife—including Laughingbird Caye National Park (a World Heritage Site) and Gladden Spit, where whale sharks congregate every year. Also under an hour away from Placencia, the southern Silk Cayes and Ranguana Caye are hard to beat, with powdery white sands and idyllic scenes straight out of a Caribbean postcard. To top it all off, the surrounding Stann Creek District offers some of the best hiking in Belize, including Mayflower Bocawina National Park, in the Maya Mountains, and the world's only jaguar preserve, Cockscomb Basin Sanctuary.

When to Go

High season is mid-December through May, which is considered the "dry season." Sunny skies and lush vegetation dominate throughout the country during the North American winter. It can change, however. November can be dry and sunny, while December, January, and even February have played host to wet cold fronts that either blow right through or sit around for days. The weather has become more unpredictable each year, as in most places in the world. And when you're visiting the cayes, weather is critical.

June, July, and August technically form the **rainy season**, which may mean just a quick afternoon shower or rain for days. This also means significantly discounted accommodations. August is most popular with European backpackers, while December and February are dominated by North Americans. Some tourism businesses shut down completely during the month of September and part of October, the peak of **hurricane season.**

Your best bet? Be prepared for clouds or sun at any time of year. A week of stormy weather may ruin a vacation planned solely around diving, but it could also provide the perfect setting for exploring the beaches, culture, or inland attractions surrounding each mainland jump-off point.

Before You Go

Passports and Visas

You must have a **passport** that is valid for the duration of your stay in Belize. You may be asked at the border (or airport immigration) to show a **return ticket** or ample money to leave the country. You do *not* need a visa if you are a British Commonwealth subject or a citizen of Belgium, Denmark, Finland, Greece, Iceland, Italy, Liechtenstein, Luxembourg, Mexico, Spain, Switzerland, Tunisia, Turkey, the United States, or Uruguay. Visitors for purposes other than tourism must obtain a **visa.**

Vaccinations

Technically, a certificate of vaccination against **yellow fever** is required for travelers aged older than one year arriving from an affected area, though immigration officials rarely, if ever, ask to see one.

In general, your **routine vaccinations**—tetanus, diphtheria, measles, mumps, rubella, and polio—should be up to date. **Hepatitis A** vaccine is recommended for all travelers over age two and should be given at least two weeks (preferably four weeks or more) before departure. **Typhoid** and **rabies vaccines** are recommended for those headed for rural areas.

Transportation

The majority of travelers arrive in Belize by air at **Philip Goldson International Airport**, nine miles outside Belize City. From the airport, short domestic connections are available to mainland coastal areas, such as Dangriga, Placencia, or Punta Gorda, via **Tropic Air** or **Maya Island Air**. A few travelers fly into **Cancún** as a cheaper back door to Belize; once there, they board a bus or rent a car and head south through the Yucatán Peninsula to reach Belize, or catch a bus and a boat over to the northern cayes.

Belize is small and extremely manageable, especially if you fly a **domestic airline** from tiny airstrip to tiny airstrip. You can also get around by **rental car, taxi,** or **bus,** which is

South Water Caye

most affordable. Another option is to let your resort or lodge arrange your airport transfers and all tours.

Water taxis are another way to get around in Belize, especially to and from Ambergris Caye and Caye Caulker and the mainland; there are regular daily routes between Belize City and these islands. For the **southern cayes**, resorts often include or arrange for round-trip transfers from the nearest mainland jump off point. Dive shops or tour operators have numerous scheduled day trips to the cayes and atolls from the mainland, particularly in the high season.

Best of the Belize Cayes

In five days, you can experience a few of Belize's most beautiful islands. This itinerary includes self-guided activities, as well as some guided tours. Caye hopping can be a bit more costly than exploring overland, so feel free to use this itinerary as best fits your budget. One thing is certain: you won't run out of islands to see or things to do!

Day 1

Arrive at **Philip Goldson International Airport** in Belize City. Hop on your connecting Tropic Air domestic puddle-jumper flight and fly to laid-back **Caye Caulker**. After dropping off your bags at the hotel, schedule a snorkel trip to **Caye Caulker Marine Reserve** for the next day, then watch the sunset at **The Split** and **Lazy Lizard Bar**, the island's social headquarters. Continue on with dinner alfresco at **Rose's Grill and Bar**. Pick your preferred fresh catch of the day and relax under a giant *palapa*.

Day 2

Today you'll head out on a half-day morning **snorkel** trip to Caye Caulker's **shark ray alley**, before hopping over to San Pedro. Swim and snorkel alongside a dozen or more nurse sharks and stingrays, among other marinelife, and admire coral gardens. Back on the island, grab your things and catch the early afternoon water taxi to bustling **San Pedro**. Spend the rest of the day walking around San Pedro Town, with plenty of opportunities to shop, eat, swim, barhop, and be merry. Grab a memorable seafood dinner at **Caramba Restaurant and Bar** or Creole specialties at **Elvi's Kitchen** and end the night with drinks at the beachfront **Señor Marlin's Sports Bar**. If you're a night owl, continue on to **Jaguar's Temple** nightclub.

Day 3

Catch the first water taxi back to Belize City, then head to **Dangriga**, in the **Stann Creek District**,

morning view from Caye Caulker

by bus or car. Take in the spectacular scenery along the **Hummingbird Highway.** Once in Dangriga, settle in and then take an afternoon trip to **Cockscomb Basin Wildlife Sanctuary,** where you can hike through the jungle past fresh jaguar tracks and chill in waterfalls under a green canopy. End the night with a fancy dinner back in Dangriga at **Pelican Beach Resort.**

Days 4-5
Catch a water taxi to **Tobacco Caye** or **South Water Caye** for diving along steep walls and snorkeling the pristine southern Belize Barrier Reef. These islands are oh-so-stunning and romantic! Stay overnight at one of several resorts for the full experience, and don't miss stargazing from your hammock. Catch your early boat transfer and flight back to Belize City's international airport.

Extend Your Stay
If you have 2-3 more days to spend in Belize,

catch the first bus or drive down to **Placencia Village**. Check into your hotel and make next-day arrangements with **Splash Dive Center** for a couple of snorkeling or dive trips or an all-day relaxing island escape to the **Silk Cayes** or **Laughingbird Caye National Park.** Back in the village, relax on the beach at **Tipsy Tuna**—swim, nap on lounge chairs, sip on local cocktails, and take in the slow vibe. Lunch on-site and join locals for a sunset beach volleyball game. Go to dinner at the local **Wendy's Creole Restaurant and Bar** or head up the peninsula to **Maya Beach Hotel Bistro** for beachfront fine dining. Back in the village, look out for some **Garífuna drumming** or other live music on the beach, at **Barefoot Bar** or **Tipsy Tuna.**

Spend the next day snorkeling, diving, fishing, beachcombing, and taking in a glorious, deserted island escape with an overnight on **Ranguana Caye** or **Robert's Caye**. Avid divers and honeymooners should just head straight to **Glover's Reef** for spectacular diving and utter seclusion.

coral off Ranguana Caye

Best Diving and Snorkeling

Whether you're an experienced scuba enthusiast or a novice snorkeler, there's plenty to see and admire at all levels and depths along Belize's great barrier reef.

Northern Cayes and Atolls

Three of Belize's top dive sites are along the northern atolls of **Lighthouse Reef** and **Turneffe**. If you're staying on Ambergris Caye or Caye Caulker, visiting these would mean a full-day trip, generally leaving around 7am and returning by 4pm If all you want to do is dive, avoid the distance and overnight at a resort on Turneffe Atoll.

Almost as popular as the Blue Hole, **The Elbow** on Turneffe Atoll is a steep drop-off going down to at least 100 feet, where you'll see large gorgonians and sponges, schools of snappers, jacks, goliath groupers, and Belize's unique species, the white spotted toadfish. Dolphins and eagle rays have also been spotted here.

Lighthouse Reef Atoll is a favorite for three good reasons. **Long Caye Aquarium**'s waters are a legendary royal blue, popping against a plethora of colorful fish, including the elusive spotted ray. Nearby, large stingrays, nurse sharks, turtles, and groupers thrive at **Half Moon Caye Wall,** where the occasional hammerhead shark roams. The infamous **Blue Hole** is the holy grail of diving, mostly due to its underground limestone formations at 100 feet. But you won't see much marinelife if you're diving, other than Caribbean reef sharks in the distance. Snorkelers will find plenty of fish to see, however, along the edges of the sinkhole.

Everyone will find their bliss at **Hol Chan Marine Reserve,** easily reached from the northern cayes or Belize City, but a less crowded and stunning alternative for snorkeling is **Caye Caulker Marine Reserve,** with its very own shark ray alley.

dive shop on Caye Caulker

Barrel sponges are found along the Belize Barrier Reef.

lionfish hovering over coral

Southern Cayes and Glover's Reef Atoll

More visitors are realizing that the **south coast and its offshore cayes** offer excellent and un-crowded dive and snorkeling opportunities. The options are limitless, with at least four nearby offshore marine reserves and the easternmost of the atolls, **Glover's Reef**. All of these sites are a boat hop away from Dangriga, Hopkins, or Placencia.

If you can only get to one dive site, make the trip to **Glover's Reef Atoll**. It's one of the least-visited cluster of islands, with more than 20 dive sites and an incredible diversity in coral and crit-ters—including reef fish, turtles, sharks, eels, and rays. Visibility is incredible, whether diving or snorkeling, even in poor weather. After the explo-ration, you can relax with a cocktail on some of the most beautiful powdery white-sand beaches along the atoll, from Long Caye to Southwest Caye.

The **Silk Cayes** and **Laughingbird Caye** are excellent picks for novice snorkelers or divers, as well as experienced ones. You'll spot plenty of coral formations, marinelife that includes lemon sharks, turtles, lobster, eels, and other colorful fish. Right off the Silk Cayes is a **shark, ray, and turtle alley** not to be missed, where giant logger-head turtles, manta rays, and lemon sharks con-gregate in one space.

South Water Caye Marine Reserve's steep wall dives are spectacular, and often missed by those who stick to the north. The reserve is home to schools of white spotted eagle rays, hawksbill turtles, green moray eels, and the gorgeous queen angelfish. Snorkelers will also be quite happy staying overnight on the island of South Water, one of the few spots in Belize where snorkeling from the beach is an option.

Gladden Spit is not to be missed for yearly whale shark dives, from March through June.

Deep South Cayes

Those fortunate enough to reach Belize's deep southern edge and venture off the coast will find two marine reserves—**Port Honduras** and **Sapodilla Cayes**—with virtually crowd-free, crystal-clear waters abundant with giant corals, leaping eagle rays, permits, loggerhead turtles, and schools of giant barracuda in these most un-touched parts of the Belize Barrier Reef.

Romantic Rendezvous

On the rise as a wedding and luxury honeymoon escape, Belize offers easy romance, but there are a few unique places and ways to experience the best of all its magic.

ROMANTIC LODGING

- Infinity pools, a beach, and all-around island glam await at **Victoria House** on Ambergris Caye. Opt for a beachfront thatch-roofed casita (page 62).

- On Ambergris Caye, **Tranquility Bay Resort** offers seclusion along a beautiful swim-to-snorkel white-sand beach (page 41).

- Dive or snorkel together daily while staying at **Isla Marisol Resort** on Glover's Reef Atoll. Stargaze, camp out on the beach, or live it up in your seafront villa with views of the Belize Barrier Reef (page 131).

FINE DINING

- Reserve a table for two at **Habaneros** on Caye Caulker, where you'll dine on a candlelit porch to the sound of live Latin ballads (page 92).

Billy Barquedier National Park

- Share a meal at the beachfront **Blue Water Grill**, where the breeze and waves drown out the otherwise bustling open dining room (page 68).

- Opt for seclusion under tiki torches at the beachfront **Barracuda Bar and Grill** in Hopkins Village, where you should splurge on a five-course meal, toes buried in sand (page 142).

- Indulge in fresh catch and unique eats like lobster wontons, before or after dipping in the pool or snuggling on the couch at **Rojo Lounge** on northern Ambergris Caye (page 69).

- Head off the beaten San Pedro path and enjoy fine dining at **Casa Picasso,** set in a residential villa turned restaurant. Savor tapas and entrées in a dimly lit, cozy dining room with a romantic turn-of-the-20th-century feel (page 69).

OUTDOOR ADVENTURES

- Catch a glorious **sunset** on **Caye Caulker** by kayaking a deux or hopping on a **sunset boat ride**. While watching the sun go down, enjoy the boat captain's freshly made conch ceviche and sip on some bubbly (page 80).

- Stop at **Billy Barquedier National Park** to enjoy the waterfalls and surrounding jade pool, sheltered by a verdant canope (page 115).

- Head off the beaten path to **Río Blanco National Park** for a park experience without the crowds (page 204).

SECLUDED ESCAPES

- Take it up a notch by renting an entire island for yourselves. Spend three blissful days in a wooden home on two-acre **French Louie Caye**, complete with a caretaker to cook your fresh catch. The sky-blue cottages on **Ranguana Caye** and its perfect blend of gin-clear seas and white sands are difficult to resist (page 169).

- Get Lost off the deep southern tip of Belize by holing up in your wooden, reef-facing cabin on **Lime Caye** (page 198).

Best Beaches

A coastline stretching along the Caribbean Sea and more than 20 offshore resort islands translates into enough beaches on and off the mainland to satisfy the most avid beach bum. The best stretches are found along Belize's eastern and southern coasts, and on the southern cayes.

Best Mainland Beaches

- **Hopkins:** Located on the eastern coast of Belize, this five-mile-long stretch of beach, lined with coconut trees, locals' clapboard homes, and colorful guesthouses, is perfect for morning walks or afternoon naps in the shade. In between swimming and beachcombing, experience Garífuna culture at its best by sampling dishes at **Laruni Hati Beyabu Diner** or **Innie's** (page 133).

- **Placencia Village, Maya Beach, and Seine Bight:** Stretching across three villages, the 16-mile-long Placencia Peninsula in southern

Belize has been dubbed "barefoot perfect," with thick, golden sand and clear water. Placencia Village's wide beach is dotted with dynamic bars and eateries frequented by a good mix of travelers and locals, but the beach itself is rarely crowded. Seine Bight and Maya Beach are quieter, with powdery soft sands, upscale restaurants, and resorts (page 149).

Best Island Beaches

- **Half Moon Caye:** Located on the southeast corner of Lighthouse Reef Atoll, crescent-shaped Half Moon Caye has a stunning beach dotted with palm trees and endless views of the Caribbean (page 99).

- **South Water Caye Marine Reserve:** Easily reached from Dangriga or Hopkins, this mile-long island is one of the few spots in Belize where you can actually swim from beach to reef. The best stretch belongs to **Pelican Beach Resort** (page 124).

Placencia Village's beach

- **Laughingbird Caye National Park and Silk Cayes Marine Reserve:** These protected marine reserves are ideal for sunning and swimming in glorious Caribbean turquoise waters. Both are also popular snorkeling and dive spots (page 171).

- **Ranguana Caye:** Day trips or overnight stays are welcome at this two-acre plot with a beautiful white-sand beach surrounded by shallow turquoise seas (page 172).

- **Sapodilla Cayes Marine Reserve:** Sapodilla Cayes' **Lime Caye** and **Hunting Caye** have beautiful turtle-nesting beaches (Oct.-Apr.). You'll likely be the only one burying your toes beneath the fine white sand (page 197).

Best Beaches for Snorkeling

Snorkeling is an easy, fun pastime while in Belize. It's not every day you get to be so close to the world's second largest reef. While the best of Belize's snorkel sites are offshore, there are still plenty of corals and colorful fish to see right off the following beaches.

- **Tranquility Bay Resort:** If you're staying on the secluded north end of Ambergris, you'll benefit from this location inside the Bacalar Chico Marine Reserve, which translates into snorkeling heaven right off the beach (page 41).

- **South Water Caye:** When you manage to leave that beach chair, swim right offshore to reach the nearby reef. South Water is one of the few islands where snorkeling from your resort's beach is an added bonus (page 124).

- **Tarpon Caye:** This fishing lodge happens to have spectacular corals and some of the Caribbean's best critters just under a five-minute swim away from shore. I was stunned by the abundant marinelife here, including permits, barracuda, schools of jacks, and grunts (page 173).

white sand beach on Ranguana Caye

Wildlife Spotting

Caye Caulker has more than 100 species of birds.

Filled with national parks and wildlife reserves, Belize is home to an estimated 145 species of mammals, 139 species of reptiles, and at least 500 species of birds, many of which can be spotted along the cayes. An island vacation doesn't mean missing out on any of the wildlife—here is what to look out for both inland and offshore.

- **Half Moon Caye National Monument:** In addition to managing Belize's protected areas and wildlife reserves, the Belize Audubon Society can arrange tours to top birding hotspot Half Moon Caye National Monument, on Lighthouse Reef Atoll (page 99).

- **The Northern Cayes:** Birders can explore the shores for unique species on **Caye Caulker's Northern Mangrove Forest Reserve** and **Bacalar Chico Marine Reserve** (pages 40 and 76).

- **The Southern Cayes:** Egrets, osprey, herons, pelicans, and other species roam daily over the southern cayes, from the **Ranguana Cayes** to **South Water** and the **Sapodilla Cayes** (page 105).

- **Cockscomb Basin Wildlife Sanctuary:** Increase your chance of an encounter—even if rare—with a jaguar, puma, ocelot, margay, or tapir with a day's hike or overnight stay. Cockscomb is easily Belize's most stunning rainforest park, with the most beautiful waterfall cascade at Tiger Fern (page 146).

- **Man-O-War Caye**: Hundreds of magnificent frigates nest and hover over this tiny mangrove plot and bird sanctuary, in addition to brown boobies (page 127).

- **Mayflower Bocawina National Park:** Often overlooked, this park is an uncrowded outdoor haven offering over 7,100 acres of lush rainforest in which to spot hundreds of bird species, including toucans and parrots, as well as howler monkeys, deer, coatimundis, tapirs, and wild cats like the ocelot. When you're done wildlife watching, cool off in one of five waterfalls (page 144).

- **Río Blanco National Park:** Beautiful butterflies flutter away in Punta Gorda's pristine park (page 204).

- **The Community Baboon Sanctuary:** Spot howler monkeys, birds, iguanas, and armadillos at this sanctuary in Bermuda Landing, less than an hour's drive from Belize City (page 231).

Underwater Guide

Stretching 180 miles along Belize's coast, from Bacalar Chico in the north all the way south to the Sapodilla Cayes, the **Belize Barrier Reef** continues to be a diving and snorkeling paradise. It's also the most abundant section of the Mesoamerican Reef System, which extends from Mexico to Honduras and has been described by National Geographic as "half the length of its famous Australian counterpart but in many ways more remarkable."

It's not surprising then, that Belize's waters are teeming with a rich underwater life. Approximately 70 hard coral species, 36 soft coral species, over 300 species of fish, and hundreds of invertebrates call these waters home. Nine protected marine reserves and an intricate system of various habitats allow these hundreds of creatures to thrive.

Divers will find guaranteed bliss off the magnificent coral atolls, while snorkelers can spot rays, turtles, and other fish directly off a caye's shores and in marine reserves. Whether you're a beginner or certified underwater aficionado, Belize's splendid down under is sure to impress. Here are the main Caribbean critters you'll encounter, north to south. The good news is, you don't have to be a diver to see them all.

Manatees

These "gentle giants of the sea" can reach between 600 and 1,200 pounds, and move ever so gracefully across the waters, rising to the surface in intervals to breathe. Belize is considered the last stronghold for the endangered West Indian manatee. In 2012, aerial surveys of Turneffe Atoll and Belize's coastline revealed 507 manatees. It's estimated that the global population of this species is less than 2,500.

WHERE TO SEE THEM

While swimming with manatees is prohibited, you can hop on manatee-watching tours. You're

diver cruising alongside coral reef at South Water Caye Marine Reserve

Belize Cayes Dive Sites

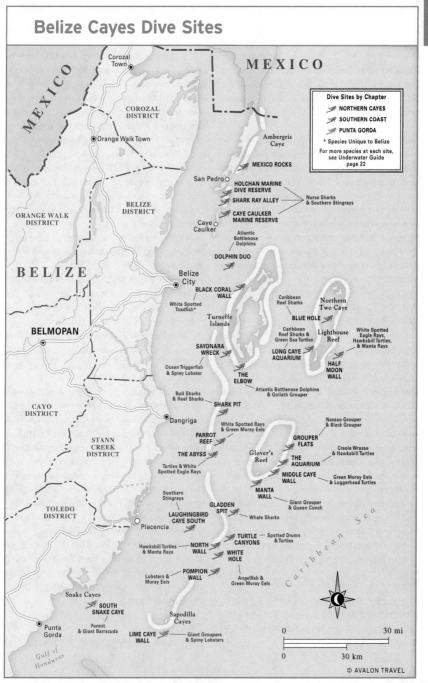

MEXICO

MEXICO

Corozal Town

COROZAL DISTRICT

Orange Walk Town

ORANGE WALK DISTRICT

BELIZE DISTRICT

BELIZE

BELMOPAN

CAYO DISTRICT

STANN CREEK DISTRICT

TOLEDO DISTRICT

Punta Gorda

Gulf of Honduras

Ambergris Caye

San Pedro

Caye Caulker

Belize City

Turneffe Islands

Dangriga

Placencia

Snake Cayes

Sapodilla Cayes

Caribbean Sea

Dive Sites by Chapter
NORTHERN CAYES
SOUTHERN COAST
PUNTA GORDA
* Species Unique to Belize
For more species at each site, see Underwater Guide page 22

MEXICO ROCKS

HOLCHAN MARINE DIVE RESERVE

SHARK RAY ALLEY — Nurse Sharks & Southern Stingrays

CAYE CAULKER MARINE RESERVE

Atlantic Bottlenose Dolphins

DOLPHIN DUO

BLACK CORAL WALL

White Spotted Toadfish*

Caribbean Reef Sharks

Northern Two Caye

BLUE HOLE

Caribbean Reef Sharks & Green Sea Turtles

Lighthouse Reef

White Spotted Eagle Rays, Hawksbill Turtles, & Manta Rays

SAYONARA WRECK

Ocean Triggerfish & Spiny Lobster

LONG CAYE AQUARIUM

HALF MOON WALL

THE ELBOW

Atlantic Bottlenose Dolphins & Goliath Grouper

Bull Sharks & Reef Sharks

SHARK PIT

White Spotted Rays & Green Moray Eels

PARROT REEF

Nassau Grouper & Black Grouper

GROUPER FLATS

THE ABYSS

Glover's Reef

THE AQUARIUM

Creole Wrasse & Hawksbill Turtles

Turtles & White Spotted Eagle Rays

MIDDLE CAYE WALL

Green Moray Eels & Loggerhead Turtles

MANTA WALL

Giant Grouper & Queen Conch

Southern Stingrays

GLADDEN SPIT

LAUGHINGBIRD CAYE SOUTH

Whale Sharks

TURTLE CANYONS — Spotted Drums & Turtles

Hawksbill Turtles & Manta Rays

NORTH WALL

WHITE HOLE

POMPION WALL

Lobsters & Moray Eels

Angelfish & Green Moray Eels

SOUTH SNAKE CAYE

Permit & Giant Barracuda

LIME CAYE WALL — Giant Groupers & Spiny Lobsters

0   30 mi

0   30 km

© AVALON TRAVEL

likely to see them on a trip along **Swallow Caye Wildlife Sanctuary** or off **Caye Caulker Marine Reserve,** particularly during the summer. Manatees also inhabit **Placencia Lagoon,** and you may come across one during a boat ride off the Placencia coast and on the way to southern cayes.

Sea Turtles

Three species of sea turtles are commonly found in Belize: the **loggerhead, the green turtle,** and the **hawksbill.** Their protected status for the past 12 years has resulted in more sightings for happy snorkelers and divers. They roam slowly in shallow coastal waters, lagoons, and open sea. But don't be surprised to notice that they are capable of fast speeds, over 20 miles an hour, especially if you attempt to follow them too closely.

WHERE TO SEE THEM

When and where you'll spot these various species of turtles will depend on several factors, including time of year, although they are quite easy to spot while exploring the southern parts of the reef. Generally, your chances of seeing green sea turtles are high at **Hol Chan Marine Reserve, Long Caye Aquarium,** and **Glover's Reef.** Loggerhead turtles can be seen off **Glover's Reef** or in the **Silk Cayes'** very own **shark and turtle alley.** The best places to spot hawksbill turtles are **Half Moon Caye Wall,** the **South Water Caye Marine Reserve,** and off **Hunting Caye.** There are several designated **turtle-nesting beaches,** including at **Half Moon Caye, Lime Caye, Hunting Caye, Hatchet Caye, Carrie Bow Caye,** and northern **Ambergris Caye.** Nesting season is from June through October.

Rays

Swimming alongside rays can be a little intimidating at first, but these are harmless creatures, as long as you leave them undisturbed. They are in abundance in Belize, home to the southern stingray, the manta ray, and the spotted eagle ray.

The **southern stingray** can reach up to five feet across, with a long and thin tail outfitted with venomous barbs 4-8 inches long. The elusive **spotted eagle rays** are mesmerizing; their glorious wing-like appendages allow them to move quickly and give them the appearance of flying through the sea. Their numerous white spots dramatically contrast with the sea wall's clear and deep blues. The spotted eagle ray has a longer tail equipped with up to five barbed spines. Its wingspan can reach up to five feet. They are considered threatened and are often hunted by sharks.

Manta rays have a wingspan reaching up to 20 feet and are often seen leaping in and out of the water up to 10 feet high.

Tip: When entering the water from the beach, particularly off the cayes, be sure to do the "stingray shuffle"—slowly rub the sandy bottom as you enter, in order not to startle any rays that may be resting on the sea floor, where they usually sit when not swimming.

WHERE TO SEE THEM

Get a close glimpse of southern stingrays on a trip to **Hol Chan Marine Reserve,** ideal for beginner and advanced snorkelers. **Caye Caulker Marine Reserve** also has its very own stingray alley, where you'll be surrounded by southern stingrays—a thrill for both adults and young ones. You'll spot them rushing towards the boat as it arrives, as they're used to the daily visits and feedings. In the south, southern stingrays and spotted eagle rays are a likely sight at **Gladden Spit, Parrot Reef** off South Water Caye, and the **North Wall** off the Silk Cayes. Manta rays can be seen from **Ambergris** and **Caye Caulker** all the way to the **Sapodilla Cayes,** where they even come right up to shore along **Lime Caye.**

Sharks

Species of sharks present along Belize's coastline

Top: loggerhead turtle swimming over corals at Trick Ridge, South Water Caye. **Bottom:** whale sharks, Gladden Spit and Silk Cayes Marine Reserve, off the coast of Placencia.

cile **nurse sharks, Caribbean** [reef sharks], **bull sharks, black tip sharks,** [sharks], **hammerheads, scalloped** [hammerheads] (though rare), and the impressive, migratory **whale sharks**. Hard as it may be at first, put aside the myth that all sharks are out to immediately attack humans. You will end up surprised when a Caribbean reef shark passes by and ignores your presence. Thanks to a complex and diverse reef system, it's not unusual to spot sharks on a dive, particularly off one of the coral atolls. The most common species are nurse sharks, reef sharks, and, in season, whale sharks.

Nurse sharks are bottom dwellers that pose no threat and are used to divers for the most part—but don't touch them! They feed on crustaceans, mollusks, and other fish, and can grow up to 14 feet and weigh over 700 pounds. Nurse sharks are in abundance in Belize and are easiest to spot in marine reserves.

Aside from nurse sharks, **reef sharks** are the most commonly encountered in Belize. They can reach up to 10 feet in length, have long and narrow fins, and have an impressive aura about them, reminding you of those Hollywood-type sharks. But not to worry—they feed primarily on reef fish and are generally harmless to humans. They can get aggressive where there is bait, however, so beware if you're out spearfishing.

Whale sharks are a primary attraction in Belize for visitors who wish to snorkel or dive with these giant creatures. They are the largest fish in the sea (up to 66 feet in length and weighing over 15 tons).

WHERE TO SEE THEM
You are guaranteed to see nurse sharks at **Hol Chan Marine Reserve**'s **Shark Ray Alley**. The thrill is to jump from the boat into waters with 20-30 of them. You can visit a similar shark ray alley at **Caye Caulker Marine Reserve**.

Divers will occasionally spot Caribbean reef sharks or the great hammerhead on trips to the atolls, particularly **Lighthouse Reef**, home to the infamous **Blue Hole**.

Whale sharks can be viewed at **Gladden Spit** during the whale shark season from April to May, three or four days before and after a full moon.

Dolphins
There's nothing like the sight of a school of dolphins at sea, jumping across Belize's emerald waters. **Atlantic bottlenose dolphins** are regularly spotted. Their appearance above and under water is often unexpected and rapid, although some have been known to hang around and swim with divers.

WHERE TO SEE THEM
Swimming with dolphins is a sure thing at dive sites off northern **St. George's Caye**. They also travel along the atolls, including **Turneffe Atoll** and **Glover's Reef**. You might see them appear randomly off the southern cayes, including **Ranguana Caye** or at **Gladden Spit**. Dolphins have also been seen traveling right along **Caye Caulker**'s **Split**.

Great Barracuda
Great barracuda are common residents of Belize's waters. Capable of speeds up to 22 miles per hour, these predators have a "bad boy" rep and are intimidating to divers with their sleek, silver bodies (up to five feet long), mean stare, and razor-sharp, fang-like teeth. But they don't go after humans; they're just as curious as you are. They may shadow you but there's no need to panic. Avoid touching or feeding them and maintain your distance. Beware that they've been known to attack people wearing bright jewelry and watches—likely a starving barracuda mistaking anything shiny for bait.

WHERE TO SEE THEM
Great barracuda can be seen on almost any dive or fishing excursion all along the Belize Barrier Reef and cayes, going north to south. They are particularly abundant and easy to spot on snorkel trips to **Laughingbird Caye National Park** and the **Snake Cayes Marine Reserve**.

Facing page: a school of spotted eagle rays at South Water Caye.

Angelfish and Butterflyfish

Angelfish are the beauties of Belize's reef. These shy creatures with large spines and rounded heads come in bright and attractive hues, gracefully roaming the waters as they feed on sponges and algae. Of about 80 species in the tropical world, at least four are found in good numbers in Belize: the **queen angelfish** (the most striking, with an electric blue body and a yellow tail), the **French angelfish,** the **blue angelfish,** and the **gray angelfish.** They love to stick close to coral or rock reefs, which makes for vibrant photographs. The **four-eyed butterflyfish** and the **spotfin butterflyfish** (with a black line running through its eye) are frequent in Belize.

WHERE TO SEE THEM

You'll spot angelfish and the four-eyed butterflyfish on literally any dive trip to the reef, including snorkeling at **Mexico Rocks** off Ambergris Caye. They are particularly abundant off the southern and deep southern cayes and the atolls.

Eels

Eels often remain tucked in reef crevices during the day, with the head poking out and the mouth open. They have fang teeth that sink deep into their prey, even if nonvenomous. The species you'll spot the most often is the **green moray eel,** which can reach up to six feet in length.

WHERE TO SEE THEM

Green moray eels are a sure thing on **Turneffe Atoll** dives, along the **North Wall** or **White Hole** of **Silk Cayes Marine Reserve,** and off the southern cayes, like **Ranguana.** Snorkelers can spot one at **Hol Chan Marine Reserve.**

Toadfish and Seahorses

The **whitespotted toadfish's** bizarre looks (a dark brown, large flattened head covered white spots and whiskers that protrude below its mouth) make it a great photographic subject. If you're lucky you'll spot one at the bottom of the sea, tucked in a reef crevice. Be careful not to step on one or come too close—their spines are poisonous.

Think the **seahorse** is a thing of the past? Not in Belize. While they're not abundant, seeing one of these minuscule creatures is a distinct possibility. Ask for Ras Creek while at the Split on **Caye Caulker** and he will gladly show you around his very own, unofficial seahorse reserve, set in the mangroves just beside the Split.

WHERE TO SEE THEM

You're most likely to see a whitespotted toadfish on dives at **Cockroach Caye Wall** or **Black Coral Wall,** off Turneffe Atoll. It takes a lot more luck to see a seahorse off the reef out at sea, but divers have encountered them off the **South Water Caye Marine Reserve.**

Damselfish and Parrotfish

These small fishes are abundant along Belize's reef. The species range from the **yellowtail damselfish** (the most striking in color) to the **threespot damselfish** and the **sergeant major,** with its unmistakable yellow and back stripes. Even more colorful are **parrotfish,** in gorgeous greens, blues, and reds. Look out for the **stoplight parrotfish** or the **princess parrotfish:** These sparkling creatures have parrot-like mouths and can reach up to 20 inches in length.

WHERE TO SEE THEM

Damselfish and parrotfish are a common sight in Belize's waters. They roam around **corals,** where they feed on algae. Spot them off the northern or southern cayes, the atolls, or in marine reserves.

Groupers, Snappers, and Grunts

The **goliath grouper** or **jewfish,** the largest species of the grouper family, can occasionally be seen in Belize. This fish can reach up to 8.2 feet long and 800 pounds. They tend to spawn in large aggregations and are now an endangered species. You'll also spot other species, including

Top: giant barracuda. **Bottom:** the colorful queen angelfish.

the **Nassau grouper**, **black grouper** (a top reef predator), and **tiger grouper**.

Look out for **yellowtail snappers**, **schoolmasters**, and **dog snappers**—major predators frequently sighted in Belize. Their bodies are silver, with near-neon yellow stripes and a yellow tail. They're fast and may be solo or in schools. You'll spot the occasional **porkfish** (a type of grunt), but schools of **Caesar grunts** are abundant, often hovering above coral.

WHERE TO SEE THEM

Groupers are spotted on wall dives, off any of the atolls, or along the northern and southern cayes. The goliath grouper has been spotted off **Glover's Reef Atoll**, and black groupers can be found at **Hol Chan Marine Reserve**. **Lighthouse Reef Atoll** and **Turneffe Atoll** have protected Nassau grouper aggregation sites. Snappers are a sure bet all along the reef and atolls, and are particularly abundant in the south.

Every year, groupers and snappers aggregate for spawning off various parts of the Belize Barrier Reef, at up to 16 different sites, from the **northern atolls** to the southern **Silk Cayes Marine Reserve** and **Sapodilla Cayes Marine Reserve**.

Tarpons, Permits, and Bonefish

Belize is world-famous for its sport-fishing opportunities, attracting avid anglers who dream of achieving the "grand slam"—catching a tarpon, permit, and snook in one day. These fish are protected by law and must be released.

WHERE TO SEE THEM

You will find schools of these fish in rivers, lagoons, and along inner mangrove islands. In the north, **Caye Caulker** has a little-known local tarpon reserve, on the "lee" side of the island just past Sea Dreams Hotel. You can purchase sardines and feed them while marveling at their incredible leaps. They are also abundant off **Ambergris Caye** and the southern cayes, like **Tobacco Caye**.

Creole Wrasses and Blue Tangs

The fluorescent blue, tiny **creole wrasses** travel in schools and often form a line above coral as they feed on plankton along the edges of walls where currents are high.

Spotted solo or in groups, the vibrant **blue tang** feeds on algae off corals, an important role in maintaining a healthy reef.

WHERE TO SEE THEM

Creole wrasses are a common sight off **Turneffe Atoll**, as well as the **South Water** and **Silk Cayes Marine Reserves**. Blue tangs can be seen off the atolls, including **Glover's Reef**, and off the **southern cayes**, including as far south as the **Snake Cayes**.

Queen Triggerfish, Spotted Drums, and Trumpetfish

The **queen triggerfish** is a beautiful sight, with its yellow and iridescent blue lines and erect spine, a protection from its predators. They swim off walls, close to the bottom, but will quickly hide in reef crevices if they sense a threat—their spines allow them to remain locked in, inaccessible to predators seeking to pull them out. Beware of getting too close, as they can get nasty. Triggerfish feed on sea urchins and crabs, among other crustaceans and mollusks. A fun fact is that they can rotate each eye independently.

Spotted drums, if you're lucky to see one, stand out because of their odd shape. Their bodies reach up to eight inches, with thick dark and light stripes. Elongated dorsal fins off their backs allow them to swim erratically.

Easily distinguishable thanks to an elongated body and equally long and narrow snout, **trumpetfish** are a common sight in Belize. They vary in color to blend in with the reef, but you'll often see them hanging vertically to hide among gorgonians and other branches while waiting on their unsuspecting prey.

WHERE TO SEE THEM

Queen triggerfish roam around **Glover's**

Top: green moray eel, off Turneffe Atoll. **Bottom:** black grouper fish alongside a school of horse-eye jack off the coast of Ambergris Caye.

Reef, Ambergris Caye, and Lighthouse Reef Atoll, among other areas of the reef. Trumpetfish are found on snorkel and dive excursions off the northern and southern cayes, like Laughingbird Caye, Tarpon Caye, and off the atolls.

Spiny Lobsters

Spiny lobsters often stay hidden during the day, in the holes along the sea floor. They have long antennae sticking that are twice the size of their body, which can range from 12 to 18 inches. Occasionally, you'll find one in the open, resting on the sand. Night dives are when these creatures come out to feed.

WHERE TO SEE THEM

Spiny lobsters are commonly spotted on dives and snorkeling trips along the reef, such as South Water Caye, Laughingbird Caye, and the Sapodilla Cayes.

Banded Coral Shrimp and Christmas Tree Worms

The banded coral shrimp and the Christmas tree worm are unusual-looking species, and you'll likely need a guide to point them out. The banded coral shrimp has long antennae used to attract fish, which it cleans by eating off any algae and parasites. Its small body is a red-orange with white stripes.

The Christmas tree worm blends in easily among corals, but its Christmas tree-shaped gills make it stand out. Tour guides like to show how the gills immediately turn inward when you reach a hand out as if to touch them.

WHERE TO SEE THEM

Christmas tree worms thrive along the reef, and are easily spotted on snorkel trips along Laughingbird Caye and the southern cayes.

You can spot banded coral shrimp in reef crevices and near sponges at Long Caye Aquarium off Lighthouse Reef Atoll or *Sayonara* wreck off Turneffe Atoll.

Queen Conch

It wouldn't be the Caribbean Sea if its waters didn't house the queen conch, resting on the sandy sea floor. These creatures have a beautiful pink inner shell and graze on algae and seagrass. They often leave a trail behind as they drag their shells across the floor. The conch-fishing season is strictly monitored and runs only from October through May, although it has been known to close earlier once quotas are met. Beware not to purchase or travel home with anything made from this endangered species, including jewelry.

WHERE TO SEE THEM

The queen conch is spotted along the reef from the north cayes to the south, but they are easier to spot in marine reserves, including Hol Chan, Caye Caulker, Laughingbird, and Silk Cayes.

Corals

More than 60 types of coral, of the soft and hard (stony) variety, inhabit Belize's waters and help make up the largest reef system in the western hemisphere. They're an unmistakable and immediate sight the minute you enter the sea. They include brain coral, elkhorn coral, fire coral, star coral, lettuce coral, mustard hill coral, and gorgonians (soft coral that includes brightly colored sea fans and sea whips). Remember that coral should never be touched— these are fragile, living organisms. All it takes to destroy generations of one species is a slight touch of the fins. Be particularly careful not to accidentally touch fire coral.

WHERE TO SEE THEM

Corals can be seen all over Belize's barrier reef. The atolls and southern cayes offer the most beautiful coral gardens, and off the Sapodilla Cayes, where you'll likely be the only one exploring, are incredibly abundant and large species.

Top: yellowtail snapper, off the Silk Cayes Marine Reserve. **Bottom:** four-eyed butterflyfish along the Belize Barrier Reef.

brain coral

Sponges

There are over 5,000 living species of sponges, and the most colorful of all inhabit the reefs of the Caribbean. While it isn't obvious to the naked eye, sponges are constantly competing for a place of attachment in the reef community, while helping the reef stay alive by recycling organic matters into nutrients for the reef. Common sights in Belize include the **yellow tube sponge, giant barrel sponge, large netted barrel sponge,** and the **azure vase sponge.**

WHERE TO SEE THEM
The azure vase sponge is found off **Ambergris Caye.** The **atolls** are also a sure bet, as are any of the **southern cayes,** particularly along **South Water Caye**'s steep walls.

The Northern Cayes

Look for ★ to find recommended
sights, activities, dining, and lodging.

Highlights

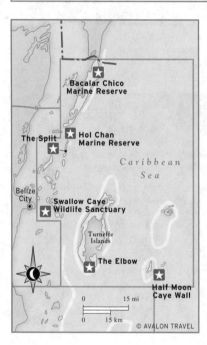

★ **Hol Chan Marine Reserve:** The second-largest barrier reef in the world is less than a mile offshore from both Ambergris Caye and Caye Caulker. Spending a day here is akin to swimming in a giant aquarium (page 40).

★ **Bacalar Chico Marine Reserve:** This UNESCO World Heritage Site at the northern tip of Ambergris Caye boasts spectacular snorkeling and diving (page 40).

★ **The Split:** Caye Caulker's best swimming beach is a unique scene where visitors and locals alike sun themselves on concrete slabs, snorkel, or dance at the on-site bar (page 74).

★ **Swallow Caye Wildlife Sanctuary:** This protected area is home to the endangered West Indian manatee and is one of several worthwhile excursions offered from the northern cayes (page 76).

★ **The Elbow:** Advanced divers visit this steep drop-off where swift currents collide, hoping to spot deep-water predatory fish as well as a wall of interesting sponges (page 96).

★ **Half Moon Caye Wall:** A birder's paradise, this beautiful crescent-shaped island is home to more than 4,000 red-footed boobies and 120 other species. It's also one of the best diving spots in Belize (page 101).

O nce the favorite hideout and play-ground of pirates, the northern cayes are Belize's greatest tourism draw, and with good reason: postcard-perfect islands, quick access to the Belize Barrier Reef and Hol Chan Marine Reserve, a dizzying array of outdoor activities, and enough lodging, restaurants, and entertainment options to fit celebrity and backpacker budgets alike.

Located close to Belize City, the northern cayes are ideal for adventurers short on getaway time. This cluster of islands includes the iconic Great Blue Hole and two of Belize's three atolls—Turneffe and Lighthouse Reef—for world-class diving, snorkeling, and fishing. And that's not all: As the most tourist-ready region in all of Belize, the northern cayes host an estimated 70 percent of visitors for their first Belizean experience. This fusion of local culture with a constant stream of international visitors makes for one lively scene.

Avid divers tend to stay on one of the atolls to minimize travel time to top dive sites; otherwise, it's a two-hour boat ride each way from Ambergris Caye or Caye Caulker. Ambergris, generally referred to as San Pedro, attracts those seeking constant activity—there is incessant hustle and bustle, not to mention pretty hotels and pools, chic lounges, fine dining, and plenty of bars and nightlife. Smaller Caye Caulker attracts the laid-back, off-the-beaten-path traveler, those who seek immersion in local island life, exploring sand-only streets on foot or bicycle (there are no cars here!). There's an amusing sibling rivalry between the two cayes—larger Ambergris Caye considers Caye Caulker slow and boring, while the smaller caye is content with the lack of noise, paved roads, and crowds. In reality, each has a varied slice of Belize to offer, excellent water sports, and island fun, and neither is a wasted visit.

PLANNING YOUR TIME

A common dilemma is whether to stay on Ambergris Caye or Caye Caulker, each unique in rhythm and scenery. The good news is that they are a mere 30-minute water-taxi hop

The Northern Cayes

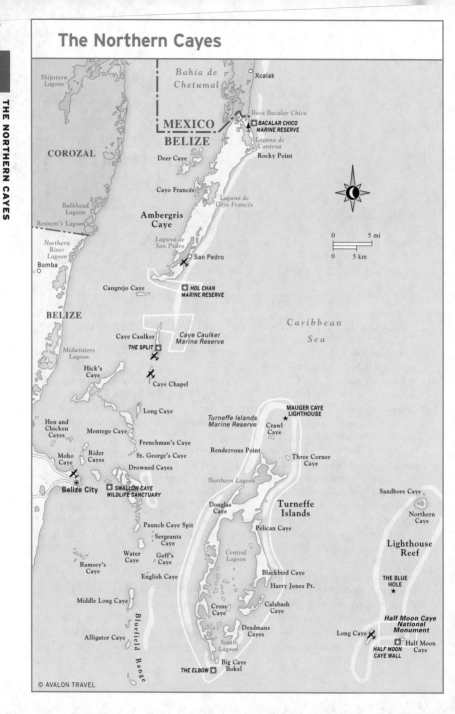

Shipstern Lagoon

Bahía de Chetumal

Xcalak

MEXICO
BELIZE

Boca Bacalar Chico

BACALAR CHICO MARINE RESERVE

COROZAL

Deer Caye

Laguna de Cantena

Rocky Point

Cayo Francés

Laguna de Cayo Francés

Bulkhead Lagoon

Bennett's Lagoon

Ambergris Caye

Northern River Lagoon

Bomba

Laguna de San Pedro

San Pedro

0   5 mi

0   5 km

BELIZE

Cangrejo Caye

HOL CHAN MARINE RESERVE

Caribbean Sea

Midwinters Lagoon

Caye Caulker
THE SPLIT

Caye Caulker Marine Reserve

Hick's Caye

Caye Chapel

Long Caye

MAUGER CAYE LIGHTHOUSE

Hen and Chicken Cayes

Montego Caye

Turneffe Islands Marine Reserve

Crawl Caye

Moho Caye

Rider Cayes

Frenchman's Caye

St. George's Caye

Rendezvous Point

Three Corner Caye

Drowned Cayes

Belize City

SWALLOW CAYE WILDLIFE SANCTUARY

Northern Lagoon

Sandbore Caye

Douglas Caye

Turneffe Islands

Northern Caye

Paunch Caye Spit

Pelican Caye

Lighthouse Reef

Sergeants Caye

Water Caye

Goff's Caye

Central Lagoon

THE BLUE HOLE

Ramsey's Caye

English Caye

Blackbird Caye

Middle Long Caye

Harry Jones Pt.

Cross Caye

Calabash Caye

Half Moon Caye National Monument

Alligator Caye

Deadmans Cayes

Long Caye

Half Moon Caye

HALF MOON CAYE WALL

Bluefield Range

South Lagoon

THE ELBOW

Big Caye Bokel

© AVALON TRAVEL

away from each other, with tours available from either base.

Ambergris Caye's foodie treasures and luxury accommodations attract travelers seeking both excellent diving and nonstop nightlife. San Pedro is considered the "trendy" part of Belize, with more resorts, bars, lounges, eateries, and general day-to-day activities than most of the country. There's a steady buzz here, and events take place year-round, attracting not only visitors but also Belizeans from the city seeking a quick, fun getaway. Hol Chan Marine Reserve is the most popular dive and snorkel site in Belize. Located on and around the northern tip of Ambergris Caye, Bacalar Chico National Park and Marine Reserve hosts an incredibly diverse array of wildlife and offers excellent snorkeling and diving.

Caye Caulker's slower yet rhythmic Caribbean vibe will appeal to the laid-back visitor while still offering excellent diving opportunities. The Split is the favorite go-to swimming and sunset rendezvous spot on the island. Swallow Caye Wildlife Sanctuary, at the north end of the Drowned Cayes, is a protected area with nearly 9,000 acres of sea and mangroves to explore.

Outside these two cayes are the upscale Turneffe Islands, with diving opportunities at The Elbow and Lighthouse Reef Atoll, home to the some of the best dive spots in the world—Half Moon Caye and Long Caye.

San Pedro and Ambergris Caye

Ambergris Caye is Belize's largest island, just south of the Mexican Yucatán mainland and stretching southward for 24 miles into Belizean waters. Ambergris ("AM-bur-giss") is 35 miles east of Belize City and about 0.75 mile west of the Belize Barrier Reef. The island was formed by an accumulation of coral fragments and silt from the Río Hondo as it emptied from what is now northern Belize. The caye is made up of mangrove swamps, a dozen lagoons, a plateau, and a series of low sand ridges. The largest lagoon, fed by 15 creeks, is 2.5-mile-long Laguna de San Pedro, on the western side of the village.

San Pedro Town sits on a sand ridge at the southern end of the island, the only actual town on the island and the most-visited destination in Belize. It is chock-full of accommodations, restaurants, bars, golf carts, and services. San Pedro is also the most expensive part of Belize, with prices for some basic goods and foods double the mainland prices and sometimes even more than similar services and restaurants in the United States.

ORIENTATION

Whether arriving by air or sea, your trip to Ambergris begins in San Pedro Town—the heart of the island's activity, where most of the restaurants, bars, nightlife, shopping, and hotels are clustered. Three streets run north-south and parallel the beach on the island's east side. Residents still refer to them by their historic names: Front Street (Barrier Reef Drive), Middle Street (Pescador Drive), and Back Street (Angel Coral Street). Another landmark is at the north end of town, where the San Pedro River flows through a navigable cut. This spot is often referred to as "the cut" or "the bridge," referring to the toll bridge that replaced the hand-drawn ferry. Past the bridge are some exclusive resorts, hotels, and lounges. You'll also hear the term "south of town," referring to the continually developing area south of the airstrip and south of San Pedro Town, accessed by Coconut Drive and starting past Ramon's Village Resort, where more posh retreats can be found, along with some casual and lively outdoor bars.

MEXICO
BELIZE

Boca
Bacular
Chico

BACALAR CHICO
MARINE RESERVE

Laguna de
Cantena

Deer
Caye

Rocky
Point

Basil
Jones

Inner Channel

Cayo
Pajaros

Punta Azul

Laguna de
Cayo Francés

Blackadore
Caye

Palermo Point

Ambergris
Caye

MEXICO ROCKS

CATALAN ROCKS

Punta Arena

Laguna de
San Pedro

Buena Vista Point

San Pedro

Caribbean Sea

ENTRANCE THROUGH
THE REEF

HOL CHAN
MARINE RESERVE

Congrejo
Caye

0   5 mi

0   5 km

© AVALON TRAVEL

SIGHTS

★ Hol Chan Marine Reserve

Once a traditional fishing ground, back when San Pedro was a sleepy village of a few hundred people, **Hol Chan Marine Reserve** (www.holchanbelize.org, US$12.50 pp) is the most popular dive and snorkel site in Belize, with tens of thousands of visitors each year. The site is four miles south of San Pedro and makes for an affordable morning or afternoon trip. In town is a small visitors center on Caribeña Street with information on the reserve. Nearly all tour operators on Ambergris and Caye Caulker offer trips to the Hol Chan cut.

Once you visit, you'll quickly understand the popularity of the reserve—and why it is important to help preserve it. Established

as a marine park in 1987, when fishing was banned, Hol Chan boasts an amazing diversity of species. The reserve focuses on creating a sustainable link between tourism and conservation, protecting the coral reef while allowing visitors to experience and learn about the marinelife living here.

Along with a stop at Hol Chan is one at **Shark Ray Alley**—a nearby zone of the reserve where stingrays and six-foot-long nurse sharks have gathered over the years thanks to anglers who often cleaned their catch in this area. Used to getting their scraps of fish, the nurse sharks anticipate the boats and are used to humans—although it is best to keep a safe distance. The thrill of jumping in waters surrounded by these creatures is something to experience at least once.

While you may see a guide or two pose with stingrays or stroke a nurse shark, note that officially it is illegal to feed or touch the fish. Even if your guide tells you differently, and even if you see other groups caressing the nurse sharks and rays, this is against the reserve rules and regulations and against all normal protocol for interacting with wildlife, as it should be. That said, San Pedro anglers and tour guides have been feeding the animals in this spot every day for over 15 years, so some argue that an exception should be made, or that there is some educational benefit to interacting with the animals. Best to leave only bubbles, I say.

★ Bacalar Chico Marine Reserve

Located on and around the northern tip of Ambergris Caye, **Bacalar Chico National Park and Marine Reserve** hosts an incredibly diverse array of wildlife, offers excellent snorkeling and diving, and is rich with history. The Bacalar Chico Canal is reputed to have been dug by Mayan traders between AD 700 and 900, creating Ambergris Caye by separating it from the Yucatán Peninsula. The reserve has a wide range of wildlife habitat; 194 species of birds have been sighted there. The landscape consists in part of sinkholes and cenotes created by the effects of weathering on the limestone bedrock of Ambergris Caye. On the eastern side of the reserve is **Rocky Point,** the only location in the Belize Barrier Reef Reserve System where the reef touches the shore. This is one of Belize's most important and prolific sea turtle nesting sites, home to at least 10 threatened species. In 1997, Bacalar Chico—along with the Belize Barrier Reef Reserve System—was designated a World Heritage Site by UNESCO.

Bacalar Chico also contains at least nine archaeological sites: Mayan trading, fishing, and agricultural settlements that were inhabited from at least AD 300 to 900. A 10th site just outside the reserve boundary is regarded as especially important for its remaining wall network throughout the settlement and its potential to provide missing information about the transition from the classic Mayan period to modern times. The reserve also contains evidence of Spanish and English habitation during the colonial period, including several Spanish-period shipwrecks offshore.

A ranger station in the northwest area of the park has a **visitors center** (tel. 501/226-2833, http://bacalarchico.org) and displays of area history, including old glass bottles and Mayan relics found within the reserve. A picnic area offers a barbecue.

ACCOMMODATIONS AND FOOD

The two places to stay nearest Bacalar are on a beautiful hard-packed white-sand beach 12 miles north of San Pedro. The boat ride from town takes anywhere from 30 to 40 minutes, well past the last stop on the water taxi. These options are for folks who want to feel like they are on another island, not for people who want to drive golf carts, party, and be "in the mix" (though all the standard tours are still available, probably with a little extra transportation cost).

Tranquility Bay Resort (U.S. tel. 800/843-2293, www.tranquilitybayresort.com, from US$139) is the only resort on the island where you can snorkel directly from the beach to the reef. Every evening, tarpon, barracuda, and eagle rays swim under the lights of the dockside restaurant, appropriately named The Aquarium. There's a budget room just off the beach, along with seven brightly painted two-bedroom cabanas and three one-bedrooms with lofts, lining one of the nicest white-sand beaches on the island. Bedrooms are air-conditioned, and each cabana is equipped with a refrigerator

the toll bridge connecting San Pedro with north Ambergris Caye

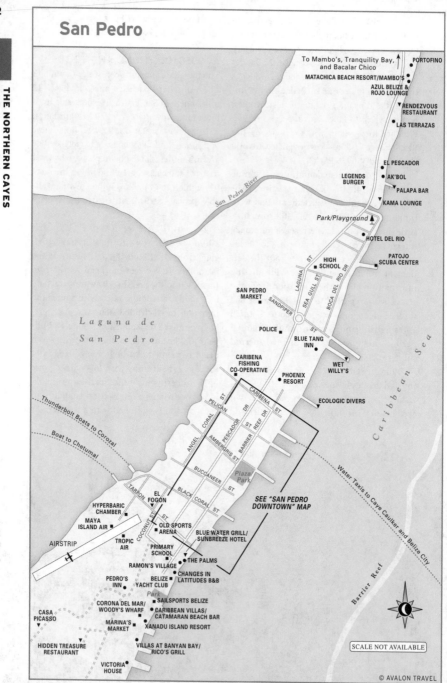

San Pedro

To Mambo's, Tranquility Bay, and Bacalar Chico

PORTOFINO

MATACHICA BEACH RESORT/MAMBO'S

AZUL BELIZE & ROJO LOUNGE

RENDEZVOUS RESTAURANT

LAS TERRAZAS

EL PESCADOR

AK'BOL

PALAPA BAR

KAMA LOUNGE

LEGENDS BURGER

San Pedro River

Park/Playground

HOTEL DEL RIO

PATOJO SCUBA CENTER

LAGUNA ST

HIGH SCHOOL

SEA GULL ST

BOCA DEL RIO DR

SAN PEDRO MARKET

SANDPIPER ST

POLICE

BLUE TANG INN

Laguna de San Pedro

CARIBENA FISHING CO-OPERATIVE

PHOENIX RESORT

WET WILLY'S

PELICAN ST

CARIBENA ST

DR

ECOLOGIC DIVERS

Thunderbolt Boats to Corozal

Boat to Chetumal

ANGEL ST

CORAL ST

AMBERGRIS ST

PESCADOR DR

BARRIER REEF DR

BUCCANEER ST

Plaza Park

SEE "SAN PEDRO DOWNTOWN" MAP

Caribbean Sea

Water Taxis to Caye Caulker and Belize City

TARPON ST

EL FOGÓN

BLACK CORAL ST

HYPERBARIC CHAMBER

COCONUT ST

OLD SPORTS ARENA

MAYA ISLAND AIR

TROPIC AIR

AIRSTRIP

BLUE WATER GRILL/ SUNBREEZE HOTEL

PRIMARY SCHOOL

THE PALMS

RAMON'S VILLAGE

CHANGES IN LATITUDES B&B

BELIZE YACHT CLUB

PEDRO'S INN

SAILSPORTS BELIZE

Park

CORONA DEL MAR/ WOODY'S WHARF

CARIBBEAN VILLAS/ CATAMARAN BEACH BAR

CASA PICASSO

MARINA'S MARKET

XANADU ISLAND RESORT

HIDDEN TREASURE RESTAURANT

VILLAS AT BANYAN BAY/ RICO'S GRILL

VICTORIA HOUSE

Barrier Reef

SCALE NOT AVAILABLE

© AVALON TRAVEL

The Marco Gonzalez Maya Site

Bone fragments discovered at the site are still being studied.

Those looking for a little Mayan history right on the island can find it at the **Marco Gonzalez Maya Site** (contact Jan Brown for a tour, 501/662-2725, www.marcogonzalezmayasite.com, US$10 site, US$8 transportation), just a 30-minute golf-cart ride from San Pedro to the south end of Ambergris Caye. Of an estimated 18 Mayan sites on the island, Marco Gonzalez was the first site to receive archaeological reserve status in 2011. History and adventure buffs will enjoy private guided tours of this virgin site, currently under study, which was inhabited by the Maya for 1,600 years. Head here with Jan Brown, a passionate expat and the reserve's chairperson, as your guide.

While the site continues to be preserved, cleaned, and examined for its history of the coastal Maya, it is literally a museum in the wild. A tour is an eco-adventure in itself, requiring careful navigation to avoid stepping on pieces of Mayan ceramics, with rainforest wildlife encounters along the way. Over the past few years, students have helped excavate parts of the site, revealing plaza structures and tombs. Human bones have been found, including skull fragments and skeletons as well as cutting tools made out of volcanic rock, thought to have been imported from Honduras and used for Mayan bloodletting rituals.

This may be the only place in the world where you can visit an ancient Maya trading city on an island and spot pieces on the site that date back to 100 BC. On the way back to San Pedro, stop along the way to enjoy the scenic views from the south side, some of the most beautiful on Ambergris Caye.

and a microwave. The cabins have Belizean hardwoods, Mexican tiles, and spectacular ocean views. The resort offers free use of kayaks, which can cover a lot of ground at this site, and there is an on-site dive shop. Fishing, snorkeling, scuba, and sailing trips are available.

The Turtleman's House (tel. 501/664-9661, http://turtlemanshouse.com) is a stilted shack above the water built out of salvaged material, much of it pieces of destroyed docks

that wash ashore after hurricanes, by Greg "Turtleman" Smith, a resident of this beach for decades and the man who is partly responsible for the creation of the reserve and protection of its wildlife. At first glance, US$80 a night with a three-night minimum seems overpriced, but you're paying for the location and the unique, albeit rustic, experience of being completely away from it all, with the barrier reef at your doorstep. Plus the meals are cheap, and you'll have the sunrise all to yourself. Guests sleep in the primitive room with a solar bag shower and sea grass compost bucket toilet, then join Greg, his wife, Rosemary, and their children in their home on the island, 50 feet away, for delicious home-cooked meals and cinnamon buns. Guests can also take advantage of Tranquility Bay's restaurant and dive shop, a stone's throw down the beach.

GETTING THERE

Most Ambergris dive shops and a few tour companies that do dive and snorkel trips to Bacalar Chico are based in San Pedro. Start with **Seaduced by Belize** (tel. 501/226-2254, www.seaducedbybelize.com, US$105 pp) and **Searious Adventures** (tel. 501/226-4202, www.seariousadventures.com, US$90), or arrange a trip with **Tranquility Bay Resort** (U.S. tel. 800/843-2293, www.tranquility-bayresort.com) or **The Turtleman's House** (tel. 501/664-9661, http://turtlemanshouse.com).

SPORTS AND RECREATION
Beaches

It is often said that you shouldn't expect the wide-open uninterrupted beaches seen in neighboring Mexico and other Caribbean destinations. The comparison is one between apples and oranges: Belize is unique in having a barrier reef, and one that's a short distance from the coastline, stopping any wave action from reaching the shores and leading to the buildup of sea grass in the shallow waters along the beach. This is a small sacrifice for a nearby natural wonder. To say there is no beach whatsoever is a stretch. It does require a little trekking away from San Pedro Town to find the better ones; the town's beachfront is nothing more than a long sandy pedestrian sidewalk, although you can still feel sand beneath your toes, and the ocean views are as beautiful as ever.

The best swimming and sunning section in San Pedro Town is directly in front of Ramon's Village Resort. This is where most head for

a swim and a snorkel. Numerous docks also give access where swimming might otherwise be difficult.

Beach enthusiasts have more choices just a short 15 to 30 minutes from town. A few of the hotels and bars on Ambergris Caye's north and south ends have wider, softer white-sand areas and better swimming entry points, although patches of sea grass are ever present.

One option is to head north of the bridge (by water taxi, bike, or cart, depending on how far you are going) and park yourself at one of the several beachfront bars or resorts—Palapa Bar is a great spot, as is Portofino resort, well worth the lengthier 30-minute boat ride with its boutique yet laid-back atmosphere, infinity pool, and calming views. Grab a meal or a cocktail and you can use the docks and dip your toes in that sand and clear water. One of the best natural swimming and snorkeling beaches is also 12 miles north of San Pedro at Tranquility Bay Resort.

Going south, lovely stretches shaded by dozens of palm trees are by Victoria House, one of the most gorgeous resorts on the island, or by Catamaran Beach Bar at Caribbean Villas. Start at any of these and hop your way along the beach.

Diving and Snorkeling

Almost every hotel on Ambergris either employs local dive shops or has its own on-site shop and dive masters. They offer similar services: resort courses, PADI or NAUI certification classes, day trips, and snorkel trips to Hol Chan Marine Reserve, Bacalar Chico, and others. Some also offer night dives, and a few have nitrox capabilities. Ultimately, what makes the difference is the experience of the instructor or dive master, the quality of the equipment, the specialty in dive sites, the size of the boat, and the size of the groups (an important factor if you want to avoid "cattle boats"). Prices are pretty standard around the island: local two-tank dives are about US$75, plus rental fees and tax; resort courses are US$160; open-water certification runs US$450-470; advanced certification is

Day Hop to Sarteneja

Sarteneja offers an authentic slice of life in Belize's fishing villages.

Looking for an off-the-beaten-path day trip or overnight getaway from San Pedro? Hop on the Thunderbolt water taxi (tel. 501/422-0026 or cell 501/610-4475, captain's cell 501/631-3400, www.ambergriscaye.com/thunderbolt, departs San Pedro at 3pm, US$42.50 roundtrip) or on a Tropic Air flight to **Sarteneja**, a beautiful fishing village in northern Belize. Located on Corozal Bay, it's still a well-kept secret—few travelers have heard about its breathtaking sunsets, sportfishing, turquoise swimming waters, wooden boat-building tradition and importance as a protected area for manatees and bird-nesting colonies in the Corozal Bay Wildlife Sanctuary. This is slowly changing, as more travelers now stop here on their way to or from the northern cayes.

Sarteneja, from the Mayan Tzaten-a-ha or "give me the water," was first settled by the Maya as an important trading area. It was occupied from approximately 600 BC to AD 1200, and period gold, copper, and shells continue to turn up in the area. Mexican refugees from the Yucatán Caste Wars settled here in the mid-19th century, attracted by the availability of drinking water. The village is known for its boat builders and free-diving lobster and conch fishers. It's also known for its annual **Easter Regatta**, during which newly painted sailboats of the artisan fishing fleet, crewed by local anglers, race against each other in a tradition that has continued since 1950. The regatta, on Easter weekend, includes live music, food, and fun local "catch the greasy pig" games.

Bring your swimwear—the water is beautiful and a stop here feels like an island getaway. Sarteneja is a great adventurer's option. You can rent kayaks from the **Tour Guide Association** office (Front St., US$5 per hour double kayak, 5 hours maximum) or hop on the Manatee Day tour to go manatee spotting (US$20 pp). The **beach** on the long, pretty coastline offers swimming and relaxing. The farther east you go, the prettier and more isolated the swimming areas get. Other options include hiking in the Shipstern Nature Reserve, exploring the Bacalar Chico Marine Reserve on the northern tip of Ambergris Caye, or fishing along Corozal Bay (US$30 pp for 2 people) with Ritchie Cruz of **Ritchie's Place** (Front St., tel. 501/668-1531).

Stay overnight for a full experience. Several guesthouses offer a decent night's sleep—opt for **Fernando's Seaside Guesthouse** (tel. 501/423-4085, www.cybercayecaulker.com/sarteneja.html, US$40-50 plus tax), with its large balconies, breezy views, and friendly staff.

If you're up for more culture and immersion, sign up for the **Sarteneja Homestay Program** (501/634-8032, sartenejahomestay@gmail.com, US$25 pp, includes meals). You can stay with a local family for a night or more in a comfortable guest room with shared bathroom.

US$380; three-tank dives to the Blue Hole are US$250-325 and to Turneffe US$235.

Beginners and experienced divers or snorkelers alike have several solid choices. **Amigos del Mar** (at the Mayan Princess Hotel beachfront dock, tel. 501/226-2706, www.amigosdivebelize.com), based on the pier across from Cholo's Sports Bar, is a bustling place with top-notch gear and a solid reputation for safety. Many clients return year after year to dive with the same long-term and friendly staff. Amigos runs frequent trips to the Blue Hole in 56- and 60-foot boats (important for the long journey to and from the famous site).

Hugh Parkey's Diving (at the SunBreeze Hotel beachfront in central San Pedro, tel. 501/226-4526 or 501/670-5239, www.belize-diving.com) specializes in local dives only. **Ecologic Divers** (tel. 501/226-4118, www.ecologicdivers.com), with the best-looking dock in town, offers regular Blue Hole and atoll journeys in the comfort of their new covered dive boat—taking no more than 12 divers at a time—as well as night dives. **Patojo's Scuba Center** (tel. 501/206-2283, patojos99@yahoo.com) is another option. All have proven reputations for safety and service.

Snorkeling gear can be rented from **Ramon's Village Resort** (Ramon's Dive Shop pier, half-day US$5, full-day US$10), and there is decent marinelife just at the end of their dock, specially created for those seeking to snorkel in town. If you decide to explore from another dock, beware of boat activity at all times, as there have been serious accidents.

Snuba and Sea Trek

To change it up a bit from regular snorkeling or for those who want to avoid diving, try snuba or sea trek. Both allow for an underwater experience and a chance for fun photo ops and videos without fretting about a tank or equalizing.

Snuba lets you explore the barrier reef at depths of up to 20 feet without getting scuba certified and without a heavy tank strapped to your back: Breathing is through a regulator, receiving air through a long 20-foot line attached to a support raft that floats safely at the surface. Training is provided in 15 minutes, and anyone over age eight can participate as long as they can swim.

Sea trek consists of hiking the sea floor, literally: Plop on a cool helmet that receives almost three times the amount of air needed through a hose. So far, the only certified outfitter to offer this new way of experiencing

This sandy stretch by Ramon's Village Resort is the best swimming beach in town.

Snorkeling and Diving off Ambergris Caye

Choose from a casual snorkel in town or a half- or a full-day snorkel or dive tour by boat. The first tion is for days when you want to stay close to shore; the second is for exploring marinelife and co a must when in Belize. Be sure to observe snorkel and reef etiquette at all times.

- **Ramon's Village Resort** (Ramon's Dive Shop pier, tel. 501/226-2071, U.S. tel. 800/624-4215, www.ramons.com) has an artificial reef that is home to a wide variety of small reef fish. Snorkel trips to the Belize Barrier Reef are available.

- **Hol Chan Marine Reserve** (reserve office on Caribeña St., www.holchanbelize.org) is the crown jewel of snorkeling, located four miles southeast of San Pedro Town.

- **Shark Ray Alley** is usually included on a trip to Hol Chan Marine Reserve. Snorkel alongside large southern stingrays and nurse sharks and view spectacular coral formations, or dive the *Amigos Del Mar* tugboat wreck.

- **Mexico Rocks,** on the reef north of town, is the place to see a huge variety of coral formations.

- **Bacalar Chico Marine Reserve,** near the northern tip of Ambergris Caye, is an incredible site with a stunning diversity of wildlife and coral—at least 187 species of fish and several important spawning aggregation sites, plus loggerhead, green, and hawksbill sea turtles.

Hol Chan is **Discovery Expeditions** (tel. 501/671-2882 or 501/671-0748, www.discoverybelize.com, US$68-74, including hotel transfers but not the US$10 Hol Chan park fee) out of San Pedro, which is also a snuba outfitter. If you're staying on Caye Caulker, you may be able to arrange the tour through your hotel and catch the water taxi over to San Pedro for a day. Another option offered is to "power snorkel"—snorkeling with a hand-held power scooter.

Boating and Sailing

Explore the Caribbean the way it was meant to be traveled: by sea. Old standby boats include the "old-school sailing trip" aboard the refurbished *Rum Punch II* (parked north of Cholo's Sports Bar, tel. 501/610-3240), operated by longtime resident and captain George Eiley, offering glass-bottom-boat snorkel tours, beach barbecues, and sunset charters.

The *Sirena Azul* is a 40-foot Belizean hardwood beauty operated out of the Blue Tang Inn. Built by a boat-building family in the northern village of Sarteneja, and with an added diesel onboard engine and restroom,

this sailboat an experience worth the extra cost. Sunset sails (US$50 pp, drinks included; private charter US$350 for 1-6 people) are popular, although the boat also goes on snorkeling day trips.

Another popular and fancy cat for private rent or for sunset sails is *Seaduction,* operated by **Seaduced by Belize** (tel. 501/226-2254, www.seaducedbybelize.com). Ecological divers now offer sailing charters aboard their two 50-foot catamarans as well as sunset dinner cruises by the reef.

For a more rustic and laid-back sail, spend the day with the Rubio brothers snorkeling, fishing, drinking aboard *No Rush,* a quaint 36-foot catamaran that can be booked through **Unity Tours** (tel. 501/600-5022, www.ambergriscaye.com/unitytours, full-day snorkel US$75 pp, half-day US$50 pp). **Reef Runners** (tel. 501/602-5055 or 501/610-1061, www.ambergriscaye.com/reefrunner, full-day snorkel US$45 adults) has 24-foot-long glass-bottom boats for snorkel tours and fishing trips, and they know these waters well. You can't miss their bright-yellow boats docked beside the San Pedro Belize water taxi terminal. **Searious**

Belize's Big Three: The Grand Slam

Chasing tail in Belizean waters is on the dream list of anglers worldwide and has been for decades. Many also head here for a chance to achieve the grand slam: catching a tarpon, permit, and bonefish in one day. Doing so is no small feat—some spend as much as a week of daily excursions and even years attempting it. Those who succeed automatically gain a spot in a de facto exclusive group of top-rated anglers.

While visitors can conduct their own grand slam fly-fishing mission year-round in Belize, Ambergris Caye holds an annual catch-and-release sportfishing tournament and event known as the **Tres Pescados Slam Tournament**. It's the fly-fishing competition of all fishing competitions, with teams descending on San Pedro from other countries and parts of Belize to compete in catching the big three in just three days. Teams consist of one or two fly-fishers and a Belize Tourism Board licensed guide. Held annually since 2009, the competition is more intense than ever to win prestigious titles, including Top Guide, Top Female Angler, Best Men's and Women's Casting, and generous cash prizes.

The money raised by the tournament supports a worthwhile cause. Up to 15 teams participated in 2012, donating US$7,000 to the Bonefish Tarpon Trust Project in Belize, benefiting bonefish, permit, and tarpon fisheries.

Nonfishing family members can have fun too, as the three-day event includes weekend long games and activities, usually held at the Central Park in San Pedro. For information contact **Tres Pescados Fly Shop** (tel. 501/226-3474, http://belizefly.com).

Adventures (tel. 501/226-4202, www.seariousadventures.com) offers sailing and snorkeling activities.

A notch up is **Belize Sailing Vacations** (tel. 501/621-0417 or 501/664-5300, U.S. tel. 800/640-2182, www.belizesailingvacations.com, from US$1,295), providing luxury sailing charters with "the amenities of an all-inclusive luxury resort aboard your own private catamaran, tailored to your own personalized itinerary." This dream itinerary goes from island-hopping to snorkeling and diving on the way or just relaxing on board. A popular choice is *Doris,* a 50-foot catamaran with four air-conditioned cabins, four baths, lounge areas, plasma TVs, and your very own chef on board.

Fishing

The area within the reef is a favorite for tarpon and bonefish. Outside the reef, the choice of big game is endless. Most hotels and dive shops will make arrangements for fishing, including a boat and a guide. Ask around the docks (and your hotel) for the best guides. Serious anglers should consider Abner Marin at **Go Fish Belize** (beachfront at Boca del Rio Dr., tel. 501/226-3121, www.gofishbelize.com), one of the most qualified and reputable guides around. Or try **Fishing San Pedro** (Front St., above Manelly's, tel. 501/607-9967, www.fishingsanpedro.com), another sure bet where half- or full-day chartered fishing trips are relatively affordable at US$325 for a full day for two people, including tackle, bait, soft drinks, and water; a fish or lobster barbecue costs a bit extra.

Kayaking

Little wave action and regular trade winds make kayaking a great option off Belize's cayes. Ideal spots to navigate are on the south side of the island near Xanadu Island Resort or Caribbean Villas, with wider open space and less boat activity. The north end also offers quieter options for rowing in safety. Many hotels offer complimentary use of kayaks. If not, check with **San Pedro Water Sports** (beachfront dock near Holiday Hotel, tel. 501/226-2888, www.sanpedrowatersports.com, single kayak US$15 per hour) or with **Ramon's Village Resort** (dockside, US$15 per hour, US$35 per day).

Wind Sports

The latest wind sports are all the rage. It's not surprising, given the often ideal weather conditions. There's that "constant breeze in Belize" that locals love to brag about—the result of Caribbean trade winds that hit the islands from November to July. Combine it with a nearby reef that creates flat waters, and voilà!

Sailsports Belize (beachfront by Caribbean Villas, tel. 501/226-4488 or 501/610-0773, www.sailsportsbelize.com) is a solid and affordable choice for windsurfing, kite surfing, and sailing. Its location is on a calm stretch of beach with plenty of open water. Lessons and courses are offered with licensed instructors (introduction to windsurfing and two-hour rental US$99; beginner kite surfing five-hour course US$303) and hotel delivery is available for rentals (windsurfing US$22 per hour, sailing US$49 per hour).

San Pedro Water Sports (dock across from Holiday Hotel, tel. 501/226-2888, www.sanpedrowatersports.com) has equipment for rent, including paddleboards (US$15 per hour) and windsurfing boards. Adrian is happy to give you pointers on paddleboarding if it's your first time.

Ramon's Village Resort's dive shop has windsurfing or Hobie Cat catamaran lessons (US$45-70 for 2 hours) and equipment rentals (windsurfing US$20 per hour, Hobie Cat US$30 per hour).

KiteXplorer (beachfront, tel. 501/635-4967, http://kitexplorer.com/kitex, 9am-6pm daily) shares a dock with Patojo's Dive Center and has two licensed instructors offering kite surfing or paddle surfing lessons (kite surfing intro US$90, stand-up paddle surfing US$45 for 1.5 hours). Rentals are also available for paddle surfing and kite surfing (US$20-120 per hour). The ideal months for these weather-influenced sports are November to July, with March to July offering the strongest winds. KiteXplorer also operates out of Caye Caulker.

A great way to relax and catch spectacular views of the island and reef, weather permitting, is to parasail with **Funtasea** (Fido's dock, tel. 501/226-3866, wwww.funtasea.net, US$77 pp, US$145 double). Funtasea also offers other boat and ecotours of the island.

Birding and Wildlife-Watching

Although many people come here for the reef, Ambergris also offers birding and nature tour opportunities.

Take a boat ride along the north of the island, where wildlife can be spotted along the beach and also in the lagoon on the back side, a peaceful, rarely visited part of Ambergris. Sightings may include egrets, great herons, and, if you're lucky, crocodiles. For customized tours and other island nature tours, check with any of the beachfront operators or with **Seaduced by Belize** (tel. 501/226-2254, www.seaducedbybelize.com). Ask about half-day trips to two bird sanctuaries, Cayo Rosario and Little Guana Caye, where you can spot more species.

Another popular bird-watching spot near town is the unique **"People Perch"** at **Caribbean Villas** (tel. 501/226-2715, www.caribbeanvillas.com, 6am-6pm daily), south of San Pedro. It's a tall viewing tower built by the owners, Will and Susan Lala, who are avid bird-watchers. The tower is reached after hiking the nature trail on the property, and at the top, there are 360-degree views over a canopy of trees and flowers and, to the east, the Caribbean Sea. Look for signs to this private sanctuary or contact the hotel for more information. Numerous species of birds can be spotted from here, but you must arrive by sunrise to spot them. Otherwise, you can glimpse and hear them in the small forest. Next door, **Xanadu Island Resort** also has a lush marked nature trail at the back of the property; stop in at the front desk for directions.

Massage and Bodywork

If your hotel lacks a proper gym and you'd rather pump iron than dive, the **Train Station** (tel. 501/226-4222, www.trainstationfitness.com) is 2.5 blocks south of the bridge. In San Pedro, you'll find both scheduled yoga classes (drop-in US$15) and

50

THE NORTHERN CAYES
SAN PEDRO AND AMBERGRIS CAYE

Land Tours from San Pedro

Lamanai's River Safari is a highlight of this inland trip from San Pedro.

While staying on Ambergris Caye provides plenty of entertainment and pretty sights, Belize's beautiful interior of rainforests, rivers teeming with wildlife, underground caves, and Mayan sites is not to be missed. Most tour operators in San Pedro offer full day trips to the mainland, or they can easily be arranged through your hotel. Take a break from the sea and hop on one of these memorable inland adventures.

If you're looking to combine these tours and save a few bucks, look into package deals and book in advance. **Searious Adventures** (tel. 501/226-4202 or 501/226-4206, www.seariousadventures. com, US$150) offers interesting ones. Remember to bring sunscreen, insect repellant and a hat or sunglasses. If touring in the summer—the rainy season—pack a light rain jacket.

LAMANAI RIVER SAFARI AND ARCHAEOLOGICAL SITE

If your schedule only allows one land tour, opt for this day-long journey through the wilderness. The trip (7am-5:30pm daily mid-Nov.-mid-Apr., US$152 pp) begins with a water taxi ride towards the mainland, just under an hour away. From there, you'll take a short 30-minute van ride that will carry you to the banks of the New River, in northern Belize. A riverboat takes you slowly along the New River—one of Belize's most beautiful bodies of water—where you'll spot howler monkeys, birds, iguanas, snakes, and, if you're lucky, crocodiles. Bring your camera, as the scenery is quite incredible. Once the boat is docked at the Lamanai site, a hike begins through a lush rainforest, leading to the archaeological site itself and the various Mayan temples. Climb up the High Temple and take in the 360-degree view of the surrounding canopy and river before descending and heading back to San Pedro in time for sunset.

CAVE TUBING AND THE BELIZE ZOO

The scenery and experience of navigating a river in a tube and floating through ancient Mayan ceremonial caves is straight out of a movie. You'll leave San Pedro early (7am-5:30pm daily mid-Nov.-mid-Apr., US$169 pp, breakfast and lunch included) and land in the mainland's western district of Cayo, one of Belize's top adventure destinations. When you're done cave tubing, it's just over an hour ride to the 29-acre Belize Zoo. Anything but typical, the zoo houses animals that are native to Belize, particularly those that were orphaned, injured, or need special care. Set in a lush rainforest and an environment that's as natural as can be, the zoo holds the country's top five cats, including jaguars, pumas, and ocelots, along with Belize's national animal, the tapir.

private sessions at **Sol Spa** (Phoenix Hotel, tel. 501/226-2410, www.belizesolspa.com, 9am-5pm daily), a small but cozy retreat offering a range of treatments and massages like Honeymoon Bliss, Solar Therapy, and Maya Abdominal Massage.

The **Asian Garden Day Spa** (Coconut Dr., across from Ramon's Village Resort, tel. 501/226-4072, www.asiangardenspasalon. com) is a family-run spa in a lovely courtyard, specializing in Thai massage, hot stone therapy, reflexology, facials, scrubs, and specials like sunset or starlight couples massage.

Jordana's Touch of Art Massage Studio (beachfront San Pedro, tel. 501/226-3357, www.artoftouchspa.com) is in the entrance to the Sunbreeze Hotel. The spa offers massages, reflexology, aromatherapy, manicures and pedicures, and even hair-braiding services for that extra tropical look (full head US$40).

A block away from Front Street is **Black Orchid Spa** (Tarpon St., Vilma Linda Plaza, 2nd Fl., tel. 501/226-3939, www.blackorchid-spa.com, 9am-8pm Mon.-Sat., 10am-5pm Sun.), with good reviews but set in the hustle and bustle of San Pedro, which might snap you back into reality too quickly as you leave the oasis.

A short distance before reaching the bridge going north, for a more casual option and an authentic Caribbean setting, look for Shirlene Santino's **Just Relax Massage** and her seaside massage chair and hut (near Wayo's Beach Bar, tel. 501/666-3536, deep tissue US$40 per hour, house calls US$55). Shirlene has special oils for any ailment ranging from sunburn to back aches. Call ahead for an appointment.

Farther up north is **Serenity Spa and Wellness Center** at Las Terrazas Resort (U.S. tel. 800/557-1553, www.lasterrazasresort.com), with the "Unbelizeable Facial" and other treatments.

Ak'Bol Yoga Retreat (tel. 501/226-2073, www.akbol.com) is one of the few places in Belize offering daily yoga classes (usually at 9am), popular among residents.

ENTERTAINMENT AND EVENTS

San Pedro boasts the best nightlife in the country, whether your idea of fun is dancing up a storm, barhopping, dining to live music, or betting on chicken poop—it's all here. San Pedranos have a weeklong calendar of places to be. Wednesday and Saturday are the biggest nights out, and water taxis actually change their schedules to accommodate revelers. But other nights are popular as well, including Monday for live *punta* music and Thursday because of the Chicken Drop. In general, the hot spots don't get going until 11pm or midnight, with lots of warming up in various bars before the bumpin' and grindin' begins.

Nightlife
BARS AND LOUNGES

Diving or touring by day and partying by night is the standard San Pedro scene, although some really do barhop all day long. There are enough watering holes on the island for serious drinkers. Lately, more upscale lounges have found their way to the north and south of the island.

Starting in the center of town, the beachfront **Cholo's Sports Bar** (tel. 501/226-2406, 10am-midnight daily) is a modest but perfect local hangout and the heart of San Pedro's social scene. You'll find the cheapest drinks in town (US$1.50 for a rum and Coke) and plenty of people-watching from the outdoor tables, as it's close to the water taxis and dive shops. Ceviche is the only bar snack. Expect to see only men on the inside, sitting at the bar or playing pool.

A few stumbling steps from Cholo's on the roadside is **Lola's Pub** (Front St., tel. 501/206-2120, 11am-midnight daily), one of my favorites and a popular after-work or weekend hangout, not to mention a great pre-party warm-up spot. Beautifully lit shelves house top-shelf liquor, and the bistro-like atmosphere is casual and friendly, with a couple of flat-screen TVs and music. If you're lucky, your bartender will be Trevor, whom I'm

Downtown San Pedro

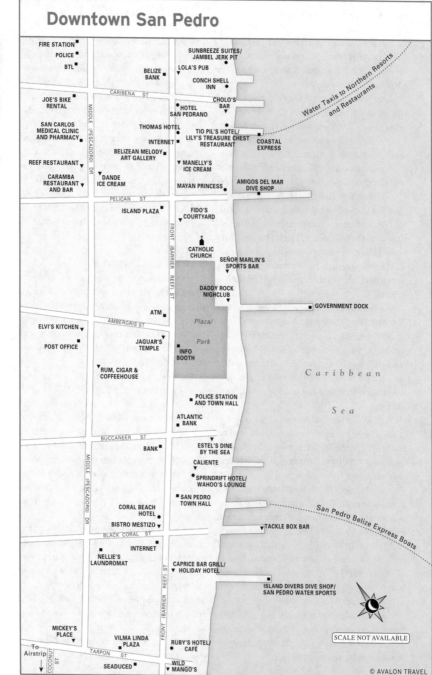

FIRE STATION
POLICE
BTL
BELIZE BANK
SUNBREEZE SUITES/ JAMBEL JERK PIT
LOLA'S PUB
CONCH SHELL INN
CARIBENA ST
JOE'S BIKE RENTAL
CHOLO'S BAR
HOTEL SAN PEDRANO
SAN CARLOS MEDICAL CLINIC AND PHARMACY
THOMAS HOTEL
INTERNET
TIO PIL'S HOTEL/ LILY'S TREASURE CHEST RESTAURANT
COASTAL EXPRESS
BELIZEAN MELODY ART GALLERY
REEF RESTAURANT
MANELLY'S ICE CREAM
CARAMBA RESTAURANT AND BAR
DANDE ICE CREAM
MAYAN PRINCESS
AMIGOS DEL MAR DIVE SHOP
PELICAN ST
ISLAND PLAZA
FIDO'S COURTYARD
CATHOLIC CHURCH
SEÑOR MARLIN'S SPORTS BAR
DADDY ROCK NIGHCLUB
GOVERNMENT DOCK
ATM
AMBERGRIS ST
Plaza/ Park
ELVI'S KITCHEN
POST OFFICE
JAGUAR'S TEMPLE
INFO BOOTH
RUM, CIGAR & COFFEEHOUSE
Caribbean
Sea
POLICE STATION AND TOWN HALL
ATLANTIC BANK
BUCCANEER ST
BANK
ESTEL'S DINE BY THE SEA
CALIENTE
SPRINDRIFT HOTEL/ WAHOO'S LOUNGE
SAN PEDRO TOWN HALL
CORAL BEACH HOTEL
BISTRO MESTIZO
San Pedro Belize Express Boats
TACKLE BOX BAR
BLACK CORAL ST
INTERNET
NELLIE'S LAUNDROMAT
CAPRICE BAR GRILL/ HOLIDAY HOTEL
ISLAND DIVERS DIVE SHOP/ SAN PEDRO WATER SPORTS
MICKEY'S PLACE
VILMA LINDA PLAZA
To Airstrip
TARPON ST
RUBY'S HOTEL/ CAFÉ
WILD MANGO'S
SEADUCED

MIDDLE (PESCADORO) DR
FRONT (BARRIER REEF) ST
COCONUT ST

Water Taxis to Northern Resorts and Restaurants

SCALE NOT AVAILABLE

© AVALON TRAVEL

convinced is one of the top three in town (try his Cadillac margarita).

Farther down the beach is **Fido's Courtyard** (Front St., tel. 501/226-2056, www.fidosbelize.com, 10am-midnight Mon.-Fri., 10am-2am Sat.-Sun.), the largest bar-restaurant complex in town, catering mostly to travelers with a live rock band almost every night in the high season and an all-day full menu that ranges from bar foods to dinner.

Place your bets at the weekly **Chicken Drop** at 6pm Thursday in front of **Wahoo's Lounge and Bar** (beachside in the Spindrift Hotel, tel. 501/226-2002) and **Caliente Restaurant** (tel. 501/226-2170, 11am-9:30pm Tues.-Sun.). A chicken is let loose on a numbered grid after revelers place bets on which number the chicken will choose to soil. The winner takes a cash prize, but not before cleaning up the poop. Warm up at Wahoo's Lounge and Bar with two-for-one rum punches and a DJ playing calypso and upbeat local sounds on the beach, or with Caliente Restaurant's two-for-one happy hour (4pm-6pm daily) and delicious nachos.

The beachfront outdoor **Señor Marlin's Sports Bar** (tel. 501/672-0212, 11am-midnight daily) was named after the massive marlin caught and brought back in the owner's canoe. Just a few steps from Central Park, the bright green exterior and the interior *palapa* decor are complemented by stiff drinks and an excellent DJ playing reggae, dancehall, and house tunes. Umbrella-covered seating is available directly on the beach.

The slightly more upscale **Caprice Bar Grill**, with interior and beachfront dock seating, is a decent choice for its popular half-price weekday happy hour (3pm-6pm Mon.-Fri.).

Also on San Pedro's beachfront, **Hurricane's Ceviche Bar and Grill** (tel. 501/226-4124, 10am-10pm Wed.-Mon.), set on a dock over the water, serves a variety of—you guessed it—ceviche. It has a very friendly barkeep and a narrow hidden top deck for views of the water and the beach. The **Rehab Bar** (Front St., open daily), a small patio bar next to the Jaguar's Temple disco, is a favorite f[] people-watching.

South of San Pedro, **Crazy Canuc[]** **Beach Bar** (S. Coconut Dr.) has live music and dancing on Monday, Thursday, and Sunday afternoon. You'll find happy customers and meet interesting characters playing cards, horseshoes, dominoes, and other games. Also on Coconut Drive directly across from Canucks, look for the **Roadkill Bar** (S. Coconut Dr., 3:30pm-midnight daily), another popular open-air hangout with joke Monday, karaoke on Wednesday, and a free beer with a shot of tequila for US$5 until 9pm. Their panty ripper cocktails are delicious.

Continuing south, you'll find a neighborhood gem in **Average Joe's Bar** (Blake St., tel. 501/602-7564, 4pm-midnight Mon., 11am-midnight Tues.-Sun.), a casual bar with the most comfortable bar stools I've sat on, live music on Wednesday and Friday, karaoke Saturday night, and special drinks (try the frozen raspberry lemon margarita). The finger licking good "dawgs" and wings menu will soak up the alcohol nicely.

A short distance before the north bridge is the lively **Wayo's Beachside Beernet** (Boca del Rio, tel. 501/661-8271, 10am-midnight daily), a casual, colorful outdoor hangout ideal for drinks, a bite, and a swim all day long, or for nighttime fun with the occasional karaoke night. Across from the bar a *palapa* and a hammock are set even closer to the water. Owner "Wayo from Cayo" will even pick you up at night and give you a ride back if needed, ideal for solo female travelers. A stone's throw away is the **Sand Bar** (across from Wet Willy's dock, tel. 501/630-1241, 11am-midnight daily), serving cheap local drinks as well as tasty bar food and pizza.

North of San Pedro, the legendary **Palapa Bar** (tel. 501/226-3111, 10am-about 9pm daily) is an absolute must-stop while on Ambergris, whether for lunch, sunset, or a lazy evening of appetizers (US$4-6), barbecue, beer, and cocktails. For the full Palapa Bar experience, bring a bathing suit so you can swim and float in an anchored inner tube and have the bartender lower you down a bucket of beer and take up your empty ones. It's a short golf cart ride north of the bridge, or US$3.50 by water taxi from the Coastal Express dock in San Pedro.

Kama Lounge (set in from the north-side road, tel. 501/610-3775 or 501/226-3709, kamalounge@yahoo.com, noon-10pm daily) raises it up a whole notch and is quite possibly the sexiest lounge and bar in Belize. This waterfront escape is a sight to be seen, with lilac voile curtains flowing over a maze of red cushy beds, a small plunge pool in the center, hookahs standing tall on every table, a full bar, and a decent-tasting menu of kebabs, ceviche, pasta, and panini. The evening red mood lighting is impossible to miss from the water, not to mention lounge beats that make you sink farther into the *camas* (beds). There are regular Tuesday hookah nights, live music or a DJ on weekends, occasional movie nights on a 15-foot screen, full moon parties, and more.

Farther up north is **Rojo Lounge** (at Azul Belize, next to Matachica Resort, tel. 501/226-4012, www.azulbelize.com, noon-close Tues.-Sat.), a trendy waterfront spot with beds and fancy cocktails.

If a quieter, pre-dinner glass of wine is more your beat, try the Friday-night wine social at **Wine de Vine** (Coconut Dr., tel. 501/226-3430, www.winedevine.com, 4pm-7pm Fri.).

DANCING

Monday is "happening" at **Crazy Canucks Beach Bar** (S. Coconut Dr.) with a live *punta* band. Get ready to throw back the cocktails, meet locals, and shake your hips Garífuna-style. The band begins around 9pm.

Wednesday is ladies' night at **Wet Willy's** (beachfront, tel. 501/226-4136), a cool thatched-roof waterfront pier nightclub, and Saturday gets going when the bars close at midnight and everyone wanders across the street to **Jaguar's Temple** (tel. 501/226-4077, www.jaguarstempleclub.com, from 9:30pm Thurs.-Sat.), the most popular and decent nightclub in Belize. The two-story interior is complete with a large dance floor, two bars with spacious standing room, air-conditioning, and just the right amount of snazzy disco lighting. After Jaguar's, the insatiable night owls often stumble over to **Daddy Rocks Nightclub** (10am-4am Thurs.-Sat., 11am-4am Sun.), just across the street in the park. It has a can't-miss-it flamboyant exterior (you'll have to see it to believe it) and stays open until 7am. The music is more the reggae

Wayo's Beachside Beernet is one of several fun outdoor bars on Ambergris Caye.

Live Music in San Pedro

Music aficionados will find their fix in San Pedro. It's the most frequent, steady, weeklong schedule of musicians and bands you'll find anywhere in Belize, although other parts of the country tend to offer more local sounds and less in Western genres. Overall, San Pedro's offerings reflect a mix that keeps visitors and locals happy on a year-round basis—from soothing Latin melodies over dinner to light rock, jazz, and blues bands catering to travelers and expats, and local *punta* rock sounds for a taste of the Afro-influenced Garífuna side of Belize. And there's no extra cover charge! Up for it? Here's your weeklong itinerary.

Monday, start out at **Crazy Canucks Beach Bar** (beachfront, tel. 501/670-8001, 7:30pm-11pm Mon.) with the local and popular Punta Boys Band. Grab a few drinks before the live Garífuna drums, turtle shells, and hip-shaking fun start around 9:30pm. The crowd is a mix of visitors, expats, and locals.

Tuesday gives you a chance to get behind the mic on Jam Night at popular **Legends Burger House** (north of the bridge, tel. 501/226-2113, noon-midnight Tues.). Ask about the other live-music nights, including Saturday. To continue the night, head to the waterfront pier bar **Tackle Box** (beachfront, tel. 501/226-4313, www.tackleboxbarandgrill.com, 9pm-close Tues.) for a mix of late-night Belizean sounds.

Wednesday, start out mellow with Cuban music and tapas at **Red Ginger** (Phoenix Resort, tel. 501/226-4623, www.redgingerbelize.com, 6pm-9pm Wed.), a more intimate option. If you're up for post-dinner fun, head to the island's biggest dance night at the infamous **Wet Willy's** (beachfront, tel. 501/226-4136), which gets going around 11pm.

Thursday, it's **Fido's Courtyard** (Front St., tel. 501/226-2056, www.fidosbelize.com, 6pm-close Thurs., 9pm-close Fri.) for a beachfront setting. A regular lineup of light rock or jazz bands fills this large indoor and outdoor space. While there isn't much "local" about Fido's, it's there if you need an option. Not to be missed, however, is the local Belizean music at the Chicken Drop event just down from Fido's at **Wahoo's Lounge** (Front St., 501/634-6008, www.wahoosloungebelize.com, 6pm-midnight Thurs.), playing a mix of calypso, reggae, *punta*, and more. It's possibly the closest you'll come to dancing barefoot to local music on San Pedro's "beach."

Friday nights are also popular at Fido's; Saturday, you can rock and roll at Wahoo's.

Sunday is "Funday" in Belize. Everything shuts down except the bars and restaurants, and everyone relaxes, swims on the beach, drinks Belikins, listens to music, and breaks out the barbecue grills. Try **Crazy Canucks Beach Bar** (noon-close Sun.) or **Caribbean Villas** (Seagrape Dr., tel. 501/226-2715, www.caribbeanvillashotel.com, 7:30am-9pm Sun.). Wherever you end up, don't forget your swimming gear to take advantage of the docks or swimming pools.

and dancehall type, while Jaguar plays a mix of all genres, from house to reggae and Latin, and attracts more of a "cool" crowd, though as a visitor you'll dance at either one. The fun gets started around 11pm-midnight and can go until 4am and later.

Festivals and Events

San Pedro's events are a year-round affair. These celebrations bring even more crowds, but experiencing them is a chance to witness the San Pedrano joie de vivre.

The **San Pedro Carnaval** (mid-Feb.) encompasses copious amounts of colorful paint splattered on the crowd, egg throwing, men dressed like women, and all-around Mardi Gras-type debauchery. The highlights of three days of partying include cultural dance performances on opening night as well as *comparsas*, or street dance groups competing for prizes.

The two-day **Lagoon Reef Eco-Challenge Kayak Race** (tel. 501/226-2247, www.ecochallengebelize.com, June, registration US$200-500) attracts professional, amateur, and junior kayakers (over age 15) from around the world to compete in a 60-mile race around the entire island. The race begins south of Ambergris, passes by the lagoon side and through mangrove cayes on day ie, and reaches the northern tip at Bacalar Chico for the night before continuing back down the island along the reef on the second day. The funds raised go toward promoting the connection between the island's lagoons and the reef—both an integral part of the island's ecosystem and vital to the livelihood of its inhabitants.

Lobsterfest (first week of June) is slowly becoming the most anticipated event on the island. It is a celebration of the opening of the lobster season with week-long bar crawl events, outdoor food festivals, and concerts in Central Park.

San Pedro holds the **Día de San Pedro** (end of June), a three-day festival in honor of St. Peter, the island's patron saint. There are traditional dances, pageants, food vendors, and music showcasing the island's mixed Belizean, Mexican, and Mayan heritage. If you can only attend one day, come opening night.

The **Costa Maya Festival** (first weekend in Aug.) is considered Belize's biggest festival—perhaps in size, because it attracts guests and participants from the neighboring Maya Mundo in one big celebration of heritage. It's worth checking out to sample all the fantastic food vendors.

The island celebrates Independence Day (Sept. 21) with the **Independence Day Parade.** San Pedro's parade rivals even the capital's, with carnival floats, costumes, marching bands, free rum and beer, beach after-parties, and children and adults dancing in the streets. It's an ideal time to visit, not least for the festivities and off-season prices.

One of San Pedro's unique and biggest year-end festivities is the **San Pedro Holiday Boat Light Parade** (http://sanpedroboatparade.com, 7pm first weekend in Dec.). In a spectacular display, illuminated boats cruise along San Pedro's shores from Boca del Rio all the way to Caribbean Villas. Children singing carols, marching bands, dancing, and loud cheers and music from the beachfront watering holes add to the holiday spirit. At the end of the course, judges pick the prize-winning boats, from most artistic to most religious.

SHOPPING

Gift shops abound in San Pedro, especially on Front and Middle Streets; they've got your postcards, beach apparel, towels, hats, T-shirts, hot sauces, and the usual knickknacks.

Arts and Crafts
Belizean Arts (Fido's Courtyard, tel. 501/226-2056, www.belizeanarts.com, 11am-7pm daily) sells art, jewelry, ceramics, and carvings by Central American and Belizean artists. The well-established shop has the largest selection of original paintings in Belize.

Paradise Gallery (Vilma Linda Plaza, tel. 501/226-4437, belizeframeshop@gmail.com, 10am-6pm Mon.-Sat.) has a small collection of local paintings and crafts and offers framing services.

Get your rocks at **Ambergris Maya Jade and History Museum** (across from town hall, 9am-6pm daily). Also a retail jade shop, it's designed "to give visitors an overview of 3,000 years of Mesoamerican jade and its importance to the cultures in the region."

Belizean Melody Art Gallery (Front St., 501/226-2787, www.belizemelodyart.com, 9am-6pm Mon.-Sat.) has carefully selected paintings, crafts, and unique handmade souvenirs, all guaranteed to be made in Belize. Transforming her great-grandmother's house into a gallery, San Pedro native, owner, and artist Melody Sanchez Wolfe—currently the visual and expressive arts director for the island's cultural committee—is passionate about providing an outlet for the success of fellow Belizean talents, some as young as 18. Hand-painted shell magnets are just an example of some unique made-in-Belize souvenir items, and the gorgeous paintings aren't to be found anywhere else.

Books
A decent book selection is available at **San**

Pedro Books (in Vilma Linda Plaza, Tarpon St., tel. 501/226-4797, 9am-5pm Mon.-Sat.).

Clothing and Jewelry

Ambar (Fido's Courtyard, tel. 501/226-2056, 10am-5pm daily) offers handcrafted jewelry made with resin ambers, Maya jade, shells, and silver.

Gourmet Goodies

Two chocolate stores in town source their cacao from Punta Gorda's Cacao Growers Association. The **Chocolate Boutique** (Front St., next to Wild Mango's, tel. 501/610-4828 or cell 501/634-9878, www.belizechoco-latecompany.com, 10am-6:30pm Mon.-Sat.) has chocolate bars, truffles, and "kakaw" powder as well as chocochino and other delicious chocolate drinks. The cacao body oil and bars make great gifts. A few steps down Front Street, right beside the water taxi alley, is **Moho Chocolate** (cell 501/633-6595, www.mohocholate.com, 9am-6pm daily), also selling chocolate bars and chocolate-anything gifts; get some free samples and then get a bottle of the Maya Cocoa Kahlua mix to make your own Belizean chocolate-based Kahlua. The owners of Moho also run the Cotton Tree Lodge in Punta Gorda, famous for its chocolate-making workshops. Moho works with several independent cacao growers in the Toledo District. The original Moho Chocolate store is in Belize City's Tourism Village.

For unique decadent gifts, the **Rum, Cigar & Coffee House** (Middle St., a block from Elvi's Kitchen, tel. 501/226-2020, 9am-9pm daily) has a walk-in humidor with Cuban and Belizean cigars as well as their own San Pedro-made Jankunu rum cream creations (which are very tasty, I might add) and delicious freshly roasted Guatemalan Arabica coffee. The coffee is available for sale and sampling (US$1 per cup), and the shop has a couple of tables should you decide to savor it on-site.

Wine de Vine (Coconut Dr., tel. 501/226-3430, www.winedevine.com) has the finest selection of imported wines in all of Belize and a worldwide selection of cheeses and meats.

They offer free wine tastings and also sell it by the glass. **Premium Wines** (tel. 501/226-3700, gisellekv@gmail.com, 9am-6pm Mon.-Sat.) on Front Street has a selection from seven countries and offers wholesale pricing: Buy 12 bottles and get a 17 percent discount. Prices range from US$17 for a California wine to US$14 for a white French table wine.

ACCOMMODATIONS

In addition to hotels and luxury lodges, there are many apartment and house rentals available around the island. To start, check the classifieds from the *San Pedro Sun* (www.sanpedrosun.net) and the *San Pedro Daily* (sanpedrodaily.com). Other sources for vacation homes are **M&M Rentals** (U.S. tel. 949/258-5268, www.mandmrentalsbelize.com) and **Caye Management** (tel. 501/226-3077, www.cayemanagement.com), which has an office that's open daily on the north edge of town at Casa Coral.

Under US$25

San Pedro has slim pickings in this category. The hands-down best is ★ **Ruby's Hotel** (tel. 501/226-2063, rubys@btl.net, US$20-40), with 23 basic, clean guest rooms in a well-maintained building right on the water in the heart of the village. Ruby's Café and pastry shop downstairs is excellent and a San Pedrano institution, and you can sit on your room's balcony or the common deck space with some fresh morning johnnycakes and watch the beach traffic below. Guest rooms have either shared or private bath with fan or air-conditioning.

The only youth hostel option is **Pedro's Inn** (Seagrape Dr., off Coconut Dr., tel. 501/226-3825, www.backpackersbelize.com, US$12.50 s, US$22.50 d), with two rows of 14 wooden stalls, each with a bed, a ceiling fan, a locker, and access to shared bath facilities. The rooms are right above Pedro's Sports Bar and poker room, so you've got an on-site nightly social scene with a lively cast of characters and pizza available for delivery. Pedro's has a small pool with lounge chairs, a deck, and

Choosing a Hotel on Ambergris Caye

At last count, Ambergris had more than 150 licensed hotels, mostly midrange and upscale lodging. The few places geared toward backpackers and extreme budget travelers are located either right in San Pedro Town or on the outskirts by the airstrip. Otherwise, here are a few things to keep in mind when deciding on a hotel.

First off, in downtown San Pedro, the word *beachfront* refers to the very narrow strip of sand that is used more as a pathway for pedestrians and boats than for lounging on sand. The views are still pretty and you can still find plenty of space to sun yourself, but as you move farther from town, either to the north or south along the island, the beaches fronting the resorts become wider, softer, and more exclusive.

Of course, what you give up in beach quality, you get back in location: "In town" means being in the middle of the buzz of cafés, bars, boutiques, dive shops, dancing, and dining. If you're more into privacy, all this action is easily accessible from any resort on the island by boat, taxi, or golf cart. And those in town can easily escape north or south for the day as well for more exclusive restaurants and scenery.

Keep in mind that rates across the board are subject to seasonal fluctuations, service charges, and government taxes. Always verify and ask about discounts before booking. Remember that rates are for double occupancy during the high season.

HONEYMOON RESORTS

Ambergris Caye is Belize's top honeymoon pick, not least for its numerous resorts, fine dining and entertainment options, and short distance to the Belize Barrier Reef. While San Pedro Town is the hub, the island is large enough that couples can choose to stay on the south or north end, secluded parts that are either a short walk to town (south) or a boat ride away (north) for added isolation. Whether spending the day in a hammock on an isolated beach stretch or exploring San Pedro Town's alley-sized streets, there are choices to suit all couples.

Most resorts offer five- to seven-day packages, which often include all meals and one snorkel or day trip for two. Picking a resort will ultimately come down to the actual hotel setting, offered amenities, and the type of getaway you seek. A few stand out from the pack and are a good place to start your research.

For a luxurious experience away from the noise but close enough to the action in town, the award-winning **Victoria House** (tel. 501/226-2067, U.S. tel. 800/247-5159, www.victoria-house.com, US$335-625) is a solid option, with beachfront villas or *palapa* roof casitas facing one of the best stretches near San Pedro and with numerous on-site amenities, including two swimming pools. The Reef Romance package is chock-full of goodies, including massage for two, champagne, and private candlelit dinner.

You'll hop on a 20-minute private boat ride from San Pedro to reach the Zen **Matachica Beach**

---

a shaded picnic area. It's back by the airstrip (you'll wake up to the morning's flights taking off overhead), a 10-minute walk from the town center or US$3.50 by taxi. Across the street, Pedro's has 30 functional hotel rooms (US$50-65) with air-conditioning, TVs, private baths, and fans.

US$25-50

Right in town, the family-run ★ **Hotel San Pedrano** (Front St., tel. 501/226-2054, sanpedrano@btl.net, US$35 with fan, US$45 with a/c) has six guest rooms, from single to triple, that make up the island's self-proclaimed "top of the low end." From the breezy upstairs veranda it's easy to eat a bite, read a book, or watch the street below. Each guest room has hot and cold water, a private bath, a ceiling fan, and optional air-conditioning. The amenities are basic, but the hotel is a stone's throw from all the action in town and steps from the water taxi pier.

Thomas Hotel (Front St., tel. 501/226-2061, US$35-43) has six cheap and barebones

The secluded Matachica Resort is a popular choice among lovebirds.

Resort (tel. 501/220-5010, www.matachica.com, from US$256), on the island's northern side. Colorful thatched roof cabanas with hammocks sit on a deserted, powdery soft white-sand beach—a postcard-perfect greeting as you near the shoreline. An excellent on-site restaurant, water sports equipment, spa, and friendly staff make this an easy pick. Honeymoon packages include two day trips, one to the reef and the other to the mainland's beautiful Lamanai archaeological site. Be sure to reserve a seafront cabana and wake early for sunrise views from your bed.

If money is no object, live it up like a rock star at **Cayo Espanto** (U.S. tel. 888/666-4282, US$1,500 or 5 nights for US$7,475), a private island where a villa comes with all the bells and whistles—private plunge pool, tailored meals, bar drinks, and your very own butler. And of course, you can't beat staying on an uncrowded, idyllic plot, surrounded by nothing but the Caribbean's turquoise waters and roaming fish.

Tranquility Bay Resort (tel. 501/236-5880, U.S. tel. 800/843-2293, www.tranquilitybayresort.com, from US$240) gets rave reviews from couples seeking peace and quiet, a sunset-facing beach, and walk-in snorkel sites. Located 12 miles north of San Pedro, the resort caters to lovebirds. You just can't go wrong with the gorgeous setting of bright blue and yellow wooden cabanas on a white-sand beach.

but clean guest rooms with private baths, fans or air-conditioning, and aged refrigerators, all 100 feet from the beach; this humble *hotelito* is more than 40 years old.

The only budget option north of the bridge is the **Ak'Bol** retreat center (a.k.a. the "yoga barracks") on the lagoon side, which has 30 guest rooms (US$35 s, US$50 d) in a long wooden building with a massive shared restroom-shower-locker room. The resort is on a narrow beach strip and has a yoga deck and an average restaurant on-site.

US$50-100

Right in the center of town and on the street side, the **Coral Beach Hotel** (Front St., tel. 501/266-2013, US$55 with fan, US$67 for a/c) offers 16 small clean guest rooms, each with a private bath, hot and cold water, and air-conditioning or a fan. The guest rooms are basic and dated for the price, but perhaps location is what you're paying for. There's a large veranda with a nice view of the hustle and bustle of Front Street.

Across the street and a few steps away is the

brighter, well-kept **Spindrift Hotel** (Front St., tel. 501/226-2174, U.S. tel. 888/705-9978, www.ambergriscaye.com/spindrift, US$54-85), a three-story building offering clean, spacious guest rooms with all the amenities, including Wi-Fi and balconies. There's a wonderful massive veranda overlooking the beach, and the hotel is sandwiched between Wahoo's Lounge, home of the Chicken Drop, and Caliente Restaurant. This is where I stayed my first time in San Pedro, and it was ideal.

Nearby **Tio Pil's Hotel** (Front St., tel. 501/206-2059, U.S. tel. 800/345-9786, www.tiopilshotel.com, US$55-70), formerly Lily's Hotel, has six good-value guest rooms with private baths, air-conditioning, and a large shared veranda overlooking the beach at the heart of San Pedro; there are a few apartments too. Lily's Treasure Chest family-run restaurant still lives on downstairs, with a new patio and additional seating. It has been known for years for offering delicious ceviche, breakfasts, and local food in plentiful family-style servings.

A few steps away is the charming pink-and-white beachfront ★ **Conch Shell Inn** (tel. 501/226-2062, conchshellinn@gmail.com, US$74-94), beside Sunbreeze Suites. It was the third hotel to open in the early days

of tourism. Renovated in 2008 and well maintained, the five upstairs single and double guest rooms have great views, tiled floors, and kitchenettes with all the amenities; the cheaper downstairs rooms are steps from the sea. All guest rooms are beachfront, and there are portable air-conditioning units (US$10) available if needed. Daily maid service and a lovely private front courtyard with hammocks and beach chairs make this a great beach vacation spot in town.

South of San Pedro, a quaint and homey option is **Changes in Latitudes Bed and Breakfast** (36 Coconut Dr., next to Belize Yacht Club, tel. 501/226-2986, U.S. tel. 800/631-9834, www.ambergriscaye.com/latitudes, US$95-115), with six small and cozy guest rooms with air-conditioning, ceiling fans, private baths, and pool privileges at Exotic Caye Beach Resort, a few doors down. They're serious about the breakfast, made fresh daily and served in the outdoor common room, and there's a board updated daily with suggested activities and nightlife. The location is ideal, just a few steps from Ramon's Village Resort, the best swimming stretch in town. Use of bicycles is complimentary, as are outdoor lockers for drying wet clothes, and there's on-site security at night.

beachfront Conch Shell Inn, San Pedro

On the north end of town, toward the bridge, **Hotel del Rio** (tel. 501/226-2286, www.hoteldelriobelize.com, US$65-145) is a quiet hotel on the beach that offers great value. Accommodations range from basic economy rooms with shared baths and cold water to bigger colorful casitas built of pimento palm, some with a king or two queen beds. There is also a larger villa (US$1,200 per month) in the back. There are hammocks to enjoy in the private beachfront courtyard.

US$100-150

The central and cheerful **San Pedro Holiday Hotel** (Front. St., tel. 501/226-2103, U.S. tel. 713/893-3825, www.sanpedroholiday.com, US$110-125), the island's first hotel and still under the original family's management, keeps getting better. The 17 clean, spacious guest rooms have air-conditioning and fans, private baths, and beachfront verandas. Lots of water sports and boats are available.

Inside an elegant three-story building of tropical colonial design, on the corner of Sandpiper Street and the sea, is the **Blue Tang Inn** (tel. 501/226-2326, U.S. tel. 866/881-1020, www.bluetanginn.com, US$120-225). The 14 tasteful guest rooms sport lots of warm, rich wood paneling and have kitchens, private baths, ceiling fans, and air-conditioning; third-floor guest rooms have whirlpool tubs. The grounds are well kept, and the rooftop balcony is breezy and pleasant.

Popular with birders, ★ **Caribbean Villas** (Seagrape Dr., tel. 501/226-2715, U.S. tel. 866/290-6341, www.caribbeanvillashotel.com, US$105-225) has a fantastic spot on the beach just south of town, offering a range of economy rooms, including a garden studio (US$99), as well as luxury suites. The loft suites—such as Hawk's Roost—are gorgeous, with immaculately clean and colorful beach decor, sea-facing balconies, kitchenettes, and large closets. The property's small bird sanctuary is one of the few remaining areas of original littoral forest on the island and has a "people perch." In addition, the guest rooms are designed to catch the cooling trade winds to reduce the need for air-conditioning.

One of Belize's only dedicated yoga resorts, **Ak'Bol** (1 mile north of the bridge, tel. 501/226-2073, www.akbol.com, US$145-165) has seven cabanas on the beach in a naturally landscaped garden, a small pool, and a shaded yoga garden within earshot of the sea. The cabanas have raised beds, local decor, a loft for the kids, unique conch-shell sinks, and private outdoor rainforest showers. There's an on-site beach bar, although the food is hit or miss and service can be slow. There are also daily yoga classes, which are popular with residents, and retreat packages.

US$150-200

The **SunBreeze Hotel** (tel. 501/226-2191, U.S. tel. 800/688-0191, www.sunbreeze.net, US$179-236) is a full-service beachfront hotel with 43 guest rooms built around an open sand area and pool. Guest rooms have two queen beds, air-conditioning, tile floors, local artwork, private baths, and direct-dial phones; Front Street starts next door, and the entrance is yards from the airstrip. There's an on-site dive shop, a top-notch restaurant (Blue Water Grill), and many other services. The SunBreeze has some of the few fully wheelchair-accessible guest rooms in the country. They also rent suites at the other end of Front Street, on the beach across from the Belize Bank, at **SunBreeze Suites** (tel. 501/226-4675, U.S. tel. 800/820-1631, www.sunbreezesuites.com, US$165-205), which offers one-bedroom suites with full kitchens, guest queen sofa beds, and air-conditioning. The suites can sleep up to four adults per room; families and children are welcome. They have less of a standard hotel feel and are more akin to self-catering condos—and are cozier for it. There is a wonderful small Jamaican restaurant on-site called **Jambel Jerk Pit**.

Ramon's Village Resort (tel. 501/226-2071, U.S. tel. 800/624-4215, www.ramons.com) is somewhat of an institution in San Pedro. So when a section of this full-service resort with 71 guest rooms was struck by an accidental and devastating fire in August 2013, the entire island came to the rescue. It's a testament to the dedicated staff that the hotel is back up and running, in just under four months of rebuilding, with brand-new cabanas and swimming pool. Standard guest rooms run from US$199 and the presidential suite goes for US$450; the guest rooms are nice, although the "kitchenettes" are not much more than a sink and a microwave. The property's 500-foot beach is practically in San Pedro Town and has decent walk-in snorkeling; it has a restaurant and bar, as well as on-site dive shops, guides, and an inland tour operator. You can rent windsurfing boards, snorkel gear, and golf carts.

★ **Xanadu Island Resort** (tel. 501/226-2814, U.S. tel. 866/351-4752, www.xanaduislandresort.com, from US$170) is one of my favorite accommodations in San Pedro. The resort is a cluster of luxury monolithic domes with thatched overlay roofs nestled in lush landscaping. There is a beachfront pool as well as a private nature walk and bird sanctuary. Nineteen suites are available with fully equipped kitchens, and there is a choice of studios and one-, two-, and three-bedroom units. The beachfront lofts are stunning, and the service is top-notch. There's a restaurant-bar next door at Caribbean Villas' **Catamaran Beach Bar** if you need coffee first thing in the morning and don't care to brew your own.

Farther south is **Mata Rocks Resort** (tel. 501/226-2336, U.S. tel. 888/628-2757, www.matarocks.com, US$145-220), a small hotel tucked on the south end of Ambergris with six suites and 11 ocean-view guest rooms centered around a pool; the guest rooms, while not huge, have plenty of basic amenities, such as air-conditioning, cable, wireless Internet, bikes, transfers, and continental breakfast at the tiny on-site bar. The architecture is unusual—all white, clean, and Mediterranean. Don't forget your sunglasses if you stay here.

US$200-300

One of the island's top class acts, ★ **Victoria House** (tel. 501/226-2067, U.S. tel. 800/247-5159, www.victoria-house.com, US$195-1,235) has a luxurious selection of suites and several multifamily mansion-like villas set along one of the nicest stretches of beach in town. Expect grand colonial elegance on a well-manicured tranquil piece of property about two miles south of San Pedro. The stucco and thatched casitas with tile floors are placed around several sleek infinity pools; you also get a full-service dive shop with private guides, the Admiral Nelson Bar, and one of the top-rated restaurants in the country (Restaurant Palmilla).

★ **The Villas at Banyan Bay** (tel. 501/226-3739, U.S. tel. 866/352-1163, www.banyanbay.com, from US$275) is a luxury family resort with all the amenities in its 32 suites, including balconies and whirlpool tubs. Lots of activities and lessons for children are available; full dive trips and inland trips can be arranged. There's also an on-site dock restaurant, Rico's, and a wedding chapel at the tip of the dock. It's close to San Pedro Town, yet away from the noise and on a nice section of the beach.

Less than three miles north of San Pedro, the family-run **El Pescador** (tel. 501/226-2398, U.S. tel. 800/242-2017, www.elpescador.com, from US$200) was constructed in 1974 as one of the world's premier sportfishing lodges, and it has evolved into a modern upscale eco-lodge resort. There are 12 seafront double rooms in the original mahogany lodge—cozy and with touches of Mayan decor—and private one-, two-, and three-bedroom villa accommodations, all of which are centered around three stunning saltwater and freshwater swimming pools and gorgeous palms. The villas can be locked off into smaller sections, and each is outfitted with a spacious seafront deck, a full kitchen with sit-up bar, baths with gorgeous tiling, and Belizean-made hardwood floors. The resort offers more than fly-fishing trips, including smaller customized ecotours and diving with resident licensed dive master Alonzo Flota. Guests mingle over communal meals on the lovely large outdoor patio and at the on-site lounge, complete with a bar and a pool table, at the end of the day's activities. You'll find that anglers and their nonfishing families (there are spa services available, yoga classes nearby, cycling, and more) are repeat visitors, and many know each other from past years.

Las Terrazas (U.S. tel. 800/447-1553, www.lasterrazasresort.com, US$225) is a slick affair of 39 fully equipped "residential townhomes" around a pool area and restaurant serving "Southwestern cuisine with Caribbean flair." This is a full-service luxury resort with many activities and packages.

A little more than four miles north of San Pedro, you'll fall in love with the über-stylish yet unpretentious ★ **Matachica Beach Resort** (tel. 501/220-5010, www.matachica.com, from US$256), with 24 spacious casitas, suites, and luxury villas clustered along a beautiful stretch of white sand, front and back. The casitas are named after fruits (mine was Cherry); each bears its own color and matching porch hammock and is styled with local art and a blend of African and Asian-tinged decor. The resort offers a full range of amenities, a spa, an infinity pool with a jetted tub, plus a vast lounge that connects to the Mambo restaurant. There are no flat-screen TVs or phones, nor will you miss them—Matachica

is all about Zen. Proximity to the reef, which is visible from the white sandy shores, makes it ideal for water sports, from paddleboarding to kayaking; all are complimentary, as are the private daily boat shuttles to town. The resort is ideal for an intimate wedding, a honeymoon (even with yourself), or a secluded couple getaway. The six-person beach mansion goes for a cool US$1,015 per night plus taxes. The view of the barrier reef from the beach is stunning.

★ **Portofino** (tel. 501/678-5096, www.portofinobelize.com, US$250-335) is another long-standing luxury lodge right on the beach, but with a deep swimming pool, an excellent on-site restaurant (meal plan available), and friendly staff. It has 15 units, including two treetop suites and a honeymoon-VIP villa with full amenities. You can use the lodge's sporting equipment to play around all day— it's only a 15-minute kayak paddle to excellent snorkeling at Mexico Rocks.

The beautiful, luxurious oceanfront suites at ★ **The Palms** (tel. 501/226-3322, www.belizepalms.com, US$204-292), a boutique condominium resort on the beach next to Ramon's Village Resort, are in a shaded compound in town. Secluded yet centrally located, the resort has a beautiful small freshwater pool in a well-kept garden and 12 one- and

the beach at the stunning Matachica Beach Resort

two-bedroom ocean-view suites, executive suites, and a poolside casita. Amenities aren't spared, and the furnishings are wonderful. The Palms feel like your own luxurious vacation home.

Over US$300

The **Phoenix Resort** (U.S. tel. 877/822-5512, tel. 501/226-2083, www.thephoenix-belize.com, US$465-795) raises luxury up a couple of notches in San Pedro. This large condo resort has 28 of the largest furnished suites on the island, with every amenity you can imagine both in and out of your room, including king beds, granite countertop kitchens, and even iPads. It has a pool, a restaurant, a gym, and a spa, all in a big walled compound toward the north of town on the beach side, and there is full concierge service for activities on and off the island. It's *très* contemporary chic.

Next door to Matachica Beach Resort, go for the full rock-star treatment in one of two 3,000-square-foot villas at **Azul Belize** (tel. 501/226-4012, www.azulbelize.com, from US$1,000, all-inclusive); watch the horizon from your private rooftop jetted tub with one of Azul's famous frozen mojitos in hand. Your enormous three-floor crib boasts a full Viking kitchen, lady-wood beams, wraparound balconies, flat-screen TV, and wireless Internet throughout the property. Or, unplug at the infinity pool or adjoining Rojo Lounge, where world-class chef Jeff Spiegel prepares some of the island's best cuisine. In 2011 Azul expanded to include several high-luxury options, including a massive 14,400-square-foot villa with its own pool, patio, swim-up bar, and beer on tap.

Open since 2012, the hottest newcomer on the Belize luxury scene is **El Secreto** (U.S. tel. 800/479-5037, tel. 501/236-5111, www.elsecretobelize.com, US$550-$1,075), which offers 13 thatched-roof, sea- or lake-facing villas outfitted with luxurious details, including marble bathrooms and 400-thread Egyptian cotton linens. Located 11 miles north of San Pedro, it's ideal for honeymooners or anyone seeking ultra pampering. It has an on-site restaurant and spa, and inland tour arrangements can be made.

FOOD

Dining out can be expensive in San Pedro, but there are cheap meals and snacks at many bakeries as well as the fast-food carts in the central park.

Bakeries and Cafés

Breakfast is serious business in San Pedro. You can smell the freshly baked bread and johnnycakes as you walk down Front Street early in the morning, starting with ★ **Ruby's Café** and **Celi's,** which for decades have been bustling every morning with workers, visitors, and party animals eating breakfast at dawn and stocking up for day trips.

Head to the **Rum, Cigar & Coffee House** (Middle St., tel. 501/226-2020, 9am-9pm daily), which, believe it or not, sells and serves some of the best coffee in town—freshly roasted Guatemalan beans. There's interior seating to enjoy, although it's limited. You might as well try their Belizean-made rum cream while you're here.

Mesa Café (tel. 501/226-3444, 8am-4pm Mon.-Fri.) serves delicious and affordable breakfasts (the coconut french toast is heaven), quiches, salads, sandwiches, burgers, and pies. It's at the entrance to the Vilma Linda Plaza, a peaceful oasis in the bustle of downtown; the tiled courtyard is filled with lush plants and a small fishpond.

Barbecue

Besides the informal street barbecues, which offer the best-value food around, a rotating schedule ensures a beach cook-up nearly every night of the week. Your choice of chicken, ribs, or fish runs US$5-10. Also on Sunday, a host of beachfront eateries offer a special barbecue menu, coupled with live music; it's a sort of tradition on San Pedro.

On Friday, you'll see a steaming grill outside the **Lions Club** building (Front St., across from Manelly's) for the weekly

Sunday Beach Barbecue

Grilling starts at dawn at Estel's Dine by the Sea for their famous Sunday beachfront barbecue.

Sunday is "Funday," as they say in San Pedro and in the rest of Belize. Businesses close, families lunch together after church, kids swim off the docks, and adults relax in the shade beside barbecue grills. Heaps of perfectly smoked chicken, lobster, and other meats come off the grill and are washed down with Belikins. The rest of the afternoon is spent fishing, competing in horseshoe tournaments, dancing to live music, or napping beside a palm tree. It's the cure for a week's hard work (or a Saturday-night hangover).

Belizeans are masters of the barbecue, and this skill manifests itself most on the weekend. If you're not lucky enough to be invited to a local's outdoor food fest, there are a few options where visitors can get a taste of this Belizean tradition. Several beachfront establishments in San Pedro Town offer a Sunday barbecue special, complete with beachside seating, pools or docks, and live music. Some also throw in games for all-around good cheer.

You can't go wrong at **Estel's Dine by the Sea** (tel. 501/226-2019, 6am-close Sun., US$12.50), a family-run gem serving succulent barbecue ribs with your choice of pork, chicken, jerk wings, sausage, and generous sides. You'll see owner Charles Worthington outside at 6:30am, perfecting the meat on a massive grill. Get your outdoor patio table early (by noon) and sip a cold beverage while you listen to a soothing acoustic band play light rock tunes.

Catamaran Beach Bar (at Caribbean Villas, Seagrape Dr., tel. 501/226-2715, US$6-15) offers a similar barbecue lunch starting at noon—from chicken to pork ribs, delicious shrimp kebabs, or lobster. A small band usually performs. Side note: The Bloody Marys are fantastic.

Sunday Funday at **Crazy Canucks Beach Bar** (beachfront, tel. 501/670-8001, US$5-10) is somewhat of an expat institution. The place attracts the largest crowd of all on Sunday afternoons, and starts later than most at 3pm. It also has a live blues band, and you can try your hand at the horseshoe tournament.

To escape the Sunday action in town, the ever-wonderful **Palapa Bar and Grill** (tel. 501/226-3111, 10am-about 9pm Sun., US$4-6), north of the bridge, is perfect almost any day, not just Sunday.

Another option is to head out on a special day's sail to a nearby caye for an island beach barbecue getaway Belizean-style. For more information, check with the **Rubio Brothers** (tel. 501/600-5022).

fund-raising barbecue. Starting at 2pm, anyone is welcome to buy a plate or "boxed lunch" of grilled chicken with generous side servings (US$4.50). There's also a bar on-site. All the money made is pooled to help members who are in need or suffer a disaster. In case you were curious, Friday night is also bingo night, so popular among the locals that many negotiate their weekly work shifts around it.

The island's only falafel joint, **Alibaba's** (across Coconut Dr. from the Tropic Air terminal and Moncho's Golf Carts, tel. 501/226-3337, 10am-10pm daily, US$5-12), is run by two cousins from Jordan and is best known for its takeout rotisserie chicken, served Lebanese style with generous portions of hummus and tabbouleh; there are also kebabs, veggie plates, and sometimes hookahs to smoke.

It's often difficult to find authentic Jamaican jerk outside Jamaica, but ★ **Jambel Jerk Pit** (Front St., beachside at Sunbreeze Suites, tel. 501/226-3515, 7am-9pm daily, US$8-20) rises to the challenge, and its weekly Wednesday all-you-can-eat buffet with live music is a great value (6pm-9pm Wed., US$20 pp). The location, on a poolside and beachfront deck with umbrellas, is wonderful.

Belizean and Central American

On the back side of the island, a few local eateries offer the cheapest stew chicken, rice and beans, or burrito dishes on the island. The popular ★ **El Fogón** (Trigger Fish St., tel. 501/206-2121, 11:30am-3pm and 6:30pm-9pm Mon.-Sat., US$4-6) is an authentic family-style eatery with flavorful Creole and mestizo dishes home-cooked on an open-fire hearth and served in a small, shaded, sand-floored space. Tucked toward the back of the island, just north of the airstrip, it will not let you down. The restaurant recently started serving dinner (US$16-30), with plenty of grilled seafood choices and kebabs along with either rice or pasta and sides.

Exactly one street back and parallel to El Fogón is **Neri's Taco Place** (Chicken St., 5:30am-11:30am and 5:30pm-9pm Mon.-Sat., 5:30am-noon Sun.), dishing out some of the best tacos (US$0.50 for 3) and cheap, delicious eats that you order at a small window. There are a couple of picnic tables outside, and it gets very crowded with locals on Sunday. It's off the beaten path but well worth finding.

On the beach side, ★ **Estel's Dine by the Sea** (on the beach behind Atlantic Bank, tel. 501/226-2019, 6am-4:30pm Wed.-Mon.,

El Fogón is famous for serving authentic Belizean food in a casual setting.

US$12.50) is a relaxed, ideal breakfast spot. Besides the morning treats, Estel's is great on Sunday with barbecue lunch and live music.

Ruby's (Front. St., 4:45am-6pm Mon.-Sat.) has the absolute best local pastries in town, from stuffed massive fry jacks to soft and crunchy johnnycakes and more, not to mention coffee early in the morning—in short, you cannot visit San Pedro and not stop in at Ruby's. Other reputable spots are **Ambergris Delights** (Middle St., tel. 501/226-2135) and **Celi's Deli** (Front St., tel. 501/226-0346, 6am-6pm daily), second only to Ruby's and popular for its plain or stuffed johnnycakes and sought-after meat pies.

Also on Front Street is a small family-style restaurant, **Bistro Mestizo** (below Coral Beach Hotel, tel. 501/226-4465, 10am-10pm daily, US$3-10), serving Central American specialties infused with a touch of Caribbean, and where I enjoyed the largest, most delicious fish tacos I've had anywhere. The Belizean-run establishment has live *cumbia* music nights (Thurs. and Sun.) to add to the cultural experience and a popular daily *hora feliz* (happy hour, 6pm-8pm), a nice change from the otherwise rock and blues offerings in town.

Mickey's Place (Tarpon St., tel. 501/226-2223, breakfast, lunch, and dinner daily, US$5.50) is the home of the huge Wednesday burrito. Mickey's has an ample menu of local fare, especially seafood and conch fritters, fresh juices, and cinnamon rolls, and offers a bit more ambience than the other Belizean places, even if it doesn't have outdoor seating.

For top-notch Latin Caribbean cuisine, ★ **Wild Mango's** (sandwiched between Ruby's Hotel and the library on the beach, tel. 501/226-2859, noon-3pm and 6pm-9pm Mon.-Sat., US$12-20) serves amazing versions of local favorites (ceviche, fish tacos, quesadillas, burritos) prepared by one of Belize's most distinguished chefs, Amy Knox. You cannot go wrong here, with offerings such as Mango's Mongo Burrito, seafood specials, Amy's Chef Salad, and rum-glazed bacon shrimp.

For fun beach-like ambience with sandy floors, picnic tables, and Latin music, **Elvi's Kitchen** (Pescador Dr., 501/226-2404, 11am-10pm Mon.-Sat., US$10-40) is a great San Pedrano experience. Doña Elvi's family-run restaurant serves the ultimate Belizean version of soul food—home-cooked, authentic cuisine with a kick. Don't miss the cheese-stuffed jalapeños, the Mayan fish, or the to-die-for coconut shrimp curry, among many other options. There's also a popular Mayan buffet on Friday nights with live Mayan music (and if you must know, they make some of the best margaritas in town).

Not far off from Elvi's is **Waruguma** (Middle St., tel. 501/651-7961, 11am-9:30pm daily, US$8-18), rightly famous for its savory *pupusas* (available for lunch but grilled outdoors on the patio in the evenings starting at 5pm) and their megasize burritos as well as other Salvadoran treats, all at a great price. So gigantic are the burritos that there's a wall of fame dedicated to those who have managed to finish one by themselves.

If you're searching for the absolute best conch fritters on the island, along with fresh seafood in all sorts of combinations—grilled, blackened, steamed, Mexican, Creole, breaded, fried, you name it—don't miss a stop at ★ **Caramba Restaurant and Bar** (Pescador Dr., tel. 501/226-4321, 11am-10pm Thurs.-Tues., US$5-15), with its lively and colorful indoor and outdoor bar and patio. Seriously, the seafood here is tasty and plentiful, as is the meat—look out for the Bacon Macho Burger. Prepare your stomach, and make reservations for dinner, as the place gets packed.

Slightly higher-end yet still casual, **Caliente** (in the Spindrift Hotel, Front St., tel. 501/226-2170, 11am-9:30pm Tues.-Sun.) offers Mexican cuisine and seafood on an open porch or in a waterfront dining room. It is famous for the lime soup (only US$4.50) at lunch (good for hangovers) and generous lobster dinners and other entrées (US$12-22). Caliente also has the best nachos in town—a perfect snack on Thursday before the Chicken Drop event next door at Wahoo's Lounge.

The old Celi's Restaurant (not to be confused with Celi's Deli) inside the San Pedro Holiday Hotel has metamorphosed into the swankier beachfront **Caprice Bar Grill** (Front St., tel. 501/226-2014, 9am-midnight Mon.-Sat., 11am-9pm Sun., US$15-32), delivering Caribbean and Latin cuisine. The quesadillas are to die for and the portions are large. The outdoor covered deck is ideal for the popular happy hour (3pm-6pm), with half-price mojitos, margaritas, and rum punch as well as US$2 beer specials.

Keep walking south and you'll run into **Hurricane's Ceviche Bar & Grill** (tel. 501/226-4124, 10am-10pm Wed.-Mon., US$8-18), set on a pier and specializing in all kinds of ceviche—including horse conch, octopus, lobster, and other seafood. The sea views and the friendly barkeep make it stand out.

Another longtime popular ceviche venue in town is the casual **Lily's Treasure Chest Restaurant** (beachside on Front St., across from Amigos Del Mar, tel. 501/226-2650, 7am-9pm daily, US$9-17), serving ceviche through the day. It has a spacious outdoor patio.

For a nice Ambergris evening away from town, take a golf cart or water taxi to one of the restaurants north of the bridge. The cheapest and most casual places are Palapa Bar and Ak'Bol. Easily accessible and a notch up in style is the chic ★ **Kama Lounge** (tel. 501/610-3775 or 501/226-3709, kamalounge@yahoo.com, noon-10pm daily, US$10-35), offering affordable "kama eats" that include bar food, salads, pastas, kebabs, paninis, and more, served under the stars in a beautiful setting of couches, hookahs, and dim red lighting.

You can get a decent burger at many restaurants in San Pedro, but only **Legends Burger House** (tel. 501/226-2113, noon-9pm Mon.-Sat., US$10), a half mile or so north of the bridge, specializes totally in beef and chicken patties. The atmosphere is tropical frat house, with live music till midnight on weekends and a popular Tuesday-night live jam. The menu is entertaining, with each burger dedicated to the owner's various heroes. The most Belizean is the Sir Barry Burger, a tribute to local legend Barry Bowen, a widely admired businessman who was tragically killed in a plane crash in 2010; it's a beef patty topped with Belikin beer-battered shrimp, representing three of the commodities Bowen produced and sold.

Italian

Pizza is available for delivery or dining in at dozens of places on the island. **Pepperoni's Pizza** (Coconut Dr., tel. 501/226-4515, 5pm-10pm Tues.-Sun.) is the most popular for both quality and price—a large 16-inch specialty pie goes for US$20 and is served deep-dish style. **Pirates** (Middle St., tel. 501/226-4663, US$4-25) is also good and does slices in the evenings.

Mexican

Mexican food lovers will enjoy the **Lone Star Grill & Cantina** (tel. 501/226-4666, noon-9pm Wed.-Mon., US$10-18), a very far trek south but well worth it both for the ambience and the tasty belly-filling dishes, including chimichangas, El Jefe burritos, chalupas, enchiladas, and more Mexican favorites. There are also "gringo favorites" of the burger-and-fries variety.

Fine Dining

San Pedro is blessed with an ever-evolving selection of trendy restaurants offering international fare and flair; if you don't pay for such indulgence with an expanded waistline, you'll surely pay for it in cash. If you're *really* dining out—an appetizer, a couple of drinks, an entrée, and a dessert—expect to pay as much as you would in a U.S. city: US$40-80 per person, more if you like your wine. Remember that many upscale restaurants add tax and a service charge, and there's a fee for using a credit card, so bring enough cash. Reservations are recommended at all of the following restaurants, especially in the high season.

Of the finer restaurants, ★ **Blue Water Grill** (on the beach, behind the SunBreeze Hotel, tel. 501/226-3347, 7am-9:30pm daily, entrées from US$19) is known to offer some of the best values and biggest portions. The menu has hints of Hawaiian and Southeast Asian cuisine; try the coconut shrimp stick with black-bean sweet-and-sour sauce. Sushi is offered on Tuesday and Thursday; there are dishes like snook with banana curry along with comfort plates like lasagna.

Red Ginger (tel. 501/226-4623, 7:30am-10:30am, 11:30am-2:30pm, and 6pm-9:30pm daily, US$9-37), in the Phoenix Resort toward the north part of San Pedro, has an indoor air-conditioned dining room and trellised outdoor patio. The food here is absolutely divine. They specialize in local cuisine with an international twist—grouper ceviche with mango, empanadas with pork, and plantains with buffalo mozzarella and sautéed basil. There are homemade bagel sandwiches for breakfast, Indian chicken curry and Cajun gumbo for lunch, and appetizers, salads, pastas, seafood, and steaks, plus a delicious and filling five-course tasting menu (US$45) for dinner; there's a big wine list, half-price wine on Monday, and tapas on Wednesday and Sunday.

★ **Casa Picasso** (Sting Ray St., tel. 501/226-4443, www.casapicassobelize.com, 5:30pm-10pm Tues.-Sun., US$10-30) is one of the best fine-dining experiences in San Pedro. The restaurant, a cozy dining room setting with art, drapes, and mood lighting, serves tapas (think lobster sliders, potato ricotta gnocchi, or pork belly in oyster sauce, yum!), salads, steaks, seafood, and unique entrées (the lobster risotto is otherworldly). Desserts aren't to be missed either, including the banana wontons. Enjoy a free pickup and return with your reservation.

Hidden Treasure Restaurant (4088 Sarstoon St., tel. 501/226-4111, www.hidden-treasurebelize.com, 5:30pm-9:30pm daily, US$15-22) is an intimate open-air restaurant, beautifully lit under a *palapa* roof. There's a long list of appetizers, lunches, dinner items, and desserts, from seafood bisque to Mayan-accented snapper and spare *buhurie* (Garífuna-spiced ribs).

The chef at **Restaurant Palmilla** (at Victoria House, 2 miles south of San Pedro, tel. 501/226-2067, 6:30am-2:30pm and 6pm-9pm daily, US$24-50) was born in Mexico City, trained in the United States, and comes from a family of renowned chefs. His unique style is "Mayan bistro," which combines the chile peppers of Mexico with fresh local produce, seafood, and meats. Start with crispy snapper cakes with chipotle beurre blanc, black beans, and roasted corn succotash; follow with black-bean or *chilapachole* (corn) soup; then savor main dishes like cashew-crusted grouper.

Glen and Colleen at the **Rendezvous Restaurant and Winery** (tel. 501/226-3426, www.ambergriscaye.com/rendezvous, lunch and dinner daily) offer free wine tasting to anyone wandering by. They blend, ferment, and bottle their own wine in recycled bottles. The restaurant has a stellar reputation for its blend of Thai and French cuisine. Start with escargot with lemon-garlic butter sauce for an appetizer (US$10), and then have grilled shrimp (US$22) or chicken with coconut red curry sauce (US$15).

★ **Mambo's** (Matachica Beach Resort, tel. 501/220-5010, www.matachica.com, lunch and dinner daily) is pure indulgence, serving rich and artful heaps of snappers, scallops, shrimp, lobsters, and calamari—you can try them all in the amazing Deep Blue entrée (US$34). Appetizers, such as soy-glazed snapper carpaccio, are US$10-16; save room for the chocolate mousse.

Rojo Lounge (at Azul Belize, www.azul-belize.com, tel. 501/226-4012, lunch and dinner Tues.-Sat., entrées from US$27) has a succulent, sophisticated menu that will leave you grasping for adjectives. Or maybe you'll just reach for your peppered cocktail in stunned silence after each bite of shrimp-stuffed grouper or conch pizza; it's spendy but worth every savory cent. The self-made chef, Jeff Spiegel, is a former punk record producer from California.

Portofino Restaurant and Green Parrot Beach Bar (tel. 501/226-5096, lunch and dinner daily, dinner entrées US$18-35) is six miles north of San Pedro, and they'll give you a complimentary boat ride to join them for dinner, although from no farther south than Fido's dock; expect local cuisine with European flair, including spider crab-laced snapper and other creative seafood specials. Lunch is also excellent with delicious chicken finger baskets and an enormous vegetarian selection (US$6-14), and they'll set up a romantic table on the end of their pier if you like.

Dessert

Go to **Manelly's** (Front St.) for homemade ice cream—it is known for its "coconut creation." Or sample the frozen custard at **DandE's Ice Cream** (Pescador St.), where a couple from Pennsylvania dairy country turn out fresh flavors every day, including soursop, from a local fruit that makes for a tart Belizean treat.

Groceries

There are several medium-size supermarkets around San Pedro; one of the cheapest is the locally owned **Marina's Market** (next to Xanadu Island Resort, Coconut Dr., tel. 501/226-3647). The best selection is at **Island Supermarket** (Coconut Dr., tel. 501/226-2972), which is large and modern and offers free delivery. **The Greenhouse** (Pescador Dr., next to St. Francis Xavier Credit Union, tel. 501/226-2084) boasts the most fresh produce and seafood, including cold cuts and unique grocery selections. **Caye Mart Supermarket** (north of Castillo's Hardware Store, tel. 501/667-4243, samirbelize@gmail.com) has wine selections as well as imported Carib beer.

INFORMATION AND SERVICES
Banks

There are plenty of banks in town. Belize, Scotiabank, Atlantic, and First Caribbean have international ATMs. There's also an ATM in the big supermarket just south of Ramon's Village Resort. **Milo's Money Exchange** (Middle St., tel. 501/226-2196) is another option. It exchanges Belizean, U.S.,

Guatemalan, Mexican, Canadian, and British currencies, and it's also a Western Union branch.

Health and Emergencies

Prescriptions and other medicines can be found at **R&L Pharmacy** (tel. 501/226-2890, open daily), by the airstrip, and there are plenty of smaller pharmacies around town. If you need medical attention, all hotels and resorts keep a list of doctors and transportation options to call in the middle of the night, including a helicopter to take you to the hospital in Belize City in the event of a major emergency. For other medical concerns, go to the **San Pedro PolyClinic II** (tel. 501/226-2536, 8am-noon and 2pm-5pm Mon.-Sat.), located behind Wine de Vine and the Island Supermarket, facing the airstrip.

Dr. Daniel Gonzalez's **Ambergris Hope Clinic** (tel. 501/226-2660), located next to Castillo's hardware store, is another option. For diving emergencies, the island has one hyperbaric chamber (tel. 501/226-2851 or 501/226-3195), or call Dr. Antonia Guerrero (tel. 501/628-3828).

The **police department** (for emergencies tel. 911, south substation tel. 501/206-2022 or 501/610-4911) and **fire department** (tel. 501/226-2372) are both in San Pedro Town near the big BTL antenna on Middle Street.

Media and Communications

Things change quickly in San Pedro, especially prices. Before your trip, always take a good look at **www.ambergriscaye.com**, by far the best portal for all things Ambergris, including a lively message board filled with opinionated characters. You'll find links to hundreds of island businesses as well as Ambergris's two weekly papers, the *San Pedro Sun* (tel. 501/226-2070, www.sanpedrosun.net) and the online *Ambergris Today* (Middle St., tel. 501/226-3462, www.ambergristoday.com), both wonderful resources. *Ambergris Today*, a favorite of mine, includes comprehensive reviews of the latest and best establishments in town, including resorts, restaurants, and more. Also check the *San Pedro Daily* (http://sanpedrodaily.com).

The **post office** (Middle St., 8am-4pm Mon.-Thurs., 8am-3:30pm Fri.) is next to Elvi's Kitchen.

There are several Internet cafés in town, some with Wi-Fi and others with desktops. **Caribbean Connection** (Front St., tel. 501/226-4664, 7am-10pm Mon.-Sat., 8am-10pm Sun., US$5 per hour) is directly across from the water taxi alley, with a speedy DSL line, wireless Internet access, coffee drinks, and air-conditioning.

GETTING THERE
Air

The 2,600-foot-long runway of San Pedro Airport (SPR) is practically in downtown San Pedro. Belize's two airlines, **Maya Island Air** (tel. 501/223-1140 or 501/223-1362, www.mayaislandair.com) and **Tropic Air** (tel. 501/226-2012, U.S. tel. 800/422-3435, www.tropicair.com) fly more than a dozen daily flights between San Pedro, Caye Caulker, and Belize City—and another five to and from Corozal. Tropic Air has a computerized system and offers more reliable service; there are flights from San Pedro to Belmopan, offering quicker access to the Cayo District. Maya Island Air is good too and sometimes gives 50 percent discounts on cash purchases; be sure to ask if a discount is available. The flight from Belize City's international airport to San Pedro takes about 15 minutes and costs US$120 round-trip. Flying in and out of Belize City's Municipal Airport is much cheaper (US$35 each way, not much more expensive than the water taxi), although you'll need to catch a taxi from the international airport to get there.

Boat

Two companies providing scheduled water taxi service between Belize City and the islands: **Caye Caulker Water Taxi Association** (San Pedro tel. 501/226-2194, Caye Caulker tel. 501/226-0992, Belize City tel. 501/223-5752, www.cayecaulkerwatertaxi.

com) and the **San Pedro Belize Water Taxi Express** (tel. 501/223-2225, www.belizewatertaxi.com) alternate schedules, each offering four daily trips between Belize City and Ambergris Caye, a 75-minute ride that costs US$17.50 one-way.

In Belize City, the Caye Caulker Water Taxi Terminal is at the north end of the Swing Bridge, with boats leaving between 8am and 4:30pm daily. The San Pedro Belize Water Taxi Express departs from the Tourism Village in Belize City. Boats depart San Pedro from Wet Willy's Pier 8am-3:30pm daily. Always check the schedule before making plans; usually there are extra boats on weekends and holidays.

Thunderbolt Travels (tel. 501/422-0026, http://ambergriscaye.com/thunderbolt) runs a once-daily trip to Corozal (3pm, US$22.50 one-way, US$42.50 round-trip), leaving Corozal at 7am. The trip takes two hours in each direction. The departure pier in San Pedro is by the old football field; ask anyone to direct you to Thunderbolt.

GETTING AROUND

Walking is feasible within the town of San Pedro; it's about a 20-minute stroll from the airstrip to the split. Once you start traveling between resorts to the south or north, however, you may want to go by bicycle, golf cart, taxi, or boat. At one time, cars were a rarity, but together with golf carts they are taking over the town streets and even the north side of Ambergris. Most of the electric golf carts have been replaced by gas-powered ones, and hundreds ply San Pedro's rutted roads. Cobbled streets mean less dust and fewer potholes downtown.

The toll bridge connecting San Pedro Town with Ambergris's north side is free for pedestrians. From 6am to 10pm, bicycles pay US$1 to cross, and golf carts pay US$5 round-trip.

Boat

Usually the smoothest and quickest way to travel up and down Ambergris Caye, water taxi service is available from **Coastal**

The Golf Carts of San Pedro

It's the most common dilemma when planning a stay on Ambergris: Do I really need a golf cart to get around? It can take a chunk out of your travel budget, so decide beforehand whether to stay in San Pedro Town or not. Carts are most useful for those staying at one of the many resorts south of San Pedro, especially if you plan on coming into town often to shop, eat, and explore, day or night. The road to the north end of Ambergris, however, gets pretty bumpy and worse in the rainy season, and it requires a toll fee (US$5 per day) to cross the north bridge. Most companies won't allow you to drive farther north than the Palapa Bar or Grand Caribe Resort, 1.5 miles north of town. To explore past that point, you either have to hike or take the Coastal Express water taxi. If you're staying right in San Pedro, everything is pretty walkable, although a golf cart could be fun for a day's exploration.

Golf carts are one of the main modes of transportation on Ambergris Caye.

Ambergris's carts all used to be electric, but now most companies have gas-powered carts. It'll set you back as much as renting an automobile on the mainland, but if you're staying south of town and have multiple passengers (a family, for example), it's probably worth it. Expect to pay more than US$75 for 24 hours and at least US$310 for a week. Drivers must be age 17 and have a valid driver's license. You will likely be required to leave a security deposit in the form of your credit card imprint or cash.

In the high season, reserve a cart in advance. Most companies will deliver to your hotel or pick you up at the airstrip. Your choices begin with **Moncho's** (Coconut Dr., tel. 501/226-4490, www.sanpedrogolfcartrental.com) and **Carts Belize** (south, next to Xanadu Island Resort, tel. 501/226-4090, www.cartsbelize.com), both close to the airstrip with relatively large fleets. Toward the north end of town, **Cholo's** (Jewfish St., in town, tel. 501/226-2406, www.choloscartrental.com) is reliable and has a small fleet of carts, and **Island Adventures Golf Cart Rentals** (Coconut Dr., near Tropic Air, tel. 501/226-4343, islandadventure@btl.net) has weekly deals and will deliver your cart. Another option is **La Isla Bonita** (north of town, tel. 501/226-3446), an extension of the Caye Mart supermarket; it's a family-run business offering reasonable cart prices. Be sure to check these companies' websites and social media pages for specials throughout the year.

When driving your cart, carry your valid driver's license and follow all normal traffic laws, including one-way street rules. Note that Front Street closes to all but pedestrian traffic on Friday, Saturday, and Sunday evenings. Make sure you park on the correct side of the street (it alternates every few weeks; just do what the locals are doing). Be sure to pay attention to the map you are given, don't speed or terrorize pedestrians into a corner, beware of unexpected bicycle riders, and watch for schoolchildren and one-way streets.

Express (tel. 501/226-2007 or 501/226-3007, www.coastalxpress.com). Boats share a dock with Amigos del Mar Dive Shop, in front of Cholo's Sports Bar, departing for points north and south 5:30am-11:30pm daily, with special late-night schedules on big party nights (Wed.-Sat.). Daily scheduled runs are posted online. The fare, usually US$5-25 each way, depends on how far you are going, all the way up to El Secreto, the farthest resort at press time. Most restaurants will radio the ferry to arrange your ride back to San Pedro Town. Coastal Express also offers private charters starting at a minimum of three people.

Taxi

Minivan taxis (with green license plates) run

north and south along the island at most hours; just wave one down and climb in. Expect to pay about US$4-7 to travel between town and points south. Within town, you'll pay around US$4. There are several drivers that you (or your accommodation's front desk) can call as well, including **Island Taxi** (tel. 501/226-3125) and **Herman Wade** (tel. 501/624-4912, 6am-9pm daily).

Bicycle

Many resorts have bicycles that their guests can use for free, and others have them for rent, as do a handful of outside shops. Rentals are available by the hour (about US$5), day (US$10), and week (US$25). Many resorts refer guests to **Joe's Bikes** (tel. 501/226-4371), so check with your hotel for referrals.

Tours

Travel & Tour Belize (just north of the airstrip, tel. 501/226-2137 or 501/226-2031, www.traveltourbelize.com, 8am-5pm Mon.-Fri., 8am-noon Sat.) is the oldest and only full-service travel agent in San Pedro; they'll handle all your bookings, both local and international, and can help with weddings and events too.

Segway of Belize (Coconut Dr., Fairdale Plaza, tel. 501/620-9345, www.segwayof-belize.com, 8am-5pm daily) offers a guided two-hour Discover San Pedro Segway tour twice a week (Wed. and Fri., US$60 pp). A second tour option is to Segway to the Marco Gonzalez Maya Site (US$75 pp). Rentals are also available and include up to 30 minutes of safety training (US$35 per hour).

Caye Caulker

About 1,300 Hicaqueños (hee-ka-KEN-yos; derived from the island's Spanish name, Cayo Hicaco) reside on this island 21 miles northeast of Belize City, just south of Ambergris Caye and a mile west of the reef. It's five miles long from north to south, but the developed and inhabited part is only a mile long, from the split to the airstrip.

It's true that there have been changes in recent years, including the arrival of boutique luxury condominium resorts as the island realizes its unique spot in Belize's growing tourism economy. Yet the authenticity of life in a small Caribbean fishing village remains—original clapboard houses dot the coastline and side streets, and the only rumble you'll hear is from the sound of the few golf carts and bicycles crushing the sand-only roads, or the daily street chatter among residents. There's a happy, familial coexistence on Caye Caulker among expats and locals, and all are determined to conserve the island's history and surroundings through community education and involvement. In the end, Caye Caulker remains more affordable than Ambergris, and

it's as laid-back as its "Go Slow" motto indicates, but no less entertaining.

ORIENTATION

The best landmark to start with is Caye Caulker's "Split"—also the most popular swimming and snorkeling spot. The Split cuts Caye Caulker into two areas: the southern inhabited part of the island, or "the Village," and the northern mangrove swamps.

Heading south from the Split, the main path lining the shore is **Front Street,** where you'll find seafront hotels, eateries, and the water taxi terminal. The other two main streets that shoot off parallel to Front Street are the simply named **Middle Street** and **Back Street.** Each leads to sandy roads with more accommodations, restaurants, and residents' homes. The entire island can be quickly explored in a couple of hours yet is big enough that it can take weeks to delve into each corner.

There's a fuel pump on the western pier. Sailors exploring nearby cayes can anchor in the shallow protected waters offshore; the re is open ocean but is still often re- as a "lagoon."

Street's south end comes to a dead- he **cemetery,** and you have a choice: he narrow beach path along the water, or turn right and then left, where you'll find another sandy avenue that leads to the airstrip at the back of the island.

Bordering the airstrip is a rapidly developing neighborhood called Bahia Puesta del Sol, which has a small grocery store and a new high school. The land opposite the airstrip, called **South Point,** consists of mangrove swamps, with a narrow path cleared for golf cart or bicycle passage, for a coastal ride through an area rich in nature—trees, birds, and crocodiles—and lined with off-the-grid solar-powered homes and docks.

SIGHTS
★ The Split

Popular long before it appeared on the TV show *The Bachelor,* Caye Caulker's infamous "Split," or "cut," as it's still called by residents, is the favorite go-to swimming and sunset rendezvous spot on the island. It resembles a perfect island movie-set—not least for having the most decent stretch of sand, although it's narrow and flat. The story most people

like to tell is that the Split came to be when Hurricane Hattie widened the channel in 1961 and "cut" the island in two, north and south. Boat captains and long-time residents will tell you that in fact the hurricane created only a tiny water passage that was later dug wider by anglers and politicians who wanted larger boats to pass. Eventually, daily sweeping tides made it as large as it is today. Either way, travelers and locals can be found here at all hours of the day swimming, snorkeling, sunbathing on concrete slabs, sharing finger foods on picnic tables anchored in shallow water, or drowning in rum punch and reggae from the on-site **Lazy Lizard Bar.** Others partake in "split jumping" into the sea, feeding magnificent frigate birds hovering over the area, or showing off their water-sports skills offshore. Those who seek peace and quiet should venture to the Split in the morning for a glorious peaceful swim.

Caye Caulker Marine Reserve

The island's very own "local channel" off the reef, where you can snorkel surrounded by dozens or more stingrays and nurse sharks as well as explore beautiful coral at the "coral gardens," is 0.5 mile from shore and just under 10 minutes by boat. It's an area often

The beach at the Split is the best on the island.

Caye Caulker

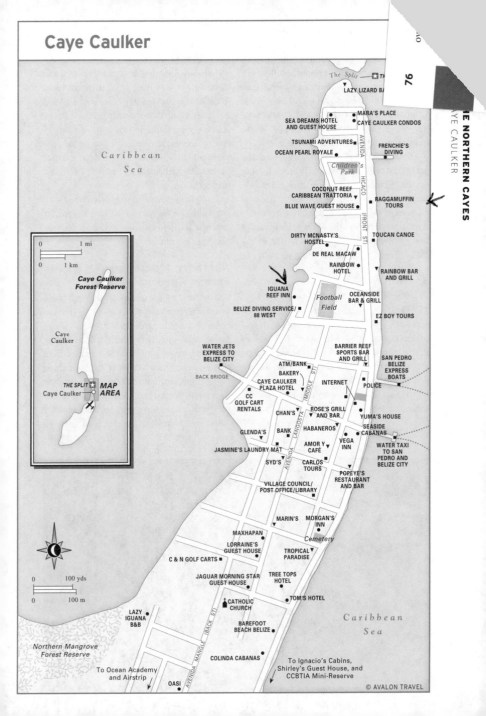

© AVALON TRAVEL

...rlooked by those who head to Hol Chan, but if you prefer a similar but less crowded experience, this is a great choice. Note that you must have a tour guide present, as these are protected waters. The tour can also be combined with other snorkel stops for a small additional fee. Let **French Angel Expeditions** (tel. 501/206-0037 or 501/670-7506, www.frenchangelexp.com) take you there.

On the north end of this reserve is a channel that attracts manatees during their mating season (May-Sept.). Two or three manatees, sometimes more, can be spotted at the surface at any time. It's a spectacular sight; just remember to respect the reserve rules and not touch or swim with the marine animals. Any of the tour companies will bring you here.

★ Swallow Caye Wildlife Sanctuary

This protected area comprises nearly 9,000 acres of sea and mangrove at the north end of the Drowned Cayes, just a few miles east of Belize City. The sanctuary is co-managed by **Friends of Swallow Caye** and the **Belize Forest Department**. Check out www.swallowcayemanatees.org for more information, including membership, tours, and manatee facts.

Many tour operators will take you to Swallow Caye, usually for US$60 per person. Chocolate's Manatee Tours was the premiere operator for Swallow Caye; unfortunately, Mr. Chocolate (a local legend on the island and in the ecotourism trade) passed away in April 2013. Mr. Chocolate was instrumental in the sanctuary's creation in July 2002. He earned environmental and tourism awards for providing quality trips to hundreds of tourists per season. Other guides are sure to uphold his legacy.

From Belize City this trip is combined with snorkeling on the barrier reef and looking for Atlantic bottlenose dolphins. Park fees are US$5 per person.

Northern Mangrove Forest Reserve

Just before the airstrip is a northern mangrove forest reserve area of about 100 acres that has been protected since 1998. Three kinds of mangroves—red, white, and black—and other trees provide an ideal habitat for crocodiles, turtles, fish, and water birds. Bird-watching is ideal here, with some 130 species, including the rufous-necked rail, the black catbird, and others that have not been spotted elsewhere in Belize. Tours can be arranged through

Caye Caulker Marine Reserve is often overlooked but has plenty of marinelife and fewer snorkelers.

Conservation Efforts on Caye Caulker

The **Forest and Marine Reserves Association of Caye Caulker** (FAMRACC, www. famracc.org) is a nongovernmental organization comprising representatives from different island organizations and service groups, including tour guides, schools, and the police. FAMRACC comanages the Caye Caulker Marine Reserve with the Fisheries and Forests Departments and works on projects like mangrove restoration, reef rapid assessments, community reef-technician training, and environmental education field trips for local children.

FAMRACC sometimes accepts volunteers to work with the mangrove and littoral forest restoration projects in the forest reserve as well as maintenance of reef mooring lines and buoys in the marine reserve. Guest researchers and scientists are also welcome.

The Caye Caulker branch of the **Belize Tourism Industry Association** (CCBTIA, www. cayecaulkervacation.com) manages a 1.5-acre private forest reserve that is just before the airstrip. This tiny but lush littoral forest reserve has a nice walking trail that winds to the mangroves on the beach, and flora and fauna along the way are identified with hand-painted signs. CCBTIA has published a trail guide to the reserve as well as two books about the plants and birds of Caye Caulker; these are for sale at Cayeboard Connection or from CCBTIA. There is no charge to walk the trails. Guided tours are also available, and there is a small interpretive center.

FAMRACC can help you plan a tour in the forest reserve. Birding tours (3 hours, US$32) leave very early, and natural history tours of the project sites can be booked, followed by snorkeling in the North Channel (US$50-70, depending on duration). Contact marine biologist and guide Ellen McRae (tel. 501/226-0178) to arrange details.

the Caye Caulker branch of the **Belize Tourism and Industry Association** (tel. 501/623-9810).

South Point

Located directly opposite the airstrip, away from town and tucked behind the abandoned Belize Odyssey Resort, is a narrow sandy path that leads to a little-visited side of the island. The trail winds through a maze of glorious landscape—mangroves, almond trees, coconut palms, and saltwater palmettos—with pockets of sea views on the left and off-the-grid solar- and wind-powered homes on the other. Keep straight on the path and follow its twists and turns until you reach a dead end, noting the last house on the right. After dousing yourself generously with mosquito repellent, hike through a small littoral forest to reach the last dock. There lies a breathtaking scene of open water, blue skies, and sailing birds at the southernmost point of the island. This is South Point, the raw inhabited Caye Caulker, where electrical poles are nonexistent and where selling seafront lots has yet to

completely change the nature that fills this area.

Don't venture here in the rainy summer months without a golf cart—not least because the occasional crocodile could very well be crossing your path as you pass. The ground could also prove particularly muddy and treacherous during rains. Golf-cart taxis can also bring you here; just ask around for a reliable driver.

SPORTS AND RECREATION

There's enough to do on this five-mile island with ideal calm waters and fewer crowds than San Pedro to keep you occupied for days if you so choose—pick from an exciting list of water activities above or below the sea, in addition to turf action such as biking, yoga, or indulging in healing spas.

Beaches

Beaches on most of Caye Caulker are of the thin, hard variety—don't expect to find a thick, soft, endless stretch of sand. Still, there's sand to feel under your toes, and the ratio of crowds versus beach space is favorable, such that finding your own sandy plot of the island is an easy feat. And if you can get past the first few inches of harmless sea grass and don't mind the lack of wave action due to the mile-distant barrier reef, you'll find the water is just as soothing and in the same jade color of Belize—all in all, a happy compromise.

The beachfront is a public area, and if you prefer to jump deeper into the sea to avoid the sea grass, docks are also a dime a dozen, unless marked "private." Just be mindful of boat activity and stay alert while snorkeling or swimming underwater.

The island is relatively small, so finding the beach merely requires going to the front or back areas of Caye Caulker. The best stretch for your towel is the Split area on the north end of the island. Other options for those looking to read quietly is the stretch of beach—formerly known as Playa Asuncion—going along the front side from the arrival dock but going south (turning left). Along the back of the island are smaller stretches of beach, and swimming may be best off a dock, but the views are still lovely. Grab a cocktail at Sea Dreams Resort's upstairs Banyan Tree Bar or at Iguana Reef and sit by their beach to watch sunset.

Diving and Snorkeling

The reef you see from Caulker's eastern shore provides fantastic snorkeling and diving opportunities right in your front yard. Snorkeling can be as simple and cheap as renting masks and fins for US$5 per day from one of the tour operators (or bringing your own) and using them off almost any dock. If renting, you may be required to leave your ID behind for the day as security. Note that several tour operators are hesitant to pass out equipment so as not to encourage snorkeling beyond the docks in the protected marine reserves without a guide.

You could snorkel at the island's most popular swimming spot: the Split. It can be crowded with sunbathers and onlookers;

avoid the heavily trafficked part and beware, as swimming here can be dangerous because of the pull of the current, which is strong enough to overpower children or weak swimmers. Your best bet is to go around the bend, only a few yards out of the Split, to avoid the dangerous boat traffic. Be mindful where you step or dive at the Split, as old construction materials have been dumped here for fill.

To snorkel the reef itself—just a mile away, leaving no excuse not to before leaving the island—boat tours are necessary, and plenty are offered for beginner or advanced snorkelers and divers. Trips can go for half a day or a full day, depending on the excursion, and there are enough to fit all budget ranges.

The most popular snorkel and dive sites are Hol Chan Marine Reserve and Shark Ray Alley, Caye Chapel Canyons, and the reefs around St. George's Caye, Long Caye Wall, and Sergeant's Caye. A common snorkeling tour package is to Hol Chan with stops at Shark Ray Alley and the Coral Gardens, San Pedro for lunch (not included), and the seahorse sanctuary behind the Split.

For snorkeling tours, you can rely on the cheerful, capable guides at **Raggamuffin Tours** (Front St., tel. 501/226-0348, www.raggamuffintours.com), who will take you out on *RaggaGal, Ragga Prince, RaggaQueen,* or *RaggaKing*—beautiful Belizean-built boats designed especially to access shallow snorkeling spots. Raggamuffin regularly sails to Hol Chan (full-day trip, US$50, includes lunch and rum punch on board). When there's enough demand, a snorkel trip is also offered via motorboat to Turneffe Atoll (full-day trip, US$75, includes lunch).

Belizean guide and dive master Shadrack Ash offers friendly, professional snorkeling, manatee watching, fishing trips, and night dives through his company **French Angel Expeditions** (tel. 501/206-0037 or 501/670-7506, www.frenchangelexp.com), which gets rave reviews from past clients. Walk straight down the street from the water taxi on Calle del Sol.

For a reggae vibe, join **Ras Creek** on his boat *Heritage Cruze,* docked at the Lazy

Lizard Bar when not plying the reef with happy reggae-crazy customers; this is one of the best ways to tour the Caye Caulker Marine Reserve (US$30). Ras Creek was the first to guide visitors to the unofficial **seahorse sanctuary** behind the Split.

Climb aboard the *Gypsy* with **Carlos Tours** (tel. 501/600-1654, carlosaya@gmail. com), which has an excellent reputation for personal attention and a focus on safety. Carlos is the only shop to offer a full-day snorkel tour to Hol Chan combined with a lunch stopover in San Pedro, where you get to eat and explore Ambergris Caye for 1.5 hours on your own (US$50 pp). Carlos loves underwater photography and will share and sell photo CDs immediately after a trip (US$15). His office is on Front Street next to Amor y Café.

Two local brothers run **Anwar Tours** (tel. 501/226-0327, www.anwartours.page.tl), and with 15 years of experience, they get positive reviews for both snorkel trips and inland tours. **Tsunami Adventures** (tel. 501/226-0462, www.tsunamiadventures.com) is near the Split and books snorkel and inland trips and rents underwater cameras (US$8 per day). **EZ Boy Tours** (tel. 501/226-0349, ezboytours-bze@yahoo.com) offers all the standard snorkel tours as well as overnight camping trips and night snorkeling.

Many visitors are willing to brave four hours (two hours each way) on a boat in mostly open ocean to dive the Blue Hole and Turneffe Islands or other atoll sites. There is no "number one" dive site, as every diver is looking for something different, but some are indeed renowned for their marine diversity; just be sure to discuss the options before booking the trip, and make sure you're comfortable with the boat, guides, group size, and gear. Consider whether gear is included in the price or not, and don't quickly jump on the cheapest package.

Caye Caulker has two main dive shops offering similar tours, albeit with slightly varying prices and packages. The main offerings include Hol Chan (US$110-125 for 2 tanks); Blue Hole, Half Moon Caye, and Lighthouse (US$190-255 for 3 tanks); Turneffe day trips (US$125 north, US$150 south); certification courses (US$325-375 open water, US$275-300 advanced); as well as snorkeling excursions and other trips.

Dive master couple Chip and Danielle Petersen run **Belize Diving Services** (Chapoose St., across from the soccer field, tel.

a stingray at Caye Caulker Marine Reserve

501/226-0143, www.belizedivingservices.com), with an excellent reputation and an operation that is all computerized and offers both recreational and technical dives at Miner's Gold and Treasure Hunt dive sites. They also offer weekly dives at the Blue Hole and the atolls thanks to their 46-foot custom Newton dive boat, equipped with showers, ideal for the long ride. Certification courses are available. **Big Fish Dive Center** (tel. 501/226-0450, www. bigfishdivecenter.com) is a Belizean-owned dive shop with knowledgeable dive masters and a 45-foot dive boat with a small onboard restroom for farther destinations, such as the Blue Hole. Note that as of 2012 the shop is no longer PADI certified, thus courses aren't available.

Snuba and Sea Trek

The new way of exploring Hol Chan is to snuba or sea trek with **Discovery Expeditions** (tel. 501/671-2881 or 501/671-2882, www.discoverybelize.com, US$68-74, includes hotel transfers but not the US$10 Hol Chan park fee) out of San Pedro. Catch the 8am water taxi over to San Pedro, where you will get picked up for your tour. The experience includes orientation before experiencing depths of 20-30 feet, enjoying marinelife and corals without needing a tank or worrying about being dive certified. Both activities are safe for anyone in good physical condition and older than age eight.

Boating and Sailing

Who doesn't love a great sail? **Raggamuffin Tours** (tel. 501/226-0348, www.raggamuffintours.com) offers sunset cruises and day sails. The best adventure has to be the unique overnight sailing trip on the 50-foot Stonington Ketch *RaggaQueen* sailboat south to Placencia (Tues. and Fri. departures), where you'll be dropped off at Tobacco Caye to continue your travels; it's three days of sun and sea and two nights camping out in style on idyllic cayes. The trip costs US$350 per person, including all gear, food, snorkeling, and fishing; expect a higher holiday rate (US$400) during the last week of December.

Fishing

Try to catch your dinner off one of the island's many piers. You can buy bait and rent fishing rods at the Badillos' house near the soccer field (look for a small porch sign). Or fish like a local with a hook, line, and weight. Or take a walk toward the back of the island, where you'll find fishers cleaning their fish, working on lobster traps, or mending their nets in the morning. Many will be willing to take you out for a reasonable fee. The main trophies are groupers, barracuda, snappers, and amberjacks—all good eating. Small boats are available for rent by the hour.

For professional fishing tours, go to **Anglers Abroad** (tel. 501/226-0602, www. anglersabroad.com, half-day US$220, full-day US$330, includes lunch) near the Split. Owner Haywood Curry sells and rents a complete selection of fly and spin gear (US$20-30 per day), and he is happy to give advice to the novice or expert fisher. He offers lessons (US$100 for 4 hours) and DIY instruction by canoe or on foot and sets up half-day, full-day, and overnight adventure trips. Group tours, as well as private lessons, are available. The shop works with well-known, award-winning, and experienced reefs and flats fishing guides, including Parnel and Kenan Coc—2011 and 2012 Top Guide title winners in the prestigious annual Tres Pescados Slam Tournament—as well as Rafael Alamilla and Eloy Badillo. Anglers Abroad now also teaches a fly-fishing high school class at Ocean Academy.

Shadrack Ash, owner of **French Angel Expeditions** (tel. 501/670-7506 or 501/670-9155, www.frenchangelexp.com, half- or full-day US$200-350), can take you catch-and-release fly-fishing, spin casting with an option to grill your catch for you, and lobster fishing (June 15-Feb. 15).

Kayaking

Toucan Canoe and Kayaks (Palapa Gardens, Front St., across from Real Macaw, tel. 501/625-8024, toucancanoe@yahoo.com) has the most comprehensive canoe and kayak tours and rentals on the island (single US$5 per hour, double US$10 per hour). Private and group lessons are offered by Canadian-Belizean owner Allie Johnstone, who is a top-placing international canoe racer and licensed tour guide and naturalist. All two-hour tours are US$25. Ask Allie about beach stargazing options, mangrove tours, and her herbal walk to learn about the various medicinal plants and other flora on the island. **Tsunami Adventures** (tel. 501/226-0462, www.tsunamiadventures.com) also offers kayak and canoe rentals (US$7.50 per hour).

Wind Sports

Nondivers can rest assured: Caye Caulker is on the cutting edge of water sports, including the latest trend of stand-up paddleboarding, in part thanks to great bump and jump conditions—shallow crystal-clear waters protected by a nearby reef and the Caribbean trade winds.

For fun in the water and the wind, find **KiteXplorer** (Front St., toward the Split, tel. 501/635-4967, www.kitexplorer.com, 9am-6pm daily), offering beginner to advanced kite surfing, stand-up paddle surfing, and windsurfing lessons (introduction to kite surfing US$90, or US$50 pp for 1.5 hours) with three licensed instructors, or equipment rentals (stand-up paddleboard US$20 per hour, windsurfing board US$15 per hour). Note that these sports are seasonal and best from October through March.

Reef Watersports (Ave. Hicaco/Front St., just before the Split, tel. 501/635-7219, www.reefwatersports.com) offers Jet Ski rentals (US$75 for 30 minutes) as well as wakeboarding, waterskiing, and boat tubing (all US$100 per hour for 2 people).

The best place to practice paddleboarding solo on the island is on the "lee side" of the island, as Hicaqueños call it—the calm, flat side starting behind the Split.

Contour Ocean Adventures (Front St., make a right turn after the arrival dock, tel. 501/635-8757, henry@countourbelize.com, 9am-noon and 1pm-5pm daily) has seven- to 10-foot paddleboards for rent (US$25 per hour, US$67 per day, includes 15-minute lesson, full damage insurance optional). Passionate water-sports couple Henry (born on the island) and Stefi Lopez, trained dive masters and surf enthusiasts, offer workout sessions and yoga on paddleboards. Surfboard rentals are also available.

Biking

An ideal way to explore the island and get

Sea kayak rentals are an affordable way to explore the island's shoreline.

a workout is by renting a bicycle (US$5-6 per day, US$25 per week) and exploring its nooks and crannies at your leisure. Most locals here are on bikes, even with their little ones in tow. The better spots to rent are **M&N Mel's Bike Rentals** (Chapoose St., off Front St., tel. 501/226-0229, US$2 per hour, US$7 per day, US$25 per week) and the Friendship Convenience Store on Front Street. Many hotels also throw in complimentary bicycle use, so be sure to check beforehand.

Birding
More than 190 species of resident and migratory birds have been identified on Caye Caulker, some of which are rarely seen elsewhere. The white-crowned pigeon, rufous-necked wood-rail, and black catbird are commonly seen here. The northernmost part of the island, part of a protected forest and marine reserve system since 1998, is ideal for birding and is made up of miles of reef, grass flats, lagoons, and mangroves. Guided ecotours can be arranged through the **BTIA Resource Center** (cayecaulkerbtia@gmail.com). Caye Caulker's South Point has plenty of birdlife; rent a golf cart and explore at your leisure.

Massage and Bodywork
You'll feel rejuvenated and have new friends after a treatment at **Purple Passion Beauty Studio** (Calle del Sol, cell 501/666-8845 or 501/633-4525, purplepassionbze@hotmail.com, 9am-noon and 1pm-6pm Mon.-Sat.), just a few steps from Rose's Grill. There's more to this green-and-purple cabin than meets the eye. Talented Belizean sisters Stacy and Gina Badillo, with more than a decade in the industry, run a tight beauty ship, offering full salon services that later expanded into spa services, including body scrubs, facials, and hot-stone massages in a cozy treatment oasis of a room in the back. The spa has a contemporary boho-chic feel, and it's a welcome respite from the outside rush of bicycles and pedestrians. Don't miss Gina's magical hands (US$50 per hour, hot stone US$65 per hour) or

Stacy's skillful nail art (get a Belizean flag on those tips). You might even pick up a couple of Creole phrases while there.

Eva McFarlane's cozy, fragrant **Healing Touch Day Spa** (tel. 501/206-0380 or 501/601-9731, www.healingtouchbelize.com) on Front Street offers everything from deep tissue and Swedish massage to Reiki, reflexology, aura cleansing, waxing, manicures, and facials. All treatments are US$60 for an hour, US$85 for 90 minutes.

Great Island Yoga (207/729-7883, www.greatislandyoga.com) offers classes from Christmas to Easter at a beautiful oceanfront location. Drop-in classes are US$7.50, if space is available, and organized groups are also welcome. **RandOM Yoga** (tel. 501/664-9444, www.randomyoga.com) is a donation-based seasonal outdoor yoga studio; for schedules, look for their sign on Front Street by Anwar Tours.

For those feeling more energetic, there is **Miss Louise's step aerobics** (Ave. Langosta, tel. 501/226-0118, 5pm-6pm Mon.-Thurs.); you can register or just drop in (US$2).

ENTERTAINMENT AND EVENTS
For a small island, Caye Caulker offers just enough "liming" (socializing over food and drink) options, from watering holes to late night dancing.

Nightlife
For drinks over sunset, head to the lively **Lazy Lizard Bar** at the Split and opt for two-for-one rum punches (Tues.-Sun., US$5) or, if you're feeling brave, the "lizard juice" cocktail, a thick, potent neon-green concoction. Lazy Lizard also serves good bar munchies, including chicken fingers and lobster burritos. The top deck has a second bar, additional seating, and a great view.

For live music, bar fare, burgers, and trivia-game nights (7:30pm Wed., Fri., and Sun.) that remind you of North America, head to the **Barrier Reef Sports Bar and Grill** (Front St., tel. 501/226-0077), directly on the beach and a few steps from the water taxi docks. The Friday guitar jam (3pm-7pm) attracts a lively crowd of visitors and residents; feel free to get up there and sing your heart out or dance. Service can be very slow at the busy bar, so go early. Tuesday nights are for free movies and popcorn, with matinees and evening screenings.

Those looking to extend sunset romance can go for an after-dinner outdoor movie under the stars at **Paradiso Lot 84 Outdoor Cinema** (Front St., next to Amor y Café, 6:30pm and 8:30pm Mon., Wed., and Fri., US$5). Having relocated from its beachfront location, it's no less appealing thanks to a giant screen, surround sound, and gated modern lounge vibe. Pick a chair and dig your toes in the sand while sipping on a fancy cocktail— mojitos to martinis—from the neon-lit bar. Movies are new and old, with the schedule announced on a chalkboard outside the venue.

Do not dare leave the island without a drink and a glimpse of the three-story **I&I Reggae Bar** (Traveler's Palm St., 4pm-1am daily), one of the best in the Caribbean with its eye-catching interior decor of all things Rastafarian, swing bar chairs, and late-night ambience of reggae and dance beats. For more of a lounge vibe, head upstairs and people-watch on the deck. A small but nicely lit VIP room with its own bar adds a special touch, although the real party is still in the main room, where tipsy sun-kissed travelers and locals on the prowl converge on a disco-lit floor until closing.

Festivals and Events

With a claim to being the original host and creator of **Lobsterfest** in 1995, now held here annually in late June, in neighboring San Pedro, and in the southern beach town of Placencia, Caye Caulker's lobster season launch celebration remains as authentic as it was decades ago and attracts visitors from across Belize. The three-day weekend event is filled with Belizean-style recreation, including a Miss Lobsterfest beauty pageant, dozens of food booths to sample the crustacean in all

its forms—grilled, stewed, or in ceviche—and beach parties with live music and games. The fun continues on at the Split for one big late outdoor party.

SHOPPING

All shops on the island are open daily. You'll find **Toucan,** the largest souvenir store, and a sprinkling of small gift shops on and around Front Street selling T-shirts, hot sauce, hammocks, art, sarongs, beachwear, postcards, photo albums, and other Belizean souvenirs. Caye Caulker's sandy streets have several skilled artisanal vendors. On Front Street is a collection of numbered stalls called **Palapa Gardens.** Here you can find hand-carved ziricote and rosewood, hand-painted T-shirts, Guatemalan textiles and handicrafts, beautiful model sailboats complete with rigging, jewelry, and music CDs. Look out for **Jacob & Stevens,** a modest art and jewelry stall just before Palapa Gardens, with longtime island resident Jacob Cabral's colorful and unusual fish-motif paintings.

Jewelry is a popular craft on the island, often sold from tables set up in the street. **Calvin** sells his cool handmade island necklaces, anklets, and earrings at his table set up between Habaneros and Rose's Grill; he started 30 years ago, well before souvenir stores opened on the island. **Celi's Music** (Front St.) is where Mr. August can be found at a small table beside the shop, cutting and polishing conch shell pieces. There's a good selection of popular Belizean music and videos.

Cooper's Art Gallery (tel. 501/226-0330, www.debbiecooperart.com, 11am-5pm Mon.-Tues., 10am-8pm Wed.-Sun., US$10-220) on Front Street sells colorful Caribbean primitive art and posters, many in funky frames, big and small, hand-painted by artist Debbie Cooper and other local Belizean artists; they make great gifts. Lee Vanderwalker's colorful Zen gallery, **Caribbean Colors Art Gallery and Café** (Front St., tel. 501/668-7205, www.caribbean-colors.com, 6:30am-9pm Fri.-Wed.,

US$6-10), across from the basketball court, serves excellent coffee as well as breakfast burritos and omelets, brownies, and delicious, daily lunch specials. The outdoor porch is ideal for watching Front Street foot traffic and sipping on a brew while waiting for a departure taxi. Make sure to take a look at the gorgeous local paintings for sale inside.

The **Go Slow Art Gallery,** in Palapa Gardens stalls 6 and 7, encourages the Belizean art community and sells paintings of different styles, including acrylic on canvas, realism, and primitive. Seek out pieces by well-known local artists Nelson Young and Marcos Manzanero, and look for beautifully crafted mini drums, handmade by Garífuna artist **Mark Welch** (tel. 501/620-1020, www.mccaribbeandrums.com, US$50).

Hair braiders along Front Street create "head art" with their lightning-fast fingers, adding colorful beads and extensions.

For clothing, **Chocolate's Gift Shop** (Front St.), run by Annie Seashore, sells high-quality Balinese sarongs, bags, and Guatemalan textiles. Several small shops sell a limited selection of imported women's clothing.

ACCOMMODATIONS

Prices given are for high-season double occupancy, but you can often get discounts year-round, especially if you're staying for five or more days. Be sure to check directly with the hotel or take note of social media pages for the latest specials. Reservations are recommended during the high season (late Dec.-Apr.), as rooms tend to fill quickly, particularly during national holidays such as Easter. The rest of the year, rooms are easy to find on the spot, and choices will be plentiful (except in October, when a few properties close for renovation).

Staying at a seafront property or by the hustle and bustle of Front Street is always lovely, but since everything is a short walk away, staying off the main drag and in the center or back of town won't hurt your vacation—particularly with the sandy streets all around. Be warned that you'll be spoiled for choice of affordable, cozy places to stay. Plenty of delightful hotels, condos, and B&B options with great sea views or relaxing gardens are spread around the island.

When arriving off the boat or plane, ignore any pushy taxi drivers or local "guides" who attempt to help with your bags and pressure you into staying at specific properties; often these individuals obtain commissions, or worse, you may end up at a hotel with low security, hence the aggressive tactics. Smile and head to your first choice of accommodations, or ask around for advice on the way to the island. Both airline and water taxi terminals often carry pamphlets and maps for visitors. My best advice, if you're completely unsure and traveling solo, is to head to Caye Caulker Plaza Hotel (Calle del Sol, across from Chan's Supermarket), which has 24-hour friendly front-desk staff.

Under US$25

There are many budget guest rooms along Front Street, or even Middle Street, that are easy to find. The best deal in town is ★ **Dirty McNasty's Hostel** (Crocodile St., off Front St. past Red Macaw, US$10-30), down a quiet side street just a stone's throw from all the action. This is the place for "world travelers." The hard-to-miss red building offers upper-floor coed dorm rooms (with bunk beds and private indoor bath) and spacious private rooms with double beds. The balcony, outfitted with hammocks, enjoys a nice breeze and a nifty view of the sea and reef. A second building houses a communal kitchen with a coffee maker, fridge, and microwave, and a game room with pool tables and a dartboard. Free Wi-Fi is included, and a swimming pool is in the works.

Yuma's House (tel. 501/206-0019, yuma-housebelize@gmail.com) is a small, waterfront hostel to your right as you walk off the town arrival dock. It offers dorm-style rooms (US$13) plus a few private rooms (US$29-30) with shared bath and kitchen. There's a dock peppered with hammocks, or you can chill in the garden while looking out at the sea. Just beware of the owner's strict rules: Nonguests are not allowed past the front gate, and no outside chatter is permitted after nightfall.

Edith's Hotel (tel. 501/206-0069, ediths-guesthouse@gmail.com, US$15-20), with small, no-frills guest rooms on ground level, is a landmark on the central street of the island. Guest rooms come with hot and cold water, ceiling fans, a communal kitchen area, and shared or private baths. Upstairs are three spacious apartment units, one with a full kitchen, for US$400 per month.

In the heart of the village, by the soccer field, are two great options for reasonable rooms and cabanas. Set in a private fenced yard is **Sandy Lane** (tel. 501/226-0117, www.belizeexplorer.com), offering nine guest rooms (US$12.50 with shared outdoor bath, US$17 with private bath) and four basic cabanas with kitchenettes, TVs, and hard beds (US$25). There is a communal outdoor cooking area as well. Across the lane is **Apartments** (tel. 501/226-0229, US$15-., which has eight basic and clean guest room. with shared baths.

A bit farther south along the beach, you'll find **Tom's Hotel** (tel. 501/226-0102, toms@btl.net, US$21-33), popular with budget travelers. There are many options among the 24 guest rooms, including a few simple bungalows. Tom's is well kept and clean, with hot and cold water, fans, louvered windows, tile floors, wireless Internet, and a sea view. Avoid walking to and from Tom's after dark, however; opt for a golf cart taxi (US$2.50) instead.

If you're packing a tent, the only place to camp is on the beach at **Vega Inn and Gardens** (tel. 501/226-0142, www.vegabelize.com, US$12 pp). The family-run site provides communal hot and cold showers, flush toilets, luggage storage, and security. They also have comfortable hotel rooms, furnished apartments, and rental homes with all the amenities.

US$25-50

For a dose of "old Caye Caulker," check in to one of the funky beachfront cabins at **Morgan's Inn** (tucked away in a cluster of palms near the old cemetery, tel. 501/226-0178, siwaban@gmail.com, US$28-45); cabins are spacious and rustic. Kayaks and windsurfing are available. Owner Ellen McRae is a marine biologist and birder who can guide interested groups.

The colorful building on your right as you get off of the water taxi is **Trends Beachfront Hotel** (tel. 501/226-0094, www.trendsbze.com, US$35-40), with seven basic guest rooms, comfortable queen beds, refrigerators, fans but no air-conditioning, and private baths. Despite a need for renovations, it's a decent choice for a one-night stopover.

Set in a private villa, **Ocean Pearl Royale** (tel. 501/226-0074, oceanpearl@btl.net, US$27.50-45) is on a side street before the Split. There are 10 guest rooms with a choice of fan or air-conditioning, single or double beds, and wireless Internet around a

...al living area and kitchen with ...rowave, and a coffeemaker. In ...en is a delightful studio-size ca- ...l kitchen and a porch, for rent ...US$250) or month (US$500), ...ditioning.

...Wave Guest House (Front. St., tel. 501/669-0114 or 501/206-0114, www. bluewaveguesthouse.com, US$25-33) has clean, basic guest rooms with shared baths, TV, an outdoor communal kitchen, wireless Internet, and a private dock. There are also private guest rooms (US$71), one of which is seafront, cozy, and clean, with a flat-screen TV; it's ideal for one or for a couple. It's a great deal for the location, just a few steps from the Split. There are also options for guest rooms with private baths.

A short walk down the end of Middle Street and past Edith's is ★ Lorraine's Guest House (tel. 501/206-0002, US$30), off the beaten path but close to town and a good deal for short budget stays. There are three clean and spacious stand-alone cabins with double beds, screened porches with street views, three fans, a coffeemaker, a full bath, and Internet access. Owners Orlando and Martha are a nice couple who live on property and are very welcoming.

US$50-100

A few steps down from the Rainbow Hotel, De Real Macaw (Front St., tel. 501/226-0459, www.derealmacaw.biz, US$50-70) is a small and rustic pet-friendly thatched-roof property whose 10 units have private baths, mini kitchens, TVs, wireless Internet, and spacious private verandas with hammocks. A condo-apartment and a two-bedroom beach house (both US$130) are also available.

Closer to the Split are the seven wood cabin rooms at Mara's Place (just before the Split, tel. 501/600-0080, maras_place@ hotmail.com, from US$85). There's a communal kitchen, and the guest rooms have private baths but are basic and small for the high rates—you decide if it's worth being just a couple of steps away from the Split. The best

feature may be the private dock with lounge chairs for guests only.

Before ★ Caye Caulker Plaza Hotel (Calle del Sol/Middle St., tel. 501/226-0780, www.cayecaulkerplazahotel.com, US$90-100) came along, traveling groups had difficulty staying under one roof, as the smaller hotels on the island lacked capacity. Located in the heart of the island, the three-story building, with 32 guest rooms, some with street-view balconies, is family-run. Past the outside concrete look, it offers great value in the heart of the action, with guest rooms that include air-conditioning, free Internet access, in-room safes, fresh coffee every morning from 6am, a top-floor terrace overlooking the island, and an invaluable 24-hour front-desk presence. Add to that friendly young Belizean staffers who are in the know, as well as easy scheduling of numerous tour options. If you don't have a reservation coming off the boat, this is a great first stop.

The Jaguar Morning Star Guest House (tel. 501/626-4538, www.jaguarmorningstar. com, US$85) is a big white building with a rainforest mural, across from the Catholic church and primary school, just a short walk from the center of town. Set in a private home, it offers a newly converted top-floor one-bedroom apartment-slash-condo with a private bath, a full kitchen, air-conditioning, a coffeemaker, cable TV, Internet access, and a massive front patio with a great ocean view and breeze as well as a back patio for privacy. The apartment comes with the use of two bicycles. In the beautiful tropical garden there is also a private stand-alone cabin with full amenities.

The southernmost beachfront option on Caye Caulker consists of the five cabins at Shirley's Guest House (south end of the beach, tel. 501/600-0069, www.shirleysguesthouse.com, adults only, US$50-75), built with beautiful tropical woods. They are clean, quiet, and comfortable, with a range of amenities, including free Internet access.

You'll find bright and spotless accommodations at Barefoot Beach Resort Belize (southern end of Front St., tel. 501/226-0205, www.barefootcariberesort.com, US$69-89), all clustered on the beach; a few bigger suites are the size of a small apartment and go for US$129-145, depending on length of stay, each with outdoor patios. The small, cheerful guest rooms have comfortable queen or king beds, ceiling fans, small refrigerators, private baths with hot showers, air-conditioning, plus their own deck or patio with seating and access to a dock. Complimentary use of one bike is provided per room, although walking to town is entirely feasible.

Just a few steps south is a quiet, postcard-perfect boutique property, secluded yet close to town, at **Colinda Cabanas** (tel. 501/226-0383, www.colindacabanas.com, US$49-139). The resort offers eight cabana rooms and a few more on the way. Standard guest rooms have fans, and the upstairs beachfront suites are spacious and tastefully decorated with Belizean paintings, with full kitchens, air-conditioning, and an amazing deck view of the barrier reef. A lovely *palapa* sunning and swimming dock is available, and all rooms have their own coffeemaker, porch, hammock, and wireless Internet access.

Quite possibly the most charming B&B on the island, ★ **Tree Tops Hotel** (tel. 501/226-0240, www.treetopsbelize.com, US$56-110) is tucked down a private side alley off the beach near Tom's Hotel. It's a luxurious little gem in a tall white building. Austria native Doris has created a wonderful ambience with her colorful ceramics and thematically decorated guest rooms—including two sea-facing suites, the African Room and the Malaysian Room, that have private balconies, TVs, fridges, full baths, and memorable decor. Two cheaper guest rooms share a bath, and each has a TV, a fan, and a fridge. The two-level rooftop has 180-degree views of the island and hammocks to enjoy them.

Maxhapan Cabañas (close to the primary school, tel. 501/226-0118, maxhapan04@hotmail.com, US$65) is another hidden gem. Belizean owner Louise Aguilar is passionate about the three self-catering cabanas she offers, originally built for her children, who ended up living abroad. Nestled to the back of a lush yard maintained by her husband, both upper- and lower-level rooms are immaculately clean and have their own verandas and hammocks, full-size beds, small fridges, coffeemakers, air-conditioning, cable TV, Wi-Fi, and full baths with hot and cold water. Bicycles are provided for each room. There is a common recreation area in the middle of the yard with lots of seating options and

Colinda Cabanas is one of a few secluded and affordable beachfront resorts on the south side of Front Street.

shade under a gigantic breadfruit tree (*max-hapan* in Mayan).

★ **Oasi** (tel. 501/226-0384, www.oasi-holidaysbelize.com, US$75-95), outside the main buzz of town toward the airstrip, gets rave reviews from its previous guests. It's no surprise—there are four quiet, self-contained, beautifully kept and decorated apartments with patios, air-conditioning, and ceiling fans, hot and cold rainwater showers, equipped kitchens, TVs, and wireless Internet. The top-floor apartment in particular is simply lovely (I could live there). The entrance is a large tropical garden with a fountain, and there are two dogs on the property. There's a recreation area in the garden with a grill for guest use. Your warm host, Luciana Essenziale, will help plan your days; complimentary use of bikes makes the five-minute ride to town easy.

US$100-150

In recent years, a host of boutique and "higher end" accommodations have sprouted on the island—offering more luxurious surroundings but still at a reasonable price compared to neighboring San Pedro.

The bright, centrally located, and long-time family-run ★ **Rainbow Hotel** (Front St., tel. 501/226-0123, www.rainbowhotel-cayecaulker.com, US$115) completed major guest room upgrades in December 2011, giving them upscale decor throughout, with quality bedding, spacious baths with glass shower doors, flat-screen TVs with premium cable, wet bars with mini fridges, coffeemakers, and microwaves. The popular waterfront Rainbow Bar and Grill is across the street.

Ideally tucked along the last side street before the Split, ★ **Sea Dreams Hotel and Guest Houses** (Hattie St., tel. 501/226-0602, www.seadreamsbelize.com, US$105-175) offers a private thatched-roof one-bedroom cabana with a partial sea view, as well as five single "courtyard" or ground-floor guest rooms and three beautiful two-bedroom apartments with full kitchens. Air-conditioning, wireless Internet,

complimentary use of bicycles and snorkel gear, and a daily hot breakfast on the second floor at outdoor table seating are included. The private dock and *palapa* for impromptu swims or sunset viewing (even better than at the Split), a rooftop deck peppered with hammocks for yoga, naps, or massages (US$65 per hour), and cocktails from the Banyan Tree Bar make it as ideal a spot for lovers—a few have left here engaged—as it is for solo travelers. Owners Heidi and Haywood Curry and their friendly staff have transformed Sea Dreams into a perfect home away from home.

At the foot of the town dock, **Seaside Cabanas** (Calle del Sol, tel. 501/226-0498, www.seasidecabanas.com, US$115-130) is a brightly painted 16-room mini resort. The smart guest rooms and cabanas are equipped with air-conditioning, cable TV, wireless Internet access, and cheerful decor surrounding a fine swimming pool and sporting lots of rooftop space. The **Uno Mas** bar is open daily until 10pm, and upstairs seating has ocean views.

Island Magic Beach Resort (beachfront, Ave. Hicaco, tel. 501/226-0505, www.islandmagicbelize.com, US$110-135) offers 11 beachfront and island guest rooms along with two fourth-floor penthouses with great views of the sea and Belize Barrier Reef in the distance. All guest rooms, with kitchenettes and baths, are spacious, although the overall decor leaves a bit to be desired. There's a lovely decent-size on-site swimming pool with a kiddy section, ideal for families, as well as a bar and a private dock.

Just off from the main dock, after making a right, you'll see a cluster of colorful guest rooms and apartment units, all family-run, including **Kokomo Beach Suites** (tel. 501/226-0777, US$99-149) and **Diana's Beach House** (tel. 501/604-1256, US$129-159).

The Lazy Iguana B&B (Alamina Dr., tel. 501/226-0350, www.lazyiguana.net, US$95-130) is a secluded three-story home toward the back side of the island. The four spacious and clean guest rooms have private baths, hot water, air-conditioning, and wireless Internet.

The residential setting is safe but isolated. The top floor is a deck for lounging with a 360-degree view of the island. Rates include a breakfast spread in the owners' kitchen. It's as far back as it gets from the village center but still an easy bike or cart ride away; bikes are available. There are rainwater showers.

The **Iguana Reef Inn** (tel. 501/226-0213, www.iguanareefinn.com, US$190) was one of the first to raise the bar with its 13 upscale rooms built around a well-kept complex on the west side of the island, behind the soccer field. Its rooms are spacious, standard in looks, and all have comfortable touches like mini fridges, porches, bathtubs, hot and cold water, and other modern conveniences. Continental breakfast is included. The bar, swimming pool, and clean beach area face the sunset and are more private and quiet than those on the island's windward side.

Apartment-style accommodations are found at **Caye Caulker Condos** (tel. 501/226-0072, www.cayecaulkercondos.com, US$99-139), near the north end of the village by the Split; eight fully furnished suites, each facing the sea, have all the amenities, including a small pool. The balconies and rooftop hangout have nice views.

Over US$150

Caye Reef (Front St., US$200-235) has the most upscale boutique accommodations on the island: six spacious luxury apartments. Although the decor isn't mind-blowing, they have all the bells and whistles. Fully furnished sea-facing units have full kitchens and two bedrooms with en suite baths; a penthouse is on the third floor. There's a swimming pool with an infinity-like view from the apartments' top-floor balconies.

Vacation Homes

Caye Caulker Rentals (tel. 501/226-0029 or 501/630-1008, www.cayecaulkerrentals.com) rents more than 20 holiday houses, cabanas, and cottages. The website sorts homes by price, location, and size and provides photos. Nightly rental rates range US$60-379,

with one luxury villa that sleeps six going for US$379. A minimum number of nights is required, and monthly rentals are available.

Caye Caulker Accommodations (tel. 501/226-0381 or 501/610-0240, www.cayecaulkeraccommodations.com) manages nine vacation properties and books suites for two upscale hotels. You can see photos and make reservations through the website.

FOOD
Bakeries and Cafés

Hicaqueños love their baked goods, street food, and mobile vendors—who wouldn't want grab-and-go pieces of home-cooked goodness at super-cheap prices?

It all begins on Back Street—you simply cannot leave the island without sampling the morning and afternoon delights at ★ **Glenda's** (tel. 501/226-0148, 7am-10am and 11:30am-1pm Mon.-Sat.), literally set up inside someone's home and offering inexpensive, ridiculously delicious Belizean breakfast and lunch options. Getting up early for her homemade cinnamon rolls and a large glass of fresh-squeezed orange juice (all for US$2) is well worth it; go early before she sells out. For lunch, try the *garnaches* (crispy tortillas under a small mound of tomato, cabbage, cheese, and hot sauce) or burritos—you won't regret it. The chalkboard menu is updated daily, and the choices will have you drooling.

No breakfast in Belize is complete without sampling fry jacks—delicious fried dough that resembles a flat beignet, best accompanied by jam or as a side to your beans and eggs. Several eateries serve them, but the best I've tried are at **Marin's Restaurant** (Traveler's Palm St., tel. 501/226-0104, 8am-2pm and 6pm-10pm daily, fry jacks with eggs US$1.50), also serving lunch and dinner on the upstairs porch, and at **Tropical Paradise** (end of Front St., tel. 501/226-0124, 7:30am-9pm Mon.-Sat.).

Two blocks south of the dock, **Amor y Café** (6am-noon daily, US$4-6) is a laid-back spot for a morning coffee (no refills) and breakfast, with seating choice between an upper deck or street-level sandy-floored patio for early bird people-watching. Omelets, waffles, grilled sandwiches, and other options are served in regular portions. It's a tad pricey for the island, but the yogurt-granola option is welcome when you tire of starch and eggs.

Happy Lobster (Front St., tel. 501/226-0064, 6am-9:30pm Wed.-Mon.) has a solid breakfast menu, with morning coffee and refills as long as you're eating; it's always good and reasonably priced.

The Internet coffee shop **La Perla Del Mar** (Middle St., beside Atlantic Bank, 7am-9pm daily) serves Cuban coffee (and it is nice and strong) with a new espresso machine for gourmet drinks, served hot or cold. Seating is available on an outdoor porch or in the air-conditioned space, although seating is limited with all the computer cubicles. Wi-Fi is free, and five desktops are available for use at US$4.50 per hour.

Paradiso Sandwich Shop (Front St., tel. 501/226-0511, 6:30am-close daily, US$6-9) has deluxe baguette deli sandwiches as well as large salads, smoothies, wine, and breakfast. There's a cute shaded seating area, ideal for a sea view while using the free Wi-Fi and people-watching along Front Street.

Barbecue

Award-winning ★ **Rose's Grill and Bar** (Front St., tel. 501/226-0407, www.rosesgrill-landbar.com, 11am-3:30pm and 5pm-10pm daily, US$10-20) is a favorite and always has a good crowd under its gigantic *palapa*; it's not surprising given its tempting outdoor dinner barbecue grill, with fresh catch-of-the-day—priced by weight—beautifully laid out for your selection and subsequently cooked as you wait, from black snapper to lobster (other entrées are available). Orders come with side choices of the day.

The barbecue dishes from **Meldy's** (Middle St., across from the bakery, tel. 501/600-9481, 7am-10pm Sun.-Fri., US$4.50) are divine, served with delicious spiced baked beans, slaw, and a warm tortilla. Wash it down with fresh fruit juice (try the soursop if it's in season).

Belizean

For fresh johnnycakes (also known as journey cakes), plain or stuffed with cheese, chicken, or beef, find the taco woman running **Rico's Tacos** (Front St., across from Sand Box), an unassuming stand that opens in the wee hours of the morning every day. The most popular orders are stuffed tortillas, and a small crowd

Glenda's restaurant is an institution.

of children and adults often forms, so be vocal about your order lest you be skipped over by other hungry souls.

Those in search of a cheap lunch snack should listen for (and will hear) the calls of the gregarious **Dukunu Man** (Mark Fitzgibbon) as he starts his rounds from the beachfront water taxi arrival dock area at 8:30am and continues along Back, Middle, and Front Streets all the way to the Split until he sells out of his US$0.50 delicious vegetarian or US$1.25 chicken-filled hot *dukunu*—a Creole version of a small tamale, made of corn and wrapped in a banana leaf. At the very least, you should meet him!

★ **Syd's** (Middle St. at Ave. Langosta, tel. 501/206-0294) is famous for its fry chicken, some of the best I've ever tasted anywhere in Belize, with a crispy, perfectly seasoned flavor, served with two large sides for just US$4.50. Orders can take about 20 minutes for the fry chicken and sell out quickly, so go by noon if you can. The stew chicken is also quite good. Those with time can enjoy the lovely garden patio seating in the back.

Directly across from EZ Boy Tours is **Martinez Fast Food** (off Front St., US$2.50-3.50), a popular local boxed-lunch spot, selling a half- or full-size lunch of rice and beans with stew chicken or the day's entrée. Even if you don't eat, you must get a cup of the refreshing, delicious homemade ginger ale juice (US$1.50). Not far from Martinez, starting at noon on "good weather" days, you will spot **Pastorina** (Front St., US$4) and her cart parked and serving fresh lunch out of her steel pots and into boxes for hungry locals. Her Creole dishes include chicken stew or beef and other offerings, with two sides.

★ **Chan's Fast Food** (Calle del Sol, tel. 501/226-0478, 7am-9pm Fri.-Wed., 7am-3pm Thurs., US$3.50-6), also known as Auntie's, comes to the rescue when you crave a quick, plentiful boxed lunch in the midafternoon to assuage post-snorkeling hunger pains. The window-service establishment dishes out everything from delicious chicken fingers to stew chicken or beef and daily local Central American specialties, such as *escabeche* (onion soup), conch soup, or barracuda, along with rice and beans or slaw. Don't judge the place by its appearance; you'll be surprised. There's a reason locals constantly flock to this window.

A little farther south off Back Street and up two flights of steep stairs is **Little Kitchen** (tel. 501/667-2178, 11am-3pm and 5pm-10pm daily, US$5-10), where you can get excellent

catch of the day on display outside Rose's Grill and Bar

appetizers, such as *salbutes* (a kind of hot, soggy taco dripping in oil), *garnaches* (crispy tortillas under a small mound of tomato, cabbage, cheese, and hot sauce), and *panades* (little meat pies, 3 for US$1); one of the best ceviches in the village; burritos; and home-cooked seafood dishes, all for very cheap. Seating is casual at outdoor picnic tables, with reggae music and a nice breeze.

Casual Dining

The beachfront **Barrier Reef Sports Bar and Grill** (9am-midnight daily, US$2-9) serves breakfast, lunch, dinner, and bar food. With options such as steaks, seafood, and pasta entrées for US$12-25 and satellite television screens showing sports, it's an easy choice for those picky eaters seeking a taste of home.

Happy Lobster (Front St., tel. 501/226-0064, 6am-9:30pm Wed.-Mon., US$4-15) offers a choice of local dishes or pastas for lunch or dinner, plus outdoor seating and free wireless Internet. Prices are reasonable and it's one of the few eateries open on Sunday.

Craving savory chicken wings and tacos? Head to **88 West** (Chapoose St., beside Belize Diving Services, tel. 501/226-0643, 8am-8pm Tues.-Fri., 8am-6pm Sat.-Sun., US$2-10) close to happy hour; these two menu options won't disappoint, and other offerings include salads. Go early to avoid a long wait.

Another great choice for a casual meal throughout the day, ★ **Tropical Paradise** (Front St., tel. 501/226-0124, 7:30am-9pm Mon.-Sat., US$4-15) has a solid menu of dishes that include Belizean, seafood, burgers, and nachos, not to mention a full bar for cocktails. The appetizers are on point—the ceviche in particular—and there are plenty of entrées. (Ask for the seafood or chicken kebab options, listed on a hidden wall menu!) The service is friendly, and the wait on orders is surprisingly short despite crowds in the busy season.

Fine Dining

Newcomer **Coconut Reef Caribbean Trattoria** (Front St., close to Raggamuffin Tours, tel. 501/206-0333, http://coconutreef-cayecaulker.webs.com, 5pm-9pm Mon.-Sat., US$10-22) gets rave reviews for its "Italian dishes with a Caye Caulker twist." Serving daily fresh seafood and fresh homemade pasta, its hits include lobster lasagna and chargrilled lime and peppercorn tuna steak. Portions are generous and there are early bird discounts offered. Pizzas are also available for delivery.

★ **Habaneros** (Front St., tel. 501/626-4911, 6pm-9pm daily, US$6-25) is the priciest restaurant and lounge by the island's standards, but its Central American cuisine is a notch above the others, with unique and absolutely delicious seafood options—from the seafood curry to coconut-encrusted snapper—and several other vegetarian and meat specialties. The raised porch is ideal to enjoy the lavishly presented meals and live music, and the indoor bar is tiny but has chic ambience. Make sure to try the frozen mojito, and the Creole voodoo cakes are to die for (watch out for the habanero pepper sauce). Reservations are highly recommended; this popular restaurant only seats 36 and gets booked as early as 7pm!

The **Rainbow Bar and Grill** (off Front St., tel. 501/226-0281, 10:30am-9pm Tues.-Sun., US$10-25) offers diners a lovely seaside ambience and view—the covered outdoor deck stretches over the water—and solid local food options. Lunch is very popular with day-trippers to the island because of the restaurant's ideal location a short walk from both the water taxi and the Split.

Dessert

Got a sweet tooth or craving dessert? **Andrew** (Front St., 6pm-close daily, US$2) starts with a sweet evening aroma as he rolls his bicycle cart filled with delicious cakes and pies, homemade daily, in addition to dinners. Try his coconut pies or banana bread, so fresh they are warm to the touch.

Groceries

Chan's Mini Mart (Middle St., across from

Caye Caulker Plaza Hotel, tel. 501/226-0165, 7am-9pm daily) is pretty much the heart of "downtown" Caulker—check the bulletin board for ads and events or go inside for a full-size supermarket minus a deli counter. **Chinatown Grocery** (Ave. Langosta and Estrella St., tel. 501/226-0338, 7am-11pm daily) also has a good selection.

There are a few great fruit, vegetable, and juice stalls around town; look near the bakery and Atlantic Bank. A favorite is **Julia's Juice** (Front St., US$2.50), where she sells watermelon, orange, lime, soursop, and mixed-fruit juice in recycled plastic bottles—you can mix and match your fruit juices. Another great stand is the newer **Seachoice Island Produce** (Pasero St., opposite Atlantic Bank, 6:30am-5pm Mon.-Thurs., 8am-noon Sun.). Rony serves freshly made fruit smoothies and mixes of your choice at **Coro's Juice Stand** (Front St.), right beside the art booths of Palapa Gardens. For fresh fish or lobsters, go to the **Lobstermen's Co-op Dock** (Calle del Sol), on the back side of the island; ask what time the fishing boats come in with their catch.

INFORMATION AND SERVICES

There is plenty of online research you can do while planning your trip to the northern cayes. Check the official website of the **Caye Caulker Belize Tourism Industry Association** (CCBTIA, www.gocayecaulker. com). The best-run and most active website is probably **www.ambergriscaye.com.** The forum also has a Caye Caulker section that is easily searched and where you'll find a large community of knowledgeable folks who are generally quick to answer. There is no tourist information booth on the island; just walk off the dock and ask around.

Tsunami Adventures (tel. 501/226-0462, www.tsunamiadventures.com), up toward the Split, acts as a local travel agency. **Seaside Cabanas** (Calle del Sol, tel. 501/226-0498, www.seasidecabanas.com) also has reliable travel agents.

Banks

Atlantic Bank (Middle St., 8am-3pm Mon.-Fri., 8:30am-noon Sat.) is the only bank on the island. Atlantic's ATM accepts international cards. A Western Union office is located in the bank, and another is down the street inside Syd's. Be warned that the ATM tends to run out of cash by noon, but it is replenished again in the afternoon. Be sure to get enough cash if you're on the island just before a weekend.

Health and Emergencies

The free **health clinic** (south end of Front St., tel. 501/226-0190, 8am-7pm) will help you with meds, if they have the supplies; it is staffed by a Cuban doctor and a Belizean nurse. For any serious emergency, your best bet is an emergency flight to the mainland; all hotels keep a list of emergency boat captains and pilots.

Media and Communications

At the south end of Front Street is the Village Council office (upstairs in the community center) and community library, health clinic, and **post office** (8am-noon and 1pm-5pm Mon.-Thurs., 1pm-4:30pm Fri.). The mail goes out every morning. **FedEx** services are available at the **Tropic Air** cargo office at the airstrip.

The **BTL Office** (Back St., 8am-noon and 1pm-5pm Mon.-Fri.) sells Digicell SIM cards for those with an unlocked phone; getting a local number requires an ID (passport or driver's license) for registration purposes.

Cayeboard Connection (Front St., tel. 501/629-3680, 8am-9pm daily, US$6 per hour) is a cozy Internet café and bookstore with an extensive collection of used guidebooks and novels, and will burn CDs and print photos; printing, scanning, and copying services are also offered. **Island Link** (Front St., tel. 501/226-0592, theislandlink@hotmail.com, 8am-9pm daily, US$6 per hour), near the Split, combines access and office copy services with a small ice-cream parlor.

Caye Caulker Ocean Academy

the Ocean Academy

The story behind the 2008 opening of Caye Caulker's first high school, Ocean Academy (near the airstrip, tel. 501/226-0321, www.cayecaulkerschool.com), speaks to the island's strong community spirit. In 2007, Hicaqueños had no option but to send their children to the mainland once they completed primary school. Only the privileged few could afford daily or even weekly commute costs to Belize City, much less the school fees and uniforms. As a result, many children on the island stopped attending school at age 12, falling behind in the most basic of skills.

Enter Heidi Curry, an American expat who left the rat race to make a new life for herself and her family in Belize. While tutoring primary schoolchildren in her free time, she learned of the alarming gap in learning opportunities. It wasn't long before her passion for the island's children led her to the idea of opening a high school. After an initial phone inquiry to the Ministry of Education (as simple, she says, as asking "How does one open a high school?") the community rallied behind her—including cofounder Joni Miller, parents, business owners, volunteers, and resident Dane Dingerson, who donated land and funded construction. Within eight months, a nonprofit high school was born. The first high school graduation ceremony took place in 2011.

In addition to core academic classes, subjects taught include marine biology, graphic design, tour guiding, and scuba certification. Environmental education has a big place here, with projects such as mangrove restoration and composting. Students are offered annual apprenticeship placements on the island, giving them a role in Caye Caulker's growing tourism industry.

Travelers have many opportunities to get involved. The school hosts service-learning groups, volunteer teachers, and mentors year-round; needed volunteer skills and school supplies are listed online. Cash donations are welcome and can help sponsor the school year-round, particularly supporting the construction of a much-needed second floor of classrooms. Guided tours of the school campus (US$5 pp) are available.

GETTING THERE
Air

Tropic Air (tel. 501/226-2012, U.S. tel. 800/422-3435, www.tropicair.com) and **Maya Island Air** (tel. 501/223-1140 or 501/223-1362, www.mayaislandair.com) make daily flights to Caye Caulker from Belize City's municipal and international airports as part of their San Pedro run. The airstrip on Caye Caulker is simple—you arrive just 15 minutes early and wait outside or on the veranda of the small building that serves all flights. Fares on

Tropic Air, slightly lower than Maya Island Air, are US$41.50 one-way to Belize City's municipal airport (about 10 minutes) and US$72 one-way to the international airport (8 minutes). Tropic Air also flies between the Belize International Airport and Cancún, Mexico, with connections to Caye Caulker and San Pedro—yet another option of flying into Belize.

Boat

The short water taxi ride between Caye Caulker and either Belize City or San Pedro is the most common and affordable way to get to the island. The Belize City-Caye Caulker trip costs US$12.50 one-way. Many boats are partially open-air, with benches for seats, although San Pedro Belize Express has a fleet of forward-facing three- and four-seat rows and covered interiors, but with less leg room. A light cardigan or rain jacket is always handy for windy trips. The boats are often packed to the point of being overloaded and sometimes depart late, although some companies are guiltier of these offenses than others. The safest bet is often the San Pedro Belize Express.

Three competing water taxi companies have alternative schedules and similar fares. Tickets for the **San Pedro Belize Express** (San Pedro tel. 501/226-3535, Caye Caulker tel. 501/226-0225, Belize City tel. 501/223-2225, www.belizewatertaxi.com) can be purchased from the ticket office on Caye Caulker's Front Street. Boats depart from the dock across the police station. Express departures to Belize City run 6am-5pm daily, to San Pedro 8am-5:30pm daily. San Pedro Belize Express Water Taxi also offers daily service to the Muelle Fiscal in Chetumal, Mexico. The boat departs from Caye Caulker at 7am or San Pedro at 7:30am and returns from Chetumal at 3:30pm. Caye Caulker connections are available. The 2.5-hour one-way trip costs US$45.

Caye Caulker Water Taxi (San Pedro tel. 501/226-2194, Caye Caulker tel. 501/226-0992, Belize City tel. 501/223-5752, www.cayecaulkerwatertaxi.com) boats depart Caye Caulker from the main pier on the east of the island; buy tickets at the office rig the dock before boarding the boat. Depar to Belize City run 6:30am-4pm daily, t Pedro 8:45am-5:45pm daily.

Water Jets Express boats (San Pedro tel. 501/226-2194, Caye Caulker tel. 501/206-0234, Belize City tel. 501/207-1000, www.sanpedrowatertaxi.com) depart from the lagoon on the back side of the island to Belize City 6:30am-4pm daily, to San Pedro 8:45am-5:45pm daily. Water Jets Express also offers daily service to Chetumal in Mexico (US$45 one-way) that departs Caye Caulker at 7am or San Pedro at 8am and returns at 3pm. It also has a daily boat that leaves San Pedro at 3pm for Corozal and Sarteneja, which returns at 7am.

GETTING AROUND

The navigable part of town—from the airstrip north to the split—is one mile long and easily explored on foot. Still, a bicycle will make things easier, particularly on hot days and if you're staying in one of the more southern accommodations. Ask if your hotel provides one, or rent at **Friendship Center** on Front Street. **M&N Mel's Bike Rentals** is also a safe bet (Chapoose St., just off Front St., tel. 501/226-0229, US$2 per hour, US$25 per week).

If you're staying far south of the village, you might consider renting a golf cart from the centrally located **Caye Caulker Golf Cart Rentals** (Ave. Mangle, across Caye Caulker Plaza Hotel, tel. 501/226-0237, US$13 per hour, US$63 per day for more than 5 hours with return by nightfall, or US$85 per 24 hours), a local family-run business with friendly owners. The other alternative is the pricier **C&N, Island Boy Rental** (Traveler's Palm St., tel. 501/226-0252 or 501/610-5236, US$88 per day).

A golf cart taxi ride is cheap and worth it when moving around the island with heavy luggage. Taxi guy **Luis** (tel. 501/624-8578, US$2.50) is responsive, friendly, and sends colleagues right away if he's busy; taxis also remain parked outside the water taxi terminals awaiting arrivals.

Diving the Northern Atolls

Belize's atolls are a sight to behold—with some of the clearest turquoise waters as well as abundant marinelife. No trip to these easterly islands is ever wasted, whether to snorkel, dive, or swim, taking in Belize's breathtaking waters, not to mention some of the most beautiful beaches.

TURNEFFE ISLANDS

A renowned diving and fishing destination about 30 miles east of Belize City, most of the Turneffe islands are small dots of sand, mangrove clusters, and swamp, home only to seabirds and wading birds, ospreys, manatees, and crocodiles. Only **Blackbird Caye** and **Douglas Caye** are of habitable size, supporting small populations of fishers and shellfish divers. In November 2012, Turneffe Atoll was officially declared a protected marine reserve.

If you're looking to hook a bonefish or a permit, miles of crystal flats are alive with both hard-fighting species. Tarpon are abundant late March-June within the protected creeks and channels throughout the islands. Those who seek larger trophies will find a grand choice of marlin, sailfish, wahoo, groupers, blackfin tuna, and many more.

Most visitors to Turneffe are day-tripping divers based in Ambergris Caye or Caye Caulker; a select few choose to book an island vacation package. There are a couple of upscale resorts and one research facility where visitors can stay.

Rendezvous Point

This is a popular first dive for overnighters out of Ambergris Caye. It provides a great opportunity for divers who haven't been under in a while. The depth is about 40-50 feet and affords sufficient bottom time for you to get a good look at a wide variety of reef life.

Angelfish, butterflyfish, parrotfish, yellowtails, and morays are well represented. This will whet appetites for the outstanding diving to come at the Elbow.

★ The Elbow

Most divers have heard of the Elbow (just 10 minutes from Turneffe Island Lodge), a point of coral that juts out into the ocean. This now-famous dive site offers a steep sloping drop-off covered with tube sponges and deep-water gorgonians, along with shoals of snappers (sometimes numbering in the hundreds) and other pelagic creatures. Predators such as bar jacks, wahoo, and permits cruise the reef, and the drop-off is impressive. Currents sweep the face of the wall most of the time, and they typically run from the north. However, occasionally they reverse or cease all together.

Lefty's Ledge

A short distance farther up the eastern side of the atoll from the Elbow is another dive to excite even those with a lot of bottom time under their weight belts. Lefty's Ledge features dramatic spur-and-groove formations that create a wealth of habitats. Correspondingly, divers will see a head-turning display of undersea life in both reef and pelagic species. Jacks, mackerels, permits, and groupers are present in impressive numbers. Wrasses, rays, parrotfish, and butterflyfish are evident around the sandy canyons. Cleaning stations are also evident, where you'll see large predators allowing themselves to be groomed by small cleaner shrimp or fish. The dive begins at about 50 feet and the bottom slopes to about 100 feet before dropping off into the blue.

Gales Point

Gales Point is a "don't-miss" dive a short

Turneffe Islands

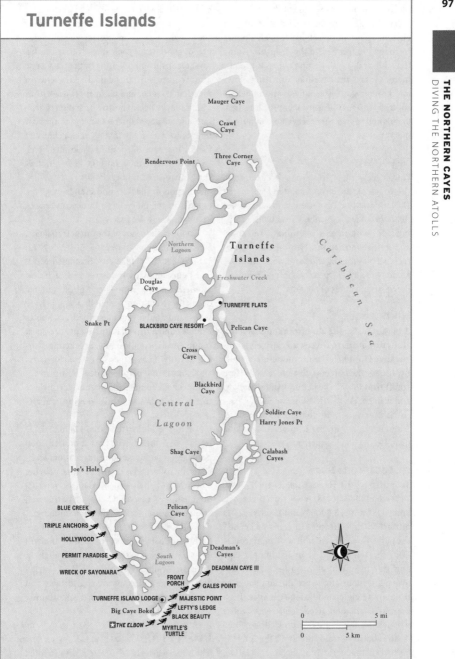

Mauger Caye

Crawl Caye

Three Corner Caye

Rendezvous Point

Northern Lagoon

Turneffe Islands

Freshwater Creek

Caribbean Sea

Douglas Caye

● TURNEFFE FLATS

Snake Pt

BLACKBIRD CAYE RESORT ●

Pelican Caye

Cross Caye

Blackbird Caye

Central Lagoon

Soldier Caye
Harry Jones Pt

Shag Caye

Calabash Cayes

Joe's Hole

Pelican Caye

BLUE CREEK

TRIPLE ANCHORS

HOLLYWOOD

PERMIT PARADISE

South Lagoon

Deadman's Cayes

WRECK OF SAYONARA

DEADMAN CAYE III

FRONT PORCH

GALES POINT

TURNEFFE ISLAND LODGE ●

MAJESTIC POINT

Big Caye Bokel

LEFTY'S LEDGE

BLACK BEAUTY

★ THE ELBOW

MYRTLE'S TURTLE

0   5 mi

0   5 km

© AVALON TRAVEL

distance up the eastern side of the atoll from Lefty's Ledge. Here the reef juts out into the current at a depth of about 45 feet, sloping to about 100 feet before the drop-off. Along the wall and the slope just above it are numerous ledges and cave-like formations. Rays and groupers are especially common here—some say this may be a grouper breeding area. Corals and sponges are everywhere in numerous varieties.

Sayonara

On the leeward, or western, side of the atoll, the wreck of the *Sayonara,* a tender sunk by Dave Bennett of Turneffe Island Lodge, lies in about 30 feet of water. Close by is a sloping ledge with interesting tunnels and spur-and-groove formations. Healthy numbers of reef fish play among the coral, and some barracuda tag along. Divers' bubbles often draw down large schools of permits.

Hollywood

A bit farther up the atoll from the *Sayonara,* Hollywood offers divers a relatively shallow dive (30-40 feet) with moderate visibility, unless the currents have reversed. Here you'll find lots of basket and tube sponges and lush coral growth. Many angelfish, parrotfish, grunts, and snappers swim here. Although not as dramatic as an eastern side dive, Hollywood has plenty to see.

Accommodations

Turneffe Island Resort (tel. 501/532-2990, U.S. tel. 800/874-0118, www.turneffesort. com, US$1,590-2,790 3-night package) is on **Little Caye Bokel,** 12 acres of beautiful palm-lined beachfront and mangroves. Book a seven-night dive or fishing package and stay in one of eight ground-floor deluxe guest rooms, four second-floor superior rooms, and eight stand-alone cabanas. It's a popular location for divers, anglers, and those who just want a hammock under the palms. At the southern tip of the atoll, the lodge is a short distance north of its larger relative, Big Caye Bokel. This strategic location offers

enthusiasts a wide range of underwater experiences—it's within minutes of nearly 200 dive sites. Shallow areas are perfect for photography or snorkeling; you can see nurse sharks, rays, reef fish, and dolphins in the flats a few hundred yards from the dock. All the dives mentioned earlier and many more are within 15 minutes by boat. The dive operation is first-rate, and advanced instruction and equipment rentals are available. Anglers have a choice of fishing for snappers, permits, jacks, mackerel, and billfish from the drop-offs. They can stalk the near-record numbers of snook, bonefish, and tarpon in the flats and mangroves. The lodge's fishing guide has an uncanny way of knowing where the fish will be.

On the eastern side of the Turneffe Islands, **Blackbird Caye Resort** (tel. 501/223-2772, U.S. tel. 888/271-3483, www.blackbirdresort. com) encompasses 166 acres of beach and jungle. It can accommodate 36 guests (double occupancy) with hot-water showers, private baths, and double and queen beds, as well as a duplex and a triplex featuring private guest rooms and air-conditioning. Snorkeling, fishing, and diving packages are offered for about US$2,000-3,000 per week, depending on activities and accommodations, and can include three dives a day, all meals, lodging, and airport transfers.

Turneffe Flats (tel. 501/232-9022, U.S. tel. 800/512-8812, www.tflats.com, US$2,000 packages) is famous among international saltwater fly fishers who know the value of being able to sight fish in wadable flats for permits, bonefish, and tarpon. Or go for barracuda, snappers, jacks, or snook and eat it up at night. Guided fishing is in the lodge's 16-foot Super Skiff flats boats. Divers are welcome and will enjoy daily forays to scores of sites throughout Turneffe Atoll and Lighthouse Reef. Varied beach accommodations are comfortable and well appointed, and meals are eaten family style.

LIGHTHOUSE REEF

The most easterly of Belize's three atolls, Lighthouse Reef lies 50 miles southeast of

Belize City. The 30-mile-long, 8-mile-wide lagoon is the location of the Blue Hole, a dive spot that was made famous by Jacques Cousteau and is a favorite destination of dive boats from Belize City, Ambergris Caye, and Caye Caulker. The best dive spots, however, are along the walls of Half Moon Caye and Long Caye, where the diving rivals that of any in the world.

Think of the atoll as a large spatula with a short handle and a long blade. At the northern tip of the spatula blade, **Sandbore Caye** is home to a rusty lighthouse and a few fishing shacks. It is also the favorite anchorage of several of the dive boats that do overnight stops, including *Reef Roamer II.*

Big Northern Caye, across a narrow strait, has a landing strip that used to serve the now-closed resort here. There are long stretches of beach to walk, beautiful vistas, mangroves, and lagoons, home to snowy egrets and crocodiles.

Halfway down the spatula-shaped atoll, about where the blade meets the handle, lies the magnificent **Blue Hole,** a formation best appreciated from the air but also impressive from the bridge of a boat.

At the elbow of the handle is **Half Moon Caye,** a historical natural monument and protected area with its lighthouse, bird sanctuary, shipwrecks, and incredible diving offshore. Finally, on the handle, **Long Caye** is a lonely outpost with a small dock, large palms, and glassy water.

Blue Hole

This circular underwater formation, with its magnificent blue-to-black hues surrounded by neon water, is emblematic of Belize itself. The submerged shaft is a karst-eroded sinkhole with depths exceeding 400 feet. In the early 1970s, Jacques Cousteau and his crew explored the tunnels, caverns, and stalactites here, angled by past earthquakes.

Most dive groups descend to a depth of about 135 feet. Technically, this is not a dive for novices or even intermediate divers, though many intermediate divers do it with a guide. It requires a rapid descent, a very short period at depth, and a careful ascent, requiring excellent buoyancy control. For a group of 10 or more, at least three dive masters should be present. The Blue Hole is everything it is hyped up to be; my own personal experience there was extraordinary, and I gasped at the sight of the gigantic formations, the infinite depth, and the Caribbean reef sharks that circled nearby. It's akin to an out-of-body experience. The lip of the crater down to about 60-80 feet has the most life: fat midnight parrotfish, stingrays, angelfish, butterflyfish, and other small reef fish cluster around coral heads and outcroppings.

Half Moon Caye National Monument

Dedicated as a monument in 1982, this crescent-shaped island was the first protected area in Belize. Half Moon Caye, at the southeast corner of Lighthouse Reef, measures 45 square acres, half of which is a thriving but endangered littoral forest; the other half is a stunning palm-dotted beach. This is also the only red-footed booby sanctuary in the western hemisphere besides the Galápagos. The US$40 per person admission fee is sometimes included in your dive boat fee, but sometimes you'll pay it directly to the park ranger when you disembark.

As you approach Half Moon Caye, you'll believe you have arrived at some South Sea paradise. Offshore, boaters use the rusted hull of a wreck, the *Elksund,* as a landmark in these waters. Its dark hulk looms over the surreal blue and black of the reef world. The caye, eight feet above sea level, was formed by the accretion of coral bits, shells, and calcareous algae. It's divided into two ecosystems: The section on the western side has dense vegetation with rich fertile soil, while the eastern section primarily supports coconut palms and little other vegetation.

Besides offshore waters that are among the clearest in Belize, the caye's beaches are gorgeous. You must climb the eight-foot-high central ridge that divides the island and

Lighthouse Reef

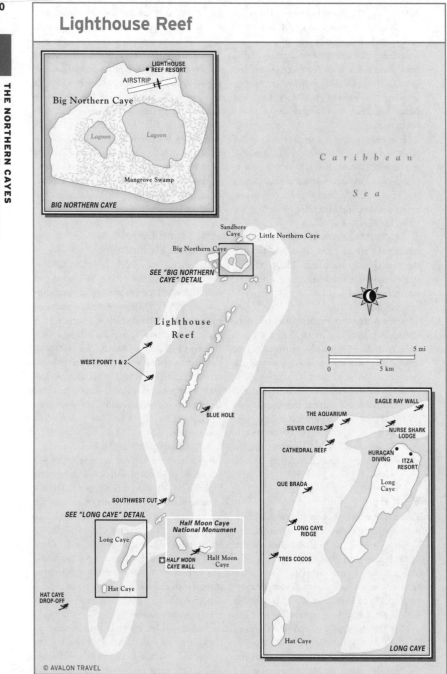

LIGHTHOUSE
REEF RESORT
AIRSTRIP

Big Northern Caye

Lagoon   Lagoon

Mangrove Swamp

BIG NORTHERN CAYE

C a r i b b e a n

S e a

Sandbore
Caye   Little Northern Caye

Big Northern Caye

SEE "BIG NORTHERN CAYE" DETAIL

Lighthouse
Reef

WEST POINT 1 & 2

0   5 mi
0   5 km

BLUE HOLE

EAGLE RAY WALL

THE AQUARIUM

SILVER CAVES   NURSE SHARK
LODGE

CATHEDRAL REEF   HURACAN
DIVING   ITZA
RESORT

QUE BRADA   Long
Caye

SOUTHWEST CUT

SEE "LONG CAYE" DETAIL

*Half Moon Caye
National Monument*

LONG CAYE
RIDGE

Long Caye

HALF MOON
CAYE WALL   Half Moon
Caye

TRES COCOS

Hat Caye

HAT CAYE
DROP-OFF

Hat Caye

LONG CAYE

© AVALON TRAVEL

gaze south before you see the striking half-moon beach with its unrelenting surf erupting against limestone rocks. Half Moon Caye's first lighthouse was built in 1820, modernized and enlarged in 1931, decommissioned in 1997, then felled by the elements in 2010. A newer lighthouse was built in 1998 and is still functioning.

Everyone should go to the **observation tower,** built by the Audubon Society in the ziricote forest; climb above the forest canopy for an unbelievable 180-degree view. Every tree is covered with perched booby birds in some stage of growth or mating. In March, you'll have a close-up view of nests where feathered parents tend their hatchlings. The air is filled with boobies coming and going, attempting to make their usually clumsy landings (those webbed feet weren't designed for landing in trees). Visitors also have a wonderful opportunity to see the other myriad inhabitants of the caye. Thieving magnificent frigates (the symbol of the Belize Audubon Society) swoop in to steal eggs, and iguanas crawl around in the branches, also looking for a snack.

It's 52 miles from the mainland to Half Moon Caye, a long boat trip over open ocean. Most visitors make the trip through one of the bigger dive shops, like Amigo's on Ambergris Caye. Otherwise, only chartered or privately owned boats and seaplanes travel to Half Moon Caye. Check with the Belize Audubon Society in Belize City for other suggestions.

★ Half Moon Caye Wall

On the eastern side of Lighthouse Reef Atoll, the reef has a shallow shelf in about 15 feet of water where garden eels are plentiful. The sandy area broken with corals extends downward till you run into the reef wall, which rises some 20 feet toward the surface. Most boats anchor in the sandy area above the reef wall. Numerous fissures in the reef crest form canyons or tunnels leading out to the vertical face. In this area, sandy shelves and valleys frequently harbor nurse sharks and gigantic stingrays. Divers here are sure to return with a wealth of wonderful pictures.

Long Caye Aquarium

Minutes from Half Moon Caye Wall, often combined with a Blue Hole trip, is a spectacular dive site ideal for photos and with the most marinelife spotting, even more than at Half Moon Caye Wall. The electrifying deep-blue waters will stun you, as will the schools

beach on Half Moon Caye, Lighthouse Reef Atoll

of bright colorful fish and the large eagle rays, sea turtles, stingrays, and nurse sharks.

Silver Caves

The shoals of silversides (small gleaming minnows) that gave this western atoll site its name are gone, but Silver Caves is still impressive and enjoyable. The coral formations are riddled with large crevices and caves that cut clear through the reef. As you enter the water above the sandy slope where most boats anchor, you'll be in about 30 feet of water and surrounded by friendly yellowtail snappers. Once again you'll see the downwardly sloping bottom, the rising reef crest, and the stomach-flipping drop into the blue.

Tres Cocos

On the western wall, "Three Coconuts" refers to trees on nearby Long Caye. The sandy bottom slopes from about 30 feet to about 40 feet deep before it plunges downward. Overhangs are common features here, and sponges and soft corals adorn the walls. Another fish lover's paradise, Tres Cocos does not have the outstanding coral formations you'll see at several other dives in the area, but who cares? There's a rainbow of marinelife all about. Turtles, morays, jacks, coral, shrimp, cowfish, rays, and angelfish are among the actors on this colorful stage.

West Point

Farther north and about even with the Blue Hole, West Point is well worth a dive. Visibility may be a bit more limited than down south, but it's still very acceptable. The reef face here is stepped. The first drop plunges from about 30 feet to well over 100 feet deep. Another coral and sand slope at that depth extends a short distance before dropping vertically into very deep water. The first shallow wall has pronounced overhangs and lush coral and sponge growth.

Accommodations

Stay overnight on **Long Caye** with **Huracan** **Diving** (U.S. tel. 518/253-7705, www.hura-candiving.com), where you can choose from either a four- or seven-night all-inclusive dive package (US$990-1,490). The four guest rooms at Huracan's lodge have private baths, king beds, ceiling fans, and screened windows. Pickup and transfer from Belize City is included in your package. A second option on Long Caye is **Itza Resort** (U.S. tel. 305/600-2585, tel. 501/223-3228, www.itza-resort.com, R&R package US$995-1,650 for 3 nights, US$1,395-2,795 for 7 nights, rates vary), a 20-room oceanfront resort offering diving, fishing, water sports (kite surfing) and "R&R" packages.

ST. GEORGE'S CAYE

The most historically significant caye—a national landmark and the first capital of the British Settlement (1650-1784)—is a little-known getaway. Nine miles or a 20-minute water taxi hop from Belize City, this small caye is home to **St. George's Caye Mangrove Reserve,** established in 2005 and covering 12.5 acres on the southernmost point of the island. One luxury resort has a full-service dive shop that also offers other water sports: **St. George's Caye Resort** (tel. 800/813-8498 or 501/220-4444, www.good-diving.com, US$168 pp includes meals). The rest of the island is lined with private villas and docks owned by affluent Belizeans who escape here on the weekends.

St. George's Caye Day is celebrated nationwide on September 10 to honor a 1798 British battle that took place here and prevented Spanish invasion. Today, the small cemetery gives evidence of St. George's heroic past and is Belize's smallest archaeology reserve.

The **St. George's Caye Research Station and Field School,** founded by ECOMAR in 2009, hosts a group of Texas State University professors and students who spend a month on the island to conduct research digs. They also conduct coral reef research and educational trips based here.

St. George's Caye Aquarium

Ever visited a professional aquarium created by a 10-year-old? Walk south of St. George's Caye Resort, past the renowned St. George's Caye cannon—where the British Baymen fought off an attempted Spanish invasion of Belize in 1798. You'll arrive at the **St. George's Caye Aquarium** (tel. 501/662-2170, 8am-5pm Mon.-Sun., karlbischof@yahoo.com), clearly indicated at the entrance to a home. In 2011, at the age of 10, Karly Bischof opened and has since managed the only indoor marine display of this kind in Belize, home to over 100 species of fish. For just US$3, he shows visitors around, describing each of the creatures that are native to Belize—from seahorses to scorpionfish and even a toadfish—and providing details on Belize's underwater life. Like his father, he hopes to become a marine biologist. No better place to prepare for it than Belize. Karly's aquarium has even appeared in overseas publications and is a worthwhile stop if you find yourself visiting the caye.

DROWNED CAYES

Spanish Lookout Caye is a 187-acre mangrove island at the southern tip of the Drowned Cayes, only 10 miles east of Belize City. There are many day-trip possibilities to Spanish Lookout Caye, including the country's first "dolphin encounter" program, a beach, kayaks, and snorkeling.

If you're not researching manatees or mangroves with Earthwatch Institute, you're most likely coming to meet the dolphins or stay at **Belize Adventure Lodge** (tel. 501/220-4024, U.S. reservations 888/223-5403, www.belizeadventurelodge.com, US$100), a full-service island facility offering 12 quasi-colonial cabanas over the water, two student dormitories, classrooms, a restaurant, a bar, a gift shop, and a dive center. Five colorful cabanas with 10 guest rooms, hot showers, and private baths are connected to the island by a dock. The resort offers popular four-night packages (US$799 per person for two) that include all meals and transfers to the island.

Diving is one of the favorite activities here, and guests can participate in educational and research programs. Manatees and dolphins are regularly seen foraging near the island. Juvenile reef fish, seahorses, lobsters, and mollusks live among the red mangrove roots and sea grass beds. Tarpon and barracuda often come into the bay to feed on the abundant silversides. The resort is only one mile

St. George's Caye is just a 10-minute boat ride from Belize City.

west of the Belize Barrier Reef and about eight miles west of central Turneffe Island.

THE BLUEFIELD RANGE

Scattered along the coast is a constellation of small cayes, some accessible by travelers, others only by drug traffickers. The Bluefield Range is one such group of cayes, a short distance south of Belize City. Accommodations are no longer available here, unfortunately, thanks to Hurricane Richard, which destroyed the range in 2010.

GOFF'S CAYE

Near English Caye, Goff's Caye is a favorite little island stop for picnics and day trips out of Caye Caulker and Belize City, thanks to a beautiful sandy beach and promising snorkeling areas. Sailboats often stop overnight; camping can be arranged from Caye Caulker by talking with any reputable guide. Bring your own tent and supplies. Goff's is a protected caye, so note the rules posted by the pier. Goff's has seen major impact from the cruise ship industry, which sometimes sends thousands of people per week to snorkel around and party on the tiny piece of sand, and a few reports have said this is destroying the coral.

ENGLISH CAYE

Although this is just a small collection of palm trees, sand, and coral, an important lighthouse sits here at the entrance to the Belize City harbor from the Caribbean Sea. Large ships stop at English Caye to pick up one of the two pilots who navigate the 10 miles in and out of the busy harbor. Overnights are not allowed here, but it's a pleasant day-trip location.

Southern Coast and Southern Cayes

Look for ★ to find recommended
sights, activities, dining, and lodging.

Highlights

© AVALON TRAVEL

★ **Gulisi Garífuna Museum:** Located on the outskirts of Dangriga, this museum offers an interactive history lesson on the fascinating Garinagu and Garífuna culture (page 112).

★ **Garífuna Settlement Day:** November 19 celebrates the arrival of the ancestral Garinagu people to Belize's shores. A colorful reenactment is followed by parades, processions, and a multitude of events from outdoor concerts to all-night drumming (page 117).

★ **South Water Caye Marine Reserve:** One of Belize's most beautiful offshore islands offers excellent snorkeling right off the beach, impressive dive sites, and a magical landscape (page 124).

★ **Tobacco Caye:** Sitting right atop Belize's barrier reef, Tobacco Caye can be a social hot spot of world travelers or an isolated island experience, depending on the time of year (page 125).

★ **Glover's Reef Atoll:** Glover's spectacular snorkeling and diving are a short journey from the southern shore, and the waters are ideal for all kinds of water sports (page 130).

★ **Lebeha Drumming Center:** In Hopkins, hourly drumming lessons provide a unique opportunity to learn about Garífuna music and dance (page 134).

★ **Mayflower Bocawina National Park:** Rappel waterfalls, zip across 7,100 acres of forest canopy, and enjoy bird- and wildlife-watching at this unique park (page 144).

★ **Cockscomb Basin Wildlife Sanctuary:** This extensive reserve is rightly famous for its multitude of birds, jaguars, and other jungle critters (page 146).

★ **Maya Beach and Seine Bight:** Maya Beach is peppered with hotels, restaurants, and bars, while Seine Bight offers low-key stretches of sand. They're a perfect jump-off point to the southern cayes (pages 149 and 151).

★ **Laughingbird Caye National Park:** Palms, sand, and excellent snorkeling are found at this national park, part of a 10,000-acre protected marine area (page 171).

J ust under two hours south of Belize City by car, the southern coast has an Afro-Caribbean soul and is the heart of the country's Garífuna culture. This district also boasts a beautiful coastline, lush rainforests, waterfalls, the world's only jaguar pre-

serve, the country's highest point, and the longest beach, stretching from unmanicured Dangriga to the tourist-heavy Placencia Peninsula. The primary towns and villages—Dangriga, Hopkins, and Placencia—provide the perfect jump-off point to the southern cayes, a mere 10-20 miles offshore.

These postcard-perfect islands, some of which can be rented in their entirety or explored on a day trip, range from a half to four-acre coral islands sitting atop or along the Belize Barrier Reef. Besides their sparkling white sands and dreamy Caribbean scenery, they offer excellent, uncrowded dive and snorkel sites—like the steep walls of South Water Caye, inhabited by spotted rays, sharks, and hawksbill turtles, and Laughingbird Caye National Park, where barracuda and angelfish thrive, among numerous other species. Besides using the various southern towns and villages as jump-off points to the islands, it's worthwhile to spend time on the mainland and explore some of Belize's most verdant and unpolluted interior, wildlife, and diverse population.

The seaside town of Dangriga, Garífuna hub and Belize's "culture capital," is home to a third of Stann Creek District's 36,000 inhabitants, and its economy is as varied as its culture and geography; tourism is as important as the orange, banana, and shrimp industries. Unassuming and untouristed, Dangriga is where independent travelers can get off the beaten path and explore African-inspired art galleries, make their own drums, and perhaps enjoy a Garífuna home. That's when they're not off trekking in the nearby Cockscomb Basin Wildlife Sanctuary, waterfall rappelling at nearby Mayflower Bocawina National Park, or cooling off in the emerald streams of Billy Barquedier National Park. It's astounding how many activities are within reach.

Previous: island near Placencia, Silk Cayes; Stann Creek River, Dangriga. **Above:** blue cabanas on Ranguana Caye.

Southern Coast and Southern Cayes

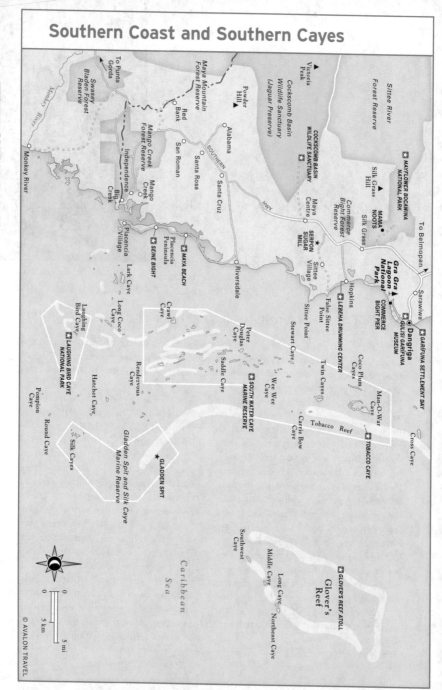

To Punta Gorda
Swasey Bladen Forest Reserve
Monkey River
Monkey River
Maya Mountain Forest Reserve
Victoria Peak ▲
Powder Hill ▲
Cockscomb Basin Wildlife Sanctuary (Jaguar Preserve)
Red Bank
San Roman
Alabama
Santa Cruz
Santa Rosa
Mango Creek Forest Reserve
SOUTHERN HWY
COCKSCOMB BASIN WILDLIFE SANCTUARY
Maya Centre
Sittee River
Forest Reserve
Sittee River
Forest Reserve
Silk Grass Hill ▲
Commerce Bight Forest Reserve
Silk Grass
MAYFLOWER BOCAWINA NATIONAL PARK
MAMA NOOTS
To Belmopan
Independence
Big Creek
Mango Creek
Placencia Village
SEINE BIGHT
MAYA BEACH
Placencia Peninsula
SERPON SUGAR MILL
Sittee Village
Riversdale
False Sittee Point
Sittee Point
Hopkins
LEBEHA DRUMMING CENTER
Gra Gra Lagoon National Park
COMMERCE BIGHT PIER
Sarawiwa
Dangriga
GULISI GARIFUNA MUSEUM
GARIFUNA SETTLEMENT DAY
Cross Caye
Lark Caye
Long Coco Caye
Crawl Caye
Stewart Caye
Peter Douglas Caye
Saddle Caye
Wee Wee Caye
Twin Cayes
Coco Plum Cayes
Man-O-War Caye
TOBACCO CAYE
Laughing Bird Caye
LAUGHING BIRD CAYE NATIONAL PARK
Rendezvous Caye
SOUTH WATER CAVE MARINE RESERVE
Carrie Bow Caye
Tobacco Reef
GLOVER'S REEF ATOLL
Hatchet Caye
Pompion Caye
Round Caye
Silk Cayes
Gladden Spit and Silk Caye Marine Reserve
GLADDEN SPIT
Caribbean Sea
Southwest Caye
Long Caye
Middle Caye
Northeast Caye
Glover's Reef
0 5 km
0 5 mi
© AVALON TRAVEL

More traveler-friendly yet still authentic, the nearby fishing village of Hopkins has uncrowded wide-open beaches, a host of lodging options to fit all budgets, drumming lessons, and plenty of Garífuna culture.

Beachcombers and dive enthusiasts looking to add pulsating nightlife to their trip will be happy to continue on to the Placencia Peninsula, one of the most rapidly developing tourist areas of Belize. With the longest (and nicest) stretch of beach on the mainland, a mixed Garífuna and Creole vibe, and the opportunity to island-hop to numerous stunning plots a quick boat ride away, Placencia offers plenty to love.

PLANNING YOUR TIME

Brace yourself: There are lots of islands to explore off the south coast. From South Water Caye, sitting atop the Belize Barrier Reef, to the three tiny specks of paradise that make up the Silk Cayes, these plots offer white sand, swaying palms, and easy-entry turquoise waters.

Remember that the mainland jump-off points (Dangriga, Hopkins, and Placencia) are equally packed with things to see and do. It would only make sense to spend some time in your stopover town, even if you're staying at a caye resort as your base, to explore Belize's lush interior alongside its incredible reef and marinelife.

How do you select one of the three mainland points? Dangriga and Hopkins—a stone's throw from each other—are the hub of Garífuna culture and offer plenty for cultureholics. They are also ideally positioned close to two major and worthwhile national parks.

If you decide on **Dangriga,** spend a half day exploring the town. Walk along the North Stann Creek Bridge and Commerce Boulevard, and then head to Y-Not Island Beach to watch Austin Rodriguez, a renowned Garífuna drum maker, at his seaside workshop. Squeeze in a visit to the **Gulisi Garífuna Museum** and the **Pen Cayetano Studio Gallery,** where you'll learn all about this Afro-Caribbean Garífuna culture. With the second half of your day, you could hike **Cockscomb Basin Wildlife Sanctuary** or tour the **Marie Sharp Factory,** where the most popular hot sauce in Belize and Central America is made and bottled. After a day or two in Dangriga, catch a boat over to **Tobacco Caye**—ideal for budget travelers and snorkelers—or **South Water Caye,** where you can stay overnight and spend your days exploring some of Belize's best snorkeling or wall dives.

Hopkins is just an hour away by bus from Dangriga. Stay right in the village for a day or two, enjoying the empty and clean stretch of beach, biking around, sampling Garífuna dishes, and taking drumming lessons at **Lebeha Drumming Center.** The nearby Sittee River offers birding and wildlife watching. From Hopkins, you could also trek to a waterfall in **Mayflower Bocawina National Park** and spend the night in **Maya Centre.** Shop for crafts, converse with herbal healers, and arrange an expedition within the **Cockscomb Basin Wildlife Sanctuary.** Continue on to Tobacco Caye or take a day trip to South Water Caye.

Placencia is dubbed the "barefoot perfect" beach of Belize and is one of the most tourist-ready areas on the mainland, with a plethora of resorts for all budgets. Journey along the gorgeous southern reef and dive to your heart's content with **Splash Dive Center.** Rent a cheap cabana on **Maya Beach** and barhop the night away, and enjoy day trips to **Laughingbird Caye** and the **Silk Cayes.** Of course, if you fall in love with the islands, you could always spend a couple of nights on charming **Ranguana Caye** or on **Coco Plum Caye.** You just can't go wrong!

If you're a major diving or water sports enthusiast, stay on **Hatchet Caye** or, better yet, spend your days with **Island Expeditions'** adventure campsite on stunning **Glover's Reef Atoll.**

Dangriga

"Mabuiga!" shouts the sign in Garífuna, welcoming you to this cultural hub and district capital. Built on the Caribbean shoreline and straddling North Stann Creek (also called Gumagarugu River), Dangriga's primary boast is its status as the Garífuna people's original port of entry into Belize—and their modern-day cultural center. But although the majority of Dangriga's 12,500 or so inhabitants are Garífuna descendants of that much-celebrated 1823 landing, the remaining few are a typically rich mix of Chinese, Creoles, mestizos, and Maya, all of whom can be seen interacting on the town's main drag.

Aside from Dangriga's ideal location for accessing the surrounding mountains and seas—and the limited visitor services available to do so—its chief attraction may just be its total lack of pretense. Dangriga, formerly known as Stann Creek Town, does not outwardly cater to its foreign visitors the way Placencia or San Pedro does—there is simply too much else going on in this commercial center, including fishing, farming, and serving the influx of Stann Creek villagers who come weekly to stock up on supplies. Consequently, this area is still relatively undeveloped for tourism, which is either a shortcoming or an attraction, depending on what kind of traveler you are. It could be intimidating for the novice traveler, but the people here are welcoming. The area is slowly evolving, finding ways to showcase its wonders—from its drumming culture to its nearby national parks. Dangriga, by the way, means something like "sweet still waters" in Garífuna.

If poking around the casually bustling vibe of Dangriga sounds intriguing, you'd do well to stay a couple of nights. And if it's culture you're looking for, with the drumming "sheds," the daily local scenes, and one of the most picturesque seaside areas in Belize, you'll want to stay a bit longer.

ORIENTATION

As you pull into town, three massive ceremonial *dügü* drums of iron will greet you. This is the *Drums of Our Fathers* monument, erected in 2003 as a symbol of Garífuna pride—and as a call to war against the erosion of Garífuna culture. Turn right to reach the deep dock at Commerce Bight or go left (north) to enter Dangriga Town. Heading north from the drums on St. Vincent Street, the old bus terminal is on your left before the first bridge. Continuing, you'll find more shops and eateries, culminating in the center of town on either side of the North Stann Creek Bridge; across the bridge, St. Vincent Street turns into Commerce Street and offers an informal market often set up along the north bank of the river. Catch a boat to the cayes from one of several places here. The airstrip is a mile or so north of Stann Creek, where you'll also find Pelican Beach Resort, Dangriga's fanciest digs and restaurant.

SIGHTS

Dangriga does not offer many traditional sights per se. A better term would be *experiences* because there is plenty going on—it's an explosion of culture, scenery, and people for any newcomer to this town. Moreover, Dangriga's central location—a detail often lost on travelers new to the area—makes it an excellent base for excursions around the region, much more so even than Placencia. You can browse the few crafts and music stores on St. Vincent Street and ask around for the drum-making workshops, one of which is set up at the Y-Not compound by the beach at Stann Creek. You might even walk away with an instrument of your own. Drums are often heard throughout the town to mark celebrations and funerals; sometimes it's simply a few people practicing the rhythms of their history. There's an abundance of artistic talent that can't be missed. Austin Rodriguez

Dangriga

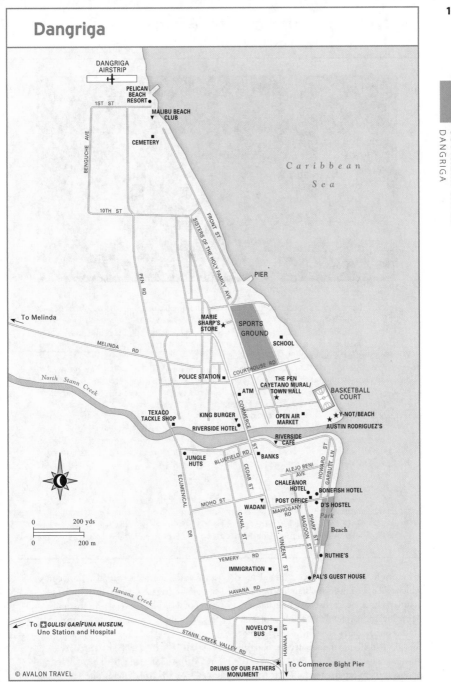

DANGRIGA
AIRSTRIP

PELICAN
BEACH
RESORT ●

1ST ST

MALIBU BEACH
CLUB ▼

CEMETERY ■

BENGUCHE AVE

10TH ST

FRONT ST

SISTERS OF THE HOLY FAMILY AVE

PEN RD

PIER

Caribbean
Sea

To Melinda →

MELINDA RD

MARIE
SHARP'S
STORE ★

SPORTS
GROUND

SCHOOL ■

North Stann Creek

COURTHOUSE RD

POLICE STATION ■

THE PEN
CAYETANO MURAL/
TOWN HALL ★

BASKETBALL
COURT

ATM ■

COMMERCE ST

TEXACO
TACKLE SHOP ■

KING BURGER ▼

OPEN AIR
MARKET ■

Y-NOT/BEACH ★
AUSTIN RODRIGUEZ'S ★

RIVERSIDE HOTEL ●

RIVERSIDE
CAFÉ ▼

BLUEFIELD RD

BANKS ■

HOWARD ST

GARBUTT LN

JUNGLE
HUTS ■

ALEJO BENI
AVE

CHALEANOR
HOTEL ■

CEDAR ST

BONEFISH HOTEL ■

ECUMENICAL DR

MOHO ST

WADANI ▼

POST OFFICE ■

D'S HOSTEL ●

MAHOGANY
RD

SHARP ST

MAGOON ST

Park

Beach

CANAL ST

ST VINCENT ST

YEMERY RD

IMMIGRATION ■

RUTHIE'S ●

HAVANA ST

PAL'S GUEST HOUSE ●

Havana Creek

HAVANA RD

← To 🏛 GULISI GARÍFUNA MUSEUM,
Uno Station and Hospital

STANN CREEK VALLEY RD

NOVELO'S
BUS ■

DRUMS OF OUR FATHERS
MONUMENT ★

→ To Commerce Bight Pier

0   200 yds
0   200 m

© AVALON TRAVEL

Drums of Our Fathers: From Poem to Monument

Drums of Our Fathers monument at the entrance of Dangriga

"In our culture, songs aren't composed, they just come from inspiration," explained Garífuna National Council cofounder, author, and educator Roy Cayetano. Cayetano's famous poem "Drums of Our Fathers" was turned into a monument erected in 2003. The structure consists of three large, equal-size Garífuna *dügü*, or ceremonial drums. It stands high at the entrance of Dangriga, greeting every newcomer to the Garífuna hub and cultural capital.

Roy Cayetano wrote "Drums of Our Fathers" in 15 minutes. It was "a call to war" and the need to act to preserve the endangered Garífuna culture, language, and heritage. At the time he dedicated the poem to his grandmother, his wife, and his child to be, symbolizing the past, present, and future.

When Sylvia Flores, then a member of the House of Representatives for the Dangriga area, mentioned her desire to commission the construction of a Garífuna monument in Dangriga, one that represented the spiritual aspect of the culture, Cayetano knew just what to suggest. The placement of three ceremonial Garífuna drums of equal size would be symbolic: the top middle drum resting on the lower two would symbolize the Garinagu present resting on the past and the ancestors and yet looking to the future. The goal was to immortalize the culture's most significant symbol, the drum, representing a sound of the people that was never quieted by the colonial masters, a sound that must continue to be heard.

Artist Steve Okeke, of Nigerian origin and based in Belize City, completed the monument within two months after it was commissioned. The resulting artwork was so impressive that a more central place was given to *Drums of Our Fathers* at the entrance to town, a constant reminder that the Garífuna culture was never silenced, the beat of the drums goes on, and its people's voices will continue to echo.

is known for his authentic Garífuna drums, which end up in musicians' hands around the country. Other local artists of national prominence include painter Benjamin Nicholas and craftswoman Mercy Sabal, who makes colorful dolls sold all over the country. Beyond this, however, what makes Dangriga unique is the opportunity to experience authentic culture.

Those with a keen eye will also notice how scenic Dangriga is—you will want to take photos of its bridges, rivers, pelicans, and anglers; it's quite the photographer's dream.

★ Gulisi Garífuna Museum

The **Gulisi Garífuna Museum** (George Price Dr., ngcbelize@gmail.com, 10am-5pm

Mon.-Fri., 8am-noon Sat., US$5) is a mile west of town on the south side of the highway; you'll see it on your right when driving into Dangriga, next to the thrusting Chuluhadiwa Garífuna Monument (taxi from downtown US$2-3). The small two-room display is packed with a wealth of fascinating information on the Garífuna people of Belize and a vast collection of artifacts, quotes, photos, and biographies of prominent Garífuna figures in Belize. The museum is named after the person thought to be the first Garífuna woman to arrive and settle in Dangriga. She had 13 sons, and many of Dangriga's modern residents believe they are descended from her. In 2008 the "language, dance, and music of the Garífuna" was inscribed on UNESCO's Representative List of the Intangible Cultural Heritage of Humanity, originally proclaimed in 2001.

Marie Sharp's Store and Factory

Be sure to save time to stop by **Marie Sharp's store** (north of Stann Creek Bridge, tel. 501/522-2370, 8am-5pm Mon.-Fri.) to stock up on the area's famous hot sauce and other products; you can purchase hot sauce here for a tiny fraction of the normal retail price. Better yet, make the trip to **Marie Sharp's Factory** (Melinda Rd., Stann Creek Valley, tel. 501/532-2087, www.mariesharps-bz.com, 9am-4pm Mon.-Fri.), just a short ride from town, where you'll be offered a free tour of the farm and factory. The factory sits on a 400-acre estate. To reach it, drive west on the Hummingbird Highway from Dangriga about eight miles and turn right after you cross a bridge and see the White Swan on your left.

Austin Rodriguez's Drum Workshop

There's little doubt that Austin Rodriguez has a deep-rooted passion for his culture and his drums. He spends all day and evening here, across from the beach at Y-Not Island, carving new drums into existence beside the sea. His purpose for setting up shop was to teach the children this dying Garífuna skill and keep the culture going. You can buy ready-made drums from him in different sizes or, with notice, watch him make one from scratch. There's no set cost for the latter, simply a donation of your choice. Be generous, because this is an invaluable experience: to witness the making of instruments that will end up being played across the country and even used during the annual Garífuna Settlement Day re-enactment events. Rodriguez doesn't play the drums himself; he simply listens and knows whether they sound right. His daughter is also a drum maker and works with her father at the workshop.

The Pen Cayetano Mural at Dangriga Town Hall

While in town, drop by the **Dangriga Town Hall** to view the impressive 2012 mural by Pen Cayetano, one of the country's foremost painters and musicians and creator of the popular Belizean music genre *punta* rock. The mural, *Hayawadina Wayúnagu* ("images of our ancestors"), depicts the Garífuna culture, including the landing of the Garinagu (plural of Garífuna) in Dangriga, and pays homage to those who have documented and perpetuated the culture. The mural also shows the interaction of other Belizean ethnic groups—the Maya, Kriol, mestizo, Chinese, and Caucasian—with the Garinagu, a glimpse of how multiethnic Belize has become. It's a "cultural mural," as he describes it, intended to further educate the young but also resist the potential disappearance of a rich history.

Mercy Sabal

Born and raised in Dangriga, with over 20 years of experience in her craft, **Mercy Sabal** (cell 501/604-6731, US$25-35) is a well-recognized name in town thanks to her striking, handmade Garífuna folklore dolls, each telling a story through art. Some have reversible outfits, and some hold firewood or other symbolic tools. They make for unique souvenirs;

Marie Sharp: The Spice Lady

the spice queen of Belize

She's a household name. Her bottles of hot sauce—ranging from Mild to Beware—are on almost every restaurant tabletop in the country and in every grocery store. Some Belizeans even carry her in their purse. You can't consume anything without an extra dash of Marie. It's the first thing to look for when served at a local eatery. And if it's not on the table or within immediate view, everyone asks "gat some Marie Sharp?"

You can visit her hot sauce factory—and if you're extremely fortunate, meet her in person—in Dangriga. It's a 10-minute ride outside town, down a gravel road and past some citrus orchards, to the 400-acre **Marie Sharp farm and factory** (Melinda Rd., Stann Creek Valley, tel. 501/532-2087, www.mariesharps-bz.com). This humble Belizean entrepreneur, mother, and grandmother is nothing short of a legend in her country, and her story is one of adversity and success.

Marie started experimenting in her kitchen with a batch of leftover peppers she didn't want to throw out. Using a carrot base that became a hit with friends, she sold her sauce out of that kitchen for three years under the name Melinda's. The real kicker? She partnered with a U.S.-based distributor who conned her out of her product's name and tied her into an exclusivity contract, attempting to force her to give up the recipe. Years of hard work and a legal battle later, Marie decided not to give up. Instead, she started over from scratch using her original recipe, which she never revealed. Marie gave the sauce her name, so no one could steal it, and her name is now known throughout the country and Central America. "I was the chief cook and bottle washer up to five years ago," she said, smiling and pointing at the small room in her factory where she started over.

Marie's factory, run with the help of her spouse, sons, and grandson, is on the verge of a major expansion, already producing nine different types of pepper sauce (the most popular is the Fiery Hot) and nine types of jams and jellies (my favorite is the guava). For all her fame, Marie Sharp doesn't want anyone to recognize her when they visit her factory. But she's proud of her success, as she should be—her products are a symbol of Belizean cultural pride. Rare is the visitor who leaves without a bottle or two in their suitcase.

you might also spot Mercy's dolls on sale at the airport gift shops. And if you're into learning more about the Garífuna people, Mercy is your lady. You can ask to spend the day with her; she'll cook a Garífuna dish or two and share tales of Garífuna life.

Sabal Farm

Three miles outside Dangriga, you can visit the country's sole cassava-producing farm. **Sabal Farm** (US$20 pp, for groups of 8 US$2.50 pp), not to be confused with Mercy Sabal, has operated for the past 25 years. Those with an interest in African culture and the Garinagu will be fascinated by this family-run operation, producing most of the cassava bread and other cassava-based products sold all around the country. Cyril Sabal and his sister, Clotilda, run the impressive 30 acres, of which six are used for harvesting other crops, including citrus. Learn the process of making cassava, from peeling a cassava root all the way to baking and roasting it the old-fashioned, organic way. Beyond the cassava, the farm is a symbol of cultural preservation at its finest.

Contact Brother David of **CD's Transfer** (1163 3rd St., tel. 501/502-3489 or cell 501/602-3077, breddadavid@gmail.com) to arrange a ride to and from the farm and to f the best day to visit.

Billy Barquedier Nationa

Established as a protected area in 20 **Barquedier National Park** (Mil... ...1/2 Hummingbird Hwy., Steadfast, http://billy-barquediernp.webs.com, 9am-4:30pm daily, US$4) is an often overlooked and little-known attraction. The park is co-managed by the Steadfast Tourism and Conservation Association, a grassroots community organization, and the Forestry Department. The approximately 1,500 acres of untouched jungle are home to abundant wildlife, including howler monkeys, numerous bird species, and even the elusive tapir. The park has a separate entrance at Mile 17 ½ for quick access to the **Billy Barquedier Waterfall**, its principal attraction. A 20-minute hike along a marked (albeit a bit run-down) trail and spelunking across some tricky rocks will lead you to a beautiful stream with a refreshing, emerald pool.

There are no accommodations in the park, but primitive **camping** (US$10 pp) is available. Accommodations are a 10-minute ride away in Dangriga, easily accessible by bus along the Hummingbird Highway.

cassava breadmaking at the Sabal Farm

Dangriga is ideally placed within a short drive of several of Belize's most stunning parks and wildlife reserves; it's just 20 miles from Cockscomb Basin and Maya Centre, 17 miles from both Billy Barquedier and Mayflower Bocawina National Parks, and 40 miles from Blue Hole National Park. This puts an incredible amount of activity at your fingertips, particularly for day trips, from birding to jaguar-track spotting, waterfall swimming or rappelling, and hiking numerous nature trails.

For input on which areas to explore and for a wealth of local wisdom, contact award-winning **C & G Tours and Charters** (29 Oak St., tel. 501/501-3641, www.cgtourscharters.com). C & G is a local tour operator, and their guides speak many languages. Unfortunately, they now only cater to large groups.

For a simple transfer to and from numerous sites, contact David Obi, or "Brother David," of **CD's Transfer** (1163 3rd St., tel. 501/502-3489, cell 501/602-3077, breddadavid@gmail.com, 2-person Cockscomb tour US$140; Hopkins Village US$65 pp; 2-person Xunantunich tour US$190). Obi is an excellent and accommodating local guide who

will take good care of getting you to and from your chosen site.

Beaches

The locals' favorite beach in Dangriga is at **Y-Not Island,** just along the Y-Not basketball court. Although erosion tends to push the beach back, it's still a lovely, picturesque stretch to take a dip, and the views of the pelicans and the anglers are reminders of Dangriga's peacefulness and authenticity. There are often events held here as well as fruit and food vendors throughout the week. Another ideal swimming beach is at **Pelican Beach,** by the Pelican Beach Resort. If you're not staying there, treat yourself to lunch or drinks and bring your bathing suit to jump off the dock and enjoy the water.

Diving and Snorkeling

The most untouched parts of the Belize Barrier Reef, along with some of the most beautiful cayes and one of Belize's three atolls, are a few miles offshore, along the **South Water Caye Marine Reserve** and the **Port Honduras Marine Reserve** off the Punta Gorda coast. The southern coast is more than a mere gateway to these idyllic plots of land, and the islands have a lot more to offer than

Y-Not Island's beach is a local favorite for swimming and relaxing.

a day trip for those who love to fish, dive, or want a "castaway" experience.

ENTERTAINMENT AND EVENTS
Nightlife

There's no such thing as a dull evening in Dangriga. You won't find big shiny nightclubs, but there's plenty of entertainment, whether it's watching lively and intense dominoes tournaments at the sheds, dancing to in-club drumming and live *punta*, or barhopping across neighborhoods. "Griga" isn't as dead as they'll have you think.

Dangriga is home to the Warribaggabagga Dancers, the Punta Rebels, the Punta Boys, the Turtle Shell Band, and the Griga Boyz, among other nationally known party bands. The music and dancing features syncopated West African-style rhythms and interesting mixtures of various southern Belizean cultures. There is often live music or drumming on weekends; ask around for where the latest event is (taxi drivers are often the best source of information, or even your hosts).

Start with some drinks and people-watching at the local "sheds" in town, where you'll find men slamming dominoes and throwing back Guinness in a thatched-roof hut. Try the **Wadani Recreation Centre** (St. Vincent St., 11:30am-midnight daily), known as "Wadani Shed"; **Waruguma** (Ecumenical Dr. at Teddy Cas St., 6pm-midnight daily); or continue to **Illagulei Sports Bar** (George Price Dr., near the entrance to Dangriga, tel. 501/666-9184, 9pm-2am Thurs.-Sun.), where there will be lively dominoes tournaments and music. At "club" time, the lights are dimmed and the tables are cleared for when the venue transforms into a full-on nightclub, starting no earlier than midnight.

Equally popular among the locals is **Di Spot** (Teachers St.), which is someone's living room-turned-dance floor. It's pitch-black save for the lit-up bar and an excellent DJ on a raised platform playing reggae and other house tunes. The crowd is decent, and there's a large outdoor yard with seating. Be advised

that Di Spot occasionally has karaoke nights, especially American country music, which is popular around these parts.

From Di Spot, hop over to **Mexicana Club** (Lemon St., tel. 501/664-6570, 8:30pm-2am Thurs.-Sat.), a spacious nightclub offering DJ music as well as live music. At last visit, the Punta Boys were playing and the sound of Garífuna drums inside the club had everyone moving.

Festivals and Events

The month of December is a festive time in Dangriga. The days leading up to Christmas are celebrated with *jankanu* dancing in the streets and dancers performing from house to house. The Institute of Creative Arts, a branch of the **National Institute of Culture and Heritage** (tel. 501/227-2110, www.nichbelize.org), sponsors the annual **Habinaha Wanaragua Jankanu Dance Contest** every December 26 (Boxing Day) at Y-Not Island. The beachfront basketball court becomes a makeshift dance floor where adult dance teams from the various Garífuna communities compete for the best *jankanu* dance team title. It's a fun, colorful event attended mostly by locals from around the country, which attests to the town's authentic vibe. The festivities usually start at 2pm; arrive early for a good seat, and wear a hat to avoid the afternoon sun. Plenty of food and drinks are sold at the venue.

★ GARÍFUNA SETTLEMENT DAY

Easily one of the most popular cultural events in Belize, **Garífuna Settlement Day** (Nov. 19) celebrates the arrival of the first Garinagu onto Belizean shores, and it's a national holiday. The biggest celebration in the country takes place in Dangriga, with a complete re-enactment of the first Garinagu arrival on the shores of Belize in dugout canoes filled with cassava, plantains, and other staple foods. The town comes alive the entire week of November 19, with concerts, art exhibits, drumming, and more; a schedule is printed that month, or you can inquire with your guesthouse or host.

The Garífuna *Jankanu* Dance

The centuries-old tradition of *jankanu*, a West African masquerade dance, dates back to the days of slavery. *Jankanu* was a celebration by the enslaved of their few days of freedom at Christmastime, during which they would dance and mock the European masters by wearing pink flesh-colored masks, white clothes, and suspenders.

In the Garífuna *jankanu* dance, the performer dictates the beat to the drummer with his movements: feet together, knees bent, arms raised, palms facing the drummers, and hips rocking quickly side to side. There are costumes that include special touches, including cowrie shells strapped above the knee and feathers shooting up from the masks.

In 2010 an annual *jankanu* dance contest was launched in Dangriga to improve the quality of the dance and pass it on to younger generations. The contest is held every December, usually the day after Christmas, at Y-Not Island in Dangriga, where the basketball court is transformed into a makeshift dance floor.

A *jankanu* dancer competes at an annual contest in Dangriga.

Almost every night leading up to Settlement Day, there is dancing and drumming under the "sheds" in town, such as Wadani Shed, from 8pm until the wee hours of the morning. On the morning of the 19th, the crowd heads over to the main bridge in town across the North Stann Creek River, lining up along the river starting at 7am, waiting for the boats to arrive and cheer them on. The merriment continues with a colorful, hair-raising procession to the church, and ends with an afternoon parade in town. Settlement Day in Dangriga is one of the best cultural experiences in all of Belize. Hotels book up months in advance, so make sure you make arrangements well ahead.

SHOPPING

Mercy Sabal's Garífuna dolls (tel. 501/604-6731, US$25-35) make for a unique gift; each is meticulously made by hand and depicts an aspect of the culture. Call ahead to view them at her home, which is currently being converted into a ground-floor shop. If you're lucky, she may treat you to a Garífuna immersion day.

Pen Cayetano Studio Gallery (3 Aranda Crescent, tel. 501/628-6807, www.cayetano.de, 9am-5pm Mon.-Fri.) is a must-see. The master painter, musician, artist, and ambassador of the Garífuna culture keeps his oil canvas collection here, along with the unique textile art of his wife and fellow artist, Ingrid Cayetano. There's also a museum section to the gallery (US$2.50 entrance fee), as well as CDs, drums, and souvenirs.

Along a side street just up from Riverside Café, you'll find a nice assortment of made-in-Stann Creek drums, turtle shells, paintings, carvings, and more at the **Garinagu Crafts & Art Gallery** (46 Oak St., tel. 501/522-2596, grigaservices@yahoo.com, 9am-6pm Mon.-Fri.). Don't miss peeking into the adjoining museum, a room displaying traditional Garífuna tools and instruments. You can get an interpretive tour from passionate owner Francis Swaso, who patiently built and collected items for this gallery for more than a decade.

ACCOMMODATIONS
Under US$25

Dangriga's main drag has a handful of low-budget options, including the **Riverside**

Hotel (north end of the bridge on Commerce St., tel. 501/660-1041, US$15 pp). Pick one of the basic front guest rooms for a chance of a breeze; all have shared baths, wood floors, a thin sheet, and fans. A better budget bet is ★ D's Hostel (tel. 501/502-3324, www.vals-backpackerhostel.com, US$12.50 pp), across from a pleasant park overlooking the ocean. Dana is a cheerful and friendly host who loves meeting her guests from around the world and putting them up in one of her cement bunk-rooms; each bed has a fan and a massive locker to stash your gear (even a suitcase). The com-munal lounge area has a chess table, a book exchange, and a movie library. Amenities in-clude wireless Internet, bikes for rent (US$5 per day), and laundry service. Val can help arrange a fishing trip, a transfer to Tobacco Caye, a night wildlife tour, or language and cultural exchange opportunities.

US$25-50

★ **Pal's Guest House** (868 Magoon St., tel. 501/522-2095 or cell 501/660-1282, palbz@ btl.net, US$43, US$60 with a/c), around the corner from the bus station, has upgraded its 16 clean, modest cement guest rooms at the corner of North Havana Road and Magoon Street. Guest rooms all have private baths,

cable TV, and optional air-conditioning. Seaside guest rooms are better, with lino-leum floors, ceiling fans, hot and cold private showers, TVs, and balconies at the ocean's edge; louvered windows on both ends of the rooms create good cross-ventilation. Wireless Internet is available for extra cost. In the high season, the Raati Grill has breakfast, lunch, and dinner options for guests.

At the towering **Chaleanor Hotel** (35 Magoon St., tel. 501/522-2587, chaleanor@ btl.net, US$23-75), friendly owners Chad and Eleanor offer a homey atmosphere in a resi-dential neighborhood. Economy guest rooms (US$21.50) are equipped with a bed and a fan; the restroom and shower are shared. The well-used standard rooms have private baths with hot water, TVs, and fans (air-conditioning is optional at extra cost). Laundry service is available. There's a gift counter in the lobby, and you can help yourself to coffee and ba-nanas all day long. Numerous tour operators book their guests in the Chaleanor, sometimes arranging a drumming or dance session on the roof.

If you'd rather hear the waves lapping below your window, try one of the four stilted wooden cabanas at **Ruthie's** (tel. 501/502-3184, ruthies@btl.net, US$28), an excellent

Garinagu Crafts & Art Gallery

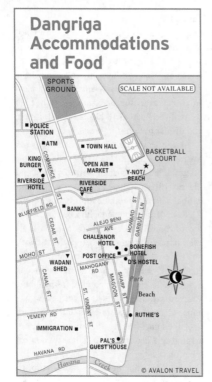

Dangriga Accommodations and Food

SCALE NOT AVAILABLE

SPORTS GROUND

POLICE STATION

ATM

TOWN HALL

BASKETBALL COURT

KING BURGER

OPEN AIR MARKET

Y-NOT BEACH

RIVERSIDE HOTEL

RIVERSIDE CAFÉ

COMMERCE ST

BLUEFIELD RD

BANKS

CEDAR ST

ALEJO BENI AVE

CHALEANOR HOTEL

HOWARD ST

GARBUTT LN

MOHO ST

POST OFFICE

BONEFISH HOTEL

D'S HOSTEL

WADANI SHED

MAHOGANY RD

CANAL ST

ST. VINCENT ST

MAGOON ST

SHARP ST

Park

Beach

YEMERY RD

IMMIGRATION

RUTHIE'S

HAVANA RD

PAL'S GUEST HOUSE

Havana Creek

© AVALON TRAVEL

three cabanas at its riverside location. All guest rooms have private baths, hot and cold water, cable TV, fans or air-conditioning, and Internet access. Screened porches allow you to listen to the frogs in the evening without mosquitoes. The on-site Garden of Eatin' Restaurant serves breakfast, lunch, and dinner to guests (when it's open, that is).

Over US$100

Griga's high end is found at the north end of town at the end of Ecumenical Drive, right next to the airstrip: ★ **Pelican Beach Resort** (tel. 501/522-2044, www.pelican-beachbelize.com, from US$135 plus taxes, includes breakfast) rests comfortably on the Caribbean. Its 17 guest rooms are open and well lit with wood and tile floors, bathtubs, and porches facing the ocean, with gorgeous views of the beach and dock. Various packages are available that include meal plans, excursions, and time spent at the Pelican's stunning sister resort on South Water Caye (easily the most beautiful caye in Belize, in this island-lover's opinion). Pelican is a full-service resort with many amenities and plenty of history behind its owners.

FOOD

Most of Dangriga's few eateries are open only during mealtimes, so expect some closed doors in the middle of the afternoon and on Sunday, when only the Chinese restaurants are open. Your best value is probably **King Burger** (tel. 501/522-2476, 7am-3pm and 6pm-10pm Mon.-Sat.), on the left as you cross the North Stann Creek bridge from the south. It offers excellent breakfast, fresh juices, sandwiches, shakes, and simple comfort dinners.

Another standby is the ★ **Riverside Café** (tel. 501/669-1473, 6:30am-9pm daily). It's popular with travelers (boats to the cayes leave from right outside) and is a gathering spot for local fishers. Grab a table or belly up to the bar and order a Guinness with your eggs and beans to fit in with the locals; it's US$4.50 for stew chicken, US$6 and up for fish and shrimp. For something different, try

value if you snag one of the seafront cabins. It's a 10-minute walk from the bus station; follow the sign from Magoon Street.

US$50-100

The **Bonefish Hotel** (15 Mahogany St., tel. 501/522-2243, www.bluemarlinlodge.com, US$95) is near the water with eight guest rooms, offering well-used private baths, air-conditioning, Wi-Fi, complimentary coffee, and a second-floor lobby and bar. It caters to active travelers who want to fish and dive—most guests continue on to **Blue Marlin Lodge** on South Water Caye, which is allied with the Bonefish. Guest rooms are clean and carpeted, with private hot and cold water baths, cable TV, wireless Internet, and air-conditioning.

Jungle Huts Resort (4 Ecumenical Dr., tel. 501/522-0185, junglehutsresort@gmail.com, US$60-90) offers 13 guest rooms and the cassava fries. Dinner is also available, with plenty of seafood options (US$9-13).

If you want cheaper food, walk back to the main drag and grab a fistful of street tacos for a few coins. There's also **Edith's** by the North Stann Creek bridge, selling burritos, *panades* (meat pies), fry chicken, and more fast food under a Coca-Cola-branded shack. Street barbecues are another common sight, offering a plate of grilled chicken with flour tortillas, baked beans, and coleslaw for about US$2.50. There are a few other local shacks with solid dishes: try **Letty's Kitchen** (62 Commerce Dr., tel. 501/665-7412, 9am-5pm Mon.-Sat., US$3.50-4) serving Creole options, including your good ol' plate of chicken stew as well as fish.

For delicious fire hearth-cooked meals, be sure to check out the yellow-and-black-painted shack **Tugucina Nuguchu** (Ecumenical Dr., close to Waruguma Shed, tel. 501/664-2017 or 501/661-2472, 11am-9pm Mon.-Sat., US$3-12), offering Creole and Garífuna specialties—rice and beans, pigtail, boil up, and fish stew in a delicious tomato sauce, conch fritters, and even *salbutes* (a kind of hot, soggy taco dripping in oil), *garnaches* (crispy tortillas under a small mound of tomato, cabbage, cheese, and hot sauce), and

other Central American goodies. Be sure to ask owner Elizabeth about her okra punch (it's an aphrodisiac!). Behind the Dangriga Market, **Zalene's Kitchen** serves the same from a modest, wooden shack.

A local favorite, **Sean's Barmouth Grill** (6pm-midnight Tues.-Sat.) is a modest *palapa* along the river with good vibes. They serve excellent home-cooked fajitas and burgers and, of course, cold beer and plenty of rum.

For Chinese, the best are **Starlight** (8am-11pm daily, closed in the afternoon, US$3-10), on the north end of Commerce Street, and **Sunlight** (8am-11pm daily, US$3-10), with good food and poor service on the south end of Commerce Street. There is "fry chicken to take" at any number of Chinese shops.

Dangriga's only proper restaurant is found at the **Pelican Beach Resort** (tel. 501/522-2044, www.pelicanbeachbelize.com, 7am-10pm daily, US$5-15) on the north end of town, where delicious food is prepared by Creole cooks and served in the dining room or in an open beachside eating area. There are occasional Garífuna dish specials offered, particularly on Sunday. Happy hour (5pm-9pm Thurs.-Fri.) is very popular, especially on the 15th and 30th of each month because they're paydays.

Ruthie's budget beachfront cabanas

A Taste of Garífuna

a plate of *hudut*

Dangriga is so authentic that you'll be hard-pressed to find public Garífuna eateries—most residents prepare and eat their traditional dishes at home. If you're lucky, you might be invited to break bread at a Grigan home. Otherwise, you can sample some of these dishes at **Tugucina Nuguchu** (Ecumenical Dr., close to Waruguma Shed, tel. 501/664-2017 or 501/661-2472, 11am-9pm Mon.-Sat., US$3-12), a small shack serving *darasa* on Wednesday and *hudut* on Saturday. The name means "my mother's kitchen." They are also able to prepare other dishes with a couple of days of advance notice (most take at least a day to gather ingredients and cook). The following are the specialties to sample when in the land of the Garinagu. All have cassava, fish, banana, and coconut as common ingredients.

- **Cassava:** You're likely to find a soothing bowl of cassava porridge in Dangriga. On Settlement Day morning, it's common to see folks warming up with a few spoonfuls of this cassava flour and coconut milk mixture while waiting on the reenactment canoes to come in. Cassava bread has the consistency of a crispy cracker or flatbread and is made in Dangriga at the only cassava-producing farm in the country, then sold in other districts. It's the Garífuna staple, a snack that symbolizes the ancestors' survival on long boat journeys in search of freedom and preservation.

- *Darasa:* These banana tamales are a Garífuna snack, with the green banana steamed in coconut milk and wrapped in green banana leaves.

- *Hudut:* Pronounced "HOO-doot," this is fish—usually snapper—simmered in a coconut milk sauce spiced with garlic, black pepper, and thyme, then served with a mound of mashed plantain all in one bowl. Grab some of the mashed plantain with your fingers, pinch a bit of fish as well, dip it in the coconut sauce, and savor away. It takes almost three hours to prepare this dish from scratch, and it's the most labor-intensive of all Garífuna dishes, so when you find it, enjoy every bite.

- *Tahara:* I first tasted this in Hopkins at Tina's Kitchen, where I learned that there is such a thing as a Garífuna breakfast. Chunks of mashed green bananas are wrapped inside heated banana leaves, left in the oven, and eventually unwrapped. The final crunchy roasted pieces are served with fried fish, sprinkled with a tomato and onion sauce.

You can't miss the **Café Casita de Amor** ("Little House of Love," Mile 16½, Hummingbird Hwy., tel. 501/660-2879, 7:30am-5pm Tues.-Sun., US$4) on the Hummingbird Highway. This heart-shaped eatery serves both German and local dishes for breakfast and lunch—everything from milk shakes, coffee, and smoothies to burgers and sandwiches. Campers are welcome to pitch a tent, and the Billy Barquedier waterfall is just down the road.

Groceries

Pick your own liquor or wine from the impressive imported selection at **Family City** (Ecumenical Dr., 8am-9pm daily); the large supermarket also has a well-stocked perfume and beauty-products counter. Another well-stocked store is **Grigalizean Shopping Center** (Stann Creek Valley Rd., tel. 501/522-3668) on the highway—look for the misspelled "Gregalizean" sign.

INFORMATION AND SERVICES

Belize Bank (8am-3pm Mon.-Thurs., 8am-4:30pm Fri.) and **Scotiabank** (8am-2:30pm Mon.-Thurs., 8am-2:30pm Fri., 9am-11:30am every other Sat.) are on St. Vincent Street near the bridge; both have ATMs.

Southern Regional Hospital (tel. 501/522-3834) is just out of town and serves the entire population of Stann Creek District.

Mail your postcards at the **post office** (Mahogany Rd., across from D's Hostel, tel. 501/522-2035, 8am-11am and 1pm-5pm Mon.-Thurs., reduced hours Fri.).

Val's Laundry and Internet (tel. 501/502-3324, 7:30am-7pm Mon.-Sat., morning Sun., US$1 per pound) is on Sharp Street near the post office. Fast and friendly satellite Internet is available (US$2.50 per hour), as well as FedEx service, local information, and organic fresh-squeezed juices. You can also get online at the air-conditioned **DNK Internet Café** (15 St. Vincent St., across from Scotiabank, tel. 501/522-0383, U.S. tel. 646/522-7939, dnkInternetcafe@gmail.com, US$2.50 per hour).

GETTING THERE AND AROUND

Dangriga is on the coast, only 36 miles south of Belize City as the crow (or local airline) flies. However, the land trip is much longer, roughly 75 miles along the Manatee Road or 100 miles via the Hummingbird Highway.

Air

Maya Island Air (tel. 501/223-1140, U.S. tel. 800/225-6732, www.mayaislandair.com) and **Tropic Air** (tel. 501/226-2012, U.S. tel. 800/422-3435, www.tropicair.com) have a number of daily 20-minute flights between Belize City and Dangriga. It's also possible to fly from Dangriga to Placencia and Punta Gorda.

Boat

You can arrange boat service from Belize City, but there is no scheduled service; they tried running a regularly scheduled shuttle, but it didn't make money. Ask around the docks by the gas station, at your hotel, or at the Belize Tourism Board. Expect to pay a fair amount for this trip (probably US$100 each way). Service to and from local cayes or other coastal villages is also dependent on how many people want to go. Only two passengers are required to make the trip to Tobacco Caye (US$35 pp); ask around the Riverside Café or the Tackle Stop. You can also check with Pelican Beach Resort as to whether you can catch a ride with them (for an additional fee) when they head to South Water Caye.

Bus

Bus service between Belize City and Dangriga takes close to three hours, including a stop in Belmopan, and costs US$6 each way; buses run between 5:15am and 6:15pm daily. There are a few express buses during the day, but the schedule is changing all the time, so be sure to check at the station.

James Bus Line (tel. 501/702-2049) operates several daily southbound buses to Punta Gorda (from 7:30am until the day's only express at 5:30pm), a three-hour trip. Buses to Punta Gorda stop in Mango Creek; from there you can make a connection to Placencia on the water taxi. As of press time, four buses go directly to Placencia (2.5 hours), thanks to Ritchie's Bus Service (tel. 501/634-8479): 11am daily, 2pm Mon.-Sat., 4:30pm daily, and 6pm daily. These buses used to stop in Hopkins and Sittee River, but that schedule is in question, so ask around the station. Buses leave from Dangriga to Hopkins at 10am daily; the first pickup is by the riverside, next to Ricky's Restaurant, where the bus will be parked starting at 9am.

Car

From Belize City, take the Western Highway to either the Coastal (Manatee) Road or Hummingbird Highway, which you follow till it ends. Taking the Coastal Road may shave 20 minutes off the Hummingbird Highway route, but the rutted, red-dirt surface may also destroy your suspension and jar your fillings loose. The unpaved Coastal Road is flat and relatively straight and is occasionally graded into a passable highway, but you'd better have a sturdy ride. Be prepared for lots of dust in the dry season and boggy mud after a rain. Numerous tiny bridges with no railings cross creeks flowing out of the west, and the landscape of pine savanna and forested limestone bluffs has nary a sign of human beings (except for the crappy road, of course). About halfway to the junction with the Hummingbird Highway, you'll find a pleasant place to stop and take a dip at Soldier Creek; just look for the biggest bridge of your trip and pull over. Watch out for snakes in the bush, and once you reach your destination, try not to spend those hard-earned extra 20 minutes all in one place.

Islands Near Dangriga

★ SOUTH WATER CAYE MARINE RESERVE

Belize's largest protected marine area, included in the sweeping World Heritage Site designation of the Belize Barrier Reef System, the South Water Caye Marine Reserve (tel. 501/661-9568, www.swcmr.org, park fee US$5, US$15 per week) covers 117,878 acres and is 15 miles southeast of Dangriga's coast, the closest jump-off point. It stretches from the Tobacco Reef all the way south to just above Wippari Caye.

Few will disagree that this marine zone includes some of the healthiest and most abundant marine and coral life along the reef, hence some of the best snorkeling, and diving along stunning royal blues. Home to sandy or mangrove cayes, in addition to littoral forests and sea grass beds, the reserve is recognized as a vital area for several critically endangered species, including the hawksbill turtle, the loggerhead turtle, and the goliath grouper, in addition to important bird nesting colonies for the magnificent frigate and brown boobies.

With depths going only to 20 feet in some parts, the area is an ideal spot for beginning snorkelers and divers, particularly right off the beach at Pelican Resort on South Water Caye, where the reef is within a swim's reach. The shallow waters off Carrie Bow Caye, across South Water, are packed with bright corals.

It's no exaggeration to say that no island trip to Belize is complete without a jaunt to the South Water Caye Marine Reserve.

Because of the protected area's sheer size and reach, some of the islands on the northern end of this protected area are more easily reached (cost and distance wise) from Dangriga or Hopkins—namely, Tobacco Caye, South Water Caye, and Glover's Reef Atoll.

Islands Near Dangriga

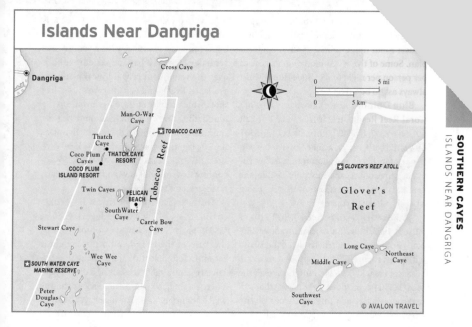

Dangriga
Cross Caye
Man-O-War Caye
TOBACCO CAYE
Thatch Caye
Coco Plum Cayes THATCH CAYE RESORT
COCO PLUM ISLAND RESORT
Twin Cayes PELICAN BEACH
SouthWater Caye
Carrie Bow Caye
Stewart Caye
Wee Wee Caye
SOUTH WATER CAYE MARINE RESERVE
Peter Douglas Caye
Tobacco Reef
GLOVER'S REEF ATOLL
Glover's Reef
Long Caye
Northeast Caye
Middle Caye
Southwest Caye
0   5 mi
0   5 km
© AVALON TRAVEL

Diving Bliss

This reserve, its surrounding islands, and numerous dive spots are also accessible to day-trippers from Placencia or Hopkins, who come here for some of the best wall dives in Belize. While it would require several trips to become familiar with this region alone, a couple of dive spots just off **South Water Caye** stand out above the rest. **Parrot Reef**'s 70-foot wall is home to nurse sharks, spotted rays, hawksbill turtles, gray and queen angelfish, lobsters, barracuda, yellowtail snapper, and schools of creole wrasse feeding on plankton, among other incredibly colorful sights of azure vase sponges and corals. You'll also see the invasive lionfish species, hovering above netted barrel sponges. **The Abyss** is a 40- to 130-foot wall that drops into an incredible abyss of blues, where turtles, nurse sharks, eagle rays, and colorful reef fish roam at various depths.

★ TOBACCO CAYE

If your tropical island dream includes sharing said island with a few dozen fellow travelers,

snorkelers, divers, rum drinkers, and hammock sitters from around the world, then **Tobacco Caye** is your place. This tiny island, located within South Water Caye Marine Reserve, has long been a popular backpacker and Belizean tourism destination, especially for divers. Tobacco Caye is just north of Tobacco Cut (a "cut" is a break in the reef through which boats can navigate).

As part of a resort package, boats will whisk you each day to snorkeling and fishing trips or to Man-O-War Caye and Tobacco Range to look for manatees. Glover's Reef, Blue Hole, and Turneffe trips are available (US$150-200); whale shark tours are usually running March-July.

Accommodations

Tobacco Caye's "resorts" offer similar packages but for a range of budgets. All accommodations are Belizean-run family affairs, each a bit different according to the owner's vision, and are comfortably crowded together on the five acres of sand. Apart from some basic differences in room quality, the more

tter the food you'll be eating—
ant thing when checking into
at also locks you into a meal
he accommodation prices are
night and include three meals;
sure.

in Lodge (formerly Gaviota
ort, tel. 501/542-2032 or cell
501/665-9837, US$40 pp private bath, US$35 pp shared bath, meals included) welcomes you to one of its four basic guest rooms or five cabanas; three boats can be used for visiting the reef and cayes. There is also a snack shop and a beach volleyball court.

★ **Paradise Lodge** (tel. 501/532-2101 or 501/621-1953, http://tobaccocayeparadisecabin.com) occupies the northern tip of the island with guest rooms (US$12.50 pp) and six clean, basic cabins with porches built right over the sea (US$40 pp, includes three meals) that will make you want to stay forever. **Lana's on the Reef** (tel. 501/532-2424, US$40, includes 3 meals) has four basic, clean guest rooms with private baths and screened windows.

Stepping things up a notch, find **Reef's End Lodge** (tel. 501/670-3919, www.reefsendlodge.com, various packages starting at $488/7 days) on the southern shore; guest rooms and cabanas have fans and hot and cold water with private baths. The newest cabana is clean, spacious, and has air-conditioning; take in the romantic sunset view from your seaside veranda. There is a bar and restaurant built over the water, and prepaid meal plans are available. Reef's End has the caye's only dive shop, which can be utilized by anyone on the island; this is an excellent location to begin a shore dive or snorkeling adventure. Dive master Eric can take you to his favorite local dive sites; dive packages range US$477-1,397 according to number of days and include meals, transfers, and two dives daily.

Tobacco Caye Lodge (tel. 501/532-2033 or 501/223-6247, www.tclodgebelize.com, US$99 pp, includes 3 meals) occupies a middle strip of the island and offers six guest rooms in four colorful cabins facing the reef. You are summoned to meals by a dinner bell. There's a small on-site bar and snack shop as well as hammocks on the beach. A few steps away, the **Tobacco Marine Station** (tel. 501/620-9116, www.tcmsbelize.org) hosts visiting scientists, and you can ask to check out their reference materials on the area's habitats and species, use the Internet (US$5 per hour), rent snorkel gear (US$7.50 per day), or head out on a night snorkel (US$10 pp) with these experts.

A hawksbill turtle feeds in the vast South Water Caye Marine Reserve.

MAN-O-WAR CAYE

Man-O-War Caye (Bird Isle) is a raucously chirping bird-choked plot of protected mangroves that is a crucial nesting site for frigates and brown boobies—one of only 10 in the Caribbean—amid beautiful turquoise waters. It's quite a sight and sound to be surrounded by the birds, even from the boat, and it makes for great photographs. It's a frequent stop on snorkel trips to Tobacco and South Water Cayes.

COCO PLUM CAYE

Coco Plum Island Resort (U.S. tel. 800/763-7360, www.cocoplumcay.com, 4 nights US$1,120-2,800, includes all water sports equipment) boasts 10 bright cabins on a 16-acre private island; they specialize in exclusive romantic packages and attract honeymooners as a result. There's no swimming pool here, but the surrounding seawater is shallow enough that you don't need one. The on-site bar and restaurant gets rave reviews for the lively staff and Belizean-inspired menu. You can rent the entire island if you choose.

A welcome addition to the southern tip of the Coco Plum Range, just under 10 miles from Dangriga, is the secluded **Fantasy Island Eco Resort** (toll-free tel. 855-350-1569, tel. 501/610-4202, www.fantasyislandecoresort.com, 3 nights US$775 pp all-inclusive). Affiliated with the popular Isla Marisol on Glover's Reef, the resort offers three delightful, bright wooden cabanas perched over the sea, with double beds, porches, and compost toilets. Various water sports and inland tours can be arranged at additional cost, and on-site PADI dive courses are offered.

THATCH CAYE

Thatch Caye Resort (U.S. tel. 800/435-3145, tel. 501/532-2414, www.thatchcayebelize.com, 3-night cabana package US$971-1,045) is an island complex nine miles from Dangriga, within the South Water Marine Reserve. The "handmade eco-resort" consists of four

Tobacco Caye

Getting There

Water taxis to Tobacco Caye leave when the captain says there are enough passengers—usually around midafternoon from the Riverside Café or the Tackle Stop farther upstream. **Captain Buck** (tel. 501/669-0869) is one option, or try Fermin, a.k.a. **Compa** (tel. 501/666-8699). The trip costs US$15 one-way or US$35 round-trip, with a return trip usually made mid-morning. **Captain Doggie** (tel. 501/627-7443) is another charter option; he will take 1-3 people for US$70; groups of 4-12 can expect to pay US$17.50 per person. Compa has the newest, largest, and most comfortable boats. All the captains usually hang out by Riverside Café, either outside or inside.

By calling ahead to Blue Dolphin, Reef's End Lodge, or Tobacco Caye Lodge, you can arrange a pickup any time from Dangriga and ensure a boat will still be there if you are arriving after midday. Be advised that if you need a boat after 3pm, you'll pay a lot more—seas get rough, and a private charter is necessary. Plan accordingly.

casitas and seven cabanas (with en suite baths, king beds, ceiling fans, and plenty of lounging room), which were constructed without the use of heavy equipment. Instead, they're run by solar and wind power. There's also a family villa and a soaring thatched-roof dining *palapa*. Various all-inclusive snorkeling packages require a three-night minimum stay; that means all meals, three guided snorkeling trips, unlimited use of sea kayaks, and round-trip water transfer from Dangriga. **Camping** (US$15 pp) is allowed on the island; campers must have their own equipment and are welcome to join other guests in the dining room for meals.

SOUTH WATER CAYE

South Water Caye is a privately owned postcard-perfect island 14 miles off the shore of Dangriga and 35 miles southeast of Belize City. The reef crests just a stone's throw offshore, sitting atop a 1,000-foot coral wall awash in wildlife. The island stretches 0.75 mile from north to south and 0.25 mile at its widest point. This southern caye is what dream getaways are made of—it's easily one of the most beautiful cayes in southern Belize. And lucky you, overnight stays are possible.

Accommodations and Food

Once a convent for the Sisters of Mercy, the ★ **Pelican Beach Resort** (tel. 501/522-2044, www.pelicanbeachbelize.com, US$325-369, includes three meals) is what every dream island resort should look like: charming yet unpretentious. It occupies the entire southern end of the island—the best end, by far—with five second-story guest rooms, three duplex cottages, and two single-unit casitas, all decently spaced from one another, and all surrounded by dozens of coconut trees and fine, powdery white sand. The beach offers some of Belize's best and rare walk-in snorkeling sites—that's if you manage to get yourself out of the dozens of hammocks on the beach. Power is from the sun, and private composting toilets help protect the fragile island ecology.

The owners also have a strip of island toward the north end that is home to **Pelican's University,** which hosts student research groups throughout the year; there are plans to refurbish it, so inquire ahead. Plenty of unique day trips are available with Pelican's guides or with one of several area dive shops, and there are kayaks and snorkel gear available; they charge US$62 per person for the boat transfer to the island.

Lesley Cottages is the common name for

frigates hovering over the protected bird sanctuary on Man-O-War Caye

International Zoological Expeditions (IZE, tel. 501/532-2404, U.S. tel. 508/655-1461, www.ize2belize.com, US$175 pp). Named for an old local fisherman, Dan Lesley, the compound here specializes primarily in student groups and "educational tourism" but also has some nice private cabins in addition to its own dive shop, dormitory, and classroom. Guest rooms are nestled to the back on the shoreline; three meals and transportation are included. It's a nice spot for couples (but check to see if you'll be sharing with student groups). There's an on-site bar and pool table, as well as complimentary glass-bottom kayaks, paddleboats, and other water sports equipment.

Blue Marlin Lodge (tel. 501/532-2104, U.S. tel. 800/798-1558, www.bluemarlinlodge. com, from US$495, includes meals), sister resort of the Bonefish Hotel in Dangriga, is on the northern tip of the island, offering 17 guest rooms, air-conditioned "igloos," and five cabanas just steps away from the sea. There's not much beach, and the sand is the hard, flat variety. The bar/dining room over the sea serves meals, snacks, and drinks. The Blue Marlin specializes in fishing trips and has a full dive shop, cable TV, and free Internet access. It's an easy and short walk along a coastal foot trail to the other parts of the island.

Getting There

South Water Caye is a 40-minute boat ri from Dangriga in good weather. You can either arrange for a pickup from Pelican Beach Resort, since it's the sister resort (US$68 pp, minimum 4 people for nonguests, but pricing varies according to space availability), or inquire with your resort on the island ahead of time.

CARRIE BOW CAYE

Just a few minutes' ride from South Water Caye, this dot of sand and palms, close to both the reef and mangrove systems and named after the original owner's spouse (Carrie Bowman), is home to the **Smithsonian Museum of Natural History's Caribbean Coral Reef Ecosystems Program** (http://ccre.si.edu), which has produced more than 800 published papers since 1972. The caye houses up to six international scientists at a time.

The public is welcome to stop by, but it's best to call ahead or arrange a visit through your resort host. Be sure to stop by the library to read and flip through the guestbook, filled with fascinating observations and drawings from visitors over the years, most of whom are scientists and marine illustrators. On your

Pelican Beach Resort

...ou can snorkel off the caye and ad-
...n very shallow waters.

...EE CAYE

...ye, affiliated with the Possum
...al Station on the mainland near
...River, hosts a tropical field station, a
marine lab, and an educational center, with
a neat system of raised catwalks through the
mangroves (it's beautiful, but there are lots of
bugs). The caye also hosts a population of boa
constrictors; contact **Paul and Mary Shave**
(tel. 501/523-7021, www.marineecology.com)
about bringing your students here.

★ GLOVER'S REEF ATOLL

The southernmost of Belize's three atolls,
Glover's (named for a pirate, of course—
John Glover) is an 80-square-mile, nearly
continuous ring of brilliant coral, flanked
on its southeastern curve by five tiny islands.
A UNESCO World Heritage Site along with
the Belize Barrier Reef, the atoll is 18 miles
long and 6 miles across at its widest point; to
the east the ocean bottom drops sharply and
keeps on dropping, eventually to depths of
15,000 feet at the western end of the Caiman
Trench, one of the deepest in the world.

The southern section of the atoll around
the cayes serves as a protected marine reserve, with the largest no-take zone in Belize.
Many travelers miss Glover's Reef, in favor of
the northern atolls, but Glover's is truly one
of Belize's remaining underwater treasures.

Diving and Snorkeling

Divers and snorkelers will find a fabulous
wall surrounding the Glover's Reef Atoll, plus
more than 700 shallow coral patches within
the rainbow-colored lagoon. There are wreck
dives and an abundance of marinelife, especially turtles, manta rays, and all types of
sharks, including reefs, hammerheads, and
whale sharks. The names of the dive sites
speak for themselves: **Shark Point, Grouper
Flats, Emerald Forest Reef, Octopus
Alley, Manta Reef, Dolphin Dance,** and
Turtle Tavern. Snorkeling is no less impressive, with amazing visibility and abundant
marinelife—spotted stingrays; barracuda;
queen, blue, and French angelfish; trunkfish;
hogfish; butterflyfish; blue tangs; groupers;
sergeant majors; and blue-headed wrasses,
among a host of other species.

Anglers will have a chance at bonefish and
permits as well as the big trophy species, including sailfish, marlins, wahoos, snappers,

Carrie Bow Caye

and groupers. There is also fantastic paddling, sailing, stand-up paddleboarding, and anything else you can dream up. Glover's is a special place indeed.

Accommodations
SOUTHWEST CAYE

The first bit of land you'll reach from the mainland is owned by the Usher clan, which runs the high-end full-service **Isla Marisol Resort** (tel. 501/520-2056, toll-free tel. 855/350-1569, www.islamarisolresort.com, 3-night all-inclusive scuba package US$1,290) for serious divers and sportfishers. There are comfortable, equipped cabanas with air-conditioning and porches, soon to be outfitted with composting toilets; or stay in one of two reef houses, with spectacular deck views of the reef and ideal for either families or honeymooners. Many all-inclusive packages are available for a three-night minimum. A lovely dockside bar is the center of nighttime activity, where guests get merry, fish, or play board games.

   Island Expeditions (U.S. tel. 800/667-1630, www.islandexpeditions.com, US$60-275 pp) is an adventure-travel outfitter with a tent camp on the north tip of Southwest Caye; it's a well-run, professional operation with daily water-sports activities of all kinds—for the novice and expert alike—and a great option if you like meeting other travelers and bonding with them on a group trip. The sturdy tents have single or double beds and kerosene lamps, and they are well sheltered from the elements. This eco-friendly camp provides shared composting toilets, cold-water showers (with outdoor warm-water hoses when the weather cooperates), and evening generator use until 9:30pm. The communal meals are excellent, and guests are welcome to head over to the bar at Isla Marisol at night. I had a great time with this dynamic group, learning a couple of water sports for the first time, including sea kayaking.

MIDDLE CAYE

There are no accommodations on Middle Caye, unless you're a Belize Fisheries Department ranger, a marine biologist with the Wildlife Conservation Society, or a PhD student with special permission. If staying on one of the surrounding cayes, ask your host about arranging a trip to see what's going on here.

LONG CAYE

The 13 acres of Long Caye form the gorgeous backdrop to the thatched-roof base

Island Expeditions' adventure camp site is on Glover's Reef Atoll.

Glover's Reef Atoll

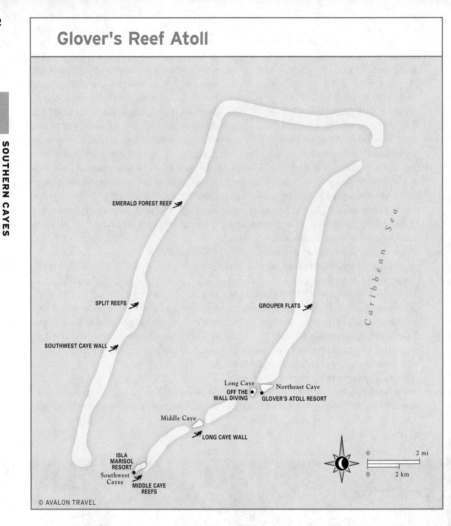

EMERALD FOREST REEF

SPLIT REEFS

SOUTHWEST CAYE WALL

GROUPER FLATS

Caribbean Sea

Long Caye
OFF THE
WALL DIVING
Northeast Caye
GLOVER'S ATOLL RESORT

Middle Caye

LONG CAYE WALL

ISLA
MARISOL
RESORT
Southwest
Cayes
MIDDLE CAYE
REEFS

0   2 mi

0   2 km

© AVALON TRAVEL

camp of **Slickrock Adventures** (U.S. tel. 800/390-5715, www.slickrock.com, 5-night package US$1,495 pp); check out the website for a range of active Belizean adventures. Slickrock has a veritable armada of kayaks, windsurfing boards, and other water toys; conditions and equipment will cover beginners and experts alike. Guests stay in very private rustic beach cabins overlooking the reef and equipped with kerosene lamps, foam-pad mattresses, and great views. Outhouse toilets are of the plein air variety,

surrounded by palm leaf "walls"—offering possibly the best views from a toilet in the entire country. Book a trip to the island, or link the trip with wild inland adventures as well (call for a catalog).

Off the Wall Dive Center (tel. 501/532-2929, www.offthewallbelize.com, US$1,395 per week all-inclusive) is a PADI 5-Star Resort. Stay on Long Caye in a rustic oceanfront cabana with access to a top-notch dive shop, gift shop, and yoga deck. The maximum capacity is 10 guests. Package prices include seven days' lodging, boat transportation, meals, diving, snorkeling, fishing, kayaking, and stand-up paddleboarding. Whale shark trips and PADI scuba certification courses are popular; yachties are welcome to come ashore and browse the gift shop.

NORTHEAST CAYE

This island is privately owned and run as **Glover's Atoll Resort and Island Lodge** (tel. 501/520-5016 or 501/614-7177, www.glovers.com.bz), a primitive island camp run by the Lomont family, which also runs Glover's Guest House in Sittee River. Their 68-foot catamaran takes you from Sittee River to

Glover's remotest caye, where you can camp or shack up for the cheapest weekly rates on the atoll: US$99 per week of camping, US$149 to stay in the dorm, or US$249-299 for rustic thatched cabins perched over the water. Prices include transportation, a week of primitive lodging, use of the kitchen, and nothing else—not even water. Show up at the guesthouse in Sittee River at 7am Saturday and be prepared for the week. It's best to bring your own food, drinking water, and a few camping basics, or pay at least US$42 per day to be provided these amenities. A dive shop and kayak rentals are also available, and the snorkeling is out of this world.

Hopkins and Vicinity

Hopkins was built in 1942 after a hurricane washed away Newtown, just up the coast; it's a scenic coastal fishing village that has steered more and more toward tourism in the past decade. More beachfront condominium developments and luxury private villas are going up on either end of the village's beautiful long stretch of beach, one of the nicest in Belize, but rest assured that nearly everything in between remains chill, spread out, and reasonably priced. There's really no place in Belize like Hopkins. Its 1,000 or so inhabitants are mostly Garífuna, making this one of the more exciting places to be to learn about the Garinagu. Traditional village life is ever-present here, and residents are holding on to it to make sure it isn't likely to disappear anytime soon. This is where you can experience culture on every corner simply by walking around or sitting on an outdoor patio. It's a much smaller area than Dangriga and is less intimidating for newcomers; those with an open mind and a thirst for cultural immersion, coupled with a love for beaches, the outdoors, and nearby cayes, will leave happy. Hopkins is just as good of a base as Dangriga, a stone's throw away, for those seeking to island-hop to nearby South Water Caye and Tobacco Caye.

With the advent of new resorts and time-share condos in Sittee, the continual trickle of backpackers that still show up in Hopkins Village, and visitors seeking a mix of beach and culture, there are a few decent makeshift art galleries, craft shops, and cafés along the main drag. There's also drumming once or twice a week, and karaoke nights are big at one or two local bars. Other than that, the sights are really just those that make up everyday village life, rarely seen elsewhere in Belize, along with, of course, the beach. On a weeknight, this means drinking beer and bitters, playing drums and dominoes, and laughing away another hot, breezy day from a hammock. Of course, things pick up considerably on festival days, Christmas, and Easter Week; expect accommodations to be in high demand during these times.

SIGHTS

The road that carries you into Hopkins from Dangriga splits the village into **Northside** (or "Baila" as the locals call it—pronounced "BAY-la") and **Southside** (or "False Sittee"). Northside is a bit denser with local flavor, while Southside hosts most of the shops, restaurants, and accommodations.

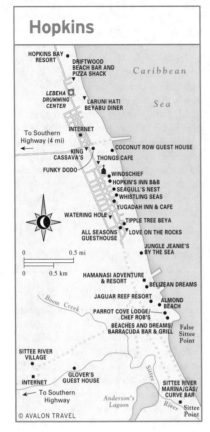

Hopkins

HOPKINS BAY RESORT
DRIFTWOOD BEACH BAR AND PIZZA SHACK
Caribbean

LEBEHA DRUMMING CENTER
LARUNI HATI BEYABU DINER
Sea

INTERNET
To Southern Highway (4 mi)
KING CASSAVA'S
THONGS CAFE
COCONUT ROW GUEST HOUSE
FUNKY DODO
WINDSCHIEF
HOPKIN'S INN B&B
SEAGULL'S NEST
WHISTLING SEAS
YUGADAH INN & CAFE
WATERING HOLE
TIPPLE TREE BEYA
ALL SEASONS GUESTHOUSE
LOVE ON THE ROCKS
JUNGLE JEANIE'S BY THE SEA

0   0.5 mi
0   0.5 km

HAMANASI ADVENTURE & RESORT
BELIZEAN DREAMS
JAGUAR REEF RESORT
ALMOND BEACH
Boom Creek
PARROT COVE LODGE/ CHEF ROB'S
BEACHES AND DREAMS/ BARRACUDA BAR & GRILL
False Sittee Point

SITTEE RIVER VILLAGE
INTERNET
GLOVER'S GUEST HOUSE
Sittee
To Southern Highway
Anderson's Lagoon
SITTEE RIVER MARINA/GAS/ CURVE BAR
River
Sittee Point
© AVALON TRAVEL

★ Lebeha Drumming Center

You can't leave Hopkins without a Garífuna drumming lesson. Drums are a key part of the Garífuna culture, a symbolic connection to their African ancestors and a sound that is considered a metaphor for the collective voice that colonial masters were unable to silence. At the award-winning **Lebeha Drumming Center** (tel. 501/665-9305, www.lebeha.com), way up on Northside (*lebeha* means "the end" in Garífuna), Garífuna drum master Jabbar Lambey offers both private (US$15 per hour) and group lessons (2 hours US$12.50 pp). He will ensure that you learn a couple of beats and have a grand time. You might even learn how to *punta* dance. Call or stop by to schedule a

lesson. Once you're there, ask him about the annual Battle of the Drums in Punta Gorda.

Serpon Sugar Mill

If you're a history buff, head to Belize's first protected historical reserve. Sitting on 114 acres of rainforest, the **Serpon Sugar Mill** (www.nichbelize.org, 8am-5pm daily) houses remnants of Belize's colonial history—a semi-mechanized sugar mill's machinery and tools, including a boiler, a locomotive, a steam engine, and more. Once considered a technological breakthrough, these old life-size machines today are nothing short of surreal. The Serpon Sugar Mill was established in 1865 and operated until the early 20th century, when it was finally abandoned after sugar production became more profitable in the north of Belize. At its peak, it produced and shipped an estimated 1,700 pounds of sugar per month.

There's a small entrance fee to this site protected by National Institute of Culture and History (US$5), and a museum offers interesting manufacturing details and a historical timeline. The mill is about a mile along the Sittee River Village access road, off the Southern Highway, and can be toured in less than an hour.

SPORTS AND RECREATION

There's plenty of inland exploration to keep you occupied near Hopkins, which is ideally located close to two of southern Belize's great parks, Cockscomb Basin Wildlife Sanctuary and Mayflower Bocawina National Park, offering plenty of hiking, rappelling, birding, and zip-lining.

For Mayflower Bocawina National Park, your best bet is **Bocawina Adventures & Eco-Tours** (tel. 501/670-2622 or 501/670-8019, U.S. tel. 928/300-1969, www.bocawinaadventures.com, single waterfall US$50 pp, zip-lining and rappelling US$150 pp, lunch included), the only company to offer waterfall rappelling from the park's five stunning chutes, including 500-foot-high Antelope

Falls, as well as birding and zooming across the canopy on the longest zip line in Belize.

Charlton Castillo (cell 501/661-8199 or 501/543-7799, charltoncastillo@yahoo.com) can guide you to the Cockscomb or to Mayflower Bocawina National Park. Charlton conducts night tours (6pm-11pm) in Cockscomb in case you want to try your luck with a jaguar encounter (US$60 pp for 2 people), daytime hiking and tubing on the South Stann Creek River (US$60 pp), and waterfall hikes at Bocawina (US$55 pp).

Beaches

Hopkins's beaches, all public, are some of the best in the country—I dare say even better than Placencia Village. Stretching nearly five miles Northside to Southside, they're wide, thick, never crowded, and have calmer waters. In the village you can take one very nice, very long beach walk, and you can lay your towel pretty much anywhere you please, except for on chairs at private resorts.

If you're looking to mingle, a great spot to hang out is in the north on the wide stretch by **Driftwood Pizza Shack** (tel. 501/667-4872, 11am-10pm Thurs.-Tues., US$8-23), where you can use Wi-Fi, eat, and hang out all day. On the south end, there's no shortage of space

either, although it tends to be quieter, if that's what you seek. In False Sittee, **Hamanasi Resort** (tel. 501/533-7073, www.hamanasi.com) has a nice pool and beachfront, both of which you can use while having lunch at the restaurant.

Snorkeling and Diving

For diving or snorkeling, you can now make plans with **Splash Dive Center** (tel. 501/523-3080 or cell 501/610-0235, www.splashbelize.com, 2-tank dive US$120, snorkeling US$90 pp, lunch included). The popular, award-winning dive shop from Placencia is setting up a second center at Jaguar Reef Resort and is sure to be up and running by publication time. A second option is **Hamanasi Adventure and Resort** (tel. 501/520-7073, U.S. tel. 877/522-3483, www.hamanasi.com, 3-tank dive at Turneffe US$185, 2-tank dive at Southern Barrier Reef US$115).

For snorkeling trips to the nearby cayes or fly-fishing, **Noel Nuñez** (tel. 501/523-7219, full-day snorkel trip US$175 for 2 people; half-day fishing US$238) is your man, located in his tour shack at the Watering Hole (his wife's restaurant). You can rent snorkel gear and even goggles with an integrated camera and video camera (US$20 per day) from Emma

Award-winning drummers teach at the Lebeha Drumming Center.

at **Motorbike Rentals** (main road, Hopkins Village, tel. 501/665-6292, www.alternateadventures.com, 8am-5pm daily).

Kayaking and Windsurfing

Most guesthouses in Hopkins rent kayaks and other small craft or provide them for guests to use. Hopkins waters are calmer than the windier northern cayes, so kayaking is a safe bet, from the sea to the lagoon at the north end of the village.

Windschief Windsurfing School and Rental (on the beach toward the south, tel. 501/523-7249 or 501/668-6087, www.windschief.com, 1pm-close Fri.-Wed., US$10 per hour, private lessons US$30 per hour, group lessons US$20 pp) has a selection of slightly used windsurfing boards of various sizes for rent and offers lessons for mostly beginner levels, as wind conditions aren't consistently ideal to offer advanced sessions.

Biking

Many guesthouses and hotels either provide complimentary bicycles or rent them at a reasonable rate. It's really the best way to navigate Hopkins's sandy, rocky roads and explore its nooks and crannies. Bike rental shops in the village include **Fred's** (6am-7pm daily, US$2.50 per hour, US$10 per day), just behind Tina's, on the main drag.

Birding

Birding in Hopkins is as easy as walking out your front door. There are over 200 species of birds in the north and south parts of the village alone. You'll see grackles crossing the street, trotting along the beach, or, especially in November and December, mass-migrating across the village's trees at sunset. It's an incredible, intense sound I have yet to hear anywhere else. On the north end, beside Hopkins Bay Resort, you'll spot pelicans and dozens of other species at sunrise. Most of the tour companies offer birding tours to the nearby national parks, and while you can ask around for the best choice to fit your budget, first try the area's highly recommended birding expert,

rappelling Bocawina Falls with Bocawina Adventures & Eco-Tours

Charlton Castillo (cell 501/661-8199 or 501/543-7799, charltoncastillo@yahoo.com, US$50 pp). Charlton also goes birding along the nearby Sittee River.

North of the village, **Fresh Water Creek Lagoon** offers plenty of birding; start early to spot beautiful herons and egrets, and navigate along the lagoon's lush mangroves. You can rent a kayak and explore solo, or take along a guide for better wildlife spotting. Keep an eye out for the 35-foot lookout tower, then climb it and take in the views. The more adventurous could ask about guided night canoeing along Boom Creek, near Sittee River.

ENTERTAINMENT AND EVENTS
Nightlife

King Cassava's (tel. 501/608-6188 or 501/503-7305, 7am-midnight daily with a 2-hour afternoon break) is at the intersection where the road from Dangriga meets the sea. Here you'll find a bar, a restaurant, taxi service, a pool hall, and the bus stop (when the buses are running, anyway). Lobster dinners go for US$10, shots of bitters are US$1, and they serve finger-lickin' barbecue. It's a great place to meet the parade of local characters.

The most local bar in town is the lively **Newtown Bar** (Back St.), a cool bamboo structure with sandy floors, drums hanging on the wall, dart boards at the back, and dimly lit Garífuna quotes, but where, to my own dismay, karaoke rules early in the evening Thursday-Saturday, followed by a DJ. The drinks are cheap and the locals do come in droves.

From Friday onward, you may find other music or entertainment around Hopkins. As far as beach bars go, **Driftwood Beach Bar and Pizza Shack** (tel. 501/667-4872 or 501/664-6611, www.driftwoodpizza.com, 11am-10pm Thurs.-Tues., US$8-23) has a nice little operation going, with daily half-price happy hours, Monday movie nights on the beach, plenty of travelers and expats, a few locals, and "jam night" on Tuesday, when anyone is welcome to pick up a guitar and a mic, followed by live Garífuna drumming by the Lebeha lads for the rest of the night (the crowd picks up close to 9pm, so come earlier if you want to sit inside rather than out by the beachside picnic tables).

A popular choice among expats is **Windschief Bar** (on the beach toward the south, tel. 501/523-7249, www.windschief. com, 1pm-11pm Fri.-Sat. and Mon.-Wed., 6pm-11pm Sun., US$4-10), particularly on Friday, when the small beachfront bar gets packed with expats playing darts and table football and nibbling on the tasty small menu of the day.

Festivals and Events

Launched in 2011 and sponsored by the Belize Tourism Industry Association, the **Mango Festival** (May) celebrates all things mango. There are more than 15 varieties of mango in Belize, and villagers—from Garífuna locals to expat residents—offer up all sorts of dishes, including mango ceviche, mango salads, and mango pies.

The last weekend of July celebrates the existence of the Garífuna village of Hopkins with a big annual festival, **Hopkins Day,** held since 2000. The fun begins on Friday evening with cultural shows and food at the village basketball court. There are games, drumming, and dancing on Saturday lasting late into the night. Sunday is for family beach time. Check local listings for a detailed schedule.

As one of the main Garífuna areas in the country, Hopkins celebrates the arrival of the Garinagu in Belize with **Garífuna Settlement Day** (Nov. 19). A reenactment of the day the Garinagu arrived in the 19th century starts in the late morning of November 19 and is smaller in scale than Dangriga's full day of celebrations, but no less intense. There is plenty of drumming, singing, and chanting on the beach. Plan for accommodations well in advance.

SHOPPING

Hopkins has its share of talented wood-carvers and drum makers. While strolling through the village, you'll find several small shops, including **David's Woodcarving** and **Kulcha Gift Shop**, with Garífuna drums made in Hopkins and Dangriga, Marie Sharp's hot sauce, and plenty of local carvings. Both are on the main road in Hopkins Village.

Save time for a bike ride just south of the village to pay a visit to **Sew Much Hemp** (11am-4pm Mon.-Sat.), where Barbara, a dreadlocked Oregonian, can teach you everything you need to know about the plant that can save the world. She sells excellent hemp products as well. If the sandflies are out, this is a great place to pick up some natural repellent.

ACCOMMODATIONS
Under US$25

On the Northside, next to Driftwood Pizza Shack, budget travelers love the **Lebeha Drumming Center** (tel. 501/665-9305, www. lebeha.com), which has campsites (US$5) and a couple of shared-bath stilted wooden guest rooms (US$25) set within the courtyard area; they are very simple (a ceiling fan, no hot water, a mosquito net, and a teakettle). There is wireless Internet.

Right in the village and hard to miss is the bright, eccentric **Funky Dodo** (tel. 501/667-0558, www.thefunkydodo.com, US$8-19), a classic small backpacker hostel with a 14-bunk bed dormitory and shared baths as well as private three-person guest rooms with outdoor baths. Camping is also available (US$4). There's a sandy courtyard, Wi-Fi, and a thatched-roof bar on-site. **Yugadah Inn** (tel. 501/503-7089, yugadahinn@yahoo.com, US$15) is another budget option, with four guest rooms and a common area.

US$25-50

From the main junction, head south on the road (or along the beach) and you'll find a few decent, affordable clusters of beachside cabins, including **Seagull's Nest** (tel. 501/663-5976, jc-seagull@yahoo.com, US$33-88), with shared-bath doubles and a nice, albeit a bit rustic, common space with a full kitchen, a dining area, and a TV. There's also a two-bedroom stand-alone beachfront casita (a great deal at US$88) on a lovely shaded stretch of beach set between local homes. Guests can also rent bikes.

Continuing south along the beach, you'll come across two rustic, stilted seafront cabanas at **Windschief** (tel. 501/523-7249, www.windschief.com, US$25-40), right next to the Windschief bar and windsurfing school.

Another budget option is **Whistling Seas Vacation Inn** (tel. 501/664-3213, williams_marcello@yahoo.com, US$38), with three small cabana guest rooms with fans and very dated bath facilities—but it's on the beach side.

A notch up yet still casual, ★ **Tipple Tree Beya** (tel. 501/533-7006, www.tippletree.com) is a longtime favorite. This well-maintained spot right on the beach offers basic guest rooms (from US$45 with private bath), en suite two-bedrooms (US$75), or a private cabin with a kitchenette (US$55). There is a shared porch with a hammock and beach chairs, and an outdoor cold-water shower if you stay in the budget room (US$30). Half-day or full-day kayak (US$15-20) and bicycle (US$5-9) rentals are available. Ask about inland tours and snorkeling trips.

Lebeha Drumming Center (tel. 501/665-9305, www.hopkinscabanas.com, US$49-80 plus tax) also has three cozy furnished cabanas set directly on a nice stretch of beach with kitchenettes, hot showers, and porches.

Seagull's Nest

US$50-100

The best in the midrange rates is ★ **Hopkins Inn Bed & Breakfast** (tel. 501/533-7283, www.hopkinsinn.com, US$69-89), with four fully furnished spacious cabanas with tiled floors, screened windows, fans, hot and cold water, a kitchenette, and a veranda; a continental breakfast of fruits and local pastries is served, and the owners are friendly. It's a deal for what you get, and it's right in the village. You'll also find good value at the **All Seasons Guesthouse** (tel. 501/523-7209, www.allseasonsbelize.com, US$49-75, includes tax and coffee). It's not right on the beach, but it's just a few steps from it, and the guest rooms in the main compound are comfortable and nicely decorated by owner Ingrid, a longtime Hopkins resident. Just next door are two fully furnished and delightful brand-new, stand-alone, two-bedroom apartments (US$98, US$600 per week), making it a more ideal spot than ever for group stays. For beachfront options, ask Ingrid about the cozy two-bedroom apartments (US$140) that she manages, just across the road and next to Tipple Tree Beya.

For those seeking a self-catering option roadside and in the village center, there's **Latitude 17°** (tel. 501/651-1322, www.latitude17.com, US$79), offering two furnished apartments across from Thongs Café, each with one bedroom and a bath, a kitchen, a living room, air-conditioning, wireless Internet access, wood floors, and a spacious outdoor deck great for people-watching.

A short distance after the pavement of Hopkins Village runs out, down the long dirt road, look for the left turn to **Jungle Jeanie's by the Sea** (tel. 501/523-7047, www.junglebythesea.com, US$55-120). This is a nice stretch of beach for guests staying in Jeanie's eight spacious rustic cabanas, three of which are beachfront. The more secluded ones, along a small network of rainforest trails, have kitchenettes, private baths, hot and cold showers, and verandas with a sea view; the Palmetto cabana, with three beds, is ideal for a family, and the tree house cabana overlooks coplum and sea grape trees. Camping (US$15

pp) is available, and in case you ei or love dogs, there are three dutiful shepherds on the property. The kitch breakfast and dinner daily (and lun quest), and there's a screened "jungle for thrice-weekly yoga sessions. Ask to see the beautiful marimba.

Over US$100

A welcome option right in the village is the colorful and immaculate ★ **Coconut Row Guest House** (tel. 501/670-3000, www.coconutrowbelize.com, US$100-145)—you can't miss the rainbow-colored beach chairs set on an idyllic stretch amid a lush garden of red hibiscus flowers and plants. There are three beachfront single guest rooms on one side, but the highlight is the two-bedroom apartments, fully furnished with a kitchenette, air-conditioning, and outdoor patios. A cute picnic area on the beach is available to guests, and the water is less than 10 steps away. There's an optional US$6 per person breakfast.

On the northern tip of town, beside the lagoon, **Hopkins Bay Resort** (tel. 501/523-7320, U.S. tel. 877/467-2297, www.hopkinsbayresort.com, US$300-750) has 19 one- and two-bedroom luxury villas that can be locked off, depending on your needs. No amenities are lacking in the homes, and there are two pools on-site, as well as a restaurant, daily housekeeping at the hour of your choosing, and complimentary use of kayaks and bikes. The resort also offers unique cultural tours, including a "cook your catch" day and a Garífuna immersion experience, among the other usual dive, snorkel, and inland tour options.

Fit for an episode of MTV's *Cribs*, **Villa Verano** (tel. 501/533-7016, U.S. tel. 877/646-2317, www.villaveranobelize.com, US$300-2,750) will have you gasping at every other step past the front door. Past the stunning open-ceiling Mediterranean courtyard are three floors, the second of which is rented as one unit (US$1,950); the remaining parts of the villa can either be locked off into separate units or rented as a whole. Some include ooms with bunk beds (with the plushest bunk mattresses I've seen) for families. Local paintings, wood carvings, granite tiling, French doors with stunning sea views, regally spacious baths with jetted tubs, library rooms fitted with gigantic plasma TVs, a 70-foot infinity pool, and top-floor terrace "game room," complete with a pool, lounge seating, and a hot tub overlooking the Maya Mountains at the back—no luxurious detail has been spared. This is an ideal place for weddings, groups of friends looking for a treat, family retreats, or just a decadent getaway. Don't miss the view of the pool and the beach from the rooftop.

FOOD

There are enough restaurants in Hopkins; most are very low-key small eateries serving either traditional Garífuna dishes or local Creole options. A couple of Western-style cafés and international or "fine cuisine" choices have popped up in the village in the past couple of years. Keep in mind that eating in Hopkins in itself is a cultural experience unlike any other, and one you will create for yourself as you explore the village.

Cafés

Morning coffee isn't quite a Garífuna tradition, so early risers will need to stock up or wait until 8am for **Thongs Café** (tel. 501/662-0110, www.thongscafe.com, 8am-2pm Wed.-Sun., US$8-12), with an outdoor roadside patio and light world music buzzing in the background; it's nice for people-watching and that first or second cup of morning coffee. The breakfast offerings range from cold sandwiches to cinnamon rolls. Steps from the village entrance on the Northside is the yellow-and-blue **Frog's Point** (tel. 501/621-3296, Fri.-Wed., US$8), run by a German expat couple and offering coffee and breakfast on an outdoor veranda.

The best local breakfast is at the small, cozy ★ **Tina's Kitchen** (along the south of the village, look for signs, tel. 501/668-3268, 7am-8pm Mon.-Sat., reduced hours Sun., US$3-7),

where you will taste the best Belizean breakfast for very cheap; her fry jacks are to die for, possibly the best I've tasted in Belize. Tina is a native of Hopkins, and you can see her cook in her open kitchen as you wait to be served. Ask her for a Garífuna breakfast if you want an even more special treat.

Garífuna

Several eateries are run by native Hopkins residents, the best way to experience authentic Garífuna cuisine. Most are casually set, with picnic tables under a thatched roof, but the meals are excellent. They require at least an hour's notice to have time to prepare, as Garífuna food is anything but the "fast" kind. The planning and wait, however, are well worth it. These dishes are also more likely to be ready on demand closer to the weekend (Fri.-Sat.). Most of these eateries also offer Belizean specialties, including stew chicken with rice and beans, or burritos, quesadillas, and other Central American fast foods.

Right on the village road going south is good but slow food at **Innie's** (tel. 501/503-7333, 7am-9pm daily, US$8-17). Her *hudut* (fried fish in a coconut broth with mashed plantains) is delicious, although you may wait at your table for over an hour, and there are several other options for dinner, including *bundiga* (coconut fish soup with green banana dumplings), fish tea, and seafood dishes. Nearby, **Yugadah Café** (tel. 501/503-7089 or 501/503-7255, 6am-2pm and 5pm-10pm Thurs.-Tues.) requires a couple of hours' notice.

Just a tad farther, don't miss the turn into **Tina's Kitchen** (tel. 501/668-3268, 7am-8pm Mon.-Sat., reduced hours Sun., US$3-7), where you'll find at least one, if not two, Garífuna options on Friday and Saturday, from *hudut* (fried fish in a coconut broth with mashed plantains) to *darasa* (banana tamales). Tina's food is excellent, Garífuna or otherwise; ask her who taught her to cook. Farther down, Jude will serve you fresh seafood, chicken, and other local treats at her longtime roadside thatched-roof restaurant,

The Watering Hole (tel. 501/614-8686, loose hours, check daily), next to her home and across from Tipple Tree.

Still my favorite of all is Marva's ★ **Laruni Hati Beyabu Diner** (Northside, tel. 501/661-5753, 10am-9pm daily), a Garífuna-owned eatery and a favorite among locals, serving the best of Belizean and Garífuna fare for just US$4-6 and in the most ideal of settings—under a thatched roof and directly on a long stretch of beach. As long as you visit during high season, you can sample *hudut,* the traditional Garífuna dish of fried fish in a coconut broth with mashed plantains. Practice eating with your fingers, breeze blowing and toes buried in the sand. Note that to date, Marva's is the only beachfront eatery run and owned by a Garífuna in Hopkins (*laru ni hati* means "clear blue sky," and *beyabu* means "seaside").

Casual Dining
You're likely to head back to the north end more than once when you discover the ★ **Driftwood Beach Bar and Pizza Shack** (tel. 501/667-4872 or 501/664-6611, www.driftwoodpizza.com, 11am-10pm Thurs.-Tues., US$8-23), where you can have amazing wood-fired pizza, play beach volleyball, or surf the Internet. The bar is one of the most social in the village, crowded with locals, expats, and travelers. On a similar social wavelength is the bar at **Windschief** (tel. 501/523-7249 or 501/668-6087, www.windschief.com, 1pm-midnight Mon.-Wed. and Fri.-Sat., 1pm-6pm Sun., US$5-7), with a daily casual dinner menu that includes delicious fish-and-chips on Friday and gyros or burgers (that you can burn off while playing darts or table football).

Fine Dining
A unique experience is at **Love on the Rocks Hot Rock Grill Restaurant** (Main St., tel. 501/672-7272, 5pm-10pm daily, US$13-25), created by chef Rob, where you can finish cooking your own entrée on 400-degree hot stones in the old way of the ancient Maya. His protégé, chef Ricky, now runs the kitchen solo, along with an attentive staff, and delivers seafood, chicken, or steak entrées with two sides—all of which are delicious. Have fun flipping your food over on the stone to your liking or warming up your sides at will. Those who don't want to "get stoned" can opt for pastas and other menu choices.

Groceries
There are five groceries and a produce stand

Beachfront Laruni Hati Beyabu Diner serves authentic Garífuna dishes.

in Hopkins, making it easier to stock up on nibbles and booze without breaking the bank; **Dong Lee's Supermarket** (9am-midnight daily) has the largest selection of liquor. The Garífuna women's group sells johnnycakes, bread, and Creole buns; look out for the kids selling their mothers' baked goods, too.

INFORMATION AND SERVICES

The **Windschief Internet café** and cocktail bar (on the beach toward the south, tel. 501/523-7249, www.windschief.com, 1pm-11pm Fri.-Sat. and Mon.-Wed., 6pm-11pm Sun., US$4-10) is where it's at, although many midrange hotels in Hopkins also offer computers and wireless service. Bring plenty of cash, as there's only one ATM in Hopkins (at the village entrance); the nearest ATMs are in Dangriga.

GETTING THERE AND AROUND

If you have your own transportation, getting to Hopkins is easy: just follow the Southern Highway until you see the well-signed turnoff on your left; from there it's a four-mile straight stretch of dirt road (which can be under water during intense rains). Figure 30-40 minutes' total drive time from Dangriga.

Motorbike Rentals (main road, Hopkins Village, tel. 501/665-6292, www.alternateadventures.com, 8am-5pm daily, US$59 per day, US$299 per week) offers up a dozen 200cc dirt- or cruiser-style motorcycles for rent. A rental, good for two, includes helmets, a map, a local cell phone, and help with designing a self-guided course to Cockscomb, Mayflower Bocawina, and other points of interest.

There are a few daily buses from Hopkins to Dangriga (8am and 5:15pm Mon.-Sat., US$2.50); buses return to Dangriga at 7am, 7:30am, and 2pm. Placencia buses used to go through Hopkins, but currently there are no buses taking that route. A popular alternative is to get off the bus at the Hopkins junction and hitch a ride to the village, or call for a taxi (contact **Mr. Abraham**, tel. 501/668-6166, or

Mr. Mac, tel. 501/665-0181). Otherwise it's an expensive hotel shuttle or local taxi—which can cost up to US$50 from Dangriga. Once in Hopkins, you can rent a dirt motorcycle at Motorbike Rentals; some people do this to get to the Mayflower reserve or other nearby hiking spots. Bicycle rentals are also easy to find and useful for exploring the village.

FALSE SITTEE POINT

A few minutes' bicycle ride south from Hopkins Village will bring you to a small ocean-side strip of upscale resorts, restaurants, and condos. The water off the beach resorts at False Sittee can be muddy at times because of the proximity of emptying rivers and streams, and depending on the time of year, sandflies and mosquitoes can get fierce. Still, this is a popular spot to stay because of the quality of the lodges as well as the location's direct access to so many inland and offshore attractions and activities.

Accommodations and Food

The most low-key lodging option in this stretch of resorts along False Sittee Point is ★ **Beaches and Dreams Seafront Inn and Pub** (tel. 501/523-7259, www.beachesanddreams.com, US$129, includes breakfast), whose four ample guest rooms have tiled floors, porches, and private baths; ask about the tree house, which is great for families. Use of kayaks and bikes is complimentary, and there's a lovely *palapa* dock, ideal for relaxing and napping by the sea. Customized tours can be arranged, and you won't have to deal with the "minimum number of people" limit; the owners are flexible and will link you with local guides. The onsite restaurant, the ★ **Barracuda Bar and Grill** (4pm-9pm or 10pm Wed.-Mon.) features chef "Alaska Tony" Marisco's amazing menu, including jerk smoked pork, aged beef, lots of seafood, and some of the best pizza this side of the Sittee River (dinner US$15-25 pp, large lobster pizza US$25, cheese pizza US$12). Set on a waterfront deck, it's a romantic dinner spot; reservations are recommended, as the restaurant can fill up quickly. Don't forget to ask chef Tony about his "Mediteribean" specials and sample the desserts made by his wife, Angie, particularly her coconut flan.

Another pleasant midrange option is next door at **Parrot Cove Lodge** (tel. 501/523-7225, U.S. tel. 877/207-7139, http://parrotcovelodge.com, US$150-400), with a handful of standard rooms and suites plus a few homes and villas for rent. It's a smaller, more intimate resort; take a kayak out to sea or lounge by the pool. A full PADI dive shop is on-site. At celebrated **Chef Rob's Gourmet Café** (tel. 501/663-1529 or 501/663-1812, 5pm-9pm Mon.-Sat., 4-course meal US$28), Rob Pronk serves up his delectable, daily-created four-course dining experience with choices like coconut soup, rib eye steak, Thai-style pork and shrimp, or Lobster Robert.

Awarded Hotel of the Year 2010 by the Belize Tourist Board, **Jaguar Reef Resort** (tel. 501/533-7040, U.S. tel. 800/289-5756, www.jaguarreef.com, US$190-275) is a full-service place with an ever-improving variety of spacious, comfortably furnished guest rooms and cottages. The Jaguar Reef end feels more like a large all-inclusive resort, but connecting next door, if you can afford it, is its charming sister property, **Almond Beach** (U.S. tel. 866/624-1516, www.almondbeachbelize.com, US$200-325), which offers a selection of more intimate, luxurious stand-alone beachfront casitas and luxury suites that fill up fairly quickly with couples. The cozy tiki swim-up bar is one of the few in Belize and has an infinity view of the sea. The two properties share a large open dining space and several more pools (including one for kiddies) and bars, along with bikes, kayaks, sand volleyball, and many activity-based packages. The ultra-luxe "beachfront vista suite" on the Almond Beach side is an outrageously decadent five-bedroom penthouse (US$870) that includes a private chef. This is a popular spot for fancy weddings, especially with the addition of the **Butterflies Spa** (8am-7pm daily, tel. 501/523-7291),

offering a full range of treatments and sc care at about the same rates as back home **Butterflies Coffee** next to it has grinds from all over Central America, roasted fresh daily, and cute patio seating.

Belizean Dreams (tel. 501/523-7272, U.S. tel. 800/456-7150, www.belizeandreams.com, US$285-625) has nine beach villas with one- and two-bedroom suite options, along with a restaurant and spa services. Area tours are available.

★ **Hamanasi Adventure and Resort** (tel. 501/533-7073, U.S. tel. 877/522-3483, www.hamanasi.com, US$275-595) is the area's premier diving operation. Sitting on 17 acres, including 400 feet of beautiful beachfront, Hamanasi offers eight beach-front guest rooms, four suites (including a honeymoon option), and five deluxe tree houses tucked away in the littoral forest, all with views and tiled baths, air-conditioning, fans, and porches. Restaurant meals include delicious pasta and, of course, fresh seafood; it's open to outside visitors as well (bring a towel). It's ideal if you just want to laze and aren't into diving or inland adventures. There's a gorgeous pool overlooking the beachfront as well as kayaks, bikes, and hammocks to use at your leisure. Hamanasi is very popular among locals as much as visitors and has a high occupancy rate; make reservations ahead of time.

Information and Services

Sittee River Marina (tel. 501/670-8525, www.sitteerivermarina.com, 6am-6pm daily) has oil, gas, diesel, snacks, restroom and shower facilities, and cold beer. They also deliver fuel at sea on request.

Getting There

Driving south on the road from Hopkins, you'll pass through False Sittee, a short drive east of the Southern Highway. There are usually two daily buses that pass through Sittee River and False Sittee Point, but the schedule varies; most accommodations will provide transfer from Dangriga.

E RIVER

...is a peaceful, riverine corner of the ...th its own calm mood. Sittee River ...a village only in the loosest sense, ...houses, a couple of riverside places ...more often than not, a few insects. Choose from the now few accommodations from which to soak up the thick, tropical tranquility. There are boats to whisk you out to the cayes, excellent fishing (snook, tarpon, peacock bass, sheepshead, and barracuda), and, only 12 miles by road to the west, the entrance to the Cockscomb Basin Wildlife Sanctuary. Sadly, businesses have become sparse in Sittee, and as of late it appears nearly abandoned, with a couple of resorts now gone, but its wildlife and natural setting remain; if you're not staying here, it's good for a drive through and perhaps a stop at a local riverside restaurant to soak in Belize's deepest and most beautiful river.

Sports and Recreation

Popular local Sittee River-born and raised guide **Horace Andrews** (tel. 501/675-8358 or 501/603-8358, www.belizebyhorace.com) does river tours on the Sittee River, snorkel trips to the cayes, fishing trips to the nearby cayes or lagoons, and inland tours such as Cockscomb, Mayflower, and Red Bank to see the scarlet macaws (in season, mid-Jan.-Mar.). He's full of life, having captained his own boats as far as Cuba and Mexico, and will help you see the best of this area; he can also take you out on fun sailing trips aboard his new catamaran.

On the road to False Sittee, past Jaguar Reef Resort, you'll find **Diversity Café and Tours** (tel. 501/661-7444), offering help with tour planning, including snorkeling, fishing, and inland trips, which they outsource to local guides. There are also golf carts for rent (US$20 for 2 hours, US$50 per day).

Accommodations and Food

Glover's Guest House (tel. 501/532-2916, www.glovers.com.bz) provides cheap, spartan lodging for both walk-ins and guests of the Glover's Atoll Resort. Stay in a bunkhouse on stilts (US$9 pp) or in one of the private, stilted, screened-in riverside cabins (US$19); meals and a cooking area are available. Camping is US$5 (bring your own tent). You can use the guesthouse's canoes and kayaks to explore the river.

A slight notch up is also the only other option in Sittee at publication time, **River House Lodge** (tel. 501/543-7044, www.river-houselodgebelize.com, US$65-75). It offers six cabanas with double beds, screened porches, and kitchenettes, and is set along the Sittee River with a small dock to gaze at the gorgeous view (but not to swim—crocodiles live in the river). There's an on-site bar and restaurant, complete with an indoor pool.

Have a sunset drink over the Sittee River under the thatched roof at the new **Curve Bar** (Sittee River Marina, tel. 501/670-8525) or grab some drinks from the convenience store at the marina.

Getting There

The Sittee River area is about a 10-minute drive east of the Southern Highway through mostly orange orchards and riverside lots. There are usually two daily buses that run through Sittee River and False Sittee Point, but this schedule is always up in the air; your accommodations will provide some sort of transfer from Dangriga. Driving south on the road from Hopkins, you'll pass through False Sittee, followed by the village of Sittee River, occupying a few bends of the slow, flat river of the same name.

★ MAYFLOWER BOCAWINA NATIONAL PARK

Located 17 miles from Dangriga and 12 miles from Hopkins, **Mayflower Bocawina National Park** (entrance fee US$10 pp) comprises more than 7,100 acres of Maya Mountain wilderness set aside in 2001 to protect and showcase the area's five waterfalls and green-fringed Mayan ruins. A trail system offers excellent hiking, and it's an adventurous climb to Antelope Falls. A hike in Mayflower Bocawina can be combined with a day trip to

Cockscomb (just to the south), or it can easily fill a whole day or more.

Guides and Tours

Ramon Guzman (tel. 501/533-7136) is a longtime park warden, and he may even greet you at the entrance. Doreen Guzman is an officer in the **Friends of Mayflower Bocawina National Park** (mayflowerbocawina@yahoo.com), an organization that comanages the park with the government.

In Dangriga, **C & G Tours and Charters** (29 Oak St., Dangriga, tel. 501/522-3641, www.cgtourscharters.com) can arrange a trip to Mayflower for large groups. The licensed guides at **Bocawina Adventures & Eco-Tours** (tel. 501/670-2622 or 501/670-8019, www.bocawinaadventures.com) will pick you up wherever you stay in the area. A day-long adventure (from US$50 pp, no minimum number of people) hiking to and rappelling from one or all five waterfalls inside the park—Antelope, Bocawina, Tears of the Jaguar, Peck Falls, and Big Drop—is well worth it. When I rappelled the smaller 125-foot-high Bocawina Falls, the drive was just a little over 30 minutes, followed by a short hike of moderate difficulty but with an impressive view. Wear adequate shoes.

Additional adventures include Belize's longest single zip line, at 2,300 feet, and bird-watching. You can overnight at the renovated **Mama Noots Eco Resort** (tel. 501/670-8019, www.mamanootsbelize.com, US$155-275, continental breakfast included), duplex cabanas set on beautifully landscaped grounds right in the park and with an on-site bar and restaurant.

For birding, the best guide is **Charlton Castillo** (tel. 501/661-8199, US$50 pp, minimum 2 people).

Getting There

The biggest challenge to enjoying Mayflower Bocawina is simply getting to the trailhead, which lies 4.5 miles west of the Southern Highway with no public transportation of any kind making the trip. (The turnoff is just north of Silk Grass Village.) Sign in at the park office and interpretive center (7am-4pm daily) and pay the US$5 per person entrance fee. There is a **campground** (US$5) at the park entrance; bring your own gear.

RED BANK

Tucked away on a red dirt road is the small Mayan village of Red Bank. Here, at the edge of the Maya Mountains, rare and impressive scarlet macaws gather to feed on the ripe fruits of pole-wood trees outside the village. This annual phenomenon was unknown to outsiders until 1997, when conservationists learned that 20 birds had been hunted for table fare; at that time it was thought Belize had a population of just 30 to 60 scarlet macaws. In response, Programme for Belize worked with the village council to form the Red Bank Scarlet Macaw Conservation Group, led by the village leader, Geronimo Sho.

The small community-based ecotourism industry offers visitors accommodations, meals, crafts, and guide services. A reserve has been established about a mile from the village, and visitors must pay a small conservation fee; ask around for Mr. Sho. The best time to visit is sometime from mid-January to March, when the annatto fruit are ripe. As many as 100 scarlet macaws have been observed in the morning when the birds are feeding. Contact the **Red Bank Bed and Breakfast** (tel. 501/660-6320, US$20) if you want to stay overnight.

Cockscomb Basin

rises gradually from the coastal plains to the Maya Mountains; driving south on the Southern Highway, you'll see the highlands to the west and flatlands to the left, mostly covered by orange and banana groves. The highway passes through a few villages and soon delivers you to the area's prime attraction: Maya Centre village and Cockscomb Basin Wildlife Sanctuary. Heavy rain along the peaks of the Maya range, as much as 160 inches per year, runs off into lush rainforest thick with trees, orchids, palms, ferns, abundant birds, and exotic animals, including peccaries, anteaters, armadillos, tapirs, and jaguars.

★ COCKSCOMB BASIN WILDLIFE SANCTUARY

Commonly called the "Jaguar Preserve," this is one of the most beautiful natural attractions in the country. A large tract of approximately 155 square miles of forest was declared a forest reserve in 1984, and in 1986 the government of Belize set the region aside as a preserve for the largest cat in the Americas, the jaguar. The area is alive with wildlife, including margays, ocelots, pumas, jaguarundis, tapirs, deer, pacas, iguanas, kinkajous, and armadillos, to name just a few, along with hundreds of bird species and even howler monkeys. The park is also home to the red-eyed tree frog and the critically endangered Morelet's tree frog. And though you probably won't spot large cats roaming during the day (they hunt at night), it's exciting to see their prints and other signs—and to know that even if you don't see one, you'll probably be seen by one.

The **Cockscomb Basin Wildlife Sanctuary** is managed by the **Belize Audubon Society** (www.belizeaudubon.org), which also conducts research and community outreach in support of conservation.

The park is open 8am-4:30pm daily. Entrance is US$5 for non-Belizeans (pay at the Maya Centre Women's Group craft shop at the head of the access road, immediately off the Southern Highway). Just past the entrance gate into the park is a gift shop and office where you'll be asked to sign in. Visitor facilities include an interpretive center, a picnic area, and an outhouse.

Victoria Peak

The second-highest point in the country is the top of **Victoria Peak** (3,675 feet). Geologists believe the mountain is four million years old, the oldest geologic formation in Central America. Reportedly, area Mayan populations thought the peak was surrounded by a lake, unapproachable by people and occupied by a powerful spirit. The first known people (a party led by Roger T. Goldsworth, governor of then-British Honduras) to reach the summit did so in 1888. Today, it is a protected natural monument, managed by the Belize Audubon Society.

Summit trips can be arranged in the dry season only (Feb.-May) and must include a permit and a licensed guide. The 30-mile round-trip trek takes three or four days; the up-and-down terrain is steep, and there are no switchbacks. Contact the **Belize Audubon Society** (www.belizeaudubon.org) for trail and campsite details; entrance is US$5 pp plus camping fees.

The Belize Audubon Society does not have guides for hire, but they can provide a list of guides with contact information. There are a few reputable mountain guides in the surrounding villages, including **Marcos Cucul** (tel. 501/670-3116, www.mayaguide.bz), who can take you rock climbing or on a backcountry trip to the top of Victoria Peak (US$500 pp).

Hiking

There are more than 20 miles of maintained

hiking trails, which range from an easy hour-long stroll along the river to a four-day Victoria Peak expedition. An early morning hike on the **Wari Loop** offers the best chance to see wildlife and to admire the large buttress roots of the swamp kaway *(Pterocarpus officinalis)* trees. At the end of the **Tiger Fern Trail,** a rigorous hike, you'll find an impressive double waterfall—the most beautiful waterfall in Belize, according to top Belizean landscape and underwater photographer Tony Rath. There are more waterfalls, including a less difficult fall with a pool, within a 30-minute hike. Check the front of the visitors center building for a detailed map.

If you climb **Ben's Bluff,** you're not just looking out over a park where jaguars live— you're at the entrance of a forest that goes all the way into the Guatemalan Petén, part of the largest contiguous block of protected forest in Central America. The bluff was named after Ben Nottingham, who monitored radio-collared jaguars with radiotelemetry. From here you can see Outlier Peak, a moderate one-day hike (about 8.5 miles round-trip) and great place to camp.

Bring your swimsuit when visiting, as you'll find cool natural waterfalls and pools for a refreshing plunge. You can also rent an inner tube and float down South Stann Creek. All visitors are encouraged to bring sturdy shoes, a long-sleeved shirt, long pants, insect repellent, sunscreen, and plenty of water. If you would like to hire a guide, there are several renowned wilderness guides who grew up in these forests and who can be found up the road in Maya Centre.

Accommodations and Camping

Bring your own tent to stay at one of three well-maintained **campgrounds** (US$10 pp). The park's overnight accommodations (US$20) begin with zinc-topped buildings with bunk space for 32 people. Expect a bed in a shared "rustic cabin" or a bunk in the main dormitory, clean sheets, shared baths with cold showers, and solar power. There are

also a few private cabins (6 beds and a kitchen US$54).

Be prepared with food and supplies if you plan to stay a few days; the only food for sale in the visitors center is chips, cookies, candy bars, and soft drinks. There are a couple of small shops in Maya Centre, so feel free to stock up there before catching a taxi into the park. You may also be able to arrange for meals to be cooked in Maya Centre and delivered to you. Otherwise, there is a communal kitchen with a refrigerator, gas stoves, and crockery and cooking utensils for rent. Again, visitors are required to bring their own food and water. A walled-off washing area has buckets, and a separate cooking area has a gas stove and a few pots.

Getting There

Cockscomb Basin is about six miles west of the Southern Highway and the village of Maya Centre; from Dangriga, it's a total of 20 miles. The road can be rough after it rains. For public transportation, catch any bus traveling between Dangriga and Punta Gorda and hop off at Maya Centre. From there, it's an extremely long—at least an hour—and hilly walk; I strongly recommend a US$15-20 taxi ride.

MAYA CENTRE

This small village is at the turnoff to the famous Cockscomb Basin Wildlife Sanctuary. Many of the 400 or so Mopan Maya who live here were relocated when their original home within the Cockscomb Basin was given protected status. Since then, they have had to change their lifestyle; instead of continuing to clear patches of rainforest for short-term agriculture, many men now work as guides and taxi drivers, while the women create and sell artwork. Still, the people of Maya Centre are struggling to support their town with tourism. Ever since they were prohibited from using the now-protected rainforest for subsistence farming and hunting, tourism has been their only hope, aside from working for slave wages at the nearby banana and citrus farms. The village has a few places to stay, eat, and experience village life, literally right down the road from the famous reserve.

At the very least, make sure that you—or the driver of your tour bus—stop at one of the three Maya crafts stores, all on the road into the park. At the turnoff from the Southern Highway, you'll find the **Maya Centre Women's Group** (7:30am-4:30pm daily), which sells local crafts and collects the entrance fee for Cockscomb. The **Nu'uk Che'il Gift Shop** is 0.25 mile farther toward the park, offering fine jewelry, slate carvings, baskets, herbs, and other crafts.

Julio Saqui runs the store next to the women's co-op and offers satellite Internet access (US$4 per hour) and taxi service as well as meals to any overnight guests in the area who need it (US$7 pp per meal, including delivery). Julio is a great guide and offers many services and tours, including to Victoria Peak; information is available on his website (www.cockscombmayatours.com).

Julio and his wife also run the **Maya Centre Maya Museum** (tel. 501/660-3903, US$7.50 pp), opened in 2010 and providing hands-on cultural activities; learn how to make corn tortillas or process coffee beans, and take home Mayan Coffee to share with friends while you tell of your adventures abroad. They also now sell their very own Che'il Mayan Chocolate bars, made from cacao beans farmed in Stann Creek.

Accommodations

There are two guesthouses in Maya Centre, owned by different families that each offer transportation in and out of the preserve, guides, meals, and other services.

★ **Nu'uk Che'il Cottages and Hmen Herbal Center** (tel. 501/533-7043 or 501/665-1313, nuukcheil@yahoo.com) offers tranquil accommodations more removed from the highway than the village's other guesthouse. Bunks with a shared bath are US$10 per person, and private guest rooms with hot showers available are US$30, tax

not included. Camping is US$4 per person, Internet access US$2.50 per hour, and bike rental US$10 per day. The place is very well kept, with beautifully planted grounds; the guesthouse has experience hosting student groups and can arrange seminars on herbal medicine, cultural performances, and the like. Proprietress Aurora Garcia Saqui's husband, Ernesto, was director of the Cockscomb Basin Wildlife Sanctuary until 2005 and is extremely knowledgeable about the area. Her late uncle, Don Eligio Panti, was a famous healer; she took over his work when he died in 1996. Aurora offers Mayan spiritual blessings, prayer healings, acupuncture, and massage (each for under US$15). Aurora also has a four-acre botanical garden and medicine trail (entrance US$2.50), offers herbs for sale, and can arrange homestays in the village for US$25 per person, which incudes a one-night stay with a local family, one dinner, and one breakfast.

Another decent option is right on the highway, about 100 yards north of the entrance to Cockscomb: **Tutzil Nah Cottages** (tel. 501/533-7045, www.mayacenter.com, US$18-22) is owned and operated by the Chun family (they helped Dr. Alan Rabinowitz in his original jaguar studies and appear in his book, *Jaguar*). There are four screened wooden guest rooms, two with private baths, two with a shared bath and shower; all have queen beds, fans, ample space, nice furniture, and a raised deck. Meals (US$6-12) are available, as camping (US$6-12) is possible on the grounds or in a separate campground about 0.25 mile into the bush. Inventive trips are available as an alternative to the standard fare, including kayak floats and night hikes.

Getting There

Maya Centre is accessed by hopping off any bus passing between Dangriga and Punta Gorda. Taxis will take you from the village to the Cockscomb Basin Wildlife Sanctuary for about US$15-20 per carload.

The Placencia Peninsula

Running parallel to Belize's southern coast, this stretch of beach and mangroves winds 16 miles southward from the coastal wetlands and shrimp farms near the village of Riverside all the way to Placencia Village, on the tip of the peninsula. The Belize Barrier Reef, surrounded by coral and mangrove islands, lies approximately 20 miles east off the coast of Placencia. This means that traveling to the nearby offshore cayes, including South Water Caye, Silk Cayes, or Ranguana Caye, is not more than an hour's boat ride, and it is just a bit longer to Glover's Reef Atoll. It can mean a day of three-tank diving, snorkeling, or just enjoying these islands' stunning beaches and scenery. All of these factors make Placencia an ideal base for those wanting to explore the southern cayes, while at the same time staying in a fun tourist beach village offering entertainment, bars, and restaurants.

It's also feasible to visit inland attractions like the Cockscomb Basin Wildlife Sanctuary, Mayan villages, and ruins of Toledo District from anywhere on the peninsula, although Cockscomb is just a bit farther than from Dangriga or Hopkins. The area offers the full range of accommodations, whether you prefer to mingle with backpackers in Placencia Village or rub elbows with fellow guests at any of a number of beach resorts, from midrange to luxurious, each with its own personality. This is also the site of several enormous, ambitious, and controversial development projects, more of which are springing up all over the area every year.

There are three main areas on the Placencia Peninsula: Maya Beach, Seine Bight, and Placencia Village, where most of the bars, restaurants, and shops are, along with the general buzz. Maya Beach and Seine Bight share a quiet, secluded vibe, with long stretches of beach, plenty of resorts sprawled along the shore, and a few restaurants. They are a bit of a distance from Placencia Village, so you'll

have to either bike (daytime only) or catch a taxi to go back and forth, which can be costly, so plan wisely. Staying in the village means being close to all the action, nightlife, general noise, and also being near the beach, even if it's not as fine and pretty as in the other areas.

Throw in the offshore islands—easily some of Belize's most beautiful, offering incredible diving and snorkeling—and it's hard to beat Placencia as a jump-off base.

★ MAYA BEACH

About halfway down the peninsula, **Maya Beach** is a strip of simple, small, boutique accommodations. They're actually quite nice, in a relaxed, isolated way, offering more value for your money than nearly anything else in the area. However, the **beach** here is more beautiful than many places in Belize, including the rest of Placencia. You just have to be content with the relative lack of services in Maya Beach, since getting to and from Placencia Village can be an expensive endeavor, even though it's only seven miles away.

Art and greenery lovers will like the retreat feel to **Spectarte** (Maya Beach, tel. 501/533-8019, spectarte@gmail.com, 9am-4pm Thurs.-Sun.), a coffee shop and "art and garden gallery" featuring 90 percent Belizean artwork: paintings, including works by Nelson Young, along with carvings and jipijapa baskets. Other items are imported works from neighboring Guatemala and Panama. There's a delightful screened greenhouse-like seating area where you can enjoy the peaceful surroundings, cookies, pies, and a hot beverage. Locals flock here on the first Sunday of the month for the weekly flea market.

For all-American fun in the tropics, try bowling at **Jaguar Lanes and Jungle Bar** (tel. 501/664-2583, jaguarlanes@yahoo.com, 2pm-8pm Wed. and Sat.-Sun., hours vary Mon. and Thurs.-Fri., US$3 per game, shoe rental US$1.25). There are four Brunswick bowling lanes, and a snack bar (US$1.50-5.50) serves hot dogs, onion rings, nachos, and pizza. Outside the air-conditioned alley there's cold beer and mixed drinks. The venue holds various theme parties, including a "cosmic" bowling night (bowling with disco lights), and Wednesday is popular among the local women bowlers of Placencia.

You can grab a drink at the **Maya Breeze Inn's** casual beachfront bar (tel. 501/666-5238 or cell 501/628-4215, 11am-midnight daily), offering a full bar with imported liquor, cocktails, and local favorites. Don't forget your swimsuit, and eat before you come here.

Accommodations

Maya Beach hotels are of the beach cabana variety, with a few furnished apartments, many with kitchenettes for cooking on your own. Most of these hotels also manage full houses and a few condos in the area; ask about weekly and monthly rates.

The first place you'll come to from the north is ★ **Maya Beach Hotel** (tel. 501/533-8040, U.S. tel. 800/503-5124, www.mayabeachhotel.com, US$90-125), with five well-kept guest rooms, a few with waterfront decks, all with wireless Internet, private baths, hot showers, and a great stretch of sand—oh, and one of the best restaurants in Placencia, the Maya Beach Hotel Bistro. It has a small pool and one- and two-bedroom beach houses (US$100-180), all with fully equipped kitchens and amenities such as bicycles. A three-bedroom house (US$400), on a private beachfront parcel, has its own infinity pool.

On the lagoon side, **Casa At Last** (tel. 501/523-3630, www.casaatlast.com, US$125-200) is a couples-only resort with four nicely furnished thatched cabanas, a pool, and a restaurant. The restaurant serves breakfast, lunch, and dinner for resort guests only.

Green Parrot Beach Houses (tel. 501/533-8188, www.greenparrot-belize.com, US$130-180 plus tax) has cozy thatched-roof A-frame cabanas with decks and loft bedrooms facing the ocean. Each sleeps four people and includes multiple beds, couches, a

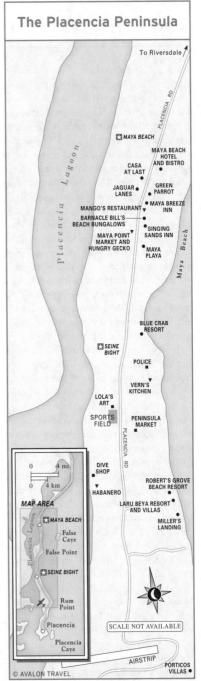

The Placencia Peninsula

kitchen, and hammocks on the decks. There's a restaurant on-site and continental breakfast is included. It's on a lovely, quiet stretch of beach, and use of bikes and kayaks is included.

Catering to relaxed couples and honeymooners, **Barnacle Bill's Beach Bungalows** (tel. 501/533-8110, www.barnaclebills-belize.com, US$110) offers two secluded bungalows on the beach, with full kitchens, fans, and hot and cold water. Each sleeps three adults, and children under 12 are not allowed. Tours, free kayaks, and wireless Internet are available.

Lovers of orchids and boutique luxury will enjoy the small but cozy **Singing Sands Inn** (tel. 501/533-3022, U.S. tel. 888/201-6425, www.singingsands.com, US$110-275 plus tax). The six thatched-roof seafront cabanas have front porches and wood floors, and the two standard guest rooms offer sea and garden views. All units have private baths, ceiling fans, and constant ocean breezes. Portable air-conditioning is available if desired. Breakfast is served in the open-air restaurant next to the pool; fresh lunches and dinners are served as well at the Bonefish Grille. Drinks and light fare can be enjoyed at Chez Albert's bar on the pier, 220 feet out into the Caribbean. Use of bikes and snorkel gear is complimentary, and golf carts, clear-bottomed kayaks, and sailboats are available for rent.

Food

When you get tired of cooking in your cabana's kitchenette, visit the **Hungry Gecko** (8am-9pm Mon.-Sat.), which serves a cheap menu of Honduran and local goodies, fresh seafood, and smoothies. One of two stores in town, the **Maya Pointe Market** (Mon.-Sat.), is open most mornings and afternoons.

Mango's Beach Bar and Restaurant (tel. 501/533-8102 or 501/610-2494, fdasilva2@yahoo.com, 4pm-midnight Wed.-Fri., noon-midnight Fri.-Sat., US$5-10) has a Belizean-Mexican menu and a breezy view to enjoy with your beer. Owner Frank da Silva was once chef at Robert's Grove. It's popular with the handful of locals, offering darts and occasional live bands at night.

The ★ **Maya Beach Hotel Bistro** (tel. 501/533-8040, 7am-9pm daily, US$16-28) is a breath of fresh air on the Belize culinary scene. Just reading the appetizer and meal choices will make your mouth water—few restaurants in the country have a menu this savory and creative. Australian chef John prepares dinner entrées like Sassy Shrimp Pot, Cacao Pork, and Mojo Roasted Chicken (with a jerk and honey glaze), not to mention fresh bread, an inspired bar food menu (honey-coconut ribs and roasted pumpkin-coconut green chile soup), a wine cellar, and a lovely assortment of breakfasts (US$6-11), including homemade bagels and imported lox (smoked salmon).

At the **Bonefish Grille** (at the Singing Sands Inn, tel. 501/533-3022, www.singingsands.com, 7am-9:30pm daily, US$10-23), everything is made from scratch: homemade pasta, ricotta cheese, breads, and the salad dressings, and there's no MSG. The menu features Asian and Italian cuisine, prepared with fresh ingredients. This place was Restaurant of the Year runner-up at the 2010 National Tourism Awards.

★ SEINE BIGHT

South of Maya Beach, a few more miles of dirt road will put you in the Garífuna village of Seine Bight. In this tiny town, most of the men are fishermen and the women tend family gardens. Some are attempting to clean up the town, with hopes it will become a low-key tourist destination, as foreign-owned resorts sprout like mushrooms up and down the coast around them. Seine Bight does have the nicest stretches of beach in the area, along with neighboring Maya Beach. There are a few casual eateries and bars. Venturing here on foot or by bicycle is where you'll get the best sense of local culture on the peninsula.

Lola's Art Gallery (behind the soccer field, follow the well-marked signs, tel. 501/523-3343 or cell 501/601-1913, lolasartgallery@yahoo.com, 7am-7pm daily) is a must-see. A renowned Creole artist, her inspired artwork includes paintings on canvas that depict scenes of village life as well as cards and gorgeous gourd masks, all in bright, primary colors. According to her parents, she started painting as a young girl, using her mother's lipstick on the walls. Lola also has a small on-site bar (10am-midnight daily) serving cold beer and soft drinks; ask her why she named it **The Fallen Angel.**

The owners of Blue Crab Resort also run a tiny chocolate factory in the house across the road. **Goss Chocolate** (north end of Seine Bight, tel. 501/523-3544, www.goss-choco-late.com, 9am-5pm Mon.-Fri., 10am-5pm Sat.) is made from 100 percent pure organic cacao and is available only in Belize; it costs US$1.50-2.50 for a bar.

Accommodations

Independent travelers may enjoy the laid-back feel of **Miller's Landing** (tel. 501/523-3010, www.millerslanding.net, US$85-150). The Millers like to keep things simple, and not much has changed since the couple opened their resort. The entrance is tucked in from the roadside, and there are three basic sea-view guest rooms and two private cabanas, all with coffeemakers and mini fridges, private baths, hot and cold water, and ceiling fans. This calm and quiet beach location is surrounded by native vegetation; watch birds and butterflies while having your complimentary breakfast. Lounge on the newly updated pool deck, or if you're feeling more active, take out a complimentary bike, kayak, or windsurfing board. It could be an ideal place to book a whole group of independent, well-traveled, and unfussy friends and family.

On a clean, shallow beach on the very northern end of Seine Bight is **Blue Crab Resort** (tel. 501/523-3544, www.bluecrab-beach.com, US$60-90). American-Belizean-owned, this humble hotel has four guest rooms with air-conditioning, fridges, coffee-makers, fans, and cable TV, plus two cabanas with high thatched roofs, louvered windows, private baths, and three fans. Blue Crab is on the primitive side, made mostly of wood and thatch, but its cabanas are more modern, and

you're likely to see a few coatimundis foraging among the fruit trees.

The **Nautical Inn** (tel. 501/523-3595, U.S. tel. 678/528-7065, www.nauticalinnbelize.com, US$65-300 pp) offers various old-school but spacious beachfront accommodations surrounding a pool, and all guest rooms have air-conditioning, ceiling fans, and cable TV. Basic guest rooms have kitchenettes, and the two-bedroom suite has a full kitchen and a living room. Ask about special group rates.

One of the well-known resorts on the peninsula, **Robert's Grove Beach Resort** (just south of Seine Bight, tel. 501/523-3565, U.S. tel. 800/565-9757, www.robertsgrove.com, from US$215) is a classic grand resort. Its various structures are situated close together along a short stretch of decent beach, so it doesn't appear overwhelming. The various guest rooms, suites, and villas have high ceilings, king beds, and updated amenities. There are three pools, a tennis court, a spa, a gym, a trio of rooftop hot tubs, and an open-air restaurant. Robert's Grove has its own dive shop on the lagoon side across the street (next to its Mexican restaurant, Habanero) and offers all kinds of underwater, offshore, and inland trips and packages. Bikes, kayaks, and sailboats are available for your own explorations. The inn is popular with couples, families, and groups; ask about trips to their private islands.

If you're going luxury, you might as well stay right next door: ★ **Laru Beya Resort and Villas** (tel. 501/523-3476, U.S. tel. 800/890-8010, www.larubeya.com, US$140-490) offers beautifully furnished beachfront accommodations and all the amenities (my favorite is the seafront balcony), with a touch of luxury yet unpretentious. The suites feel more like your own private condo than a resort. Penthouse suites have a ladder to a private rooftop jetted tub with a great view. It's a stone's throw from the beach, and you'll fall asleep to the sound of waves. The **Quarter Deck** restaurant and bar (7am-10pm) serves international cuisine and caters for destination weddings.

Food

Vern's Kitchen (main road, Placencia, 6am-2pm and 4pm-9pm Thurs.-Tues., US$2-5) serves up local dishes and often a Garífuna specialty. Besides Vern's, you'll have to wander up to Maya Beach, up the road, to get some cheap local food.

The **Seaside Restaurant** (just south of Seine Bight, tel. 501/523-3565, 7am-9pm daily, US$12-28) at Robert's Grove has an international menu: sandwiches, pizza, wings, and quesadillas for lunch; seafood appetizers and entrées, imported steaks, and à la carte options for dinner. The bar is open till midnight. **Habanero Mexican Café and Bar** (tel. 501/523-3565, noon-10pm daily Dec.-May, US$9-15) is an excellent lagoon-side Mexican restaurant across the road from Robert's Grove Marina.

If you need groceries, the **Peninsula** (main road Placencia to Seine Bight, 9am-10pm daily) has the widest selection.

PLACENCIA VILLAGE

A fishing village since the time of the Maya and periodically flattened by hurricanes (most recently by Iris in 2001), Placencia continues rebuilding and redefining itself, in large part to accommodate the influx of foreigners.

Placencia Village is still worlds away from the condo-dominated landscape of San Pedro on Ambergris Caye, and most locals claim it will never go that way, but time will tell. There are plenty of bulldozers, swaths of cut mangroves, golf carts for rent, and a brand-new pier and marina completed in 2013.

It's everyone's hope that despite area development, this town will remain the *tranquilo* ramshackle village it is today for years to come. Find a room, book some day tours, pencil in a massage before happy hour, and relax. Oh, yeah, and feel free to drink the tap water as you explore: Placencia's *agua* is piped in from an artesian well across the lagoon in Independence, reportedly the result of an unsuccessful attempt to drill for oil, and it's clean and pure.

Sights

There are few sights per se in this beach village. What you'll find, however, is plenty of sand, water sports, food, active bars and nightlife, and all the options you can think of to embody a fun beach vacation.

The north-south Placencia Road runs the length of the peninsula, doglegs around the airstrip, continues along the lagoon, and then parallels the famous central sidewalk

There are several upscale resorts in Seine Bight, including Laru Beya Resort and Villas.

as it enters town. You'll see the soccer field on your right before the road curves slightly to the left, terminating at the Shell station and the main docks. If there is a "downtown" Placencia, it's probably here, in front of the gas station and dock. This is where buses come and go, taxis hang out, and most dive shops are based.

Aside from the beach, the main attraction in Placencia is the world-renowned **main-street sidewalk,** cited in the *Guinness Book of World Records* as "the world's most narrow street." It is 24 inches wide in spots and runs north-south through the sand for over a mile. Homes, hotels, Guatemalan goods shops, craft makers, and tour guide offices line both sides. Several side paths connect it to the main road in the village. No bikes are allowed; pedestrians only.

Sports and Recreation

There's no shortage of guide services in Placencia, where most tour operators offer service to all nearby destinations: Cockscomb Basin Wildlife Sanctuary, Monkey River, snorkeling and fishing trips with lunch on a beautiful caye, the Mayan ruins of Lubaantun and Nim Li Punit, and a variety of paddling tours. For any of these trips, also refer to the dive shops and fishing guides listed in this chapter.

Many tour operators have their offices in shacks clustered in the village or by the main dock area in town, just past the gas station; most are subcontracted by the hotels that offer tours to their guests. If you're going it on your own, ask around and know that prices are often based on a minimum number of passengers, usually four. Prices vary little, but it's definitely worth comparing. Monkey River day trips, for example, range US$60-75 per person, depending on whether lunch is included and the size of the boat. Half-day snorkel trips are about US$35-75 per person, depending on group size. Most tours require that you sign up the day before; reef tours typically leave around 9am, inland tours around 7am.

I highly recommend **Splash Dive Center** (tel. 501/523-3080 or cell 501/610-0235, www. splashbelize.com) for inland trips, snorkel and dive tours to the cayes, or whale shark experiences. The guides and drivers are professional and very friendly, and no request is ever too much for owner Patty Ramirez, who loves to meet travelers and is absolutely top-notch—she goes above and beyond to make sure you're taken care of and happy. The good

Splash Dive Center offers numerous diving and snorkeling trips to the reef and cayes.

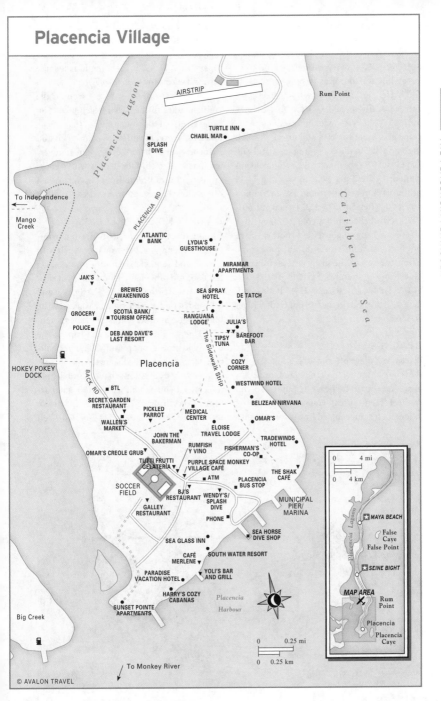

Placencia Village

Placencia Lagoon

AIRSTRIP

Rum Point

TURTLE INN
CHABIL MAR

SPLASH DIVE

PLACENCIA RD

To Independence

Mango Creek

ATLANTIC BANK

LYDIA'S GUESTHOUSE

MIRAMAR APARTMENTS

JAK'S

BREWED AWAKENINGS

SEA SPRAY HOTEL

DE TATCH

GROCERY

SCOTIA BANK/ TOURISM OFFICE

RANGUANA LODGE

JULIA'S

POLICE

DEB AND DAVE'S LAST RESORT

TIPSY TUNA

BAREFOOT BAR

HOKEY POKEY DOCK

BACK RD

Placencia

The Sidewalk Strip

COZY CORNER

WESTWIND HOTEL

BTL

BELIZEAN NIRVANA

SECRET GARDEN RESTAURANT

PICKLED PARROT

MEDICAL CENTER

OMAR'S

WALLEN'S MARKET

ELOISE TRAVEL LODGE

JOHN THE BAKERMAN

RUMFISH Y VINO

FISHERMAN'S CO-OP

TRADEWINDS HOTEL

OMAR'S CREOLE GRUB

TUTTI FRUTTI GELATERÍA

PURPLE SPACE MONKEY VILLAGE CAFÉ

ATM

PLACENCIA BUS STOP

THE SHAK CAFÉ

SOCCER FIELD

BJ'S RESTAURANT

WENDY'S/ SPLASH DIVE

GALLEY RESTAURANT

PHONE

MUNICIPAL PIER/ MARINA

SEA GLASS INN

SEA HORSE DIVE SHOP

CAFÉ MERLENE

SOUTH WATER RESORT

PARADISE VACATION HOTEL

YOLI'S BAR AND GRILL

Placencia Harbour

Big Creek

HARRY'S COZY CABANAS

SUNSET POINTE APARTMENTS

To Monkey River

Caribbean Sea

0   4 mi
0   4 km

MAYA BEACH

False Caye
False Point

SEINE BIGHT

MAP AREA

Rum Point

Placencia

Placencia Caye

Placencia Lagoon

0   0.25 mi
0   0.25 km

© AVALON TRAVEL

news is, they will be opening a second location in Hopkins.

Nite Wind (tel. 501/503-3487 or cell 501/660-6333, doylegardiner@yahoo.com) is reliable for tours, as is **Seahorse Dive Shop** (tel. 501/523-3166, www.belizescuba. com). Locally owned **Ocean Motion** (tel. 501/523-3363, www.oceanmotionplacencia. com) gets great reviews and offers snorkeling and fishing tours to Ranguana and Silk Cayes (US$70 pp, lunch and equipment included; US$325 per boat for fishing 11-19 miles offshore). Hubert and Karen Young's **Joy Tours** (tel. 501/523-3325 or cell 501/601-0273, www.belizewithjoy.com, Monkey River US$63 pp, Laughingbird Caye snorkel US$75 pp) is across from Tim's Chinese restaurant. Clint, the son of the proprietress of Lydia's Guesthouse, operates **Pelican Tours** (tel. 501/634-8476 or 501/630-2795, lydias@btl. net); he'll take you to the reef or Monkey River (US$65 pp).

BEACHES

Placencia Village offers a long uninterrupted stretch of thick golden sand, good for walks, jogs, and dips. The beach is public, so you can feel free to spread your towel anywhere, as long as it's unoccupied by a resort's lounge chairs. The water isn't perfect Caribbean turquoise-clear, but it's clear enough and refreshing. Popular stretches are just across from Tipsy Tuna, ideal for grabbing lunch, some sun, and even some beach volleyball.

The prettiest beaches I have seen on the peninsula are in the Maya Beach area. You can pick any of the restaurants in that area—Robert's Grove, for instance—for lunch and swim off the beach for the day. A great unpretentious spot to chill for the day with a cocktail is the Maya Breeze Inn's beach bar; just bring a towel and your own snacks.

DIVING AND SNORKELING

Although the beach is usually fine for swimming and lounging, you won't see much with a mask and snorkel except sand, sea grass, a few fish, and other bathers. A short boat ride, however, will bring you to the barrier reef and the kind of underwater viewing you can write home about. Snorkel gear is available for rent (US$5 per day) everywhere, and trips to the cayes and reefs cost around US$50 per half-day, depending on the distance.

The few dive shops have comparable prices, and you can either let your hotel arrange everything or do it yourself. **Splash Dive Center** (tel. 501/523-3080 or cell

Placencia Village beach

501/610-0235, www.splashbelize.com, 2-tank dive US$120, snorkeling US$90 pp, lunch included) has two locations in Placencia: an appointment and tour booking desk at **Wendy's Creole Restaurant** and a top-notch dive center on the north end, across from Chabil Mar Resort. The dive center is where Splash's six boats, including a 46-foot Newton, are docked, and from where trips depart. Splash has the most professional operation I've seen in Belize, from the way they handle their gear to the attention they pay to their customers, first-timers or experienced. They take care of everything, from pickups to fittings to food. Owner Patty Ramirez—named a Sea Hero in 2012 by *Scuba Diving* magazine for her dive center's contributions to community building and marine environmental awareness—left a banking career 13 years ago to pursue her passion. Along with her partner, Ralph, they're a classic example of a passion turned into a success story. Splash is in the midst of launching a second location in Hopkins, at Jaguar Reef Resort, starting in March 2014. They also offer inland tours across the Stann Creek District, and can assist in finding suitable accommodations if needed.

Seahorse Dive Shop (near the town dock, tel. 501/523-3166, www.belizescuba.com, whale shark dive US$185 pp, 2-tank local reef dive US$110 pp) is highly recommended. Farther north from the village, you'll find a couple of other serious dive operations linked to their respective resorts, with professional shops at Robert's Grove Beach Resort and Turtle Inn.

FISHING

Placencia has always been a fishing town for its sustenance, but with the advent of tourism, it has gained a worldwide reputation for sportfishing. Deepwater possibilities include wahoo, sailfish, marlin, kingfish, and dolphinfish; fly-fishing can hook you a grand slam—bonefish, tarpon, permit, and snook (all catch-and-release). Fortunately, serious angling means serious local guides, several

of whom (like the Godfrey brothers, Ea̶ Kurt) have been featured on ESPN and in m̶ tiple fishing magazines. Hire Earl at **Trip'N Travel Southern Guides Fly Fishing and Saltwater Adventures** (Placencia Office Supply Bldg., tel. 501/523-3205, lgodfrey@btl.net). Most tour operators listed in this chapter offer fishing trips, and a few specialize in them, like **Tarpon Caye Lodge** (tel. 501/523-3323, www.tarponcayelodge.com, 3- or 4-night all-inclusive fishing trip US$2,160 pp), boasting decades of experience. Charlie Leslie Sr., owner and head guide, has a stellar reputation and now works with his son and a wonderful team read to take you to a variety of spots, from inshore places that include nearby flats to Tarpon Caye and the remote Ycacos area. Check www.placencia.com for more options.

KAYAKING AND PADDLEBOARDING

An unforgettable and underrated way to explore the near-shore cayes, mangroves, creeks, and rivers is by paddle. Plastic open kayaks are available to guests at most resorts, and many tour operators and dive shops have some for rent as well. Located behind the peninsula, the **Placencia Lagoon** is home to birds, saltwater crocodiles, manatees, and mangroves. While it's easily explored solo by kayak, I recommend going with a guide if you're not an experienced kayaker, in case of a surprise croc encounter. **Eric Foreman** (tel. 501/664-8121) offers guided lagoon kayak trips (US$125 or $160 for two, half day, includes kayaks) as well as sea kayak tours to the nearby inner reef cayes (US$225 pp half day, lunch not included); rentals are also available for US$40/day.

Stand-up paddleboarding classes are available with the energetic Tony of **BelizeFit Tony's Gym** (tel. 501/631-7427, www.belizefit.com, hours vary, call ahead, private lessons US$25 per hour, board rental US$12.50 per hour from booth next to Tipsy Tuna). Tony offers morning beach workouts (US$10) and introductory lessons.

AND SAILING

ies abound for day trips, sunset
rkel voyages, and sail charters,
floating around the gorgeous
.yes. A sure bet is Jeff Scott's
r Catamaran Charters (tel.
7, www.daytripperbelize.com,
US$75 pp with lunch), based on the dock
at Yoli's Bar & Grill. Jeff will take you on a
fun, leisurely snorkel trip to the nearby cayes,
under an hour away—including the Lark
Range or Lighthouse Caye—where you'll
spot stunning corals and marinelife. You'll
likely be the only ones in the area. Expensive,
high-end The Moorings (tel. 501/523-3351,
U.S. tel. 800/535-7289, www.moorings.com,
US$500-1,700, minimum 3-day rental) has a
dock for multiple catamaran adventures on
their beautiful 40- to 46-foot cats, based on
the lagoon side north of the airstrip and just
across from Laru Beya Resort. Bring your own
crew or charter one with a crew and all the
bells and whistles for a weeklong sail. Belize
Sailing Charters (tel. 501/523-3138, www.
belize-sailing-charters.com) has bareboat and
crewed yacht charters. Just across from town,
Placencia Yacht Club (tel. 501/523-3500 or
501/653-0569, http://placenciayachtclub.com)
is on Placencia Caye, featuring the Tranquilo
Restaurant and Bar. The über-exclusive mem-
bership-based Tradewinds Cruise Club has
headquarters here, in case you were wonder-
ing, on the lagoon side across from Sunset
Pointe Condominiums. They'll pick you up
from across the lagoon if you wave. Their 50-
feet luxury cats will have you gawking.

MASSAGE AND BODYWORK

Sign up for a massage or other treatment at
The Secret Garden Massage and Day
Spa (behind Wallen's, tel. 501/523-3420 or
cell 501/624-6096, www.secretgardenplacen-
cia.com), where a one-hour massage costs
US$50 and a special four-hands treatment
costs a bit more. If you need relief from the
sun and barefooting on the beach, try the sunburn treatment and foot massage for US$50.

Robert's Grove Beach Resort Spa (just
south of Seine Bight, tel. 501/523-3565), north
of town, offers a full range of treatments—for
premium prices, of course. The Turtle Inn (1
mile north of the village, tel. 501/523-3244 or
501/523-3150, www.turtleinn.com) also has
pampering services, as does the Siripohn's
Thai Massage (tel. 501/620-8718, www.
thaimassagebelize.com, 10am-6pm Mon.-Sat.,
massage from US$75 per hour), right on the
front street in Placencia Village, run by experienced Thais who offer seaweed treatments
and papaya body polish. Also on the main
drag, check into the affordable Serenity Day
Spa (tel. 501/523-3513 or cell 501/669-7113,
zelmac96@yahoo.com, massage US$50 per
hour), a small one-massage-bed cabin run by
Belizean certified masseuse Zelma. It's right
on the strip, but she gets rave reviews for her
"magic hands."

If you're up for a workout, check out Tony's
BelizeFit (tel. 501/631-7427, tony@belizefit.
com, hours vary, call first), with an indoor
gym located in the RE/MAX building across
Scotiabank, in Placencia Village. Tony offers
Beach Boot Camp, Thai stretch classes, and
more.

Entertainment and Events

NIGHTLIFE

Placencia's bars, restaurants, and resorts do a
decent job of coordination, so special events
like beach barbecues, horseshoe tournaments,
karaoke, and live music are offered through
the entire week—especially during the high
season. Your best bet is to check the *Placencia
Breeze* (www.placenciabreeze.com) newspaper
and look for current schedules, because bars,
clubs, and parties come and go with the wind.

The Barefoot Bar (tel. 501/523-3515,
11am-midnight daily) is the only constantly wildly popular venue in the high
season. Flip-flop clad revelers choose from
hundreds of froofy cocktails and bar food;
there's live music (Fri.-Sun.) and happy hour
(5pm-6pm daily) as well as never-ending
theme parties. Another party constant is

the beachfront **Tipsy Tuna** (now directly next door to Barefoot Bar, tel. 501/523-3089, tipsytuna@hotmail.com, 11:30am-midnight daily), with Garífuna drumming on Wednesday nights and a general all-day-long party vibe. The happy hours are excellent too, with fifty-cent wings and $1.50 local rum drinks 5pm-7pm daily.

Another happening and locally popular bar and restaurant a bit farther down the harbor is **Yoli's,** with barbecue and ring toss starting at 3pm on Sunday. Stop by the **Pickled Parrot** (between the sidewalk and the main road, just off the soccer field, tel. 501/636-7068, 11:30am-9:30pm daily), where you can have a Belizean panty ripper via Jell-O shot or a three-rum Parrot Piss cocktail; maybe you'll have enough of those to graduate to their so-called secret VIP section.

FESTIVALS AND EVENTS

The biggest party of the year happens the third week of June, during **Lobsterfest.** The whole south end of town closes down for lobster-catching tournaments, costumes, and dances, and there are food booths everywhere. **Easter weekend** is popular, as Placencia is a destination for many Belizeans as well as foreign visitors; they typically book their rooms months in advance, so be prepared for the crowds. Look for a Halloween celebration, complete with a parade and trick-or-treating for kids and adults alike.

Another annual gig, the **Mistletoe Ball,** wanders to a different hotel before Christmas every year and doubles as a fund-raiser for the local Belize Tourism Industry Association chapter. **New Year's Eve** sometimes consists of one big outdoor party out on the soccer field, with all-inclusive drinks, hats, and more for just US$2.50 pp, or a no-cover beach party at **Barefoot Bar** and **Tipsy Tuna**. The local humane society organizes various fund-raising events as well; keep an eye out.

Shopping

Despite plenty of gift stores featuring Guatemalan crafts and clothes, there are a couple of talented Belizean artists and wood-carvers worth checking out and supporting. Stop by the father-and-son-operated shop **A Piece of Belize Wood Carvings** (sidewalk shortcut across from Omar's, tel. 501/621-1595 or 501/628-1279, apieceofbelize01@yahoo.com, 9am-6pm daily, US$15-50, prices vary according to the item). Bob and Tyrone Lockwood make beautiful pieces using rosewood and ziricote wood, found only in Belize, including bowls, bracelets, and home decor pieces, even customized carved doors. Feel free to bargain with them. Just steps away, still on the sidewalk, is **Made in Belize** (tel. 501/205-5511 or cell 501/627-5125, 9am-5pm daily), where Leo has a shack filled with all sorts of creative carvings, including pieces made out of driftwood, mahogany, and ziricote.

Strike A Pose (main road, Placencia Village, 9am-7pm Tues.-Fri., 10am-6pm Sat., strikeapose.placencia@gmail.com) has a random selection of trendy clothes imported from Los Angeles, including plus-size options and evening dresses, in case you need a new outfit for a hot date.

Accommodations

All of Placencia's budget lodgings are found on or within shouting distance of the sidewalk, and most of the high-end resorts are strung along the beach north of town. Remember, these are high-season double occupancy prices; expect significant discounts and negotiable rates between May and November.

UNDER US$25

Right on the sidewalk, **Omar's** (tel. 501/634-4350, US$13 shared bath, US$22.50 private bath) is a wooden flophouse. If the office is closed, head to Omar's Creole Grub to inquire. Near the Anglican school, **Eloise Travel Lodge** (tel. 501/523-3299, US$20-25) has four guest rooms with private or shared baths and a communal kitchen. There is no reception office; ask for Miss Sonia Leslie.

A better budget bet is ★ **Lydia's Guesthouse** (tel. 501/523-3117, lydias@btl.net, US$25), toward the north end of the sidewalk. Lydia's is a longtime favorite among backpackers. The eight clean, private guest rooms with a shared tile-floor bath also share a sociable two-story porch, a communal kitchen, fans, hammocks, and a 30-second walk to the beach. Miss Lydia will make you breakfast if you make arrangements the day before; she also makes fresh Creole bread and guava jam.

If you're out of options, stop by **BJ's Restaurant** (the building on the corner of the soccer field, up the stairs, US$20-30) and ask Miss Betty about her two budget guest rooms—they're basic and nothing more than a place to crash but cheap. One has a double bed, fans, and a shared bath; the second has three single beds and a private bath, ideal for backpacking friends.

US$25-50

As you enter Placencia, there is a gate by the Placencia Bazaar gift shop; ★ **Deb & Dave's Last Resort** (tel. 501/523-3207 or 501/600-6044, US$25) consists of four small, clean guest rooms surrounding a tidy sand courtyard and tropical garden favored by hummingbirds. The common screened-in porch space is excellent for meeting your neighbors and telling war stories from the day's paddling and snorkeling trips; there are clean shared baths for all, free Wi-Fi, and a coffeemaker.

Claiming to be the "first established hotel on the Placencia Peninsula" (since 1964), the **Sea Spray Hotel** (Placencia sidewalk, tel. 501/523-3148, www.seasprayhotel.com, US$25-65) is a decent choice, although staff friendliness can be hit or miss. It's 30 feet from the ocean and has 20 guest rooms with private baths, refrigerators, hot and cold water, and coffeepots. There are economy guest rooms and nicer units closer to the water, where guests can relax in hammocks and chairs under palm trees. **De Tatch** seafood restaurant, on the premises, is popular for breakfast and serves up lunch and dinner.

US$50-100

A good deal right on the beach is **Julia's** (tel. 501/503-3478, www.juliascabanas.com, US$65-70), with simple stand-alone cabanas complete with double beds, mini fridges, wireless Internet, porches, and hammocks. The decor is a bit of a hodgepodge, but the price is right.

Well located within the village, right off the sidewalk, is **Sea View Suites Hotel** (beside Purple Space Monkey Village Restaurant, tel. 501/523-3777, www.seaviewplacencia.com, US$75), which gets rave reviews and has nine immaculately clean tile-floor guest rooms with a beach ambience, double or king beds, coffeemakers, microwaves, beach towels, and cable TV.

At the extreme southern end of Placencia Village, look for the brightly painted **Tradewinds Hotel** (tel. 501/523-3122, trdewndpla@btl.net, US$75-95), on five acres near the sea, offering nine cabanas with spacious guest rooms, fans, refrigerators, coffeepots, and private yards just feet from the ocean. It's a bit dated but the interior is clean.

The **Cozy Corner Hotel** (tel. 501/523-3280 or 501/523-3540, cozycorner@btl.net, US$50-70) has 10 decent guest rooms with private baths and basic amenities, right behind the Cozy Corner bar-restaurant on the beach, with a nice breezy second-story porch; some guest rooms have air-conditioning. Next door, the Tipsy Tuna plays loud music at night.

The newly renovated **Sea Glass Inn** (formerly Dianni's Guest House, tel. 501/523-3098, www.seaglassinnbelize.com, US$79) is a lovely new addition to the village, with six immaculate guest rooms with twin or double beds, air-conditioning, coffeemakers, fridges, ceiling fans, and verandas looking onto a nice quiet stretch of sand with a dock, even if it's not quite a typical beach. Walk-ins are welcome, and the inn is well located, just a few steps from the sidewalk strip and the action in the village.

★ **Paradise Vacation Hotel** (Placencia sidewalk, tel. 501/523-3179 or U.S. tel. 904/564-9400, www.belize123.com, US$89-159) has 12 air-conditioned guest rooms, each beautifully appointed, and an on-site seaside restaurant and bar, a spa, and a gift shop. Ask about room 12 if you want to live it up a little. There is complimentary use of bikes and kayaks as well as a rooftop hot tub with views of the Maya Mountains. **Harry's Cozy Cabanas** (Placencia sidewalk, tel. 501/523-3234, www.cozycabanas.com, US$30) has three simple cabanas with screened porches.

Westwind Hotel (tel. 501/523-3255, www.westwindhotel.com, US$80-150) has 10 guest rooms with views, light tile floors, sunny decks, private baths, and fans (air-conditioning is optional and costs a little extra if you turn it on); there's also wireless Internet access. The family unit goes for US$150. The hotel has a friendly vibe and a nice beach to relax on, although it's a little close to the pounding music at Tipsy Tuna. The **Ranguana Lodge** (tel. 501/523-3112, www.ranguanabelize.com, US$88-94) has five private cabanas: three air-conditioned beach cabins and two cabins set back with garden views. All are spacious and have nice wood floors, walls, and ceilings.

US$100-150

Captain Jak's (Placencia Village, tel. 501/523-3481, www.captainjaksbelize.com, US$90-120) is a quaint lagoon-side resort set in a tropical garden, with cabanas, two-story cottages, and a spacious villa (US$300). Each unit has a full kitchen, hot and cold water, and plenty of space to relax.

Easy Living Apartments (tel. 501/523-3481, www.easyliving.bz, from US$135, US$810 per week) offers four slightly dated, carpeted, but fully furnished two- and three-bedroom air-conditioned units; they are ideally located off the sidewalk. ★ **Miramar Apartments** (toward the north end of the

sidewalk, tel. 501/523-3658, www.miramarbelize.com, US$125-235) is a favorite of mine; the hot pink building, opposite Lydia's Guesthouse and next to De Tatch, has studio (my favorite, on the first floor facing the beach), one-bedroom, and three-bedroom units. Each has a king bed, a full kitchen, air-conditioning, and cable TV. The three-bedroom unit has hardwood flooring, beautiful decorations, original artwork, and a large seaview balcony. It's a great place for a family getaway or solo traveler.

OVER US$150

Belizean Nirvana (tel. 501/523-3331, www.belizeannirvana.com, US$150-275) is one of the newer additions to the village and lives up to its boutique-hotel status. It's right in the heart of the action, with five one- and two-bedroom suites adorned with Belizean artwork, full kitchenettes, bathrobes, balconies with direct views of the beach and the sea, air-conditioning, and continental breakfast delivered to your suite at your chosen hour of the morning. Amenities are plentiful, including use of bicycles, wireless Internet, a rooftop grill (don't miss the incredible view from up there), with hammocks and a kitchen area, local cell phones you can top up during your stay, and a magicJack for calls overseas. The hotel can also book Tropic Air flights for you, or pick you up from Belize City at additional cost.

At **Chabil Mar** (tel. 501/523-3606, www.chabilmarvillas.com, US$375-525), the privately owned luxury villas have richly decorated interiors and are furnished with all the modern conveniences one could ask for. On the beach less than a mile north of Placencia Village, the exclusive Café Mar provides butler service so you can dine where you please: at poolside (there are two), on the pier or a private veranda, or in the comfort of your villa. It's a popular spot for small weddings.

One of the few truly upscale options that's actually in Placencia Village, **Sunset Pointe Apartments** (Placencia Lagoon, tel. 501/664-4740, U.S. tel. 904/471-3599, www.sunsetpointebelize.com, US$250-275) offers luxury two-bedroom condos for short- or long-term rental, often advertised online. They're back on the lagoon side, but they all have raised roof decks with a breeze. It's only a 10-minute walk to the beach from here, and there are many accessible restaurants and shops.

Turtle Inn (tel. 501/523-3244 or 501/523-3150, www.turtleinn.com) is one of the nation's premier luxe destinations, one of U.S. film producer Francis Ford Coppola's two Belizean properties. It is about a mile north of Placencia Village. Prices start at US$375 per night for the garden-view cottages and go up to US$1,850 per night for the master two-bedroom pavilion house with a private entrance, a pool, and a dining pavilion. Even if you're not staying here, swing by to treat yourself to a fine meal with beautifully framed views of the ocean. Turtle Inn has seven luxury villas and 18 cottages on offer. The guest rooms are designed along Indonesian and Belizean lines, with lots of natural materials and airy space. The high thatched ceilings absorb the heat, so there are fans only, no air-conditioning, but there are music players for your iPod as well as fancy shell phones. Amenities include two swimming pools, the über-mellow Laughing Fish Bar on the beach, and one of the peninsula's premier restaurants, the Mare Restaurant. There's also an on-site spa, dive shop, and more dining options; Auntie Luba's Belizean eatery and the Gauguin Grill are open for dinner 6pm-9pm daily.

Food

Placencia has a small number of restaurants, but there's enough variety to keep you stuffed during your visit: seafood cooked in coconut milk and local herbs, Creole stews and fry chicken, sandwiches, burritos, burgers, French, Italian, and adequate vegetarian options nearly everywhere you go.

BAKERIES AND CAFÉS

John the Bakerman (7am-close daily) makes great breads, cinnamon buns, and coffee bread, available all day; he also sells his brother's meat pies. Look for his sign on the sidewalk and get it fresh out of the oven around 5pm.

You can get your latte or cappuccino fix at the small **Brewed Awakenings** (main road, Placencia Village, tel. 501/668-1715, 6:30am-5pm Mon.-Sat.), serving up Belizean coffee freshly roasted daily from a small shack with little seating but plenty of street action. Flavor options to blend in your coffee range from Kahlua to Nutty Irishman, and options include iced cappuccino and other fancy coffee concoctions.

In Placencia Village Square, ★ **Tutti Frutti Gelatería** (tel. 501/620-9916, tizi.lory@virgilio.it, 9am-9pm Thurs.-Tues.) serves up some of the best homemade gelato you'll have outside of Italy; it's made fresh daily with local fruits and traditional flavors. The fruit sorbets are dairy-free, and espresso drinks and iced coffees are served.

Up the road, just across from the town dock, look for **The Shak Beach Café** (tel. 501/622-1686, 7am-7pm daily), which has 21 smoothie flavors, all made with fresh fruit, along with a healthy vegetarian menu, a view of the water from the dockside tables, and good breakfasts of banana pancakes or omelets with coffee or tea (US$5-6).

BELIZEAN AND INTERNATIONAL

Omar's Creole Grub (tel. 501/634-4350, 7am-2:30pm and 6pm-9pm Sun.-Thurs., 6pm-9pm Sat.) will take care of you all day, with a lobster omelet, handmade tortillas, and guava jelly (US$9) to start the day off, then a burrito for lunch (US$4) and Creole-style barracuda steak (from US$7), pork chops, conch steak, or lobster for dinner. Chef Omar Jr. won the 2009 Lobsterfest Cook-Off with his stuffed lobster. Come for the seafood and stay for the conversation with the vivacious Omar and family, whose children all work at the restaurant. No alcohol is served.

Dawn's Grill n'Go (tel. 501/602-9302, grillngo@yahoo.com, 7am-3pm and 5:30pm-9pm Mon.-Sat., US$10-15) has finger lickin' good fried chicken—served on Friday—and a cozy spot on the main road where Miss Dawn loves to serve up her creative specials, whether local favorites or international dishes, including pastas, seafood, fajitas, and lobster burgers. There's nothing "fast" tasting about the food here. Be sure to sample her decadent banana bread pudding with One Barrel rum sauce—a bit pricey at $3.50 for a small slice, but yum!

BJ's Belizean Bellyfull (on the corner of the soccer field, 7am-7pm Mon.-Sat., 7am-4pm Sun., US$2.50-10), "where good food and God's people meet," has an upstairs outdoor porch (sometimes downstairs tables in busy season) and cheap fare: sandwiches from US$2.50, a buffet lunch, seafood and stir-fry dinners for US$10. Next door, ★ **Wendy's Creole Restaurant and Bar** (tel. 501/523-3335, 7am-9:30pm daily, US$3-23) offers varied, consistently tasty Creole and international dishes at reasonable prices, the best outdoor people-watching veranda in the village, plus a glassed-in, air-conditioned seating area and a full bar. This is a great place to come to for Creole and Mexican cooking (they have the best stuffed fry jacks for breakfast, by the way), burgers (US$3-7.50), burritos (US$4.50-8), and fancier steaks and seafood items like Creole fish and curry lobster (US$13-23). There's no hit or miss at Wendy's no matter what you order.

The long-standing **Galley Restaurant** (behind the soccer field, tel. 501/523-3133, 11am-2:30pm and 5:30pm-9pm Mon.-Sat., US$4-30) is popular among the locals not only for offering some of the cheapest local eats but also for the freshly made seaweed punch, which Belizeans say "give yuh strong back"; draw your own conclusions. The thick crust pizzas are also a hit among residents.

The Cozy Corner (Placencia sidewalk, tel. 501/523-3280, cozycorner@btl.net, 7am-10pm Tues.-Sun., US$8-13) has a relaxed open-air atmosphere and is one of the nicer beach bars. For breakfast in Belize you can never go wrong with eggs, beans, and fry jacks; it also offers a lobster burger, fish dinners, and good bar food.

Dragonfly Moon (main road, Placencia Village, tel. 501/523-2662, rongdi.chen@yahoo.com, 6pm-10:30pm daily, $5-20) is a welcome addition, serving the only authentic Chinese dim sum in Belize, in addition to creative fusion dishes like the sweet and sour chicken with cassava. The dim lighting, lounge atmosphere, and Asian furnishings add to the restaurant's uniqueness. Don't leave without trying the dumplings. Look out for a striking centerpiece at the bar involving a snake and a shot—try at your own risk.

FINE DINING

The revamped ★ **Secret Garden Restaurant** (main road, Placencia Village, tel. 501/634-9789, www.secretgardenplacencia.com, 5pm-11pm Mon.-Sat., US$14-17) is a breath of fresh air, offering up tasty Caribbean and Latin and Asian-fusion dishes, including delicious pasta, seafood gumbo, chicken Maya, and Argentinian steak, among others. There's a full bar and a wonderful ambience, with a garden patio or indoor seating. Don't miss the signature stacked ceviche or their Belizean lime tart, when available. The place fills up quickly, so be sure to make reservations.

Rumfish y Vino Wine and Gastro Bar (main road, Placencia Village, tel. 501/523-3293, www.rumfishyvino.com, 2pm-midnight daily, US$7-15) opened in 2008; the Solomons bought the place while honeymooning. Pamela, a wine specialist, imports Italian and Californian wine, and John works his magic in the kitchen. The menu features a mix of international comfort food, from fish-and-chips to pastas, short ribs, and more.

Most of the resorts north of town have fine restaurants to brag about. Grab a fistful of dollars and a taxi and bon appétit. At the Turtle Inn's **Mare Restaurant** (main road, 1 mile north of the village, tel. 501/523-3244 or 501/523-3150, www.turtleinn.com, 9am-10pm daily, US$15-35), the chef prepares meals with greens from his own on-site organic herb garden, as well as those grown in their upland sister resort's extensive organic vegetable garden. In fact, this is the best place to come for a fresh green salad in Placencia—as well as seafood, pasta, and oven-baked gourmet pizza.

The **Seaside Restaurant** (tel. 501/523-3565, 7am-9pm daily, US$12-28) at Robert's Grove Beach Resort serves mouthwatering seafood and imported U.S. steaks. Don't forget **Habanero Mexican Café and Bar** (tel. 501/523-3565, 3pm-9pm daily Oct.-May, US$9-15) for excellent Mexican food, just south of Seine Bight and across from Robert's Grove. A few miles farther north, **Maya Beach Hotel Bistro** (tel. 501/533-8040, 7am-9pm Tues.-Sun., US$14-28) has Placencians raving and unanimously declaring that the food is well worth the US$15 taxi trip from town (or US$1 on the afternoon bus). The options here are unique—try the four sampler platters—and owner Ellen Lee can help you pair your menu choice with the right wine.

GROCERIES

Wallen's Market (8:30am-noon and 1:30pm-5:30pm Mon.-Sat.) is on the main road, close to the soccer field, and sells groceries, dry goods, and sundries. **Everyday Supermarket** (7am-9pm daily) is in the center of town.

Information and Services
TOURIST INFORMATION

The **Placencia Tourism Center** website (www.placencia.com) is one of the most organized and useful in the country. Upon arrival in town, head straight to the **Tourism Office** (back of the Scotiabank Bldg., 2nd Fl., tel. 501/523-4045, placencia@btl.net, 9am-5pm Mon.-Fri.) in Placencia Village Square. After reading the various postings on the wall,

pick up a copy of the latest *Placencia Breeze* (www.placenciabreeze.com), a monthly rag with many helpful schedules and listings, including happy hours and house rentals. The tourism office also sells books, maps, music CDs, and postcards, and it has a mail drop; the office will not recommend one business over another.

The **BTL telephone office** (8am-5pm Mon.-Fri.) is at the bottom of the big red-and-white antenna.

BANKS

Belize Bank (8am-3pm Mon.-Thurs., 8am-4:30pm Fri.) is by the marina and has a 24-hour ATM. **Atlantic Bank** (8am-3pm Mon.-Thurs., 8am-4:30pm Fri.) has an ATM in town, across the road from Wendy's Creole Restaurant. **Scotiabank** (8am-2:30pm Mon.-Thurs., 8am-3:30pm Fri., 9am-11:30am Sat.) has an ATM just north of the BTL office.

HEALTH AND EMERGENCIES

The **Placencia Medical Center** (tel. 501/523-3326, 8:30am-4:30pm Mon.-Fri.) is behind the school. For after-hour emergencies, **Dr. Alexis Caballero** (tel. 501/523-4038) makes house calls, should you have a severe shellfish reaction. The village of Independence, a short boat ride away, has the nearest 24-hour clinic to Placencia. If a medevac to Belize City is not possible, this is where a patient will be taken in an emergency. There is a **private clinic** (tel. 501/601-2769) on Water Side Street, a public hospital providing health care to the poor, and a **pharmacy** (above Wallen's Market, on the main road, close to the soccer field, tel. 501/523-3346).

For **police,** contact the Placencia police station (tel. 501/503-3142), the Seine Bight station (tel. 501/503-3148), or the Tourism Police (tel. 501/503-3181).

MEDIA AND COMMUNICATIONS

Placencia Office Supply (tel. 501/523-3205, fax 888/329-6302, plaofficesupply@gmail.com, 8am-5pm Mon.-Sat., closes at lunchtime), tucked off the main road in the town center, has a copy machine and Internet access, and can send faxes; they will let you plug into their ethernet or use their wireless Internet (US$4 per hour).

Getting There

There are a number of ways to travel the 100-plus miles between Placencia Village and Belize City. The tip of the long peninsula is not as isolated as it used to be, and various options exist for continuing on to points south and west, including Guatemala and Honduras.

AIR

At last check, there were more than 20 daily flights in and out of Placencia's precarious little airstrip, to and from various destinations throughout Belize. Planes generally hop from either of Belize City's two airports to Dangriga, Placencia, and Punta Gorda (in that order, usually landing at all three), then turn around for the reverse trip north. For current schedules and fares, check directly with the two airlines: **Maya Island Air** (tel. 501/223-1140, U.S. tel. 800/225-6732, www.mayaislandair.com) or **Tropic Air** (tel. 501/226-2012, U.S. tel. 800/422-3435, www.tropicair.com). There is sometimes air service between nearby Savannah Airport (near Independence Village) and San Pedro Sula in Honduras; three flights a week cost about US$160.

CAR

The 21-mile excuse for a road from Placencia Village to where the peninsula hits the mainland was a rutted, dusty nightmare for decades. Then, in July 2008, the highest officials in the land gathered at Robert's Grove Beach Resort and signed the papers to begin the paving project that was completed in 2010. And the people rejoiced. It's now about a three- or four-hour drive from Belize City. From Belize City, most people drive via the Hummingbird and Southern Highways. About half an hour after turning south before Dangriga, look for a left turn to Riverside, where you'll begin the peninsula road.

The **gas station** (6am-7pm daily) is by the M&M hardware store in the center of the village.

BUS

Placencia Village is served by three daily bus departures and arrivals (in high season, anyway; service is spotty the rest of the year). Buses come and go from the center of the village, right next to the M&M hardware store, and current schedules are available at the Placencia Tourism Office and inside the Placencia Breeze. Buses to Dangriga (Ritchie's Bus Service, 501/523-3806) depart at 6:15am, 12:45pm, and 2:30pm Monday-Saturday, and 7am, 12:45pm, and 2:30pm Sunday. There's also a 6:15am express bus to Belize City (air-conditioned, US$13 pp). Otherwise, you'll need to change in Dangriga to reach Belize City. Cost is about US$5 or less for each leg of the journey. The more common—and quickest—bus route is via the boat to Mango Creek and Independence Village.

BOAT

For those traveling to points south, like Punta Gorda or Guatemala, or for those who want to avoid the Placencia Road, a boat-and-bus combo will get you back to the mainland and on your way. **Hokey Pokey Water Taxi** (tel. 501/523-2376, 501/601-0271, or 501/601-8897) provides regular service between the gas station dock behind M&M Hardware in the center of the village and the dilapidated landing at Mango Creek, charging US$5 one-way for the 15-minute trip through bird-filled mangrove lagoons. Boats leave Placencia at 6:45am, 10am, 12:30pm, 2:30pm, 4pm, and 5pm daily, and 6pm Monday-Saturday; the same boat turns around for the reverse trip: 6:30am, 7:30am, 8am, 10am, 11am, noon, 2:30pm, 4:30pm, and 5:30pm. Hokey Pokey is a reliable family-run operation, proudly steered by captains Pole, Lito, and Caral.

Bus connections to all points are

Cruise Ship Tourism in Placencia

In 2013, the Government of Belize signed a $50 million contract with Norwegian Cruise Lines (NCL), authorizing NCL to develop Harvest Caye—a 75-acre untouched island of mangroves and beach, just under three miles off the coast of Placencia Village—into a "eco-friendly" cruise destination. This planned development will bring thousands of cruise ships passengers to the south, an otherwise uncrowded, pristine part of Belize.

The project has met fierce resistance from Belize's top conservationists, local businesses, and industry stakeholders, who are against mass tourism and are striving to protect the southern coast, as well as the country's reputation as a leading eco-friendly destination in the region. While NCL vows to adhere to Belize's environmental standards and to provide jobs for locals, the magnitude of the project leaves much to be desired: an island pier, a marina, a hub for mainland tours, a lagoon for water sports, and planned cultural entertainment using the various cultures of Belize. There's little doubt that dredging and development on this scale will harm the surrounding coral habitat, mangroves, and the Placencia Lagoon—one of three main habitats for the endangered West Indian manatee.

Despite ongoing protests, however, the project is advancing at a rapid pace. Cruise ships are expected as early as spring 2015.

coordinated with the 10am and 4pm boats from Placencia, so the traveler need only worry about stepping onto the correct bus when the boat lands in Independence after the quick taxi shuttle (US$0.50) to the bus depot by Rosa's Restaurant (5:30am-3pm daily). The last bus to Punta Gorda leaves at 8pm, sometimes later, and the last ride to Dangriga and Belize City is at 5:30pm. The earliest northbound bus from Punta Gorda arrives around 7am, and the James Bus express arrives at 9am.

TO HONDURAS AND GUATEMALA

The ship to **Puerto Cortés** (tel. 501/202-4506 or 501/603-7787, Honduras tel. 504/665-1200) leaves at 9am every Friday, returning at 2pm Monday afternoon. The trip costs US$60 and takes roughly four hours, stopping in Big Creek, Belize, for immigration purposes, and carrying a maximum of 50 passengers. Buy tickets at the Placencia Tourism Office. Every now and then (sometimes as often as a couple of times a week), a boatload of passengers arrives in Placencia from Livingston, Guatemala, and seeks passengers to take with them back to Livingston (with an immigration stop in Punta Gorda). Inquire at Caribbean Tours and Travels.

Getting Around

Placencia Village itself is small enough to walk, and if you're commuting on the sidewalk, walking is your only option (riding a bike on the sidewalk can earn you a US$50 fine). Speaking of two-wheeled options, there are plenty of bicycle rentals in town. If bicycling north on the road, know that Seine Bight is five miles from Placencia and Maya Beach another 2.5 miles. The cheapest way (besides walking) to get up and down the peninsula is to hop on a bus as it travels to or from Dangriga.

TAXIS

There used to be a free shuttle service up and down the peninsula, but no longer. In the meantime, there are at least a dozen green-plated taxis hanging around the gas stations and the airstrip. Rides from town to the airstrip cost US$6 for one or two people, to the Seine Bight area one-way US$12, to Maya Beach US$15. Ask around the gas station and tourist office, and look for posted rate lists to know what you should be paying. The more trusted and long-standing taxi services include **Radiance Ritchie** (tel. 501/523-3321) and **Traveling Gecko** (tel. 501/523-4078).

My own preferred driver is Noel of **Noel Taxi Service** (tel. 501/600-6047 or 501/632-0980); he works late in the night, ideal for solo female travelers.

CAR RENTAL

Rent a car for do-it-yourself land tours to the Jaguar or Mayflower nature reserve, or for trips to the ruins near Punta Gorda. Otherwise you'll pay US$50-100 per person to join a tour group. **Barefoot Rentals** (tel. 501/523-3066 or cell 501/629-9602, www.barefootservicesbelize.com) has a selection of cars (US$65-85 per day), golf carts (US$32-49 per day), and scooters (US$9 per hour). **Captain Jak's** (tel. 501/622-7104, www.captainjaks.com), right in the center of the village, rents golf carts.

MONKEY RIVER

An easy 35-minute boat ride from Placencia brings you to the mouth of the Monkey River and the village of the same name. Founded in 1891, Monkey River village was once a thriving town of several thousand loggers, *chicleros*, banana farmers, and anglers; that was then. Now, the very sleepy village of 30 families (about 150 people) makes its way with fishing and, you guessed it, tourism, though

the latter has been slow as of late. M lagers are trained and licensed tour g who work with hotels in Placencia to prov unique wildlife-viewing experiences.

Ninety percent of the structures you see have been rebuilt since Hurricane Iris destroyed the town in 2001. The village is accessible by boat—most often through the mangroves from Placencia—but there is also an 11-mile road from the Southern Highway that ends across the river from the village.

If you're on a tour from Placencia, after negotiating the mangrove maze your guide will take you into the river's mouth and dock up in town for a restroom break and a chance to place your lunch order for later in the day. Then you'll be off upstream, all eyes peeled for animals. You'll beach up at the trailhead to explore a piece of **Payne's Creek National Park,** a 31,000-acre reserve that is surrounded by even more protected area. You'll hike through the dense brush, now a regenerating broadleaf forest that will take decades to reach its pre-Iris glory. Then it's back down the river for lunch and a stroll through the village. Most head back to their guest rooms in Placencia, but you may wish to consider staying a night or two, either to experience the village life or to get some serious fishing time in.

Monkey River

lations and Food

Monkey River are casual inns, d by those who enjoy isolation urroundings. Most offer a set fferent entrée served each day. re required for meals, but all afés will serve drop-ins some-thing, such as a burger or a beer.

Near the breezy part of town by the mini basketball court, **Alice's Restaurant** (tel. 501/543-3079, noon-3pm, US$6) offers meals served in a large dining room with a view of the sea; renting one of her airy wood guest rooms in a neighboring building costs US$23, with a fan and a shared bath with hot and cold water. **Sunset Inn** (tel. 501/720-2028, www.monkeyriverfishing.com, US$50) is a two-story green structure with eight musty guest rooms with private baths, fans, and hot and cold water. Decent meals can be had for about US$8. Monkey River native and owner Clive Garbutt knows the area inside out, and can easily guide fishing and snorkel tours. The **Black Coral Gift Shop, Bar, and Restaurant** (US$5-15) is one street back from the riverfront and offers simple fare, local crafts, and Internet access. The family that runs this hotel has an acclaimed guide service too, especially for sportfishing trips.

All hotels and resorts offer sea and land tours and trips. Local guides and fishers are experts. Sorry, there's no dive shop yet, but bring your snorkeling gear. Overnight caye trips are available, as are river camping trips: You're dropped off at the Bladen bridge and canoe down the river, stopping at night to camp.

Islands Near Placencia

GLADDEN SPIT AND SILK CAYES MARINE RESERVE

Belize's famous seasonal whale shark site is the protected **Gladden Spit and Silk Cayes Marine Reserve** (tel. 501/523-3377, www.seabelize.org), 26 miles from the coast of Placencia. Gladden Spit, known as "the elbow" of the Silk Cayes Marine Reserve, is where whale sharks congregate once a month March-June to feed off spawning fish. Divers have the unique opportunity to swim alongside these giant creatures. For such a memorable experience, contact **Splash Dive Center** (tel. 501/523-3080 or cell 501/610-0235, www.splashbelize.com).

SILK CAYES

The **Silk Cayes**, also known as the **Queen Cayes,** are part of the Silk Cayes Marine Reserve: three tiny plots of land ranging from a half to four acres, located a mile inside the barrier reef. One is a protected birding area. They are easily the most photogenic islands of Belize, and what the Silk Cayes lack in size they make up for in diving bliss, with rich marinelife that includes stingrays, giant barracuda, and lobsters. Snorkeling is decent as well, with coral and reef fish to explore just steps off the islands' white-sand beaches.

Most dive shops offer full day trips to the Silk Cayes, just under an hour away from Placencia or approximately 22 miles offshore. The main island, with restroom facilities and wooden picnic tables, is straight out of paradise, with frigates soaring above shallow turquoise and jade waters replete with coral. Across from this main island, you'll spot the second Silk Caye, this one a mere plot of sand and resident pelicans. Several tour company boats anchor here in high season—my advice is to come very early if you want some solo time before the crowds arrive, or to pick a weekday for your trip.

Snorkeling around these islands consists of colorful coral and small reef fish like sergeant majors and angelfish. The entry is easy and the water shallow, if rocky at first. It's an

Private Island Dreams

Where else in the Caribbean can you rent your own Caribbean island and live out your *Lost* fantasies? If you've got cash to spare or a big group to split the cost, then you've got exclusive access to a handful of Belize's most stunning cayes.

- **French Louie Caye** (tel. 501/523-3636, www.frenchlouiecayebelize.com, 3-night package US$1,260): The caye is about eight miles east of Placencia Village, with its own beach, coral reef—ideal for walk-in snorkeling—fishing dock, and a two-bedroom wooden house with verandas. You can even pitch a tent for the kids if you choose, just for kicks. Accommodations are rustic but cozy and eco-friendly. An on-site caretaker cooks "catch and eat" meals and can take you on a night snorkel tour. No other guests will be there when you book—you'll have the entire island to yourself.

- **Hatchet Caye** (tel. 501/533-4446, www.hatchetcaye.com/belize-private-island-rental, US$250-300): Located 17 miles east of Placencia, the island accommodates 26 guests for weddings, group retreats, and more. Features include a beautiful beach, a swimming pool, and a restaurant on-site, plus a full-service dive shop.

- **Lime Caye** (tel. 501/722-0070 or cell 501/604-3548, www.garbuttsfishinglodge.com, 2-day package US$345, 4-day package US$700, includes cabin, food, snorkeling, transportation, and park fee): This island, off Belize's deep south coast and sitting in the Sapodilla Cayes Marine Reserve, is the site of turtle nesting. It offers basic seafront huts sitting atop the sea (with outdoor showers and rustic bathrooms), a pretty white sand beach, and excellent snorkeling, where you're likely to be the only one exploring the reef. It doesn't get more distant or authentic than Lime Caye.

- **Ranguana Caye** (U.S. tel. 800/565-9757, tel. 501/523-3565, www.robertsgrove.com/belize-private-islands, 3-night package US$1,035): A private island two acres in size and 18 miles (90 minutes by boat) from the Placencia Peninsula, Ranguana is dreamy. Three rustic cabanas on stilts have private baths, and there's a housekeeper. The surrounding scenery of turquoise and jade seas is breathtaking.

- **Robert's Caye** (U.S. tel. 800/565-9757, tel. 501/523-3565, www.robertsgrove.com/belize-private-islands, US$490): This one-acre semiprivate island 10 miles from the Placencia coast has four thatched-roof cabanas and access to a small bar and restaurant.

- **Cayo Espanto** (U.S. tel. 888/666-4282, www.aprivateisland.com, US$1,995) is as exclusive as it gets. This five-star, award-winning hideaway for the super rich is just three miles from Ambergris Caye and provides lodging and service with all the bells and whistles: beachfront villas with private plunge pools, private docks, luxury designer bed sheets, and your very own "personal houseman."

- **Coco Plum Island Resort** (U.S. tel. 800/763-7360, www.cocoplumcay.com/belize-island-group-rental, 7-night package for 24 guests at $49,216), located on Coco Plum Caye, offers 14 cabanas for rent, for up to 28 people, on a gorgeous 16-acre island. The island rental package is attractive, and includes all meals, unlimited local beers and rums, water sports gear, and up to five tours, two of which can be to the mainland. What folks rave most about here is the friendly staff.

ideal spot for beginner snorkelers or divers, or for an all around nice day of sun, swim, and beach. As compared to Laughingbird Caye, snorkeling at Silk is average—except for a unique snorkeling site now called Shark, Ray, and Turtle Alley, just a couple of minutes from the main island, where thanks to lobster fishers cleaning their catch from a traditional wooden sailboat, you can see giant, magnificent, three-foot-long loggerhead turtles and impressive, large southern stingrays, as well as lemon and reef sharks. Observe from a healthy distance, as these creatures can all get aggressive even among themselves while vying for the scraps being thrown into the sea. Splash Dive Center includes this snorkel stop on day trips to the Silk Cayes.

Diving at Silk Cayes is excellent, with a couple of walls to explore. The North Wall is one of the top sites in the reserve and in Belize, going down to 80 feet and offering a look at many of the Belize Barrier Reef's beautiful species in one place: hawksbill turtles, spotted eagle rays, moray eels, manta rays, black groupers, and the occasional reef shark. White Hole is a 30- to 70-foot dive that begins in a sandy area (resembling a white hole from the surface), where you'll spot yellowtail snappers, groupers, nurse sharks resting, passing spotted eagle rays, four-eyed butterflyfish traveling in pairs, angelfish, gorgonians, and walls of corals. Loggerhead and hawksbill turtles can also be spotted at the Turtle Canyons dive site, which goes to 60 feet, along with smaller species like spotted drums and arrow crabs.

HATCHET CAYE

The latest hit among couples and honeymooners, this 7.1-acre private resort (18 miles offshore from Placencia Village, tel. 501/523-3337 or 501/533-4446, www.hatchetcaye.com, US$250-300) offers eight decent casitas with all the amenities, outdoor decks, and an on-site dive shop with complimentary sports gear—from kayaks to Hobie Cats, paddleboards, and fishing gear. There's also a cute, small beachfront swimming pool and on-site bar and restaurant. The caye has a bit more of an upscale vibe, and it gets rave reviews from vacationing lovebirds. The beach is decent on the island, if flat in some parts. The island's location is ideal, however, a stone's throw from excellent snorkeling and diving sites off nearby Laughingbird Caye and off the Silk Cayes, which are visible from shore.

The Silk Cayes offer one of the best day trips off the coast of Placencia.

★ LAUGHINGBIRD CAYE NATIONAL PARK

Located close to the Silk Cayes, Laughingbird Caye National Park is an important protected area encompassing over 10,000 acres. With swaying palms, small beautiful beaches, an absence of biting bugs, shallow sandy swimming areas, roaming pelicans, and interesting snorkeling and diving, it's a popular day trip from Placencia, just 11 miles from shore or a mere 45-minute boat ride.

Laughingbird National Park was designated in December 1991 and gained World Heritage status along with the Belize Barrier Reef in 1996. It's managed by the nonprofit **Southern Environmental Association** (SEA Belize, office near Placencia town dock, tel. 501/523-3377, www.seabelize.org, US$10 park fee), also in charge of the Sapodilla Cayes, Placencia Lagoon, and Gladden Spit and Silk Cayes Marine Reserve, a famous whale shark site.

The reserve is visited regularly, mostly by researchers and travelers brought out by tour operators from Placencia for picnics, snorkeling, and diving. In high season, it's not unusual to see several tour groups on the island. Private yachts and sea kayaks also use the site

regularly, and some mooring buoys have b[e]en installed to prevent anchor damage to the surrounding reef. There is one **trail** through the center of the caye. A park ranger remains on the caye at all times and greets daily visitors to give them a five-minute briefing on the park, including dos and don'ts in this no-take zone. Named after laughing gulls that once inhabited the island, this particular kind of caye is referred to as a *faro*; the arms on each end make a kind of enclosure around a lagoon area on the leeward side. In this way, the island acts much like a mini atoll. It's also a 100 percent no-take zone. All of this is good news for those wishing to **dive** or **snorkel** the front or the eastern side of the island.

The snorkeling in particular is spectacular, and ideal for beginners. You'll find a lot of coral, sponges, and plentiful fish life. Starting in shallow waters, there are three designated snorkel entries. At the front side of the island, you'll spot sergeant majors, stoplight parrotfish, hogfish, porkfish, giant lobsters, sea cucumbers, and schools of blue striped grunts hovering over corals. Ask to see the **elkhorn coral harvesting station**, where healthy elkhorn is planted and eventually used to replace dead coral in other parts

Hatchet Caye is a favorite among honeymooners.

of the reserve, which you can also see while you snorkel—proof of Belize's continued dedication in maintaining its reef's health. The leeward or back side of the island offers even more dazzling snorkeling—be sure not to forget a waterproof camera to capture large barracuda preying on smaller fish, healthy soft and hard corals, bonefish, blue tang, and even rays and nurse sharks, sergeant majors, trumpetfish, porkfish, schools of black jacks, princess parrotfish, and surrounding silversides.

Shutterbugs should stay at the back of the boat upon leaving the island, around midafternoon, to capture Laughingbird Caye's gorgeous full-length view.

Both the Silk Cayes and Laughingbird Caye can be enjoyed in a one-day trip (no overnights allowed) if you charter a boat, but a full day on each would be a much better plan.

RANGUANA CAYE

Located 18 miles away or about an hour from Placencia, Ranguana Caye is yet another paradisiacal plot. Perched atop the Belize Barrier Reef, this privately owned caye, operated by **Robert's Grove Resort** (U.S. tel. 800-565-9757 or tel. 501/523-3565, 3-night all inclusive

package US$1,035), is a cozy two-acre island with a stunning white-sand beach at the front, swaying palms jutting out of its center, and all around blissful scenery.

There's a casual restaurant and bar onsite. Four charming blue wooden cabanas on stilts are tucked at the back of the island under the shade of coconut trees. No phones, no Internet, no problem.

Swim and snorkel off the beach in shallow waters or get some sun with a cocktail in hand. Entry starts at the ankle level, and visibility is incredible at lower depths. Divers will find decent sites to explore just a couple of miles off Ranguana Caye, including the **Fox Hole**, a wall dive going to 100 feet, where hawksbill turtles, angelfish, nurse sharks, barracuda, ocean triggers, and queen triggerfish all roam in deep blue waters. Splash Dive Center and several other tour operators offer a full-day excursion to Ranguana.

But you don't have to be a diver or snorkeler to enjoy this island. Rent a cabana, take in the turquoise views to the sound of birds and gentle waves, and walk the edge of the plot to feel as if you're walking on water. This island's glorious scenery encapsulates what Belize's cayes are all about.

Laughingbird Caye National Park is a great island getaway for the day.

ROBERT'S CAYE

It may not sound like it, but even a smaller, one-acre island just 10 miles from Placencia is plenty big enough to live out your castaway fantasies. Robert's Caye, owned by **Robert's Grove Resort** (U.S. tel. 800-565-9757 or tel. 501/523-3565, 3-night all inclusive package US$906), offers four red-roof cabanas partially towering over the sea. It feels much more like a resort and a man-made island, in contrast to Ranguana Caye, but the surrounding waters are no less striking. A boat ride is needed to snorkel or dive off the caye.

The on-site restaurant's outdoor deck is a perfect place to shoot the breeze.

TARPON CAYE

Fifteen miles east of Placencia Village or a 45-minute boat ride away, the five-acre plot of Tarpon Caye is easily a fisher's dream: A tarpon lagoon surrounds the caye's entrance, while along its edges, permit glide by all day long. That was Charles Leslie Sr.'s goal when he opened **Tarpon Caye Lodge** (tel. 501/523-3323, www.tarponcaye.com, $150 or 3-day fishing package $1,420) in 1996. Tarpon Caye continues to be family-owned

and Belizean-operated and is one of the preferred getaways for avid anglers in search of a local experience.

Right off the three bright cabins on stilts, perched over the sea and equipped with porch, hammock, double beds and solar power, is *spectacular* snorkeling, thanks to the Leslie family chasing off fishers and turning the surrounding waters into an unofficial marine reserve. On-site is the waterfront **Pesky Permit** restaurant, serving up excellent home-cooked Belizean meals and fresh catch. While the lodge caters primarily to anglers, it won't turn away couples seeking a no-frills, Belizean island getaway. One thing's for sure: Evenings on this caye are anything but dull, from the starlit skies to the local jokes shared at the dinner table.

WIPPARI CAYE AND WHIPRAY CAYE LODGE

Avid anglers will find their bliss staying at **Whipray Caye Lodge** (tel. 501/610-1068, www.whipraycayelodge.com), a family-run fishing lodge where they can chase daily after bonefish, permit, tarpon, barracuda, king mackerel, and more, when they're not relaxing in a hammock on this three-acre

The white sand beach on Ranguana Caye is postcard-perfect.

island. The lodge caters to an upscale clientele, but the eco-friendly accommodations are simple, with two cabanas of two rooms each and generator-powered electricity limited to a few hours in the evening. The **Sea Urchin Bar and Restaurant** gets excellent reviews and dining is family style.

LARK CAYE RANGE, LIGHTHOUSE CAYE AND FRIGATE CAYE

Directly east of Placencia is a series of inner reef cayes—small, uninhabited plots ranging from mangrove plots that are home to bird colonies to larger plots with not much more than a wild beach. Just 10 to 15 minutes away by boat, these cayes all have some things in common: bright corals surround them, the depths are shallow, and there's excellent visibility, even from the boat.

Several day-trip catamarans offer all-day snorkel trips for up-close reef encounters along these cayes: Lark Caye, Lighthouse Caye, and Frigate Caye. Jeff of **Daytripper Catamaran Charters** (tel. 501/666-3117, www.daytripperbelize.com, US$75 pp lunch) is an excellent choice—explore every corner at your leisure and take in the sheer beauty of this area.

POMPION CAYE

Occasional dive trips (no snorkeling) are offered to Pompion Caye, just south of the Silk Cayes. Many divers rave about the vertical wall dives here—up to just 40 feet deep—sites that are teeming with eels, octopus, toadfish, manta rays, large kingfish, and the occasional reef shark. The island itself, privately owned, offers some beach respite for day trippers.

Punta Gorda and the Deep South

Highlights

West African *djembe* drum, keeping Punta Gorda's African diaspora culture alive (page 181).

★ **Market Days:** Punta Gorda comes alive on market days, with eateries, shopping, music, and vendors and goods from all the district's villages (page 186).

★ **Snake Cayes:** A short ride from Punta Gorda, the protected Snake Cayes offer spectacular snorkeling in crystal-clear waters teeming with permits, rays, schoolmasters, barracuda, and other stunning marinelife (page 196).

★ **Sapodilla Cayes Marine Reserve:** This distant yet alluring cluster of cayes offers rarely visited dive and snorkel sites with abundant marinelife, giant corals, powdery white-sand beaches, and utter seclusion (page 197).

★ **Lubaantun Archaeological Site:** The ancestors of today's Maya used this ceremonial center, which boasts stunning views, thick forests, and several long-standing legends (page 201).

★ **Río Blanco National Park:** In addition to waterfalls, this beautiful national park offers diverse flora and fauna plus the possibility of jaguar sightings. Bring your camera (page 204).

★ **Blue Creek Cave:** Swim up to 600 yards inside this stunning cave—the source of the Río Blanco—near the village of Blue Creek (page 205).

★ **Drum Schools:** Two renowned drum masters teach how to play the Garífuna drums or the

The Toledo District is the real back-country of Belize to many—or what it used to be before the influx of tourism—and is the farthest in distance from Belize City, as well as the least marketed part of the country. Because of these factors,

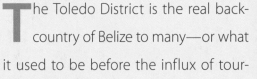

few pick "PG," as Belizeans affectionately call this area (short for Punta Gorda), and its off-shore Snake and Sapodilla Cayes over the more touristed Cayo District and the northern cayes. But just an hour and a half on a regional flight from Belize City will land visitors in the real backcountry of Belize, where they'll find all that is authentically Belizean in one place: virgin rainforests, waterfalls, five Mayan archaeological sites, a diverse population, and, more importantly, proximity to the most pristine and uncrowded of Belize's offshore islands for snorkeling, diving, and sportfishing in two adjacent marine reserves.

The Toledo District has the lowest per capita income in Belize, yet it is also the most expensive in which to live. The Creole, the East Indians, the Garinagu, and the Maya all coexist here. More than 10,000 Q'eqchi' and Mopan Maya are subsistence farmers in the Toledo countryside. This is chocolate country, home to organic cacao farms that supply all four of Belize's quality chocolate producers.

The district is also home to the least visited islands, clustered around the very last tip of the Belize Barrier Reef. The Snake Cayes, resting inside the Port Honduras Marine Reserve, are a day-tripper's dream, with virtually no other boats and waters teeming with marinelife at shallow depths. The farthest at just over an hour from shore, the Sapodilla Cayes—a designated UNESCO site along with other parts of the Belize Barrier Reef—beckon for a longer stay with two stunning islands and white-sand coral beaches at Lime Caye and Hunting Caye that are some of Belize's best stretches.

While tourism isn't yet booming in these parts, the mainland continues to grow. More restaurants are sprouting, jungle lodges continue to thrive while new ones appear, and the cacao trail is growing. The cayes, easily accessible by boat from Punta Gorda,

Previous: the beach and "natural pool" on West Snake Caye; view of Seven Hill Range from Punta Gorda's coast. **Above:** cabin on Lime Caye.

Punta Gorda and the Deep South

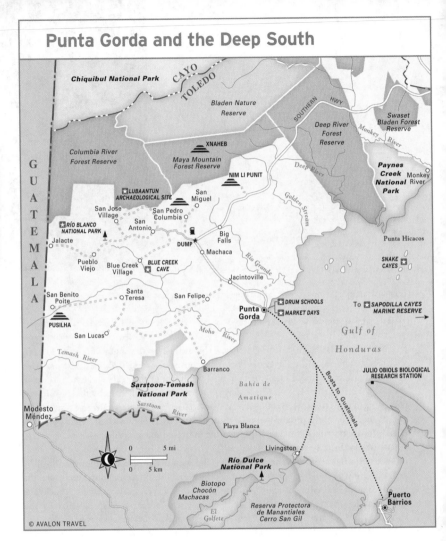

© AVALON TRAVEL

are slowly receiving more attention as the northern islands and southern cayes become more popular. Rapid improvements to the Southern Highway and San Antonio Road, giving easier access to sights and villages, and daily air service to and from Punta Gorda are helping to put Toledo on the map. There's never-ending hope that visitors will realize this is the most untouched part of Belize.

PLANNING YOUR TIME

To best get a taste of the Toledo District before or during your getaway to the Snake or Sapodilla Cayes you'll need to set aside at least 4-5 days. Spend your first half day exploring **Punta Gorda,** the urban heart of the deep south. Take a walk along **the waterfront,** stop by at one of the **drum schools,** and definitely time your visit to coincide with one of Punta Gorda's **market** days. Spend the rest of the day on a scheduled **chocolate trail** tour, to get a glimpse of a traditional Mayan village.

Make a day trip to **Port Honduras Marine Reserve** and its **Snake Cayes,** where you can snorkel and spot stunning coral and fish, dive, or simply soak in West Snake Caye's gin-clear natural swimming pool and relax on its coral white-sand beach.

Add on a couple of days of relaxation and adventure in the **Sapodilla Cayes,** where you'll snorkel and dive amid shipwrecks before lazing on the prettiest of beaches at Lime Caye and catching the sunset over the reef from your porch.

If you have time to spare, add on a final day trip for a visit to the inland **Lubaantun Archaeological Site,** a notable Mayan ruin. A sure bet is **Río Blanco National Park,** a 45-minute drive from Punta Gorda, offering a spectacular waterfall, hiking trail, caves, and plenty of stunning scenery. See where the Río Blanco begins at stunning **Blue Creek Cave.**

Punta Gorda

Toledo District's county seat and biggest town, PG is simultaneously the lazy end of the road and an exciting jumping-off point to upland villages, offshore cayes, Guatemala, or Honduras. Punta Gorda's 5,000 or so inhabitants live their daily lives getting by from hurricane to hurricane.

Punta Gorda is a simple port, with no real beach but plenty of swimming spots, and its winding streets are framed by some old dilapidated wooden buildings and newer concrete ones. The majority of inhabitants are of Garífuna and East Indian descent, although there are representatives of most of the country's ethnic groups. Fishing was the main support of the local people for centuries; today many anglers work for a nearby high-tech shrimp farm. Local farmers grow rice, mangoes, bananas, sugarcane, and beans—mainly for themselves and the local market. Fair trade-certified and organic cacao beans are an important export as well, used to make chocolate by the Green & Black's company in England.

ORIENTATION

Punta Gorda is a casual village with few street names. Arriving from the north, you'll cross a bridge over Joe Taylor Creek—next to which is the famous Garbutt's Marine and Fishing Lodge operation—and then be greeted by the towering Sea Front Inn, with the Caribbean on your left. After the road splits at the Uno gas station, it forms North Park Street (a diagonal street one block long) on the right and Front Street on the left. Following Front Street will take you through town, past the boat taxi pier, the immigration office, the market, and several eating establishments; continue all the way south to Nature's Way Guest House at the bottom of Church Street, followed by Blue Belize Guest House. The municipal dock and town plaza, just a couple of blocks in from the sea, form the town center.

If you arrive by bus or at the town dock from Guatemala, prepare to be greeted by a few local hustlers; feel free to shake them off by firmly refusing their services.

SIGHTS
The Waterfront

Even though there is no real lounging beach or developed waterfront, people go swimming and sunning off the dock just north of Joe Taylor Creek. The waterfront is rocky but quiet and tranquil, with small waves lapping the shoreline, and a walk along its length, especially at sunrise, should be a top priority of your visit.

Central Park

The **town park,** on a small triangle of soil

Punta Gorda

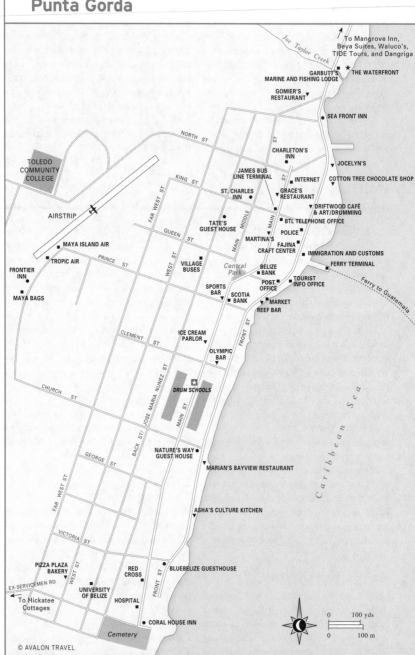

To Mangrove Inn,
Beya Suites, Waluco's,
TIDE Tours, and Dangriga

THE WATERFRONT

GARBUTT'S
MARINE AND FISHING LODGE

GOMIER'S
RESTAURANT

SEA FRONT INN

Joe Taylor Creek

TOLEDO
COMMUNITY
COLLEGE

NORTH ST

CHARLETON'S
INN

JOCELYN'S

JAMES BUS
LINE TERMINAL

KING ST

INTERNET

COTTON TREE CHOCOLATE SHOP

ST. CHARLES
INN

GRACE'S
RESTAURANT

DRIFTWOOD CAFÉ
& ART/DRUMMING

FAR WEST ST

AIRSTRIP

TATE'S
GUEST HOUSE

BTL TELEPHONE OFFICE

QUEEN ST

MARTINA'S

POLICE

FAJINA
CRAFT CENTER

IMMIGRATION AND CUSTOMS

MAYA ISLAND AIR

PRINCE ST

WEST ST

VILLAGE
BUSES

Central
Park

BELIZE
BANK

FERRY TERMINAL

TROPIC AIR

MAIN ST

MIDDLE ST

TOURIST
INFO OFFICE

Ferry to Guatemala

FRONTIER
INN

POST
OFFICE

SPORTS
BAR

SCOTIA
BANK

MARKET

MAYA BAGS

REEF BAR

FRONT ST

CLEMENT ST

ICE CREAM
PARLOR

OLYMPIC
BAR

JOSE MARIA NUNEZ ST

CHURCH ST

DRUM SCHOOLS

MAIN ST

BACK ST

NATURE'S WAY
GUEST HOUSE

GEORGE ST

MARIAN'S BAYVIEW RESTAURANT

FAR WEST ST

Caribbean Sea

ASHA'S CULTURE KITCHEN

VICTORIA ST

PIZZA PLAZA
BAKERY

RED
CROSS

BLUEBELIZE GUESTHOUSE

WEST ST

EX-SERVICEMEN RD

UNIVERSITY
OF BELIZE

FRONT ST

To Hickatee
Cottages

HOSPITAL

CORAL HOUSE INN

Cemetery

0   100 yds
0   100 m

© AVALON TRAVEL

roughly in the center of town, has an appropriately sleepy air to it, though plenty of activity swirls around it. At the north end is a raised stage dedicated to the "Pioneers of Belizean Independence." In the center of the park is a dry fountain, along with a few green cement benches, and a giant clock tower on the south end. On market days, this is an especially pleasant spot to take a break, enjoy the blue sky, and watch the activities of the villagers who have come in to sell their produce.

★ Drum Schools

PG's diverse population provides a chance to learn drumming from two African-rooted cultures: Garífuna and Creole. For Garífuna drumming, Raymond "Ray" McDonald of the **Warasa Drum School** (New Rd., tel. 501/632-7701, www.warasadrumschool.com, 4:30pm-8pm Mon.-Fri., 9am-8pm Sat.-Sun., US$12.50 per hour drum lesson, US$25 per hour drum making) is one of Belize's top drummers and a local star in Punta Gorda for his undeniable skills. He offers an introductory class on Garífuna drumming; learn about the various rhythms, how to produce the correct sound, and then start jamming. Ray also teaches drum making (ask to see

his very own custom collection) and drumming at various lodges in town, particularly at Hickatee Cottages. The school's location in a Garífuna Reserve area on the edge of town is currently being upgraded with a large new thatched hut.

Continue your drumming tour of Belize's south with the **Maroon Creole Drum School** (main contact at Driftwood Café & Art, 9 Front St., tel. 501/632-7841 or 501/668-7733, methos_drums@hotmail.com, 7am-4pm daily, US$10 per hour), run by renowned Belizean musician and drum master Emmeth Young, previously located in San Pedro Colombia and now in his new home in Punta Gorda town. Emmeth, originally from the Creole village of Gales Point, is a talented man whose drumming and efforts to preserve Belizean culture have been featured on the Travel Channel, among other media. Emmeth's *sambai* rhythms, which he learned as early as age eight, can be traced half a millennium back to the Ibo people of West Africa. Ask Emmeth about his "Drums not guns" initiative. At the school's location near Joe Taylor's Creek, they host "Black Pot Fridays"—an evening complete with hearth-cooked meals, drinks, drumming, and chanting under a massive *palapa*.

Central Park

SPORTS AND RECREATION
Fishing, Diving, and Snorkeling

The waterways around Punta Gorda offer anglers the rare chance to bag a grand slam (permit, tarpon, bonefish, and snook). Fly-fishing is generally possible between November and May, in shallow areas around the cayes, mangroves, and river mouths. Reel fishing is possible throughout the year, up the rivers or in the ocean; cast for snappers, groupers, jacks, barracuda, mackerels, or kingfish. Most guides help you bring your fish back and find someone to cook it up for you. Fishing trips can run upward of US$400-500 for four people.

Garbutt's Marine and Fishing Lodge (tel. 501/722-0070 or 501/604-3548, www.garbuttsfishinglodge.com), next to Joe Taylor Creek, at the entrance to Punta Gorda, is a top-notch operation run by the Garbutt brothers, who were raised in nearby Punta Negra and grew up exploring these waters. They offer the most reliable way to get out to the cayes and go fly-fishing, diving, or snorkeling. Fishing charter packages for groups include on-site seafront cabin lodging (7 nights US$2,865 pp, all-inclusive). They are also dive masters and offer PADI classes and certification as well as self-guided (US$5 per hour) or guided (half-day US$12.50) kayak rentals.

TIDE Tours (1 Mile San Antonio Rd., tel. 501/722-2274, www.tidetours.org, 7:30am-4:30pm Mon.-Fri., reduced hours Sat.) offers snorkeling (US$145 pp for 2 people) and fishing trips to the Snake Cayes or Sapodilla Cayes. TIDE Tours is the customer service branch of the Toledo Institute for Development and Environment (TIDE), Belize's only "ridges to reef" NGO. TIDE does much of the guide training in the area, helping to teach people sustainable, often tourism-related, skills. TIDE staff promote tours to protected areas and give presentations on their work in the Port Honduras Marine Reserve, in Paynes Creek National Park, and on the Private Lands Initiative. They also do

Drum master Emmeth Young teaches at his Maroon Creole Drum School.

tours to archaeological sites, caves, and other inland attractions. Revenue generated from TIDE Tours is used for education and outreach efforts.

BlueBelize Tours (tel. 501/722-2678, www.bluebelize.com) is owned and run by Dan Castellanos, a local fisherman, guide, and PADI dive master who specializes in fishing (US$325 for 2 people) and snorkeling tours (US$250 for two). He has led National Geographic and BBC film crews around the area.

Kayaking

TIDE Tours (41 Front St., tel. 501/722-2129, www.tidetours.org, 7:30am-4:30pm Mon.-Fri., reduced hours Sat.) offers numerous inland and sea trips, including river kayaking (US$90 pp for 2 people). Kayak rentals (US$2.50 per hour) are also available. Many guesthouses also include complimentary kayak use. In town, you can explore Joe Taylor Creek, and if you're staying inland, the riverside lodges are ideal to launch your canoe.

Caving

With the largest number of Mayan villages in Belize, it's not surprising that Punta Gorda offers some of the country's most off-the-beaten-path caving and hiking sites. **Toledo Cave and Adventure Tours** (tel. 501/604-2124, www.travelbelize.de, US$95-115) is your best bet for trips to some of Belize's lesser-known attractions, including **Yok Balum Cave, Tiger Cave, Gibnut Cave,** and **Oke'bal Ha.** Owner Bruno Kuppinger, longtime resident of Punta Gorda, is an adventure junkie who loves to get deep in the bush. He also runs Sun Creek Lodge and offers countrywide tours and group pickups from Belize City.

For some cave tubing fun, folks rave about **Big Falls Adventures** (Southern Hwy., Big Falls, tel. 501/634-6979 or 501/631-3497, www.bigfallsextremeadventures.com, 8am-4pm daily, US$48-60, lunch US$10 extra), offering tubing along the Río Grande, followed by a dip in a local hot spring before getting back down into the river (I opted for the zip line across Big Falls).

Tours and Day Trips

Toledo offers more cultural tours than any other district, thanks to its diverse population, which includes East Indians, Maya, Garinagu, Creoles, and more. You can spend the morning in a Mayan community and the afternoon at a seaside Garífuna fishing village a couple of hours later, observing two entirely different worlds and lifestyles.

The most unique immersion experience in Toledo is to sign up for a Mayan village homestay. You can arrange this with the **Toledo Ecotourism Association** (TEA) program—contact Chet Schmidt at **Nature's Way** (tel. 501/702-2119, teabelize.org); with the **Aguacate Belize Homestay Program** (tel. 501/633-9954, www.aguacatebelize.com/homestay-program, US$9 pp per night, meals US$3.50 pp per meal, US$5 registration fee); or with the village of **San Jose** (contact Justino Pec, tel. 501/722-0109 or 501/668-7378, peck.justino@gmail.com).

Otherwise, if you're short on time and would rather spend the most of your time on the cayes, but still want a taste of Mayan life, an excellent option is to go on **Eladio Pop's Cacao Trail** in San Pedro Colombia. Eladio is a one-of a-kind individual, full of enthusiasm and knowledge of organic farming. He will walk you through his cacao orchards and land, showing you the cacao process from bean to chocolate. You'll end up at his home,

Garbutts Marine and Fishing Lodge offers day trips to the nearby cayes and overnight stays on Lime Caye.

where you'll get to watch cacao roasting and grind some yourself before tasting a delicious cup of hot chocolate the way the Maya used to have it. Tours are arranged through local lodges and operators, including **Toledo Cave and Adventure Tours** (tel. 501/604-2124, www.travelbelize.de, US$90 pp) or **Cotton Tree Lodge** (tel. 501/670-0557).

The Cho family runs **Ixcacao Maya Belizean Chocolate** (formerly called Cyrila's Chocolate, tel. 501/742-4050 or cell 501/660-2840, www.ixcacaomayabelizeanchocolate.com, US$32.50 for two) in the village of San Felipe. They offer a five-hour chocolate tour beginning with a visit to an organic cacao farm and continuing with lunch in Cyrila's home. She and her daughter then lead a chocolate-making session. They also offer shorter, two-hour chocolate-making lessons.

TIDE Tours (41 Front St., tel. 501/722-2129, www.tidetours.org, 7:30am-4:30pm Mon.-Fri., reduced hours Sat.), the tour operating arm of PG's leading NGO, specializes in cultural visits, including half a day in **Barranco**, a traditional Garífuna village, where you'll get to tour, sample Garífuna food, and visit the museum and the sacred ceremonial temple (US$95 pp for 2 people). Another option is a craft lesson in the village of San Miguel, coupled with a visit to Lubaantun (US$65 pp for 2 people). TIDE offers several tour combos.

ENTERTAINMENT AND EVENTS
Nightlife

There are a handful of small bars scattered around town, some with pool tables, all with lots of booze. The nightlife in Punta Gorda is a bit scattered, and there's no one best hot spot. You pretty much have to hop from one spot to another to find the crowd, or ask around. The most consistent place you'll find is on weeknights at **Reef Bar** (Front St., tel. 501/622-9783, 5pm-midnight Mon.-Tues., noon-midnight Wed.-Sat., 6pm-midnight Sun., US$3-5), where you can enjoy a drink on a top deck overlooking the waterfront. There's dancing and live drumming, mostly

as it gets closer to the weekend. The **Olympic Bar** (Clement St.) is also good spot to get a drink after dinner before taking it up a notch.

Waluco's Bar & Grill (Mile 1, San Antonio Rd., tel. 501/630-3672 or 501/664-7186, 7am-2pm and 5pm-10pm Mon.-Thurs., 7am-midnight Fri.-Sat., US$3.50-10) is right across from the sea, a short walk north of town, although at night a taxi or bicycle is best. The name means "son of the soil" in Garífuna. It's sometimes a happening spot, with live music and drumming on Friday and Sunday as well as during festival times. You'll find plenty of karaoke and some pool tables at **Seaside Heights** (tel. 501/722-2450, 10:30am-3pm and 5pm-midnight Mon.-Wed. and Thurs.-Sun.), just a block away from Waluco's. A little outside of town, you'll find a few more bars and nightclubs, open only on random weekends (9pm-2am), including **Roots Rock Reggae** and **Embassy** on the Southern Highway just outside of town.

Festivals and Events

Toledo's biggest event is the annual **Chocolate Festival** (Front St., www.chocolatefestivalofbelize.com, 3rd weekend in May) at the park. It's a weekend-long tribute to Belizean chocolate and the organic cacao farmers of the Toledo District. From a Wine and Chocolate Evening to open-air concerts with traditional Mayan and Garífuna music and chocolate tastings, Cacao for Kids storytelling and games, chocolate-flavored cocktails, and an all-day food and crafts fair on Front Street, there are events from Friday evening through Sunday to entertain both children and adults, who come from all over Belize. Be sure to reserve accommodations ahead of time, and bring plenty of small change—there's no telling how much chocolate or art you'll be tempted to take home. The best part is that all the funds from the festival go to support community projects.

The **Deer Dance Festival** takes place over a week in August in the village of San Antonio. There are Mayan arts, crafts, music, and food showcased, but the highlight is the

Toledo's Chocolate Trail

The cacao tree (*Theobroma cacao*, "food of the gods") has gained renewed importance in the culture and economy of the Maya in southern Belize. Thousands of years ago, Mayan kings and priests worshipped the cacao (or *kakaw*) bean, using it as currency and drinking it in a sacred, spicy beverage. A revival of southern Belize's cacao industry has since led to choco-tourism. A few area lodges and families have found ways to connect ancient cacao farming with the modern craze for high-quality fair-trade food and products.

Today, farmers sell their cacao crop to the **Toledo Cacao Growers Association** (TCGA, one block north of the town park on Main St., Punta Gorda, tel. 501/722-2992, www.tcgabelize.com), a nonprofit coalition of small farms that sells the beans to acclaimed chocolatier Green & Black's, a United Kingdom-based company specializing in fair-trade and organic-certified chocolate bars. Some beans remain in Belize, used by a few Mayan families and small-batch chocolate makers to produce chocolate for the domestic market.

Sustainable Harvest International (SHI, tel. 501/722-2010, U.S. tel. 207/669-8254, www.sustainableharvest.org) is a nonprofit organization working to alleviate poverty and deforestation throughout Central America. The organization works with more than 100 cacao-growing families, helping them develop multistory forest plots that mimic the natural forest; this provides a diversity of food and marketable produce for the families, plus a home for threatened plants and animals. Coffee, plantains, and other shade-loving crops are planted alongside the cacao trees, under a hardwood canopy. Sustainable Harvest Belize estimates that for every acre converted to multistory cacao forest, five acres are saved from destructive slash-and-burn practices. The organization offers sustainable chocolate tours and other voluntourism opportunities at work sites in southern Belize. Accommodations range from rustic homestays to the stilted cabins of Cotton Tree Lodge, where SHI maintains a demo garden.

costume performance of the deer dance, an ancient ritual that reenacts the hunting of a deer, from chase to capture, acted out to traditional Mayan harps and violins. This is one of the most off-the-beaten-path cultural events you could attend.

One of the largest Garífuna cultural events in the country, the **Battle of Drums** (50 Main St., www.battleofthedrums.org) takes place in Punta Gorda, usually the weekend preceding November 19, Garífuna Settlement Day. While there are weekend-long events celebrating Garífuna culture through concerts and food fetes, the main event takes place on Saturday night, when drumming teams from all of Belize's Garífuna towns and villages, and from neighboring Honduras and Guatemala, compete for the title of best Garífuna drumming team. It's a spectacular display of music and dance and culture. Hotel rooms book up almost half a year in advance, so be prepared, and check the local papers for ticket prices, event times, and location details. You can

also contact **Beya Suites** (tel. 501/722-2188 or 501/722-2956), the chief organizers of this event, for more information.

Mayan culture is celebrated in all its glory on **Maya Day** (Tumul K'in Center of Learning, Blue Creek, Mar.) in the village of Blue Creek. Folks descend from all over Belize to attend this event, which includes traditional dancing and performances, tortilla-baking competitions, firewood-splitting contests, plenty of *caldo* tastings, and other Mayan-inspired recreation. Get a copy of the latest *Toledo Howler* from the **BTIA Tourist Office** (Main St., tel. 501/722-2531) or pick up a local newspaper for details.

SHOPPING

Next door to the airstrip, at **Maya Bags** craft workshop (tel. 501/722-2175, www.mayabags.org, 9am-5pm Mon.-Fri.), about 90 women from eight Mayan villages participate in this craft and export venture. The women make hand-woven bags (US$50-140), embroidered yoga mats (US$43), beach bags, jipijapa purses, and other unique products. The bags are absolutely gorgeous, especially the clutches. If you have time, you can order a custom embroidered design; the craftsmanship is so good that the bags were featured in *Vogue* magazine in 2010 and sold in Barneys for several years. They also make home decorating items, from vases to throw pillows.

Tienda La Indita Maya (24 Main Middle St., 9am-5pm Mon.-Fri.) carries handmade jewelry, wooden bowls, pottery, and other handicrafts. The store lies just north of Central Park, at the end opposite the clock tower. Also check the **Fajina Women's Group Craft Center** on Front Street near the ferry pier (7am-11am Mon.-Sat.). It's a small co-op for quality Mayan crafts run by the Q'eqchi' and Mopan women. You'll find jipijapa baskets, *cuxtales* (bags), slate carvings, calabash carvings, jewelry, textiles, and embroidered clothes—when they're open, that is. If the door is closed, ask upstairs at the restaurant to get it opened up.

You can find Creole drums at the **Driftwood Café & Art** (9 Front St., tel. 501/632-7841, 7am-4pm daily), made by locally renowned Creole drummer Emmeth Young, as well as other African-inspired crafts, clothing, and souvenirs.

For beautiful furniture pieces, made solely from Toledo District woods, mahogany to gorilla, stop by the showroom at **Belize Wood Works** (Front St., across from Reef's Bar, tel. 501/604-2124 or 501/665-6778, www.belize-woodworks.com, 8am-noon Mon., Wed., and Fri., 8am-4pm Sat., US$100-800), where you'll see sample dressers, chairs, and hand-carved Mayan doors. Exports are available to Canada and the United States. There are plenty of other shops along the market in town, though most of the wares are likely from neighboring Guatemala.

If you're a chocolate lover, don't miss the **Cotton Tree Chocolate Shop** (2 Front St., just south of the Uno station, tel. 501/621-8772, www.cottontreechocolate.com, 8am-noon and 1:30-5pm Mon.-Fri., 8am-noon

Sat.). They make milk, white, and dark chocolates; in addition to free chocolate samples, tours are available by appointment. A small gift shop sells chocolates, cocoa mix, cocoa butter, whole vanilla beans, and handmade chocolate soap by Dawn and Jo's Soap Company, which looks good enough to eat.

★ Market Days

Although there are four weekly market days, Wednesday and Saturday are the biggest. Monday and Friday are smaller but still interesting. Many Maya vendors sell wild coriander, yellow or white corn, chile peppers of various hues, cassava, tamales wrapped in banana leaves, star fruit, mangoes, and much more. Many of the women and children bring handmade crafts as well. Laughing children help their parents. If you're inclined to snap a photo, ask permission first—and perhaps offer to buy something. Folks here are the most sensitive to photos that I've encountered in Belize. If you're refused, smile and put your lens cap back on.

ACCOMMODATIONS
Under US$25

Punta Gorda's few hotels and guesthouses occupy the blocks of Front Street near the main dock as well as a couple farther back; a good rule of thumb is not to book a room that is accessed via a smoky bar and pool hall (for example, at the Mira Mar). Quieter options are only a few blocks or a few minutes off the waterfront and an easy walk or bike ride away.

You're apt to run into all sorts of interesting travelers from around the world at **Nature's Way Guest House** (65 Front St., tel. 501/702-2119, natureswayguesthouse@hotmail.com, US$19-24), which really is more akin to a hostel. Set at the back of a lush well-kept garden are six small, very basic fan-cooled guest rooms with bunk beds, all sharing baths. Three basic guest rooms have private baths and showers, although they are not much different in decor. Nature's Way serves a good breakfast, and you'll have access to all the activities in the area. The place is run by Chet Schmidt and his Belizean wife. Chet is an American expat and Vietnam veteran who has been here for over four decades; he also spent 13 years teaching in the surrounding villages. He can help arrange kayak trips, rainforest treks, camping, exploration of uninhabited cayes, visits to archaeology sites, and Maya and Garífuna guesthouse stays with award-winning TEA.

Located on a quiet street toward the very back of the town center is the **Circle Inn** (117 West St., tel. 501/722-2726), a Garífuna-owned guesthouse, run by Aurora "Rhoda" Coe, who does a good job of making sure her seven basic guest rooms are clean and fresh; four are shared with double or single beds (US$13-18), and three have double beds and private baths (US$20). It's a decent place to rest your head if everything else is booked in town, and about a 15-minute walk to the town center.

US$25-50

St. Charles Inn (23 King St., tel. 501/722-2149, stcharlespg@btl.net, US$32.50 or US$43.50 with a/c) is centrally located, with a dozen guest rooms and a shady veranda that allows you to observe village life below. The well-kept guest rooms include springy mattresses, private baths, fans, and small TVs.

As you leave the airport, you'll see the **Frontier Inn** (3 Airport St., tel. 501/722-2450, frontierinn@btl.net, US$35), a white two-story cement building. Twelve good value, immaculate tile-floored guest rooms have TVs, wireless Internet, private baths, hot water, and colorful bedspreads and walls; there's even a standby generator. The place is owned by a local airplane pilot. It's a short two-minute bike ride from here to the center of town.

Tate's Guest House (34 Jose Maria Nunez St., tel. 501/722-0147, tatesguesthouse@yahoo.com, US$19-45) is a comfortable home with five double guest rooms in a quiet neighborhood setting. Ask for room 4 or 5; they are spacious, with ceiling fans, TVs, sunrooms, louvered windows, and tile floors, and each

has an additional entrance through the backyard. Internet access is available.

Charlton's Inn (9 Main St., a block from Uno gas station, tel. 501/722-2197, www.charltonsinn.com, US$44) is close to everything in town, and there's a James Bus stop across the street. The 27 guest rooms are well kept, with hot and cold water, private baths, TV, air-conditioning, wireless Internet, and fans; there are also nine furnished apartments available with monthly rates.

US$50-150

Occupying a breezy, ocean-looking rise next to the hospital, **Coral House Inn** (151 Main St., tel. 501/722-2878, www.coralhouseinn.net, US$90-100) is an excellent seafront bed-and-breakfast with a small pool and bar and a quiet yard. It was opened after the owners drove to Belize from Idaho in their VW Microbus. The four guest rooms are pleasantly decorated with soft colors, local artwork, and comfortable beds; continental breakfast, use of bicycles, and wireless Internet are free for guests. This is where one of Belize's recent former prime ministers used to stay when in Punta Gorda. Ask about the nearby Seaglass Cottage, a little one-bedroom, one-bath, small-kitchen option, pitched on a bluff above the ocean (US$125).

One mile outside Punta Gorda, up Ex-Servicemen Road, **Hickatee Cottages** (tel. 501/662-4475, www.hickatee.com, US$80-120) is a wonderful option on the edge of the rainforest. Your expatriate British hosts are knowledgeable about local flora and fauna, passionate about their "lifestyle business," and strive to run a green hotel and involve the local community as much as possible. After you've settled into your well-appointed wooden cottage (private bath, hardwood furniture, ceiling fans, and veranda) or the garden suite (more space, furnishings, and a kitchenette), take a walk through the beautiful grounds and nature trail, followed by a dip in the plunge pool. Hickatee Cottages is very popular with birders and naturalists; guests wander on a rainforest trail, participate in

Jungle Lodges Near Punta Gorda

Staying at one of Punta Gorda's several jungle lodges is a great way to immerse and get a feel for this lush, verdant district. The choices are surprisingly many, for a region that isn't as far up on the tourist trail as the western, Cayo region. But it's a great option for those who wish to experience the cayes but still want a taste of Belize's inland magic, even for a night.

Tucked away on the San Felipe Road, only eight miles outside Punta Gorda, **Tranquility Lodge** (tel. 501/677-9921, www.tranquility-lodge.com, US$110-135) offers four well-appointed guest rooms popular with avid bird-watchers and orchid lovers; both have plenty to explore right here on Tranquility's 20 lush acres (only five of which are developed at the lodge area). There were 75 species of orchids at last count and more than 200 identified species of birds. Rates include breakfast; guest rooms have clean tile floors, private baths, air-conditioning, and fans. When there are no other guests, it's like having your own private lodge. Upstairs from the guest rooms is a beautiful screened-in (but very open) dining room, where you'll enjoy gourmet dinners (US$15-25). All rates are negotiable in the off-season. There's direct access to an excellent swimming hole on the Jacinto River, as well as walking trails.

Cotton Tree Lodge (tel. 501/670-0557, U.S. tel. 212/529-8622, www.cottontreelodge.com, US$179-219, US$419 pp all-inclusive) is 12 miles up the Moho River from PG and is accessed either by boat or via the road to Barranco. Its 16 stilted thatched-roof cabins along the river's edge are connected by a raised plank walkway; ask about the deep-rainforest tree house. The lodge is one of several in the area trying to take "green" to new levels; Cotton Tree conducts "voluntourism" projects with Sustainable Harvest International, has developed a unique septic system using banana plants, and raises 50 percent of the food it serves in its own organic garden. Available activities include the cacao trail, treks to Blue Creek Cave, mountain hikes, river and village trips, visits to ruins, and the like, plus hands-on classes in subjects like chocolate making and Garífuna drumming. Sportfishing and fly-fishing trips are available as well. There is one honeymoon suite with a jetted tub and one cabin with wheelchair access.

Hugging a lush bend of the Río Grande as it sweeps near the roadside village of Big Falls, **The Lodge at Big Falls** (tel. 501/732-4444 or 501/610-0126, www.thelodgeatbigfalls.com, US$160-265) is an elegant and quiet retreat in a peaceful, well-maintained, green clearing. The nine cabanas are ideal for a nature-loving couple looking for a comfortable base from which to explore the surrounding country or just to laze in the pool and listen to the forest sounds. Special rates are offered for multiple

howler monkey research, watch orchid bees at work while having a cup of Toledo organic coffee, and observe the wild creatures of the night on the bug board. Bicycles are available to get to and from town. Ask about visiting the on-site farm, fruit trees, nursery, and orchid collection (40 native species at last count); rates also include a free visit to **Fallen Stones Butterfly Farm** (Wednesday afternoon, advance reservations required, maximum four people—an incredible opportunity). Also on-site, **Charlie's Bar** offers home-cooked healthy meals (breakfast and lunch about US$8, dinner US$17.50). Hickatee sometimes offers cultural nights, including weekly drumming lessons with Ray McDonald, a local Garífuna musician.

★ **BlueBelize Guest House** (tel. 501/722-2678, www.bluebelize.com, US$75-135 plus tax) is owned by renowned marine biologist Rachel Graham and managed by a lovely couple, Kate and Adam. The five cozy furnished suites—including one for honeymooners—are large enough to feel like apartments and are tastefully decorated, with one or two bedrooms, en suite baths, kitchenettes or full kitchens, hot and cold water, ceiling fans, lovely seating areas, and wireless Internet. The guest rooms open onto verandas or patios literally a stone's throw from the water's edge. Use of bikes is complimentary, as is continental breakfast, served on your veranda or in your suite. BlueBelize is very popular with visiting doctors, scientists, and

The Lodge at Big Falls is one of several jungle lodges just outside Punta Gorda.

nights and for families; it's a 20-minute drive to the town of Punta Gorda, and many day trips are available, as the Lodge at Big Falls is centrally located in the Toledo District.

Sun Creek Lodge (tel. 501/604-2124 or cell 501/665-6778, www.suncreeklodge.com, US$40-100) offers four octagonal cabanas with central posts and thatched roofs. Some have shared rainforest showers and toilets, a few have private baths, and the spacious Sun Creek Suite is for families or groups. Sun Creek is popular with European backpackers in that comfy-yet-primitive way. The on-site tour company **Toledo Cave & Adventure Tours** will take you wherever you want to go in the area, with active hikes being their forte—including trips and expeditions unavailable anywhere else. Sun Creek Lodge is at Mile 14 on the Southern Highway, about two miles from "Dump," near the Shell gas station. Owner Bruno Kuppinger, longtime PG resident and adventure tour guide, will pick you up from the Punta Gorda airstrip or arrange pickup from Belize City for large groups.

volunteers, as well as travelers escaping cold dark winters up north.

You can't miss the **Sea Front Inn** (4 Front St., tel. 501/722-2300, www.seafrontinn.com, US$119, includes continental breakfast) as you enter town: It comprises two towering stone buildings across the street from the sea. The 14 guest rooms and three apartments are also available for monthly rentals. Guests find comfortable, spacious guest rooms, no two alike, with TVs, fans, air-conditioning, private baths, and handmade furniture built with hardwoods. The third floor is the kitchen, dining room, and common area, overlooking the ocean.

Also on the waterfront, just before the bridge taking you into town, the Garífuna-owned and tourism board award-winning **Beya Suites** (tel. 501/722-2188 or 501/722-2956, www.beyasuites.com, US$75-175) looks like a giant pink-and-white wedding cake. Inside you'll find cheery staff to show you to one of the comfortable, air-conditioned, tile-floored guest rooms with large baths and a sinus-clearing floral scent. There's a rooftop, a restaurant (breakfast only), a bar, a conference area, and fast Internet. Ask about apartments and weekly rates. Owner Darius Avila is the founder of the popular Battle of the Drums, an annual Garífuna cultural event held in Punta Gorda every November.

Over $150

The area's sole rainforest-luxe property is

Belcampo Belize (tel. 501/722-0050, www.belcampoinc.com/bz, US$470), atop a forested perch high above the Río Grande and a gorgeous expanse of rainforest, five miles north of PG. This is a unique spot targeting a unique market. Belcampo's property encompasses 12,000 acres of rainforest and organic citrus, coffee, and cacao farms, including 4.5 miles of riverfront (reached by a rainforest elevator!) and Nicholas Caye, a pristine island in the Sapodilla Cayes. The sea is a 20-minute boat ride down the river, where you'll head for your sportfishing and snorkeling tours. Amenities include a pool, a farm-to-fork restaurant, kayaks and mountain bikes, a breakaway sitting room and veranda, and a spa as well as a screened rainforest veranda in your canopy-level tree house suite (there are 12); you may see a brightly colored toucan from your shower window or get a wakeup call from a howler monkey.

FOOD

Punta Gorda offers mainly cheap local eats, with the added benefit of fresh seafood and a few excellent vegetarian options. Many restaurants are closed on Sunday and for a few hours between meals. The town has several good bakeries, and fruit and veggies are cheap and abundant on **market days** (Mon., Wed., Fri.-Sat.). Some of the best breakfast and lunch joints in the market building are also only open these days; look closely just behind the market stands, along the wall, and you'll see hungry souls chowing down on Central American treats and coffee for dirt cheap. Notice which has the most crowds and place your order. Ask at any corner store for a sampling of the local Mennonite yogurt and bread and be sure to try a seaweed shake, which you can buy fresh and cold at Johnson's Hardware Store, across from the market. Keep an eye out for **Ms. Adriana,** who is one of the few Garífuna women at the market, commuting all the way from the village of Barranco; she sells cassava cake, kola nuts, and other interesting items on the sidewalk across from the market.

Barbecue

Don't miss Belizean barbecue chicken on Saturday, a tradition in much of Belize. The best in town is at **Kay's Barbecue Spot** (Queen St., near Jose Maria Nunez St., close to the park, 8am-3pm Mon., Wed., and Fri.-Sat.). You'll see her grill steaming up the block while she fills the stream of orders. The chicken comes with generous sides of rice and beans and a large fresh tortilla, all for US$3. Get here early, as she can run out by 2pm.

Belizean

There are some great fast-food places surrounding Central Park. **Grace's Restaurant** (Main St., tel. 501/702-2414, 6:30am-10:30pm daily) is a long-standing joint with typical Belizean fare like stew chicken (US$4), tasty conch soup (US$9), and eggs and beans with fry jacks. It gets traffic all day long, especially at breakfast, and there's a ton of seating space. Close to Charlton's Inn, **El Café** (6am-2pm and 6pm-10pm Mon.-Sat., 7am-2pm Sun., US$4-10) has cheap diner-style Belizean food all day long.

Waluco's Bar & Grill (Mile 1, San Antonio Rd., tel. 501/630-3672 or 501/664-7186, 7am-2pm and 5pm-10pm Mon.-Thurs., 7am-midnight Fri.-Sun., US$3.50-10) serves up daily local lunch specials, including stew chicken and fry fish, with the usual sides of rice and beans, callaloo (leafy green vegetable), or coleslaw. The dinner menu is more varied, with pastas, burgers, and barbecue. There may be music to go along with your meal if you come on a Friday or Sunday night.

Just next door to the Hibiscus Cafe is **Seaside Heights** (tel. 501/722-2450, 10:30am-3pm and 5pm-midnight Mon.-Wed., 10:30am-midnight Thurs.-Sun., US$4-10), serving Belizean, Central American, and East Indian options. Entrées range from burritos to *tarkari* (East Indian curry), and there's a full bar and a huge top-deck seating area overlooking the waterfront. Add to that a pool table and plenty of karaoke nights.

★ **Martina's Kitchen** (Main St., tel. 501/623-3330, 7am-3pm Mon.-Fri., US$3) is where the best johnnycakes are baked. They serve good ol' Belizean breakfast and lunch plates; orders are taken from a small window, and there's decent seating space. You'll get a basket of four johnnycakes with your eggs and coffee. Locals flock in and out with their take-out bags.

★ **Jocelyn's Cuisine & Catering** (Front St., tel. 501/661-9267, 6am-9pm daily, US$2.50-4) is a cozy little seaside shack across from the Uno gas station with a lot of charm, serving delicious plates of local breakfast—freshly made johnnycakes, fry jacks, and even waffles—and a lunch of jerk chicken or Belizean stews and seafood. There's seating under the tree on picnic tables, with a lovely breeze from the water.

The **Snack Shack** (near BTL parking lot, tel. 501/702-0020, 7am-3pm Mon.-Fri., 7am-1pm Sat.) is an expat favorite for breakfast, especially its giant US$3 egg burritos, a "gringo breakfast" option, fruit shakes, pancakes, and bagels. For lunch, there's a "build your own" tortilla option (US$5), with flavored tortillas of your choice. It's walking distance from the Immigration Office and good for a snack before you leave.

Chinese

A few Chinese restaurants offer reliable chop suey; some expats call **Hang Cheon** (Main St., tel. 501/722-2064, 10am-2pm and 5pm-midnight daily, US$3-10) the best Chinese in town.

Creole

★ **Olympic Grill** (Main St., tel. 501/702-0078, 7am-2pm and 5pm-10pm Mon.-Sat., US$4-9) is a local favorite, serving up Creole cuisine, including stews, pig tail, and fry fish. Perched over the water, steps from BlueBelize, is **Asha's Culture Kitchen** (80 Front St., tel. 501/632-8025, 4pm-10pm Fri.-Wed., US$5-13), a wooden casita with quite possibly the best outdoor deck and dinner setting in town. Asha's serves Creole seafood dishes made to order as well as curries and other entrées. A bright chalkboard menu with blue checks lists the day's availability, served up with two sides in generous portions (the garlic mashed potatoes are good). There is occasional live drumming here.

A couple of restaurants have opened their doors on the highway out of Punta Gorda. Look for Miss Aida's **Hibiscus Café** (Wild Cone St., tel. 501/632-7859, 9am-9pm daily, US$9-13), serving up authentic Creole cuisine—including boil-up, seafood curries, and local pastries

Asha's Culture Kitchen offers lovely views with dinner.

and juices—served under a tastefully decorated *palapa*, or the front and back garden, filled with hammocks and more seating options. Miss Aida cooks with spices from her garden and makes her own wines. I toured her cooking quarters and I can tell you, it looks like a museum, or rather, your grandmother's kitchen, filled with dozens of jars on shelves, juices, ice cream, and all sorts of goodies.

East Indian

An easy place to recommend for lunch or dinner is **Marian's Bayview Restaurant** (76 Front St., tel. 501/722-0129, 11am-2pm and 6pm-10pm Mon.-Sat., noon-2pm and 7pm-9pm Sun., US$5), located on a rooftop over the water on the south edge of Punta Gorda, across from Nature's Way. Marian's serves East Indian cuisine, seafood, or a good ol' plate of rice and beans from her buffet—all with a view of Guatemala and Honduras across the sea.

Ital and Vegetarian

The best Ital restaurant is ★ **Gomier's Restaurant** (5 Alejandro Vernon St., tel. 501/722-2929, 11am-2pm and 5pm-10pm Mon.-Sat., US$3-9), set in a small, humble space at the north entrance to town across from the Punta Gorda welcome sign. Expect a healthy haven of whole grains, homemade tofu, and lots of "good for you" options with a delicious veggie, vegan, and seafood menu. The tiny restaurant offers tasty and creative daily specials, such as barbecued tofu served with baked beans, bread, and coleslaw, plus a veggie grain casserole served with a salad (about US$5), a bulging soysage burger (US$3), delicious conch soup (in season), and tofu pizza. Other options include fresh local fruit juices (try the golden plum), soy milk, and soy ice cream. Ask Gomier about his vegan cooking classes.

Mayan

If you don't have the time to visit the Mayan villages, be sure to stop by **Fajina Restaurant** (Front St., tel. 501/666-6141 or 501/666-6144, fajina.craft.center@gmail.com, 7am-8:30pm

daily, US$3.50) for traditional Maya fare, typically a delicious bowl of *caldo* (Mayan chicken soup served with corn tortillas). The small casual eatery is run by the same women's group that operates the craft shop downstairs. Occasionally you'll find callaloo (leafy green vegetable), boiled plantains, or cohune cabbage on the daily menu.

Mexican

Palma's Tortilla Factory (Main St., 7am-1pm Mon.-Sat.) makes fresh tortillas every day and sells them for US$2.50 per pound; they also make tacos (3 for US$0.50), *panades* (little meat pies), tamales, and the like.

Seafood

The **Reef Bar** (Front St., tel. 501/622-9783, 5pm-midnight Mon.-Tues., noon-midnight Wed.-Sat., 6pm-midnight Sun., US$3-5) is a convivial rooftop affair on the water's edge, above the market, with the best view in town. The friendly Garífuna women in the kitchen and bar serve good seafood options, including conch and lobster in season, along with other local dishes. There's drumming and dancing on Friday night, and Garífuna *hudut* (fish simmered in a coconut milk sauce, then served with a mound of mashed plantain) on the weekend, as well as Belizean boil-up, both of which you should sample while in Belize. Saturday is barbecue day, and the grills smoke away while reggae music plays over the waterfront.

Casual Dining

As you follow the highway north out of Punta Gorda, look for a driveway and sign on your left just as the road is about to turn away from the sea. Here you'll find ★ **Mangrove Inn and Restaurant** (tel. 501/623-0497, 5pm-10pm daily, US$6-10), a family affair with a charming dining balcony, complete with a bar, cozy lighting, and African decor. The cook, Iconie, has worked in fancy resorts across Belize but prefers working at home. Expect savory fish dishes, pot pies, pasta, fresh salads, and rolls.

Tucked at the back of town, the **Pizza**

Plaza Bakery (121 West St., tel. 501/702-2676, 11am-9pm daily), on the south end of town, one street behind the university, occasionally has baked goods, including brownies, cookies, bagels, Creole bread, and honey whole-wheat oatmeal bread. Miss Norma also makes grilled sandwiches or pizza for lunch, although you'd better call and check first.

Groceries

Check at one of the two **Supaul's** stores for local yogurt. Sophia Supaul's store on Alejandro Vernon Street (known locally as Green Supaul's, 10am-7pm daily) carries imported cheeses (French brie in PG!), Mary's Yogurt (a must-try, in many flavors, including coconut), local jams and honey, a decent wine selection, couscous, white chocolate, vegetables, and fruits.

INFORMATION AND SERVICES
Tourist Information

Look for the **Toledo Tourism Information Center** (Front St., tel. 501/722-2531, btiatoledo@btl.net, 8:30am-4:30pm Mon.-Fri., 8:30am-noon Sat.), not far from the town dock and run by the Belize Tourism Industry Association. This is a concerted effort by local businesses to provide excellent and organized information to visitors; they'll recommend accommodations, tour companies, transportation, and more. You can pick up a print or PDF copy of *The Toledo Howler* (www.belizenews.com/howler), a local magazine published by the BTIA, for upcoming events and updated transportation schedules, often including a recent map of the area.

For information on the **Toledo Ecotourism Association** (TEA) and how you can you sign up to stay in one of the six village guesthouses or visit the villages, contact Chet Schmidt at **Nature's Way** (tel. 501/702-2119, www.teabelize.org). Near the municipal dock, you'll find the **Immigration Office** (tel. 501/722-2247, 8am-close daily), for departures to and arrivals from Guatemala and Honduras. The departure tax is US$15 if you spent up to 24 hours in Belize, plus the US$4 PACT fee if you've been here longer.

Banks

The **Belize Bank** (tel. 501/722-2326, 8am-3pm Mon.-Thurs., 8am-4:30pm Fri.) is right across from the town square and has an ATM. Continue one block south for **Scotiabank** (8am-2:30pm Mon.-Thurs., 8am-4pm Fri., 9am-11:30am Sat.), which has a 24-hour international ATM. Grace's Restaurant (Main St., tel. 501/702-2414, 6:30am-10:30pm daily) is also a licensed *casa de cambio* (moneychanger) and can change dollars, Guatemalan quetzales, or traveler's checks. You may also find a freelance moneychanger hanging around the dock at boat time.

Media and Communications

Opposite the Immigration Office are a couple of government buildings, including the **post office.** There are two Internet places just north of the park on Main Street, both with nice air-conditioning and decent machines: **Dreamlight Computer Center** (Main St. and North St., tel. 501/702-0113 or 501/607-0033, dreamlightpg@yahoo.com, 6:30am-8:30pm Mon.-Sat., 9am-1pm Sun., first hour US$1.50 per hour, US$2 per hour thereafter) and **V-Comp Technologies** (29 Main St., tel. 501/722-0093 or 501/601-0342, 8am-8:30pm daily, US$1.50 per hour), a nice operation with printing, copying, scanning, and even DVDs for sale.

Health and Emergencies

Punta Gorda has a **police department** (tel. 501/722-2022), a **fire department** (tel. 501/722-2032), and a **hospital** (tel. 501/722-2026 or 501/722-2161) for emergencies. **NJV's Pharmacy** (Front St., tel. 501/722-2177, 8am-1pm and 4pm-8pm Mon.-Sat.) is a well-stocked drugstore, with everything from a pharmacy to books and office supplies.

GETTING THERE

If you're coming to the area by bus, plan on nearly a full day of travel on either end of your trip south (at least 5-6 hours from Belize City). Consider taking the quick flight from Belize City, Placencia, or Dangriga to Punta Gorda.

By Air

Daily southbound flights from Belize City to Dangriga continue to Placencia and then to Punta Gorda. This is the quickest and most comfortable way to get to PG. For the return trip, **Tropic Air** (tel. 501/226-2012, U.S. tel. 800/422-3435, www.tropicair.com) and **Maya Island Air** (tel. 501/223-1140, U.S. tel. 800/225-6732, www.mayaislandair.com) each offer five flights to Placencia, Dangriga, and Belize City between 6:30am and 4pm daily. Tropic is usually more reliable and frequent in southern Belize.

By Car and Bus

Punta Gorda is just under 200 miles from Belize City, a long haul by bus, even with the newly surfaced Southern Highway speeding things up. Count on 3-4 hours by car, 5-6 hours by express bus, or seven hours on a nonexpress bus. **James Bus Lines** (tel. 501/722-2049) has a centrally located terminal in Punta Gorda, at King and Main Streets, and runs up to 10 buses daily between Punta Gorda and Belize City, departing 3:50am-3:50pm Sunday-Friday, with one express at 6am. The first departure from Belize City is a 5:30am express, and then service continues until 3:45pm; the only other express is this last bus of the day. The fare is US$11 one-way. The James Bus makes a loop through PG before heading out of town. A few other bus lines make the trip, but much less regularly.

Remember that you can get off in Independence and take a boat to Placencia, or you can get off at any other point, like Cockscomb Maya Centre (Cockscomb Basin Wildlife Sanctuary) or Dangriga.

GETTING AROUND

Ask your hotel if it provides free use of a bicycle, or rent one at **Gomier's Restaurant** (5

Alejandro Vernon St., tel. 501/722-2929, 11am-2pm and 5pm-10pm Mon.-Sat.), near the entrance to Punta Gorda (US$10 per day). It's a great way to navigate the town, which can sometimes be a tad spread out on foot.

Bus

Every day has a different schedule, but buses go to the Maya villages on Monday, Wednesday, Friday, and Saturday, generally around 11am, departing from Jose Maria Nunez Street (between Prince and Queen Street). From here it's possible to get to **Golden Stream, Silver Creek, San Pedro, San Miguel, Aguacate, Blue Creek, San Antonio,** and other villages. Some buses drop you off at the entrance road, leaving a walk of a mile or two. It's possible to make it a day trip and return later in the afternoon. Check the Toledo Tourism Information Center on Main Street for updated village bus schedules, or grab a copy of the latest *Toledo Howler* newspaper in town.

Taxi

Punta Gorda's taxis will take you anywhere within city limits for about US$3-4; look for their green license plates. It's US$10 to drive the six miles to Belcampo and US$12.50 to Jacintoville and the Tranquility Lodge. Or you can call on **Jonathan Supaul** (tel. 501/669-4823 or 501/628-0460, 5am-10pm daily). Also try **Castro's Taxi** (tel. 501/602-3632).

Car Rental

The folks at **Sun Creek Lodge** (tel. 501/604-2124 or 501/665-6778, ibtm@gmx.net) will deliver a rental car anywhere in Punta Gorda (if you're not staying with them); the cost is US$75 per day with a three-day minimum, or US$480 per week for a 4WD vehicle. They can also deliver to Belize City for a two-week minimum rental. Fill your gas tank at the **Uno Station** (Front St.), right across from the ocean; it accepts traveler's checks and credit cards.

Islands Near Punta Gorda

The Toledo District is the gateway to the least visited of Belize's offshore Caribbean islands—the Snake Cayes and the Sapodilla Cayes. For those who make the time and take the chance to venture this far south, the snorkeling and dive sites are rewarding, and with fewer boats (if any at all), you're likely to be one of the few out in the water. It's no exaggeration to say that you'll have the entire last end of the Belize Barrier Reef to yourself. Just be sure not to attempt the boat journey from Punta Gorda in rough weather. On a glorious day, this is as close as you can get to paradise.

Closest to Punta Gorda, a mere 30-minute boat ride away, are the **Snake Cayes**, part of the Port Honduras Marine Reserve. These are ideal for snorkeling, diving, and swimming, thanks to protected, no-take zones. These islands, along with the more remote **Sapodilla Cayes**, are not one bit about luxury—it's about adventure and experiencing Belize's nature and barrier reef at its best, with simple accommodations on two cayes and plenty of neighboring plots to explore above or under water. Relax in a phone and Internet-free environment in your cabin or camping at **Lime Caye**, and crash in basic rooms on **Hunting Caye**, home to one of Belize's most stunning beaches. You might not even use your room, it's that pretty outside. Try to stay at least two days in the Sapodilla Cayes area if you're heading that far. The Snake Cayes are an easy day trip from either Punta Gorda or the Sapodilla Cayes.

PORT HONDURAS MARINE RESERVE

The limits of the **Port Honduras Marine Reserve** (park fee US$5 pp) begin just three miles outside Punta Gorda, stretching as far as 160 square miles and encompassing mangrove forests and approximately 138 mangrove islands, plenty of fresh water from five rivers that flow into the reserve, and, in the distance, a seven-hill range with its peaks towering over the reserve. The **Snake Cayes** and a few other gorgeous islands are accessible for top-notch snorkeling and sportfishing—you'll likely notice private yachts on your way across the reserve, as top anglers head here for the best fly-fishing in the area, dubbed "the permit capital" of the world, not just Belize.

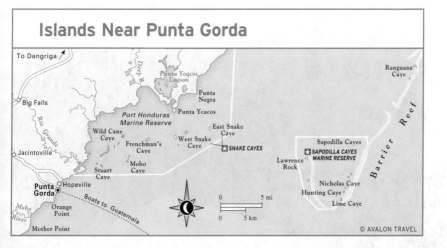

Islands Near Punta Gorda

The Port Honduras Marine Reserve is comanaged and funded by the nonprofit **Toledo Institute for Development and Environment** (TIDE, tel. 501/722-2274, info@tidebelize.org), based in Punta Gorda. Their marine conservation efforts in the area are significant, the most notable of which has been the protection of, and increase in, the number of West Indian manatees. Seven years after gaining protected status, the reserve now boasts the second-largest population of these gentle sea cows. The park rangers play an important part in monitoring illegal fishing activity and removing gill nets, as well as protecting Middle Snake Caye, a strictly no-entry caye used for monitoring mangroves and marinelife research.

Abalon Caye

Your first stop in the Port Honduras Marine Reserve may be at **Abalon Caye,** in the center of the reserve. Abalon Caye is home to the ranger station and six full-time rangers. It's a great place to learn about the area, included as a World Heritage Site along with the Belize Barrier Reef. Whatever you do, don't miss climbing up the 60-foot-tall ranger station's **observation tower,** used to spot vessel activity. A steep, narrow wooden staircase leads to views of the reserve. The 180-degree panorama includes the Snakes Cayes as well as neighboring Guatemala and even the Cockscomb range.

★ Snake Cayes

Shortly past Abalon Caye, you'll spot four plots in the distance, almost aligned from left to right. They are East Snake Caye, Middle Snake Caye, West Snake Caye, and South Snake Caye. Boa constrictors once lived here, hence the name.

The **Snake Cayes** make up the main area of the reserve used for daytime recreation purposes only—swimming, snorkeling, diving, and sportfishing—except for **Middle Snake Caye,** which is a strictly off-limits zone to everyone except researchers, with boats not being allowed to come within a half mile of the island.

Three of these accessible plots, ranging 1-2 acres, offer an incredible marine environment of healthy corals and reef fish on this end of the Belize Barrier Reef, and are a worthwhile day trip from Punta Gorda. Snorkel stops include South Snake and East Snake, before ending at West Snake for swimming.

At two acres, **West Snake Caye** (also called Lagoon Snake Caye) has a beautiful

view from observation tower on Abalon Caye

white-sand beach—the only one among these islands—facing a turquoise stretch of water 250 feet wide and 3.5 feet deep for ideal swimming. Even if not snorkeling, it's great for all around frolicking in a natural pool. There's a *palapa* on site for barbecues and not much else but glorious fine sand, making this one of the most romantic southern islands and fun daytime hangout spots.

South Snake Caye tops all for marinelife, with stunning schools of fish hovering amid bright corals. You'll need your underwater camera, as you'll likely gasp at the sight and abundance of fish in these parts, thriving in crystal-clear waters at relatively shallow depths. Giant barracuda, Caesar grunts, permits, schoolmasters, dog snappers, angelfish, porkfish, and porcupine fish are among the numerous species in these parts. **East Snake Caye**, home to a lighthouse, is popular for its stunning coral gardens.

While you get in or out of the boat on snorkel trips, keep your eyes peeled for spotted rays leaping up to one foot out of the water!

★ SAPODILLA CAYES MARINE RESERVE

One of the seven wonders of the Belize Barrier Reef Reserve System and the most southern of Belize's protected areas, the **Sapodilla Cayes Marine Reserve** (park fee US$10 pp, paid at Hunting Caye) is as remote as it gets. Few people make it out here from the mainland; most visitors venture over from neighboring Honduras and Guatemala, as well as a few locals from Placencia. Located 35 miles or 1.5 hours by boat from the shores of Punta Gorda—or an additional 45-minute ride from the Snake Cayes—it might seem like quite the trek (don't even attempt it on a cloudy, choppy day), but it's not that far to go for top-notch snorkeling and diving, gorgeous white-sand beaches on **Lime Caye** and **Hunting Caye**—the two available islands for overnight stays—and an overall stunning landscape of deep turquoise waters, flocking birds, and marinelife. These make it worth the extra journeying.

The reserve—co-managed by the Fisheries Department and the **Southern Environmental Association** (SEA, tel. 501/523-3377, www.seabelize.org)—covers approximately 80 square miles and is divided into a preservation zone, a conservation zone, a general use zone, and special management areas. It's also home to approximately 14 mangrove and sandy islands, many of which are privately owned, spread across its clear waters.

East Snake Caye

The sandy islands are considered to be among the most beautiful of Belize's southern cayes, and I agree wholeheartedly.

This last edge and boundary of the Belize Barrier Reef forms a hook or J-letter shaped curve, within which the Sapodilla Cayes are clustered. This is an area teeming with underwater life, where a ray jumping out of the sea or a loggerhead turtle swimming right up to the beach at sunset is no rare sight.

The reserve protects several endangered species, such as the West Indian manatee, three turtle species—with designated turtle-nesting beaches at Hunting and Lime Cayes—and over a dozen fish species. To add to its uniqueness, the Sapodilla Cayes Marine Reserve counts spawning aggregation sites, with whale shark sightings every year.

Lime Caye

Owned and operated by the Garbutt family, who run the successful **Garbutt's Marine and Fishing Lodge** based in Punta Gorda (tel. 501/722-0070 or cell 501/604-3548, www.garbuttsfishinglodge.com, 2-day package US$345, 4-day package US$700, includes cabin, all meals, snorkeling, transportation, and park fee), this rustic and gorgeous 3.5-acre island and resort is your best bet for an overnight stay in these parts.

An often-deserted soft white sand beach—a designated turtle-nesting site—will greet you upon arrival, while the rest of the island is white sand shaded by grape trees and coconut trees.

Stays range 2-6 days in one of five no-frills wooden cabins painted in bright pastel colors. Two larger, front cabins hold a mixture of bunk beds and a double bed, for up to six persons per cabana. The bathrooms are en suite, with clean and rustic shower tubs and toilets. Farther to the edge of the beach is a sea-facing wooden bunk-bed house, ideal for groups of 16—bathrooms are of the shared, outdoor variety.

For more privacy, opt for one of two adorable, stand-alone and basic **reef-facing cabanas on stilts** at the very back of the island, ideal for couples or solo travelers. These are nothing more than a double bed, nightstand, and shutters, but the atmosphere is cozy and the porch offers stunning views of the reef crest ahead, where the sun rises. Shared toilets and showers are a short walk away from the cabin. Bring sufficient towels as well as a rain jacket, as it can get cool in the mornings and evenings in high season. If

The Sapodilla Cayes have some of the prettiest beaches.

Hunting Caye

Under five minutes from Lime Caye is **Hunting Caye**, known for having one of the most beautiful crescent-shaped white-sand beaches in Belize, accented by a lighthouse.

A turtle-nesting site, the island serves as a base for staff from the Belize Coast Guard, Port Authority, the Fisheries Department (rangers), a lighthouse keeper, and the University of Belize (UB). Because of this, the island has a fun local vibe. You'll hear punta music in the background and voices chatting in Creole.

Luckily, UB does rent its basic, double bed rooms to visitors (contact Victor Jacobs, tel. 501/602-4546, vrrjacobs@yahoo.cm or vjacobs@ub.edu, US$40 pp). Camping is allowed (US$5 pp, bring your own tent). There's a large kitchen for use on site, if groups choose to cook for themselves. Otherwise, on-site meals are available with advance notice.

Hunting Caye feels a lot more spread out than Lime Caye, but it's equally as laid-back and charming, if it weren't for the small crowd of folks who live there. If you're staying on Lime Caye, ask for a ride to Hunting Caye for an hour or more of lounging on that gorgeous beach.

If you get the chance, meet the lighthouse keeper, Domingo Lewis, an interesting character who served 25 years in the British Army and has interesting travel tales to share.

Diving and Snorkeling

There's little doubt that this deep southern area of Belize offers some of the best visibility for snorkeling and diving. Few make it this far, but those who do will have an entire reserve to themselves.

The Shipwreck is right off Lime Caye, a 10- to 15-foot-deep dive site where you'll spot abundant marinelife—blue tangs, white grunts, angelfish, butterflyfish, lionfish, schoolmasters, and vibrant coral—surrounding a massive sunken ship. There are colorful schools of fish and amazing clarity, even in cloudy weather. The waters surrounding **Ragged Caye** offer decent snorkeling.

Lime Caye

you're up for it, you can get even closer to the elements by camping on the island (US$10 pp).

Haphazardly placed hammocks and iguanas shuffling in distant mangrove trees at the beach's end add to this remote, deserted island feel. Be sure to miss neither the sunset nor the sunrise, both of which are visible from the island—quite a rare treat!

On site is **Sanny's Kitchen**, run by the lovely Sandra Garbutt, serving delicious daily meals that are enjoyed family style on outdoor picnic tables three times a day. They consist of fresh seafood and Belizean specialties as well as classic cocktails. You'll likely spend time reading prior guests' messages and signatures along the dining area's wood pillars and walls.

On Sundays, a local family or two might occasionally show up from Placencia for the day, unless a group reserves the caye in its entirety. Activities from Lime Caye—besides tanning, swimming, and strolling around the island—include diving, fly-fishing, and snorkeling.

Lime Caye Wall is a top dive site, with plenty of big fish, such as groupers, snappers, giant spiny lobsters, and moray eels. Whale sharks also pass here, in season.

Snorkelers will be equally amazed at the health and brilliance of the coral and the spectacular Caribbean sea, with those vibrant turquoise hues, similar to the waters surrounding Belize's atolls. They wash over lush coral gardens, densely packed and teeming with fish life. At **Vigilante Shoal**, right off Hunting Caye, you'll spot densely packed corals, many in giant form, at a depth of barely eight feet. Within a hand's stretch, you'll spot huge spiny lobsters, 15-pound dog snappers, blue hamlets, blue tangs, bluehead wrasses, rock beauty fish, and other Caribbean reef species, like the stoplight parrotfish, sergeant majors, and angelfish. Impossible to miss are the massive mountainous star corals, pillar corals, and grooved brain coral. No other boats showed up while my guide and I snorkeled at our leisure.

Garbutt's Marine and Fishing Lodge (tel. 501/722-0070 or cell 501/604-3548, www.garbuttsfishinglodge.com) offers a range of trips, from snorkeling to "Discover Scuba" courses and fishing.

REEF CONSERVATION INTERNATIONAL

If you're looking for a vacation that combines conservation education and recreation, Reef Conservation International (ReefCI, tel. 501/702-0229 or 501/629-4266, www.reefci.com, divers US$1,195 per week, nondivers US$895 per week, all inclusive) offers weekly and monthly dive trips to stay on **Tom Owens Caye,** a small one-acre private island in the Sapodilla Cayes with incredible snorkeling. The boat leaves Punta Gorda on Monday morning and returns on Friday afternoon. Reef Conservation offers scuba certification courses. It's worth stressing that not only will you be diving in the Sapodilla Cayes, but you'll most likely be the only dive boat in the water (nondivers are also welcome). ReefCI offers various packages; there's often a discount for walk-in travelers and last-minute bookings. ReefCI customers have the opportunity to get involved in a number of projects, such as helping with the removal of the invasive lionfish and other preservation projects in the Sapodilla Cayes Marine Reserve. They also have the unique opportunity to get involved with the survey work, learn about the environment, and identify fish, coral, and

Hunting Caye's gorgeous crescent shaped beach is the least-visited in all of Belize.

invertebrates—and to combine this with recreational dives and other activities.

GETTING THERE

You'll find it more affordable to get to the Snake Cayes or the Sapodilla Cayes for a day trip when there's a group of at least four people heading out. Check your dates with **Garbutt's Marine and Fishing Lodge** (tel. 501/722-0070 or cell 501/604-3548, www. garbuttsfishinglodge.com) or with **TIDE** (tel. 501/722-2274, info@tidebelize.org), both solid transfer options; they can keep you posted on availability and tour dates. If you're staying on Lime Caye, the Garbutts will arrange for your transportation to and from the resort.

Mayan Upcountry

The wild, unique, and stunning southwestern chunk of Belize is referred to as "upcountry" or simply "the villages." The Toledo District settlements to the west of Punta Gorda are home to Q'eqchi' or Mopan Maya, whose descendants fled to Belize to escape oppression and forced labor in their native Guatemala. Anthropologists now believe that the Mopan were probably the original inhabitants of Belize, but that they were forcibly removed by the Spanish in the late 17th century. The Q'eqchi' were close neighbors with the Mopan and the Manche Ch'ol, a Mayan group completely exterminated by the Spanish. The older folks continue to maintain longtime traditional farming methods, culture, and dress. Modern machinery is sparse—they use simple digging sticks and machetes to till the soil, and water is hand-carried to the fields during dry spells. It's not an easy life.

On the outskirts of each town, the dwellings are relatively primitive; they often have open doorways covered by a hanging cloth, hammocks, and dirt floors, and animals may wander throughout. People use primitive latrines or just take a walk into the rainforest. They bathe in the nearest creek or river, a routine that becomes a source of fun as much as cleanliness.

Within the towns, past the thatched homes on each side of the road, it becomes apparent that the effects of modern conveniences are only beginning to arrive. When a family can finally afford electricity, the first things that appear are a couple of lights and a refrigerator—the latter allows the family to earn a few dollars by selling chilled soft drinks and such. After that, it's a television set; you can see folks sitting in open doorways, their faces lit by the light inside.

★ LUBAANTUN ARCHAEOLOGICAL SITE

Located on a ridge between two creeks, Lubaantun ("Place of the Fallen Stones") consists of five layers of construction and is unique compared to other sites due to the absence of engraved stelae. The site was first reported in 1875 by American Civil War refugees from the southern United States and was first studied in 1915. It is believed that as many as 20,000 people lived in this former trading center.

Lubaantun was built and occupied during the Late Classic Period (AD 730-890). Eleven major structures are grouped around five main plazas—in total the site has 18 plazas and three ball courts. The tallest structure rises 50 feet above the plaza, and from it you can see the Caribbean Sea, 20 miles distant. Lubaantun's disparate architecture is completely different from Mayan construction in other parts of Latin America.

Most of the structures are terraced, and you'll notice that some corners are rounded—an uncommon feature throughout the Mundo Maya. Lubaantun has been studied and surveyed several times by Thomas Gann and, more recently, in 1970

Maya Upcountry

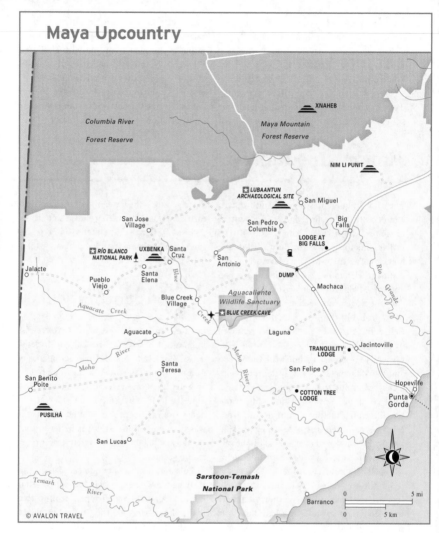

Columbia River
Forest Reserve

Maya Mountain
Forest Reserve

XNAHEB

NIM LI PUNIT

LUBAANTUN
ARCHAEOLOGICAL SITE

San Miguel

San Jose
Village

San Pedro
Columbia

Big
Falls

LODGE AT
BIG FALLS

RÍO BLANCO
NATIONAL PARK

UXBENKA

Santa
Cruz

San
Antonio

Jalacte

Santa
Elena

DUMP

Machaca

Pueblo
Viejo

Blue
Creek

Aguacaliente
Wildlife Sanctuary

Aquacate Creek

Blue Creek
Village

BLUE CREEK CAVE

Rio Grande

Aguacate

Laguna

TRANQUILITY
LODGE

Jacintoville

Moho River

Santa
Teresa

San Felipe

Hopeville

San Benito
Poite

Moho River

COTTON TREE
LODGE

Punta
Gorda

PUSILHÁ

San Lucas

Sarstoon-Temash
National Park

Temash River

Barranco

0   5 mi

0   5 km

© AVALON TRAVEL

by Norman Hammond. Distinctive clay whistle figurines (similar to those found in Mexico's Isla Jaina) illustrate lifestyles and occupations of the era. Other artifacts include the mysterious crystal skull, obsidian blades, grinding stones (much like those still used today to grind corn), beads, shells, turquoise, and shards of pottery. From all of this, archaeologists have determined that the city flourished until the 8th century AD. It was a farming community that traded with the highland areas of today's Guatemala, and the people worked the sea and maybe the cayes just offshore.

To reach Lubaantun from Punta Gorda, drive 1.5 miles west past the gas station to the Southern Highway, then take a right. Two miles farther, you'll come to the village of San Pedro. From here, go left around the church to the concrete bridge. Cross and drive almost one mile—the road is passable during the dry season.

The Unspoiled South: Toledo's Conservation Trail

Belize has the highest percentage of forest cover in Central America and the largest barrier reef system in the western hemisphere. These rich natural resources have survived relatively intact, primarily due to Belize having the lowest population density in the Central American region. This enviable status, however, is at risk, particularly in the south, where the country's most pristine environment—in the lush Toledo District—is faced with rapid population growth and immigration, combined with increasing deforestation and illegal fishing along marine and terrestrial borders.

Nonetheless, the Toledo District has managed to fight back and continues to rise as an example in protecting its fragile ecosystems. Since the late 20th century, conservation efforts in the heavily forested and biodiverse district have strengthened. As early as the 1990s, commercial interest from Malaysian logging was met with fierce resistance from local indigenous activists. The bulldozing of Toledo's forests had damaged drinking water supplies, leading to opposition from downstream communities. The late Mayan leader Julian Cho organized and led resistance to unsustainable logging on traditional Mayan land. The Government of Belize responded by canceling these companies' licenses.

More recent conservation successes are owed to the implementation and use of a comanagement program, created by the Belizean government, whereby areas designated officially "protected"—such as the 100,000-acre no-public-access Bladen Nature Reserve—are monitored by nongovernmental organizations and residents of communities close to these protected areas, all working together and sharing in the financial burden of accomplishing the gigantic task. This comanagement system promotes both sustainable development and conservation, helping the local communities who depend on the health and sustainability of these resources.

Today, hope lies in the appointment of one of Toledo's own residents and award-winning conservationist Lisel Alamilla as the Minister of Forestry, Fisheries, and Sustainable Development. Of note is Alamilla's 2012 moratorium on the logging of rosewood from Toledo's forests. A few busts of illegal harvesting have since been made, including in January 2013, when up to 700 pieces of the precious wood intended for export were discovered adjacent to Tambran Village. The export-quality logs were seized and set ablaze by the minister herself, in the presence of the media, to send a clear message to the perpetrators. The remaining logs were handed to local communities for traditional house building.

Toledo has unique tropical forests and pristine coral reefs that provide livelihoods to the most culturally diverse population in Belize. If the protection of its resources continues in this vein, this district can be a globally recognized example of sustainable development.

(Contributed by Lee McLoughlin, manager of the Protected Areas Management Program at Ya'axché Conservation Trust.)

SAN PEDRO COLUMBIA

San Pedro is one of the biggest of the villages and is home to well-known Mayan musicians as well as Eladio Pop's Cacao Trail. A small Catholic church in town has an equally small cemetery; it sits on a hilltop surrounded by a few thatched dwellings.

Eladio Pop's Cacao Trail is a fantastic experience. Eladio is a one-of-a-kind Maya who will take you all over his farm and show you how the Maya once made chocolate, from the cacao tree all the way to his home, where his wife will roast, grind, and make hot chocolate the old-fashioned way. Contact **Toledo Cave**

and **Adventure Tours** (cell 501/665-6778) to arrange a trip to Eladio's.

Two miles upriver from San Pedro Columbia you'll find **Maya Mountain Research Farm** (MMRF, tel. 501/630-4386, www.mmrfbz.org), a registered NGO and working demonstration farm situated on 70 acres. Maya Mountain promotes sustainable agriculture, renewable energy, appropriate technology, and food security using permaculture principles and applied biodiversity. The farm also operates on solar power and offers courses. The property has more than 500 species of plants (including lots of cacao), and the

he Skull of Doom: Mystery Solved

1924, Anna Mitchell-Hedges, the daughter of explorer F. A. Mitchell-Hedges, allegedly found a rfectly formed quartz crystal skull at the Lubaantun archaeological site on her 17th birthday. The bject has been the subject of much mystery and controversy over the years. Was it made by the Maya to conjure death? Atlanteans? Aliens? Did Mitchell-Hedges plant it for the pleasure of his daughter? Is the whole story a hoax?

The world got its answer in 2007 when the Smithsonian Institute put the Mitchell-Hedges skull under a scanning electron microscope. Researcher Jane MacLaren Walsh concluded, "This object was carved and polished using modern, high-speed, diamond-coated, rotary cutting and polishing tools of minute dimensions. This technology is certainly not pre-Columbian. I believe it is decidedly 20th century."

The skull currently resides in North America with the widower of Anna Mitchell-Hedges. Despite the Smithsonian's findings, some still warned of dire consequences if the skull was not returned to Lubaantun by December 21, 2012, but that also proved untrue.

staff are working to establish an ethnobotanical garden of useful plants with their Q'eqchi' Maya names and uses. Accommodations are simple rustic affairs, with solar lighting and Internet access.

From the turnoff for Punta Gorda at Mile 86 on the Southern Highway, take the road north. At about Mile 1½, a turnoff on the right heads for San Pedro Columbia and other villages. The **Chun Bus** makes the run from Punta Gorda to nearby San Antonio (11:30am Mon.-Sat., about US$4 round-trip) but doesn't stop in San Pedro Columbia; instead you will have to leave the bus at the road and trek in several miles.

★ RÍO BLANCO NATIONAL PARK

Established in 1994 and comanaged by the **Río Blanco Mayan Association** (the people of Santa Cruz, who volunteer their time as the park wardens, and chairperson Jose Mes) and by the government, Río Blanco National Park is a favorite, providing stunning scenery and

village of San Pedro Columbia

natural beauty for the visitor and an alternative income for members of neighboring villages. The park is 105 acres and encompasses a spectacular waterfall that is 20 feet high and ranges from a raging 100 feet wide during the rainy season to about 10 feet during the dry season. Locals say the turquoise pool under the waterfall is bottomless (one claims to have dived 60 feet and never touched bottom, though another says he touched it at 20 feet). The adventurous can jump off the surrounding rocks and fall 20 feet into crystal-clear water. There are also several pools to the back of the falls, plenty of space for a picnic, and two miles of nature trails, which include the cave where the Río Blanco river enters the mountain and a suspended cable bridge over the river.

Río Blanco National Park (tel. 501/628-9535, US$5) is a community-based effort, and 10 percent of entrance fees goes back into the surrounding villages, home to indigenous Maya. On-site, visit the **Craft & Snack Shop** (run by the Río Blanco Women's Association) for things like baskets, jewelry, and embroidery, plus the only cold beverages in the area. There is a picnic area under the visitors center.

Getting There

Río Blanco National Park is about 30 miles west of Punta Gorda, between the villages of Santa Cruz and Santa Elena on the road to Jalacte. From Punta Gorda Town, the park is a smooth one-hour drive or an easy hop off the bus. It's also an easy two-minute hike from the visitors center (at park entrance) along a clear rainforest trail to reach the waterfall.

Two small bus companies serve the village of Jalacte, leaving from Jose Maria Nunez Street in Punta Gorda at 11:30am (Chun Bus, Mon.-Sat.) and 4pm (Bol Bus, Mon., Wed., and Fri.-Sat.); they return from the village on the same days at 3pm. Double-check the latest copy of the *Toledo Howler* to ensure the schedule hasn't changed, as it so frequently does around these parts.

BLUE CREEK VILLAGE
★ Blue Creek Cave

This village of some 275 Q'eqchi' Mopan Maya was first settled in 1925, also called Ho'keb Ha, "the place where the water comes out," describing the spot where the Río Blanco emerges from the side of a mountain and becomes Blue Creek, home to an extensive cave system. You'll need a guide who's familiar with these caves; ask at Punta Gorda or at one of the nearby Mayan villages. Many of these folks know the nearby caves well. You can swim up to 600 yards into the cave; it's pretty stunning, with a small waterfall in the cave. Bring a flashlight and a swimsuit.

To get here, Kan's bus leaves Punta Gorda at 11:30am Monday-Saturday; Teck's bus leaves at noon on Monday, Wednesday, Friday, and Saturday.

BARRANCO

Barranco is an isolated, authentic Garífuna village, where activities include fishing along the river and traveling by dugout canoe up the river into the **Sarstoon-Temash National Park** to see howler monkeys, hickatees (river turtles), and iguanas. Many of Barranco's 600 inhabitants have traveled far from their village to become some of Belize's most renowned musicians, painters, and researchers; many have earned advanced degrees in their fields, giving Barranco one of the highest per capita PhD percentages in Central America.

Go on a tour of the village with **Alvin,** a local resident and tour guide who will share Garífuna culture and history along the way. Visit a traditional Garífuna thatched-roof home—including the home of famous Garífuna artist Andy Palacio—and view the inside of the impressive *dügü,* or Garífuna temple, used for family reunions. Sample a Garífuna lunch of fried fish stewed in coconut broth, and visit the **Barranco House of Culture** for more on this fascinating Afro-Caribbean culture. Return for a refreshing

Andy Palacio: Garífuna and Belizean Legend

Barranco's pride and joy is Andy Palacio, whose pictures are still plastered around the village—clipped from old magazines, at the bar, inside homes, at the local museum, and on the village bulletin board. The talented artist, popular singer, and Garífuna activist was born in Barranco and was buried in his home village far too soon; the star suffered a heart attack in 2008 at the age of 47, and his death left behind a grieving nation.

Palacio's legacy is undisputed. Anxious to preserve the Garífuna culture and language, he used music as his medium. The Afro-influenced rhythms of *punta* and *paranda* are accompanied by moving lyrics that carry socially conscious messages: "Our ancestors fought to remain Garífuna / Why must we be the ones to lose our culture?"

His last album, *Wátina*, was recorded with the Garífuna Collective, a group of Garífuna musicians from Belize, Honduras, and Guatemala. *Wátina* won worldwide acclaim and awards and put Garífuna music back in vogue, especially with the younger generation. (If you can, grab or download a copy; I still listen to it regularly.)

A year before his death, Andy Palacio was awarded the prestigious WOMEX and named a UNESCO Artist for Peace. You can visit both his childhood home and his grave in Barranco.

glass of *hiu* (a spicy drink made of cassava and sweet potato) at the local bar and an evening of drumming.

You can get to Barranco by bus from the park in Punta Gorda, by boat from the Punta Gorda dock, or with your tour operator.

TIDE Tours (41 Front St., Punta Gorda, tel. 501/722-2129, www.tidetours.org, 7:30am-4:30pm Mon.-Fri.) is your best bet for a trip to Barranco. If you can, arrange to return by boat—it's a lot faster and more pleasant than the 2.5-hour bumpy ride back to Punta Gorda.

Stopover in Belize City

Belize District

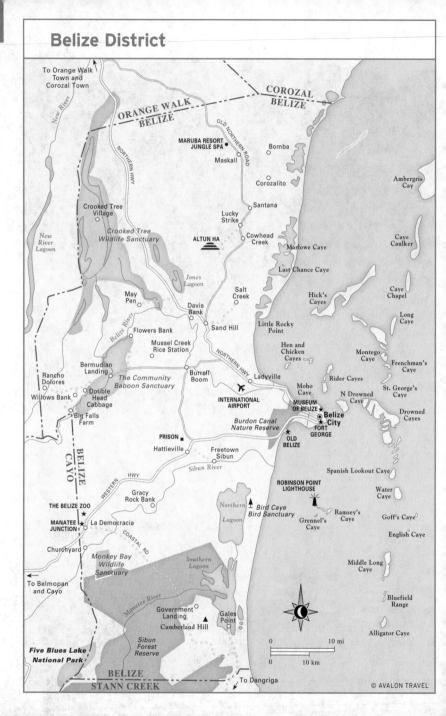

To Orange Walk Town and Corozal Town

New River

ORANGE WALK BELIZE

COROZAL BELIZE

NORTHERN HWY

OLD NORTHERN ROAD

MARUBA RESORT JUNGLE SPA •

Maskall

Bomba

Corozalito

Santana

Crooked Tree Village

Crooked Tree Wildlife Sanctuary

New River Lagoon

Jones Lagoon

Lucky Strike

ALTUN HA

Cowhead Creek

Marlowe Caye

Last Chance Caye

Ambergris Cay

Cave Caulker

Caye Chapel

May Pen

Davis Bank

Salt Creek

Sand Hill

Hick's Cayes

Little Rocky Point

Long Caye

Belize River

Flowers Bank

Mussel Creek Rice Station

NORTHERN HWY

Hen and Chicken Cayes

Montego Caye

Frenchman's Caye

Bermudian Landing

The Community Baboon Sanctuary

Burrell Boom

Ladyville

Rider Cayes

St. George's Caye

Rancho Dolores

Double Head Cabbage

Moho Caye

N Drowned Caye

Drowned Cayes

Willows Bank

BELIZE CAYO

Big Falls Farm

INTERNATIONAL AIRPORT

MUSEUM OF BELIZE ★
★ Belize City
FORT GEORGE

Burdon Canal Nature Reserve

PRISON ■

Hattieville

Freetown Sibun

OLD BELIZE

WESTERN HWY

Sibun River

Spanish Lookout Caye

Gracy Rock Bank

ROBINSON POINT LIGHTHOUSE

Water Caye

THE BELIZE ZOO ★
MANATEE JUNCTION ★

La Democracia

Northern Lagoon

Bird Caye Bird Sanctuary

Grennel's Caye

Ramsey's Caye

Goff's Caye

COASTAL RD

Churchyard

Monkey Bay Wildlife Sanctuary

Southern Lagoon

English Caye

Middle Long Caye

To Belmopan and Cayo

Manatee River

Government Landing

Gales Point

Bluefield Range

Cumberland Hill

Sibun Forest Reserve

Alligator Caye

Five Blues Lake National Park

BELIZE STANN CREEK

To Dangriga

0   10 mi
0   10 km

© AVALON TRAVEL

Belize City is often the first introduction to the country, and while this Central American city's reputation leads many to transfer immediately to the northern cayes or to their final south coast destination, those who have a day or two to spare will find that the nation's most populated district has more to offer than meets the eye: the hustle and bustle of Belize City, the black howler monkeys of Burrell Boom, the lush mangroves and crocs of the Old Belize River, the tranquil Kriol villages and their cashew wines, and the Mayan archaeological site of Altun Ha.

Although it hasn't been the capital since 1961, Belize City remains central to the life of Belizeans. At the heart of the country's British colonial past, it's the center of Creole culture and commerce, offering museums, art, markets, and authentic eateries. The rice and beans shacks, boisterous fish markets, men playing dominoes in the park, roadside drink stalls, and slow-paced surrounding villages give this district a distinctly Caribbean feel, the only one in an otherwise Spanish-speaking Central America.

Thanks to the city's central coastal location, nowhere is too far, making Belize City a hub for exploring other parts of the country. Transportation options are plentiful—from water taxis to the northern cayes to buses and flights connecting the mainland jump-off points, for more boat rides to islands along the south coast.

And if Belize City itself fails to appeal on first glance, its outskirts will surprise. A visit here means proximity to inland hiking and wildlife watching—from crocs to howler monkeys.

PLANNING YOUR TIME

A half-day's exploration of Belize City is a must for anyone interested in a bigger picture of the country—even if you have only a few hours between bus and boat connections. You can see all the sights in a few hours and get a sense of the true Caribbean, or "Kriol," spirit of this town. Favorite stops include the **Belize Museum,** the **House of Culture,** and the busy Swing Bridge area leading to downtown

Previous: archaeological site Altun Ha; view of Belize City harbor and Princess Marina from Princess Hotel.
Above: The Belize River Lodge at Old Belize River.

Belize City

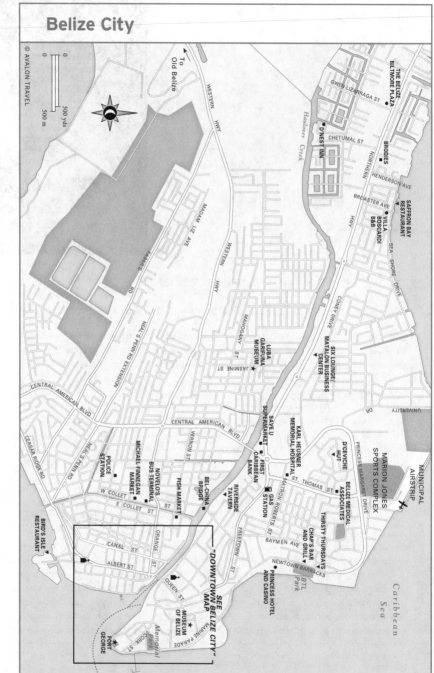

© AVALON TRAVEL

0   500 yds
0   500 m

To
Old Belize

Haulover Creek

Caribbean Sea

THE BELIZE
BILTMORE PLAZA

GWEN LIZARRAGA ST

D'NEST INN

CHETUMAL ST

BRODIES

HENDERSON AVE

NORTHERN HWY

BROADSTER AVE

SAFFRON BAY
RESTAURANT

VILLA
BOSCARDI
B&B

SEA SHORE DRIVE

CONEY DRIVE

WESTERN HWY

MADAM LIZ AVE

FABER'S RD

NEAL'S PENN RD EXTENSION

WESTERN HWY

MAHOGANY ST

LUBA
GARIFUNA
MUSEUM

JASMINE ST

SIX LOUNGE/
MATALON BUSINESS
CENTER

UNIVERSITY DR

CENTRAL AMERICAN BLVD

CENTRAL AMERICAN BLVD

CEASAR RIDGE RD

NEAL'S PENN RD

POLICE
STATION

MICHAEL FINNEGAN
MARKET

NOVELO'S
BUS TERMINAL

FISH MARKET

VERNON ST

BEL-CHINA
BRIDGE

SAVE U
SUPERMARKET

KARL HEUSNER
MEMORIAL HOSPITAL

FIRST
CARIBBEAN
BANK

RIVERSIDE
TAVERN

GAS
STATION

ST. THOMAS ST

MATRON ROBERTS ST

MARION ROBERTS ST

D'CEVICHE
HUT

PRINCESS MARGARET DRIVE

BELIZE MEDICAL
ASSOCIATES

MARION JONES
SPORTS COMPLEX

MUNICIPAL
AIRSTRIP

BTL
Park

THIRSTY THURSDAYS

CHAP'S BAR
AND GRILL

BAYMEN AVE

FREETOWN ST

BIRD'S ISLE
RESTAURANT

W COLLET ST

E COLLET ST

CANAL ST

ALBERT ST

ORANGE ST

QUEEN ST

NEWTOWN BARRACKS

PRINCESS HOTEL
AND CASINO

"DOWNTOWN BELIZE CITY"
MAP

SEE

MARINE PARADE

MUSEUM
OF BELIZE

Memorial
Park

PORT
GEORGE

CORK ST

Albert Street (with its lovely views of sailboats). Although Belize City lacks the evolved dining scene of more touristed parts of the country, there are enough decent restaurants and authentic local eateries to get by for a day or two, including the country's best Creole cuisine.

You have the option of skipping the city entirely and instead spending a day exploring its surroundings, which offer plenty of nature, wildlife, and history. Spend an afternoon at The Belize Zoo—enjoyed by adults and children—or at the Community Baboon Sanctuary, both a mere hour away by car and easily reached by bus. Hop on a river tour for wildlife spotting or hike the Mayan site of Altun Ha.

ORIENTATION

The old Swing Bridge spans Haulover Creek, connecting Belize City's Northside to its Southside, and it is the most distinct landmark in the city. North of the bridge and creek, Queen Street and Front Street are the crucial thoroughfares. On this side of the bridge, you'll find the Caye Caulker Water Taxi Terminal, an important transportation and information hub. Across from the

water taxi are the post office and the library, which has a quiet sitting room and Internet access. Walking east on Front Street, toward the sea, you'll find several art galleries and shops before you come to the second water taxi terminal to the north cayes, the San Pedro Belize Express, and to the Tourism Village, the hopeful, Disneyesque name for the cruise-ship passenger arrival area, its access closed to the outside world. The rest of the adjoining Fort George historic area is, in contrast, genuine and interesting to see. Some of the higher-end restaurants and best cafés are also here.

On the Swing Bridge's south end, Regent Street and Albert Street make a V-shaped split and are the core of the city's banking and shopping activity. There are a few old government buildings here too, as well as Battlefield (Central) Park and a couple of guesthouses. Southside has a seedier reputation than Northside (aside from downtown, don't go south), which is monitored more closely by the police. For a walking map of the city, stop by the Belize Tourism Board office (tel. 501/227-2420, www.travelbelize.org) on Regent Street; the map includes a great walking tour of the city's main sights.

Sights

A morning stroll through the weathered buildings of Belize City, starting in the Fort George Lighthouse area and walking toward the Swing Bridge, gives you a feel for this seaside population center. This is when people are rushing off to work, kids are spiffed up on their way to school, and folks are out doing their daily shopping. The streets are crammed with small shops, a stream of pedestrians, and lots of traffic. One thing Belize City isn't is boring.

FORT GEORGE

The Fort George area, a peninsula ringed by Marine Parade Boulevard and Fort Street,

is one of the most pleasant in Belize City. Meander in the neighborhood and you'll pass some impressive homes and buildings, including a few charming old guesthouses. The Baron Bliss Memorial and Fort George Lighthouse stand guard over it all.

The sea breeze can be pleasant here, and you can glimpse cayes and ships offshore. Once you round the point, the road becomes Marine Parade and runs past the modern Radisson Fort George Hotel and Memorial Park, a grassy salute to the 40 Belizeans who lost their lives in World War I.

From the Radisson Fort George marina, you'll get a good view of the harbor. Originally

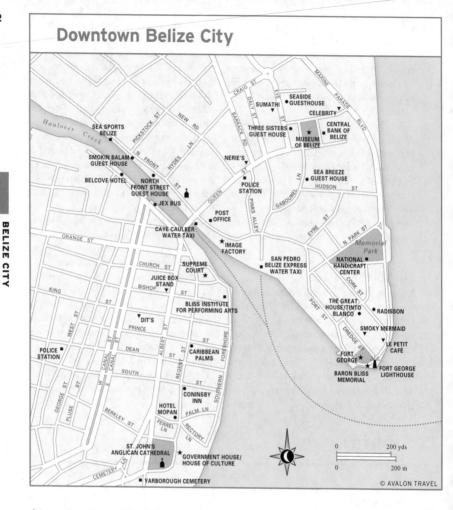

Downtown Belize City

this was Fort George Island; the strait separating the island from the mainland (the site of today's Memorial Park) was filled in during the early 1920s. The entire area is easy to navigate on foot.

Baron Bliss Memorial

Henry Edward Ernest Victor Bliss, also known as the "Fourth Baron Bliss of the Former Kingdom of Portugal," was born in the county of Buckingham in England. He first sailed into the harbor of Belize in 1926, although he was too ill to go ashore because

of food poisoning he had contracted while visiting Trinidad. Bliss spent several months aboard his yacht, the *Sea King,* in the harbor, fishing in Belizean waters. Although he never got well enough to go ashore, Bliss learned to love the country from the sea, and its habitués—people on fishing boats and officials in the harbor—all treated him with great respect and friendliness. On the days that he was only able to languish on deck, he made every effort to learn about the small country. He was apparently so impressed with what he learned and the people he met that before his death, he drew up a will that established a trust of nearly US$2 million for projects to benefit the people of Belize.

More than US$1 million in interest from the trust has been used for the erection of the Bliss Institute, the Bliss School of Nursing, and Bliss Promenade as well as contributions to the Belize City water supply, the Corozal Town Board and Health Clinic, and land purchase for the building of Belmopan.

An avid yachtsman, Bliss stipulated that money be set aside for a regatta to be held in Belizean waters, now a focal point of the gala Baron Bliss Day celebrations each March, an important holiday that is now called National Heroes and Benefactors Day. The baron's white granite tomb is at the point of Fort George in Belize City, guarded by the Fort George Lighthouse and the occasional pair of late-night Belizean lovers.

Fort George Lighthouse

Towering over the coastline and facing the Belize Harbor, the **Fort George Lighthouse** was built as part of the memorial for Baron Bliss, Belize's greatest benefactor. In fulfillment of his dying wish and financed with the generous proceeds he left the country, the tall structure was erected next to his tomb and memorial. While the public cannot enter the lighthouse, it remains an important, historic landmark in Belize City and is easy to spot while touring the Fort George area. The views from there also make for a nice photo op.

MUSEUM OF BELIZE

Housed in the old city jail (Her Majesty's Prison was built in 1857 and served as the nation's only prison until the 1990s), the small but worthwhile **Museum of Belize** (8 Gabourel Lane, tel. 501/223-4524, www.museumofbelize.org, 9am-4:30pm Tues.-Fri., 9am-4pm Sat., US$5) includes historical artifacts, indigenous relics, and rotating displays on topics such as *Insects of Belize,* *Maya Jade,* and *Pirates of Belize*. Philatelists and bottle collectors will love the 150 years of stamps and bottles on display.

IMAGE FACTORY

A few doors up from the Swing Bridge, the **Image Factory Art Foundation** (91 N. Front St., tel. 501/223-4093, www.imagefactorybelize.com, 9am-5pm Mon.-Fri., 9am-noon Sat.) is the official pulse of the Belizean art and literary scene. In addition to offering the best book selection in the country (both

Belize City is a small but active Caribbean town.

local authors and some foreign titles), there is gallery space for semi-regular art events, usually held on Friday evenings at happy hour. There's also a separate arts and crafts shop at the back filled with gorgeous Belizean paintings, sculptures, and other unique creations.

ST. JOHN'S ANGLICAN CATHEDRAL

The lovely old **St. John's Anglican Cathedral** (S. Albert St. at Regent St., 7am-6pm daily), across from the House of Culture, is one of the few typically British structures in the city. It is also the oldest Anglican church in Central America. In 1812, slaves helped erect this graceful piece of architecture, using bricks brought as ballast on sailing ships from Europe. Several Mosquito Coast kings from Nicaragua and Honduras were crowned in this cathedral with ultimate pomp and grandeur; the last was in 1815. The church is surrounded by well-kept green lawns and sits next to a lively schoolyard. It's usually okay to walk right in and quietly admire the impressive interior with its stained-glass windows, mahogany pews, and the antique organ. You can leave a little something in the donation box on your way out.

One block from the cathedral is the **Yarborough Cemetery,** the city's first burial ground, with the graves of Belizean citizens dating back to the 18th century, as well as some who died during World War II.

GOVERNMENT HOUSE AND HOUSE OF CULTURE

Opposite St. John's Cathedral, at the southern end of Regent Street and facing the Southern Foreshore, is the **House of Culture** museum in the old **Government House** (tel. 501/227-3050, www.nichbelize.org, 8:30am-5pm Mon.-Thurs., 8:30am-4:30pm Fri., US$5), which, before 1961's Hurricane Hattie and the ensuing construction of Belmopan, was the home and office of the governor-general, the official representative of Queen Elizabeth. (Today's governor-general can be found in Belmopan, at Belize House.) For a long time these grounds were used as a guesthouse for visiting VIPs and a venue for social functions. Queen Elizabeth and Prince Philip stayed here in 1994. The elegant wooden buildings (built 1812-1814) are said to be based on designs by acclaimed English architect Christopher Wren. Sprawling lawns and wind-brushed palms facing the sea surround Government House, making it ideal for the year-round

The Museum of Belize is within walking distance of the city center.

Crime and the City

Like many Central American countries, Belize has its share of problems with drugs, gangs, and violent street crime. However, due to its extremely small population—70,000 inhabitants, compared to millions in most Central American capitals—Belize City's problems are nowhere near as severe as those of El Salvador, Honduras, and Guatemala's cities. Still, violent crime has increased in Belize City, mostly in the form of petty theft and shootings. Much of this violent gang culture is imported from the United States by deported Belizean youths.

Most—but not all—violent crime occurs in the Southside part of Belize City, many blocks away from the traditional walking paths of visitors, but occasional incidents have occurred throughout the city and in broad daylight. The government has taken steps to battle crime, including stiffer enforcement of the law and deployment of a force of tourist police, recognizable by their khaki shirts and green pants.

For the most part, you'll be fine sticking to the sights and general city center, where there's lots of pedestrian traffic and daytime activity. Most locals are friendly and helpful with directions or other questions. To be safe, use the same common sense you would in any city in the world:

- Before you venture out, have a clear idea of how to get where you're going and ask a local Belizean, like your hotel desk clerk or a restaurant waiter, whether your plan is reasonable.

- Don't walk around at night if you are at all unsure of where you're going or if the neighborhood is safe.

- Taxis are plentiful and inexpensive—use them. Generally, only those with green license plates should be considered. But most Belizeans have a personal taxi driver whom they know and trust; ask if they would be willing to call one for you at the local price.

- Don't flash money, jewelry, or other temptations; if threatened with robbery, hand them over. Report all crimes to the local police and to your country's embassy.

outdoor functions, art events, and concerts that are still held here.

Wander through the wood structure and enjoy the period furniture, silverware, and glassware collections, plus a selection of paintings and sculptures by modern Belizean artists. Stroll the grounds, on the water's edge, and enjoy the solitude. Also on-site is the headquarters of the National Kriol Council, with some Kriol language phrasebooks for sale, although its doors have remained closed in the months before press time.

Sports and Recreation

You'll find the best diving, fishing, and other water activities while on the cayes, north to south. Aside from these, Belize City offers river and wildlife tours, as well as your classic city park or spa pampering, if you prefer to take it easy.

RIVER TOURS
Explore the waterways, marshlands, and mangroves of the **Almond Hill Lagoon** and **Indian Creek** from a 450-hp airboat via **Chukka Caribbean Adventures** (Mile 9, Western Hwy., tel. 501/635-1318, U.S. tel. 877/424-8552, www.chukkacaribbean.com, US$55 pp). This is a great way to glimpse some of Belize's birds and wildlife in just an hour; if you're lucky, you'll spot 15-foot crocs. Chukka's enthusiastic and knowledgeable guides make it a fun experience with a few speedy twists and turns. Chukka also offers

adventure tours out of Jaguar Paw that get rave reviews, with cave tubing, rappelling, and more.

PARKS

A simple, enjoyable way to spend an afternoon or watch the sun go down in Belize City is to hang out "seaside" (as the locals call it) in one of the city parks. **BTL Park** (www.btlparkdirectory.com), within walking distance of the Princess Hotel, is; grab a drink and some fresh tacos or plate of rice 'n' beans from one of several food booths, and sit back on the benches while the breeze blows all along the seaside. There are also swings and other distractions for kids. You're likely to spot lovers as well as families, who come here in the early evening to stroll, wind down, jog, or just chat. Going seaside is popular on Sunday, with lots of families taking a breather from their long week. Another popular seaside spot is across from Memorial Park and along the Marine Parade promenade.

MASSAGE AND BODYWORK

The Radisson Fort George Hotel offers spa services at the **Nim Li Punit Spa** (2 Marine Parade, tel. 501/223-3333, sam.rah@radisson.com). Or put yourself in the hands of **Harold Zuniga** (85 Amara Ave., tel. 501/604-5679, haroldzuniga@yahoo.com), a U.S.-trained physical therapist, masseur, and acupuncturist.

If you're up for relaxation coupled with a day trip, tucked in the village of Maskall just a 1.5-hour drive from the city is the unique **Maruba Resort Jungle Spa** (U.S. tel. 713/799-2031, Mile 40½ Old Northern Hwy., www.maruba-spa.com, US$50-100). The offerings are numerous, but don't miss getting the Mood Mud Massage; you'll leave not only with baby-soft skin but also a memorable photo of your body covered in nothing but mud and . . . a hibiscus flower. You can also get manicures, pedicures, and facials.

Explore the Old Belize River via Chukka Caribbean Adventures.

Entertainment and Shopping

Belize City is even more alive during the September Celebrations, a month packed with events, music, dancing, and a full-blown carnival parade along Central American Boulevard. It's quite possibly one of the most interesting towns in the Caribbean, one you must dig into to appreciate. Just don't listen when they tell you to skip it.

Bliss Promenade skirts the waterfront and brings you to the towering **Bliss Center for Performing Arts** (Southern Foreshore, tel. 501/227-2110, www.nichbelize.org), which hosts social functions, seminars, arts festivals, and drama series throughout the year. It is also the location of a theater, a museum, and a library, as well as the Institute of Creative Arts. Step in to grab a calendar of events.

NIGHTLIFE

Thursday is the biggest night for dancing in Belize City, followed by Friday, especially those that fall on a payday. Nightclubs come and go like hurricanes; keep your wits about you and ask where the latest safe place to party is. At the moment, one of the best nightspots for dancing is **Club Next** (Princess Hotel, Newton Barracks, tel. 501/223-2670, 10pm-4am Thurs.-Sat.), offering bottle service and international DJs. For a notch up, the trendy **Six Lounge** (Matalon Business Center, Coney Dr., 6th Fl., tel. 501/637-4722 or 501/223-2821, 8pm-2am Thurs.-Sat.) is where you'll rub elbows with Belize's elite. This rooftop nightclub serves expensive cocktails in a roomy, disco-lit interior or outside on the Vegas-like open-air terrace lounge, complete with red lounge sofas, tables, a bar, and a nice city view. Serious dancing usually doesn't get started until after 11pm, and the crowd gets younger or rowdier as the hours pass.

For a quiet, relaxing evening away from the crowds, try **Tinto & Blanco Wine Bar** (13 Cork St., tel. 501/223-5700, tintoandblanco@ gmail.com, 4pm-midnight Tues.-Sun.), tucked inside the Great House building. Its dim, cozy interior is perfect to enjoy wine by the glass or bottle without music drowning out your conversation, and before turning in for the night.

Ask around to find out where the best happy hours are held—they often feature live music and free *bocas* (deep-fried something, probably). The bars at the **Radisson Fort George Hotel** (2 Marine Parade, tel. 501/223-3333), the **Biltmore** (Mile 3, Northern Hwy., tel. 501/223-2302), and **Princess Hotel** (Barrack Rd., tel. 501/223-2670) are popular and provide safe, contained venues—and some of the highest drink prices in the city. **Bird's Isle** (90 Albert St., past the House of Culture, tel. 501/207-6500), or "Island" as locals call it, is popular for karaoke on Thursday (5pm-1am). **Riverside Tavern** (2 Mapp St., tel. 501/223-5640), or just "Tavern," has plenty of bar fare and cocktails on Friday as well as other weekday happy hours.

FESTIVALS AND EVENTS

September is Belize's golden month. For three weeks—from September 1 all the way through September 21 (Independence Day)—the city hops on one long party train to celebrate the country's freedom from Great Britain in 1981. Along the highways, you'll spot massive billboards listing events in districts countrywide leading up to Independence Day. The streets, lights, and bridges in Belize City are decked in the national colors—red, blue, and white—and everyone is on a celebration high. It's quite the time to visit Belize City, particularly if you're a culture and history buff (not to mention the prices in low season are oh-so-right).

St. George's Caye Day (Sept. 10) commemorates the 1798 Battle of St. George's, when British forces repelled a Spanish invasion of Belize. The day begins around 10am with a ceremony full of pomp and circumstance at Memorial Park on Marine Parade Boulevard, just a few steps from the Radisson, where you'll glimpse the prime minister along with other important figures. A colorful citizens' parade follows around noon, with plenty of music and dancing, from the park all the way to Albert Street.

Catch the **Independence Day Parade** (Sept. 21) celebrating Belize's independence from Great Britain. Similar to the St. George's Caye Day, Belize City holds its own with uniform parades, marching bands, floats, and children and adults all wearing the blue-red-white national colors and waving flags. The celebrations usually begin at Memorial Park around late morning and continue on throughout the afternoon and evening.

Carnival

Belize's Caribbean spirit is on full display during a Caribbean-flavored Carnival (mid-Sept.). You'll see colorful floats, men and women in sexy, extravagant costumes, trucks and massive speakers blasting either *punta* or *soca* music as the crowd and revelers hop and dance all along Central American Boulevard. The parade often starts on the south side of town around 2pm; be sure to arrange a taxi ride to and from the event and arrive about an hour early if you want to save a spot. After Carnival, the celebrations continue at the BTL Memorial Park with an all-night outdoor concert, food and drink vendors, and plenty of seaside dancing.

SHOPPING

Gift shops, craft stalls, and street vendors line Front Street near Tourism Village as well as just south of the Swing Bridge. In the Fort George area, check out the **Belize Handicraft Market Place** (Memorial Park, 8am-5pm Mon.-Fri., 8am-4pm Sat.), near the Radisson. Across from Memorial Park, look for the **National Handicrafts Center** (8am-5pm Mon.-Fri., 8am-4pm Sat.), an official

Chamber of Commerce-sponsored shop with fine crafts purchased directly from artisans around the country.

There is a **flea market** (at the Catholic Church, N. Front St.) at 7am on Saturday. Also seek out the **Mennonite Furniture Market** (47 N. Front St., daylight hours Fri.-Sat.), next to Smokin' Balam Guest House, for nice handmade wooden furniture at reasonable prices (but they don't do shipping).

Wine is increasingly sought out in Belize. Once difficult to find, it's now fairly well stocked at the super-size **Brodie's** (Mile 2½, Northern Hwy., tel. 501/223-5587, 8am-9pm Mon.-Sat., 8am-2pm Sun.) and at the Belize City retail location of **Wine de Vine** (Northern Hwy., tel. 501/223-2444, www.winedevine.com), where you can even find Dom Pérignon.

At the **Traveller's Liquors Heritage Center** (Mile 2½, Northern Hwy., tel. 501/223-2855, www.onebarrelrum.com, 10am-6pm Mon.-Fri., bar until midnight Fri.-Sat.), Belize's premier rum producer offers a fun stop on your way in or out of town. The Heritage Center consists of a historical display, a selection of their many products at bargain prices, an open-air bar and restaurant, and most importantly, a tasting bar where you can sample all 27 varieties of Traveller's Liquors rum. Ask about the "vintage edition rum" to bring home some premium spirits.

A few stores have small but pertinent book selections featuring several shelves of Belizean and about-Belize books. The **Image Factory** (91 N. Front St., tel. 501/223-4093, www.imagefactorybelize.com, 9am-5pm Mon.-Fri., 9am-noon Sat.) has the best collection, including an art gallery. **Angelus Press** (10 Queen St., tel. 501/223-5777, 7:30am-5:30pm Mon.-Fri., reduced hours Sat.-Sun.), right around the corner from the Image Factory on Queen Street, has a complete corner of books and maps behind all the office supplies and services.

Accommodations

All room rates are for double occupancy in the high season and may or may not include the 9 percent hotel tax. If you're traveling alone or from May to November, expect discounts at some, but not all, of the following hotels.

UNDER US$25

The **Seaside Guest House** (3 Prince St., tel. 501/605-3786 or 501/632-7660, www. seasideguesthouse.org, US$20-45) is popular among backpackers. The guesthouse is down a narrow, quiet alley off Regent Street, near the Belize Tourism Board. The couple of guest rooms are tiny, barely bigger than the beds, but the common spaces both upstairs and downstairs are good for meeting travelers from all over the world. Choose from shared bunk space or private guest rooms. There is hot water in the community bathroom, a breeze on the ocean-facing porch, and a friendly family-run atmosphere in this former Quaker house. Three cheap meals a day (US$3-5 each) are available, though there are plenty of outside eateries in this central area. If you know you're coming to town, make a

reservation—the Seaside can sometimes fill up fast.

On North Front Street, a short walk from the Swing Bridge, is the quiet family-run ★ **Smokin' Balam Guest House** (59 N. Front St., tel. 501/628-2003, smokinbalam2@ yahoo.com, US$15 s, US$30 d), with four cozy and clean rooms, all airy with fans, two with private baths; all have access to a caged balcony over Haulover Creek at the back (with a small dock for sunning, if you choose) and a nice upper-floor balcony with street views as well as a nice downstairs café (meals from US$2). There's a gift shop, a pay phone, and Internet access on the ground floor. The guesthouse also offers weekly and monthly rates, bag storage (US$2 per bag per day), and a friendly atmosphere.

US$25-50

The ★ **Belcove Hotel** (9 Regent St. W., tel. 501/227-3054, www.belcove.com, US$33-52), centrally located on the south bank of Haulover Creek, just west of the Swing Bridge, is well taken care of, clean and bright, and easy

Smokin' Balam Guest House

to recommend. There are 13 guest rooms on three floors; options include shared or private baths with fan or the works (a/c and TV). The porch over the creek is fun to watch boats from, and cheap lively eats are right next door at Deep Sea Marlin's Restaurant & Bar. It's a great base for a walking tour of the city, and tour packages can keep you busy on the reef or at inland sights. The only downside is the slightly seedy two blocks on Regent Street between the hotel and the Swing Bridge; take a cab to and from the hotel door at night.

Three Sisters Guest House (36 Queen St., tel. 501/203-5729, US$32) has three big, clean guest rooms with private baths and fans plus a massive cavernous common space, all on the second floor of an old building on Queen Street. There's even one guest room with three or four beds. It's good for groups looking simply for a place to rest, and it's friendly, clean, and has a small secure front gate. Ask about the additional guest rooms for rent at the Isabel Guest House on Albert Street, by the Swing Bridge.

US$50-100

Built in 1973, the ★ **Hotel Mopan** (55 Regent St., tel. 501/227-7351, www.hotelmopan.com, US$50-65) is an old standby with a very pleasant rooftop lounge area. There are 12 guest rooms, some with ocean views, all with tile floors, private baths, TV, free wireless Internet, mini fridges, and air-conditioning. Balcony rooms are worth the extra couple of dollars. On the same street, **Coningsby Inn** (76 Regent St., tel. 501/227-1566, www.coningsbyinn.com, US$50-60) has 10 rooms with TV, private baths, air-conditioning, wireless Internet, and minibars. There's a second-story bar and restaurant with a front balcony; breakfast is US$6. Common-area carpets are run down, but guest rooms are clean and the staff is friendly. Both Hotel Mopan and Coningsby Inn are in Southside, steps from the House of Culture and the Tourism Board.

Next to the Fort George Radisson, the **Chateau Caribbean** (6 Marine Parade, tel. 501/223-0800, www.chateaucaribbean.com, US$89) resides in an old wooden building with wide porches, ocean breezes, and plenty of character, although overall it is in need of some TLC. The 19 guest rooms are a bit worn but have clean beds and private baths, cable TV, fridges, wireless Internet, and air-conditioning. The lounge areas, restaurant, and bar have big east-facing bay windows; definitely ask for an upstairs room. The restaurant, serving a range that includes Chinese, international, and Belizean dishes, is popular with locals, and the food is actually quite good.

Just a few minutes farther north, located in Buttonwood Bay, an upscale residential area just three miles north of downtown and seven miles south of the international airport, ★ **Villa Boscardi Bed & Breakfast** (6043 Manatee Dr., tel. 501/223-1691, www.villaboscardi.com, US$75 plus tax, includes breakfast) is an excellent value and wonderful retreat from city noise. It's just a block away from the sea and from the prime minister's home, and a 10-minute drive into the city. Owner Françoise, an interior decorator by training, takes pride in her villa, ensuring the spotless guest rooms convey the cozy at-home atmosphere of a bed-and-breakfast but with a notch up. Guest rooms and suites are located inside the house or at the back of the property with garden views. A honeymoon suite is also available. Hot breakfast is included and served fresh daily, courtesy of the friendly housekeeper, Anna. There's free Internet access and a common desktop and kitchen, and taxis are easy to come by as the guesthouse keeps a list of drivers handy. It's an ideal place to return to after a long day of activities. Shopping and several restaurants are within walking distance, including the delicious Saffron Bay Restaurant just a street behind on Seashore Drive.

US$100-150

The six-floor **Princess Hotel and Casino** (Barrack Rd., tel. 501/223-2670, U.S. tel.

888/790-5264, www.princessbelize.com, US$120) has 170 concrete guest rooms, some recently updated and with new bedding but still slightly worn baths, and all with the same air-conditioning, cable TV, and breakfast. Overall, you'll find much better value elsewhere, particularly at the B&Bs. But if you're looking for lots of on-site entertainment, the Princess houses Belize City's only cinema and bowling alley; there's also a pretty but shallow pool, a gift shop, a beauty salon, a conference room, bars, restaurants (the one over the dock has lovely views), and a tour desk. The on-site marina has docking facilities and water sports, and the popular casino and disco are open midnight-4am.

After World War II, visiting dignitaries from England came to Belize with plans for various agricultural projects, but they couldn't find a place to stay. As a result, the **Radisson Fort George Hotel** (2 Marine Parade Blvd., tel. 501/223-3333, U.S. tel. 800/333-3333, www.radisson.com/belizecitybz, US$139-174 plus tax) was built, and it remains the premier lodging in town. The Radisson's 102 nicely appointed full-service guest rooms sport all the amenities you'd expect, including outrageously priced minibars. This resort-style hotel has two swimming pools (for guests

only), a poolside bar, the Stone Gri licious burgers), and fine dining an breakfast buffet in St. George's Dir All the restaurants host special happy hours. Full catering faciliti quet rooms are available. All kin such as diving, caving, and golfing, are organized right out of the hotel. The Villa Wing across the street includes restrooms, a new business center, a gym, and an expansion of Le Petit Café, connecting it to the Villa Lobby with expanded seating and wireless Internet (for guests only).

The Belize Biltmore Plaza (Mile 3, Northern Hwy., tel. 501/223-2302, U.S. tel. 800/528-1234, www.belizebiltmore.com, US$140) is the local Best Western branch, three miles north of the city center (seven miles south of the international airport) on the Northern Highway. The Biltmore is popular with business travelers; its 75 midsize guest rooms surround a garden, a pool, and a bar and have cable TV, phones, and modern baths. There's also Internet service, an excellent gift shop, an overpriced dining room (US$12-20) with mediocre international food, and a lounge. The hotel may be convenient for flights, but the Biltmore is walking distance to nothing, so you may feel a bit trapped.

Villa Boscardi

✦ The Great House (13 Cork St., tel. 501/223-3400, www.greathousebelize.com, US$150) is a charming colonial-style boutique hotel, built in 1927 and renovated to show off its 16 unique, spacious, and colorful guest rooms (there are no elevators, just stairs). Both tiled and hardwood floors offset the pastel walls and modern furniture; the guest rooms in back have more charm than the rest. Internet access is included in the room rates, as is a light continental breakfast at the best café in town, Le Petit, next door. Downstairs, you'll find a high-end real estate company, a business service center, a delightful wine bar, and the Smoky Mermaid restaurant, with a sushi bar extension.

Food

Belize City's upscale restaurant scene has yet to explode, but in its place you'll find a host of tasty, reasonably priced, and authentic Belizean food. Residents often grab a boxed meal on the way to work, home, or the next errand. Lunch is big, often consisting of stewed meat and rice and beans, seafood, soup, and other Creole and Latin specialties. Pastries and desserts are popular as well, and you'll find plenty of street vendors selling fast foods, snacks, fresh fruit juices, and more.

CAFÉS

European in flavor is **Le Petit Café** (2 Marine Parade, tel. 501/223-33336, ext. 750, 6am-8pm daily), attached to the Radisson Hotel in the Fort George area. It offers delicious twice-daily baked Belizean and European pastries and cakes, ham-and-cheese croissants, and possibly the best cup of freshly brewed coffee in town. They also make excellent johnny-cakes, plain or stuffed.

Dessert and ice cream junkies can find their joy at **Zero Degrees** (18 St. Thomas Place, tel. 501/223-5132, zerodegreesicecream@yahoo.com, 9am-8pm Mon.-Thurs., 10am-9pm Fri.-Sat., 2pm-9pm Sun.), also serving ice cream cakes.

BELIZEAN

The city is packed with traditional Creole eateries. A long-standing local option is **★ Dit's** (50 King St., tel. 501/227-3330, 8am-6pm Mon.-Sat., 8am-3pm Sun., US$4-6), a fifth-generation family-run Creole institution, serving freshly baked pastries—you must try the jam rolls—as well as pies and other traditional Creole desserts along with the wide menu of local specialties. It's always packed with Belizeans—a good sign. **Nerie's** (Queen St. and Daly St., tel. 501/223-4028, 7:30am-10pm daily, US$5-9) was featured on the Travel Channel in a program about traditional Belizean fare; order stew chicken, fish fillets, soups, and daily specials, including oxtail, jerk, and Garífuna *serre* (fish stewed in a broth of green banana and coconut milk and spiced with garlic, black pepper, and thyme).

A couple of streets from the swing bridge are the infamous meat pies at **Dario's** (33 Hyde's Ln., US$0.75), delicious hot, flaky pastries filled with meat or chicken. Go early if you want them fresh. **Pou's Meat Pies** (New Rd.) is also nearby; try both and decide who rules the city's meat pie district.

Deep Sea Marlin's Restaurant & Bar (Regent St. W., tel. 501/227-6995, 7am-9pm Mon.-Sat., US$4) is on Haulover Creek, next to the Belcove Hotel. It's a cheap and sometimes raucous fishing joint, with tasty Belizean and American staples and simple seating with breezy waterside views. The breakfast fry jacks are said to be out of this world. **Tropicolada Cocktail Hut** (7 Fort St., tel. 501/223-1066, 11am-10pm Tues.-Sat., US$6-10), near Tourism Village, serves some of the best ceviche in Belize City as well as a wide range of Belizean and Central American

Wah Belly Full: Kriol Eats

Stew beef or stew chicken served with coconut rice and beans are typical Kriol dishes.

The most authentic Belizean Kriol food you'll find is right here in Belize City, the heart of the Kriol or Caribbean culture. There's no way you could starve here, between the coconut-based dishes, the meats, the multitude of baked treats, and the very affordable meals. Here's what you shouldn't miss.

- **Boil up:** This isn't served frequently, but when it's available, you should jump at the chance to taste this uniquely Caribbean stew mix of pig tail, fish, hard-boiled eggs, yams, plantains, sweet potato, cassava and yam—all *biled up* in a sauce of tomatoes, onions, and peppers.

- **Meat pies** are serious business—so much so that there's a constant debate on who makes the best: **Dario's** (33 Hyde's Ln.) or **Pou's Meat Pies** (New Rd.)? Join the club and be the judge.

- **Pastries and sweets** are a part of Kriol life. You'll find children selling their mothers' Creole bread, buns, and johnnycakes, often baked with coconut oil. Stop by **Dit's** (50 King St., tel. 501/227-3330, 8am-6pm Mon.-Sat., closes earlier Sun.) to sample traditional jam rolls, hot off the oven by noon. While you're at it, sample their bread pudding, coconut pie, or some "plastic" pudding, made with cassava.

- **Soup:** Of the more than a dozen Kriol soups you could sample, the best-known are beef soup (head to Bird's Isle on Tuesday for the best) and cow foot soup.

- **Stew chicken** is the unofficial national dish of Belize. Often served family style on Sunday, it's also sold throughout the week at various eateries. Along those same lines, you'll find stew beef on the menu and some sort of fry fish or fry chicken. These dishes are almost always served with a heap of coconut rice and beans (not to be confused with beans and rice, which is white rice and stewed beans served separately) or plantains and coleslaw. For some of the best, head to **Deep Sea Marlin's** (Regent St. W., tel. 501/227-6995, 7am-9pm Mon.-Sat.), by the Swing Bridge, or **Nerie's** (Queen St. and Daly St., tel. 501/223-4028, 7:30am-10pm daily).

- **Wine:** Fermenting fruits, plants, and herbs is a tradition in the Belize River Valley. Locally made and potent (6-12 percent alcohol) but delicious wines are worth sampling, particularly the blackberry, cashew, or rice wine. These can be found in villages across the district, including Burrell Boom, on the roads to Altun Ha and Maskall Village, and in Crooked Tree.

dishes and pretty cocktails. Tropicolada closes earlier on Tuesday and later on karaoke Friday.

★ **Bird's Isle Restaurant** (tel. 501/207-2179, 10am-midnight Mon.-Sat., US$5-13), or "Island" as the locals call it, has a longstanding reputation and an excellent waterfront location on a small islet to the south of downtown Belize City. Any taxi driver will know it, or just walk south past the Anglican Church on Albert Street until you can't walk any more. This is a casual affair in a gorgeous outdoor setting, with a spacious yard as well as indoor seating and a waterfront deck where you can watch the fish and birds glide by. Expect large portions of local comfort dishes, including stew beans, hamburgers, and sandwiches.

A couple of blocks past the Princess Hotel, **Thirsty Thursdays** (164 New Town Barracks, tel. 501/223-1677, thirstythursdaysbz@gmail.com, 10am-10pm Mon.-Thurs., 10am-midnight Fri.-Sat., US$8-15) is a popular pre-party joint with a savory menu and breezy patio overlooking the ocean.

CHINESE

There are more authentic Chinese restaurants in Belize City than you can imagine. They all make decent greasy dishes, but a few stand out, such as **Chon Saan Palace** (1 Kelly St., tel. 501/223-3008, 11am-11:30pm Mon.-Sat., 11am-2:30pm and 5-11:30pm Sun., US$4-7). In addition to Chinese standards, there are many seafood and steak options.

Mama Chen's (7 Eve St., tel. 501/223-4568 or 501/620-4257, 10am-6pm Mon.-Sat., US$4-6), on the corner of Eve and Queen Streets and close to the Belize Museum, is a good choice for vegetarians. Choose from veggie chow mein, spicy beef dumplings, crispy spring rolls, sushi, and bubble tea (the "bubbles" are sweet seaweed balls that are slurped up through a thick straw).

ITALIAN AND MEXICAN

Pepper's Pizza (4 St. Thomas St., tel. 501/223-5000, 10am-10pm daily, US$17) offers free delivery within city limits.

Across from the BTL Park, ★ **Chap's Bar and Grill** (160 Newtown Barracks Rd., tel. 501/223-1299, 11am-10pm Tues.-Sat., noon-6pm Sun., US$7-11) is a welcome addition. This Mexican restaurant specializes in savory *arrachera* (grilled marinated flank steak) as well as many other Central American dishes, sandwiches, and bar eats. There's a nice outdoor poolside terrace with partial views of the

Bird's Isle Restaurant's excellent setting make it a popular stop for lunch or dinner.

seaside park. The pool is run by a membership club along with the tennis courts next door, but you're welcome to bring your bathing suit and cool off for US$7.50 per person.

INDIAN

For East Indian curries and dal, ★ **Sumathi** (31 Eve St., tel. 501/223-1172, 11am-3pm and 6pm-11pm Tues.-Sun.) is a solid choice. It's got a great weekly lunch buffet (US$5), plus air-conditioning and a large Indian menu with plenty of vegetarian options. It also offers takeout and delivery anywhere in the city. The food is so good that expats from as far away as San Pedro or Punta Gorda order takeout via plane.

FINE DINING

Belize's Belikin brewing family runs the ★ **Riverside Tavern** (2 Mapp St., tel. 501/223-5640, 11am-10pm Mon.-Thurs., open later Fri.-Sat., US$15-35), an upscale sports bar whose massive "gourmet burger" (10-ounce patty US$9, super-size 16-ounce patty US$12.50), made of Belizean beef from the Bowens' Gallon Jug Estate, is one of the best in the country. The Cuban burger is also delicious, but the King Kong just sounds scary. Or try the coconut-crusted shrimp,

other rich bar foods, pastas, and seafood options. There's beer on tap, and the very convivial atmosphere is popular at happy hour or for Thursday karaoke; it's a meeting place for Belize's who's who crowd. There's just one downside to this place: Table service can be very slow.

Celebrity Restaurant and Bar (Volta Bldg., Marine Parade Blvd., tel. 501/223-2826 or 501/223-7272, www.celebritybelize.com, 11am-10pm daily, US$9-20) is near the water, next to the national bank and museum. You enter through a dark, swanky lounge, emerging into a bright restaurant with a huge variety of seafood, pasta, steaks, and salads. The best deals are Celebrity's takeout menu (US$5) and the giant plate of fish and chips. It's also open for hearty breakfasts on Saturday and Sunday (8am-3pm). Folks rightfully rave about the quesadillas and Budapest Chicken.

The **Smoky Mermaid** (13 Cork St., opposite the Radisson, tel. 501/223-4759, www. smokymermaid.com, 7am-10pm daily, US$12-20) specializes in smoked fish, meats, and assorted fresh breads. Breakfast, lunch, and dinner feature Belizean cuisine and freshly baked Creole bread served on a lovely dining patio under thatched roofs surrounding a porcelain mermaid. Inside the Smoky Mermaid,

Located in the Smoky Mermaid, Nautical Fusion is a delightful sushi bar.

but also with a separate street-side entrance, is a delightful sushi bar. The **Nautical Fusion** (tel. 501/672-4759, 11am-2pm and 5pm-10pm daily, US$7-10) serves classic and tasty sushi offerings as well as noodle bowls, teriyaki dishes, a dessert or two, and wines (even local cashew wine) by the glass or bottle. It's a great date night choice, with soothing music and colorful seating.

The **St. George's Restaurant** (Radisson Fort George Hotel, 2 Marine Parade, tel. 501/223-3333, 6:30am-10am, 11:30am-2pm, and 6:30pm-10pm daily, US$20) serves a grand buffet and has a standard menu of international fare and seafood. Outside around the bar, the **Stonegrill Restaurant** (10am-10pm daily, US$ 15-20) offers a fun, meat-sizzlin'

meal inside or on the heavily vegetated outdoor patio. The burgers are surprisingly good.

GROCERIES

Brodie's (Albert St. and Regent St., tel. 501/227-7070, 8am-6pm Mon.-Fri., closes earlier Sat.-Sun.) is a department store, supermarket, deli, drugstore, and more—a Belizean institution. You can also stock up on your way into or out of the north edge of town at **Save-U Supermarket** (San Cas Plaza, tel. 501/223-1291, 8am-9pm Mon.-Sat., 8am-2pm Sun.). This modern air-conditioned market sells everything any supermarket in the United States would carry, and it's reasonably priced, though not necessarily less than Brodie's.

Information and Services

TOURIST INFORMATION

The central office of the **Belize Tourism Board** (BTB, 64 Regent St., tel. 501/227-2420, U.S. tel. 800/624-0686, www.travelbelize.org) is in the Southside, near the Mopan Hotel and the House of Culture. If offers an excellent free first-timer's map with a suggested walking tour of the city. The **Belize Tourism Industry Association** (10 N. Park St., tel. 501/227-1144, 8am-5pm Mon.-Thurs., shorter hours Fri., www.btia.org) can also answer many of your questions and provide lodging suggestions. **The Belize Hotel Association** (BHA, 13 Cork St., tel. 501/223-0669, www. belizehotels.org) is a nonprofit industry group representing some of the country's most respected resorts and lodges; staff can help you decide where to stay.

BANKS

Most of the city's banking is clustered in one strip along Albert Street, just south of the Swing Bridge. This includes **Atlantic Bank** (tel. 501/227-1225), **Scotiabank** (tel. 501/227-7027), **First Caribbean International Bank** (tel. 501/227-7211), and **Belize Bank** (tel.

501/227-7132). Most banks have ATMs and keep the same hours (8am-1pm Mon.-Thurs., 8am-1pm and 3pm-6pm Fri.).

HEALTH AND EMERGENCIES

For **police, fire,** or **ambulance,** dial 90 or 911. Another ambulance service is **B.E.R.T.** (tel. 501/223-3292). **Belize Medical Associates** (5791 St. Thomas St., tel. 501/223-0302, www.belizemedical.com) is the main private hospital in Belize City. The fairly modern 25-bed facility provides 24-hour assistance and a wide range of specialties. Or try **Karl Heusner Memorial Hospital** (Princess Margaret Dr., tel. 501/223-1548, www.khmh. bz).

MEDIA AND COMMUNICATIONS

The main **post office** (150 N. Front St., tel. 501/227-2201, www.belizepostalservice.gov. bz, 8am-5pm Mon.-Thurs., 8am-4:30pm Fri.) is across from the Caye Caulker Water Taxi Terminal. A second post office is at Queens Square on the Southside (corner of Dolphin

St. and Racoon St., tel. 501/227-1155, 8am-5pm Mon.-Fri.).

As elsewhere in the country, an increasing number of hotels and guesthouses offer at least a single computer for guests or even wireless Internet for your laptop. There are a few broadband Internet cafés in Belize City, though not as many as in San Ignacio or San Pedro.

The **Turton Library's Computer Center** (9am-7pm Mon.-Fri., 9am-1pm Sat.), tucked away in a narrow air-conditioned room above the library, has five speedy computers; they are the cheapest in town at US$1.25 per hour. On the Southside, try **KGS Internet** (29 King St., tel. 501/207-7130, 8am-7pm Mon.-Fri., reduced hours Sat., US$1.50 per hour), a few steps from Dit's Restaurant. It's a clean, organized space with quite a few desktops and fast cable connections. **Angelus Press** (10 Queen St., tel. 501/223-5777, 7:30am-5:30pm Mon.-Fri., reduced hours Sat.-Sun.) has a few machines available for US$1.75 per hour. More expensive options are available in Tourism Village and in the business centers of fancier hotels.

Getting There and Around

Most sights are relatively close together in Belize City, and you can walk from the Southside's House of Culture to the National Museum in about 30 leisurely minutes. This route is generally safe during the day, even more so if you are traveling in a group; I have walked it solo several times.

Check with the travel agencies in the main Caye Caulker Water Taxi Terminal; they may be able to hold your backpacks for the day or arrange for longer storage (US$1 per hour, US$5 per day). The nearby **Smokin' Balam Guest House** (N. Front St., US$2 per bag) offers storage for the day if you're passing through. Ask your guesthouse if you can leave a bag there as well.

AIR

The **Municipal Airport** (TZA), called "Muni," is on the waterfront behind the Marion Jones Sports Complex, one mile from the city center. Belizean commuter planes (Tropic Air or Maya Island Air) provide steady service in and out of Belize City to outlying airports all over the country. It's cheaper to fly to local destinations from here.

From **Philip Goldson International Airport** (BZE, 10 miles west of town, 501/225-2045, www.pgiabelize.com), it's a 20-minute taxi ride to downtown Belize City (US$25), less in the opposite direction. There are no other transportation alternatives unless a friend is picking you up.

BUS

Domestic bus service to mainland jump-off points is handled almost entirely out of **Novelo's Terminal,** on West Canal Street at the western terminus of King Street. If you arrive by bus, it's about 10 blocks to walk downtown to the Swing Bridge. From Novelo's, cross the canal and stay on King Street until you reach Albert Street, then make a left. Continue three blocks to the Swing Bridge and Water Taxi Terminal. You can also cross the street and take a right on Orange Street just one block up, then stay on Orange Street all the way to town; it's always busy with foot traffic. This walk is usually safe during the day but should not be attempted at night. When in doubt, take a taxi, and have one referred if possible; a good rule of thumb is not to walk any streets that appear deserted. International bus service to Guatemala and Mexico and ferry service to Honduras is offered by a handful of companies with offices in the **Caye Caulker Water Taxi Terminal** (north end of the Swing Bridge).

BOAT

The country's two water taxi companies have their terminals in the city, with an all-day schedule of departures and returns to the northern cayes. The islands are very close; Caye Caulker is a mere 45-minute ride, San Pedro is 1.5 hours away, and St. George's Caye is a 25-minute ride. Travelers passing through will find it well worth the time.

Three water taxi companies offer regular service to San Pedro and Caye Caulker. The **Caye Caulker Water Taxi Terminal** (San Pedro tel. 501/226-4646, Caye Caulker tel. 501/226-0992, Belize City tel. 501/223-5752, www.cayecaulkerwatertaxi.com) is at the north end of the Swing Bridge, with boats leaving between 8am and 5pm.

San Pedro Belize Express (tel. 501/223-2225, www.belizewatertaxi.com) departs just a few blocks farther down, near the Tourism Village, between 7:45am and 5:30pm daily.

Water Jets Express (tel. 501/207-1000, www.sanpedrowatertaxi.com) leaves between 8am and 5pm daily from Bird's Isle Water Taxi and Marina.

Verify first and last departures, as those tend to change seasonally. Boat transit to Caye Caulker takes about 45 minutes, then it's another half hour to Ambergris Caye. The trip to Caulker costs about US$10 one-way; to San Pedro costs US$15 one-way. The trip is pleasant on calm sunny days when the boat isn't full, but otherwise be prepared to squeeze on, and it can be a cold and wet ride if the sky to the east is dark.

TAXI

To hail a taxi, look for the green license plates, but better yet, ask your hotel or guesthouse to call you one, and keep the numbers or make arrangements with the driver for the duration of your stay. From the international airport to Belize City, the flat fare is US$25; from the municipal airstrip, expect to pay US$5 or less. The fare for one passenger carried between any two points within Belize City or any other district town is US$3-5. If you plan to make several stops, tell the cabbie in advance and ask what the total will be; this eliminates lots of misunderstandings, as taxis often charge by the stop. They can also be hired by the hour (about US$16-25). For occasional trips to or from town, try Kenneth Bennett of **KB Taxi Service** (tel. 501/634-2865).

TOURS

If you prefer to delegate the logistics of your trip, local travel agencies can book local and international transportation, tours, and accommodations across the country. **S & L Travel and Tours** (91 N. Front St., tel. 501/227-7593 or 501/227-5145, www.sltravel-belize.com) is easy to find, next door to the Image Factory. Belizean owners Sarita and Lascelle Tillet run a first-class and very personable operation; they've been in business for more than 30 years. They can get as creative as you like, whether you want a custom vacation, a photo safari, a bird-watching adventure, or anything else you can imagine.

Day Trips

If you have a full day to spare while passing through Belize City, it's worth hopping on one of the following day trips to see the real interior beauty of the Belize District—home to Mayan sites, monkeys, and Creole villages.

ALTUN HA

Altun Ha (9am-5pm daily, US$5) is 34 miles north of Belize City and has become one of the more popular day trips for groups and individuals venturing from Belize City, Ambergris Caye, and Caye Caulker; it is the most visited archaeological site in Belize. A Mayan trading center as well as a religious ceremonial site, it is believed to have accommodated about 10,000 people. Archaeologists, working amid a Mayan community that has been living here for several centuries, have dated construction to about 1,500-2,000 years ago. It wasn't until the archaeologists arrived in 1964 that the old name, Rockstone Pond, was translated into the Mayan words "Altun Ha."

A team led by Dr. David Pendergast of the Royal Ontario Museum began work in 1965 on the central part of the ancient city, where upward of 250 structures have been found in an area of about 1,000 square yards. So far, this is the most extensively excavated of all the Mayan sites in Belize. For a trading center, Altun Ha was strategically located— a few miles from Little Rocky Point on the Caribbean and a few miles from Moho Caye at the mouth of the Belize River, both believed to have been major centers for the large trading canoes that worked up and down the coasts of Guatemala, Honduras, Belize, Mexico's Yucatán, and all the way to Panama.

Altun Ha spans an area of about 25 square miles, most of which is covered by trees, vines, and rainforest. It was rebuilt several times during the Pre-Classic, Classic, and Post-Classic periods. The desecration of the structures leads scientists to believe that the

site may have been abandoned because of violence.

A gift shop and restroom facilities are at the entrance. Local tour guides (US$10 per group per half hour) are available at the entrance. If you're coming to Altun Ha as part of a package, consider insisting that your tour provider use a local guide; this ensures that local communities benefit from the site.

Rockstone Pond

Located near Plaza B, the reservoir, also known as **Rockstone Pond**, is fed by springs and rain runoff. It demonstrates the advanced knowledge of the Maya in just one of their many fields of expertise: engineering. Archaeologists say that an insignificant little stream ran through the rainforest for centuries. No doubt it had been a source of fresh water for the Maya—but maybe not enough. They diverted the creek and then began a major engineering project, digging and enlarging a deep, round hole that was then plastered with limestone cement. Once the cement dried and hardened, the stream was rerouted to its original course, and the newly built reservoir filled and overflowed at the east end, allowing the stream to continue on its age-old track. This made the area livable.

Today, Rockstone Pond is surrounded by thick brush, and the pond is alive with rainforest creatures, including tarpon, small fish, turtles, and other reptiles.

Sun God Temple

The concentration of structures includes palaces and temples surrounding two main plazas. The tallest building is the **Sun God Temple,** rising 59 feet above the plaza floor. At Altun Ha, the bases of the structures are oval and terraced. The small temples on top have typical small rooms built with the Mayan trademark—the corbel arch.

Temple of the Green Tomb

Pendergast's team uncovered many valuable finds, such as unusual green obsidian blades, pearls, and more than 300 jade pieces—beads, earrings, and rings. Seven funeral chambers were discovered, including the Temple of the Green Tomb, rich with human remains and traditional funerary treasures. Mayan scholars believe the first man buried was someone of great importance; he was draped with jade beads, pearls, and shells.

Next to his right hand, the most exciting find was located—a solid jade head now referred to as **Kinich Ahau** ("The Sun God"). Kinich Ahau is, to date, the largest jade carving found at any Mayan site. The head weighs nine pounds and measures nearly six inches from base to crown. It is reportedly now housed far away in a museum in Canada. The two men who discovered the jade head some 40 years ago, Winston Herbert and William Leslie, still reside in Rockstone Pond and Lucky Strike villages. On November 29, 2006, they were honored by the National Institute of Culture and History for their discovery.

Because of its proximity to Belize City, Altun Ha is Belize's most visited Mayan site.

Altun Ha

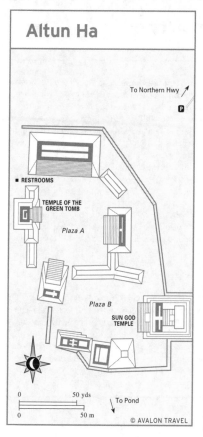

To Northern Hwy

RESTROOMS

TEMPLE OF THE
GREEN TOMB

Plaza A

Plaza B

SUN GOD
TEMPLE

| 0 | 50 yds |
| 0 | 50 m |

To Pond

© AVALON TRAVEL

Getting There

To reach Altun Ha from the Northern Highway, continue past the Burrell Boom turnoff (to the baboon sanctuary) and continue to about Mile 19, where the road forks; the right fork is the Old Northern Highway, which leads to Altun Ha and Maskall Village. The entrance is 10.5 miles from the intersection. The road is in horrible condition and is not getting any better with the increased traffic.

Altun Ha is close enough to Belize City that a taxi ride is your best bet (US$100 round-trip). Kenneth Bennett of **KB Taxi Service** (tel. 501/634-2865) is an excellent driver who will wait for up to 2.5 hours while you tour the site. You can also opt for a tour operator that

specializes in these trips, such as Mr. Lascelle of **S & L Travel and Tours** (91 N. Front St., tel. 501/227-7593 or 501/227-5145, www.sltravelbelize.com).

Note that Altun Ha is a popular destination for cruise-ship passengers (usually Tues. and Thurs.), so if you don't want to share your experience with busloads of tourists, check with the park before coming. In general, it's easy to avoid the crowds if you get here when the park first opens.

THE COMMUNITY BABOON SANCTUARY

The Community Baboon Sanctuary (CBS, tel. 501/245-2009 or 501/245-2007, www.howlermonkeys.org, 8am-5pm daily, US$7) is a nonprofit organization consisting of 220 members in seven local communities who have voluntarily agreed to manage their land in ways that will preserve their beloved "baboon" (the local term for the black howler monkey). Because of community-based efforts to preserve the creature, there are now 3,000 individual monkeys living freely in the forests and buffer zones between people's farms. Since 1998 the CBS Women's Conservation Group has overseen the organization and its members, with a female representative from each of the seven villages. More recently, the CBS member landowners received US$15,000 in microgrants to improve their small businesses and communities. CBS feels remote but is less than an hour's drive from Belize City, making it both a popular day trip and a destination for anyone who'd rather wake up to the throaty roars of Belizean howler monkeys than the bustle of Belize City.

There are enough trails, rivers, and guided tours to keep you busy here for a couple of days. All activities are arranged through the **CBS Visitors Center** (tel. 501/245-2009 or cell tel. 501/622-9624, www.howlermonkeys.org, 8am-5pm daily) in Bermudian Landing; group trips and guides from local hotels are also available. A basic nature walk is included with the entrance fee to the visitors center and museum (feel free to tip your

History of the Community Baboon Sanctuary

One of the six species of howler monkeys in the world, the black howlers, *Alouatta caraya*, are the largest monkeys in the Americas. Robert Horwich of the University of Wisconsin-Milwaukee was the first zoologist to spend extended time in the howler's range, which covered southern Mexico, northeast Guatemala, and Belize. The results of his study were disturbing. In Mexico the monkeys were being hunted for food, and their habitat was fast disappearing. Conditions in Guatemala were only slightly better. Here, too, the monkeys were hunted by locals in the forests around Tikal, and as the forest habitat shrank, so too did the number of howler monkeys.

In the Belizean village of Bermudian Landing, however, the communities of monkeys were strong and healthy, the forest was intact, and the locals seemed genuinely fond of the noisy creatures. This was definitely the place to start talking about a wildlife reserve. Horwich, with the help of Jon Lyon, a botanist from the State University of New York, began a survey of the village in 1984. After many meetings with the town leaders, excitement grew about the idea of saving the "baboon." Homeowners agreed to leave the monkey's food trees—hog plums and sapodillas—and small strips of forest between cleared fields as aerial pathways for the primates, as well as 60 feet of forest along both sides of waterways.

An application was made to World Wildlife Fund USA in 1985 for funds to set up the reserve. Local landowners signed a voluntary management agreement set forth by Horwich and Lyon, and a sanctuary was born.

According to sanctuary manager Fallett Young, who died in 2009, there have been successful relocations of some of the thriving monkey troops around the country, including to the Cockscomb Basin Wildlife Sanctuary, where howlers hadn't been heard since they were decimated by yellow fever decades ago.

In the case of the Community Baboon Sanctuary, educating people about conservation and encouraging their fondness for nature was more successful than stringent hunting laws. The managers of the sanctuary are villagers who understand their neighbors; much of their time is spent with schoolchil-

guide), which is small but has very informative displays on a range of topics—from the history of CBS to the local Kriol culture and Belize's wildlife.

There are 90-minute and three-hour **canoe tours** and a two-hour **driving tour** of some of the different sanctuary villages. Those staying overnight should definitely take advantage of the nighttime trips, such as the 3.5-hour crocodile canoe trip up Mussell Creek and the two-hour night hike into the surrounding forest. If you'd like to experience the local culture, request a **Kriol cultural package** (groups of 12 or more, US$15 pp), with food and dance performances.

If you're lucky, between February and August you might catch a village softball game or cricket match.

Getting There

Bermudian Landing is only 26 miles from Belize City, or about a 45-minute drive. From Belize City, drive north on the Northern Highway for 13 miles, then turn left toward Burrell Boom (notice a sign to turn left for the Black Orchid Resort). Follow signs to the **Community Baboon Sanctuary Museum and Visitors Center**, located across a soccer field. Try not to get confused by the distracting private tour guide signs posted en masse just prior to the museum, and ignore any gestures for you to stop. This is not the official CBS site, and you won't be supporting the community by skipping CBS, who have very competent guides, know the history of the sanctuary, and work with the villages. Look for the CBS logo.

a howler monkey at the Community Baboon Sanctuary

dren and adults in the villages concerned. Part of their education includes basic farming and sustained land use techniques that eliminate the constant need to cut forest for new milpas (cornfields).

Another result is the unhindered growth of 100 species of trees, vines, and epiphytes. The animal life is thriving—anteaters, armadillos, iguanas, hickatee turtles, deer, coatis, amphibians, reptiles, and about 200 species of birds all live here.

A lively debate continues among traditional conservationists about allowing people to live within a wildlife preserve. However, Belize's grassroots conservation is proving that it can succeed.

Two bus companies travel between Bermuda Landing and Belize City. In Belize City, McFadzean buses depart from the corner of Cemetery Road and Amara Avenue, and Russell buses leave from Euphrates Street and Cairo Street. Seven buses depart Belize City between noon and 9pm Monday-Friday; there's a shorter schedule on Saturday. There are no buses in either direction on Sunday. The bus takes about an hour. Four early-morning buses leave Bermudian Landing 5:30am-7am, and there are two in the afternoon at 3:30pm and 4pm Monday-Saturday.

The sanctuary is close enough to the city or the international airport that you can consider a taxi or an escorted tour for a day trip. Negotiate taxi prices ahead of time. The Community Baboon Sanctuary can arrange airport transfers for reasonable prices.

THE BELIZE ZOO

Established in 1983, **The Belize Zoo** (Mile 29, Western Hwy., tel. 501/822-8000, www.belize-zoo.org, 8:30am-4:30pm daily, US$15) is set on 29 acres of tropical savanna and exhibits more than 125 animals, all native to Belize.

The zoo keeps only orphaned animals, those injured and rehabilitated, those born in the zoo, and those received as gifts from other zoos. The environment is as natural as possible, with thick native vegetation, and each animal lives in its own wildlife compound. Displays include Tapir Town; ask about Lucky Boy, a beautiful black jaguar the zoo helped rescue and rehabilitate.

In collaboration with the Panthera organization, the government of Belize, and the U.S. Fish and Wildlife Service, the Belize Zoo also runs the only problem **jaguar rehabilitation** program and in situ jaguar research program in the world. Problem jaguars, which prey on livestock and domestic animals, are trapped and brought to the zoo for behavior modification training—instead of a bullet. In difficult cases, the animals are transferred to zoos in the United States; the Milwaukee and Philadelphia zoos have received problem cats from Belize.

In 2010, Hurricane Richard tore through the zoo, destroying many of the cages and structures. With superhuman efforts, the zoo staff and an army of volunteers participated in immediate reconstruction. And it was literally an army—in addition to Belizean volunteers, tour operators, students, ambassadors, and Belize Zoo fans from abroad, U.S. Special Forces and British Forces Belize took part. The zoo was up and running again in only six weeks. The zoo continues to do amazing work with Belizean wildlife, but it needs all the help—and visitors—it can get.

Getting There

The zoo is at Mile 29 on the Western Highway. It is included in many day tours from Belize City and often as a stop during airport transfers. Independent travelers can easily jump off the bus from Belize City; bus fare from Belize City is US$1-2.

Background

The Landscape

GEOGRAPHY

Belize lies on the northeast coast of Central America, above the corner where the Honduran coast takes off to the east. Belize's 8,866 square miles of territory are bordered on the north by Mexico, on the west and south by Guatemala, and on the east by the Caribbean Sea and the Belize Barrier Reef. From the northern Río Hondo border with Mexico to the southern border with Guatemala, Belize's mainland measures 180 miles long, and it is 68 miles across at its widest point. Offshore, Belize has more than 200 cayes, or islands. Both the coastal region and the northern half of the mainland are flat, but the land rises in the south and west to over 3,000 feet above sea level. The Maya Mountains and Cockscomb range form the country's backbone and include Belize's highest point, **Doyle's Delight** (3,688 feet). Mangrove swamps cover much of the humid coastal plain.

Cayes and Atolls

Belize's more than 200 cayes (pronounced "keys" and derived from the Spanish *cayo* for "key" or "islet") dot the blue waters off Belize's eastern coast, ranging in size from barren patches that are submerged at high tide to the largest two, Ambergris Caye—25 miles long and nearly 4.5 miles across at its widest point—and Caye Caulker, five miles long. Some cayes are inhabited by people, others only by wildlife. The majority are lush patches of mangrove that challenge the geographer's definition of what makes an island (that's why you'll never see a precise figure of how many there are).

Most of the cayes lie within the protection of the 180-mile-long **Belize Barrier Reef**, which parallels the mainland. Without the protection of the reef—in essence a breakwater—the islands would be washed away. Within the reef, the sea is relatively calm and shallow.

Beyond the reef are three of the Caribbean's four atolls: **Glover's Reef, Turneffe Islands,** and **Lighthouse Reef.** An atoll is a ring-shaped coral island surrounding a lagoon, always beautiful, and almost exclusively found in the South Pacific. The three types of cayes are **wet cayes,** which are submerged part of the time and can support only mangrove swamps; **bare coral outcroppings** that are equally uninhabitable; and **sandy islands** with littoral forest, which is the most endangered habitat in Belize due to development pressure. The more inhabited cayes lie in the northern part of the reef and include Caye Caulker, Ambergris Caye, St. George's Caye, and Caye Chapel.

Reefs

The polyps of reef-building corals deposit calcium carbonate around themselves to form a cup-like skeleton or corallite. As these small creatures continue to reproduce and die, their sturdy skeletons accumulate. Over eons, broken bits of coral, animal waste, and granules of soil contribute to the strong foundation for a reef that will slowly rise toward the surface. In a healthy environment, it can grow 1-2 inches a year.

Reefs are divided into three types: atoll, fringing, and barrier. An **atoll** can be formed around the crater of a submerged volcano. The polyps begin building their colonies on the round edge of the crater, forming a circular coral island with a lagoon in the center. Thousands of atolls occupy the

---

world's tropical waters. Only four are in the Caribbean Sea; three of those are in Belize's waters.

A **fringing reef** is coral living on a shallow shelf that extends outward from shore into the sea. A **barrier reef** runs parallel to the coast, with water separating it from the land. Sometimes it's actually a series of reefs with channels of water in between. This is the case with some of the larger barrier reefs in the Pacific and Indian Oceans.

The Belize Barrier Reef is part of the greater Mesoamerican Barrier Reef, which extends from Mexico's Isla Mujeres to the Bay Islands of Honduras. The Belizean portion of the reef begins at Bacalar Chico in the north and ends with the Sapodilla Cayes in the south. At 180 miles long, it is the longest reef in the western and northern hemispheres.

CORAL

Coral is a unique limestone formation that grows in innumerable shapes, such as delicate lace, trees with reaching branches, pleated mushrooms, stovepipes, petaled flowers, fans, domes, heads of cabbage, and stalks of broccoli. Corals are formed by millions of tiny carnivorous polyps that feed on minute organisms and live in large colonies of individual species. Coral polyps have cylinder-shaped bodies, generally less than half an inch long. One end is attached to a hard surface (the bottom of the sea, the rim of a submerged volcano, or the reef itself). The mouth at the other end is encircled with tiny tentacles that capture the polyp's minute prey with a deadly sting. At night, coral reefs really come to life as polyps emerge to feed. Related to the jellyfish and sea anemone, polyps need sunlight and clear saltwater not colder than 70°F to survive. Symbiotic algal cells, called zooxanthellae, live within coral tissues and provide the polyps with much of their energy requirements and coloration.

Estuaries

The marshy areas and bays at the mouths of rivers where salt water and fresh water mix are called estuaries. Here, nutrients from inland are carried out to sea by currents and tides to nourish reefs, sea grass beds, and the open ocean. Many plants and animals feed, live, or mate in these waters. Conchs, crabs, shrimp, and other shellfish thrive here, and several types of jellyfish and other invertebrates call this home. Seabirds, shorebirds, and waterfowl of all types frequent estuaries to feed, nest, and mate. Crocodiles,

Caye Caulker

Belize Coral Watch

Belize's world-class reefs are impacted by overfishing, coastal development, sewage, sedimentation, coral bleaching, and inappropriate or uninformed marine tourism practices. Linda Searle, Belize Coral Watch Program Coordinator and founder of ECOMAR, says that when you touch coral, you are destroying the thin layer of living tissue that keeps the coral healthy. It's like when people get a cut on their skin, she explains; the area becomes more susceptible to invasion by bacteria and disease. When a "cut" on a coral does not heal, this space can become invaded by a disease that can spread to the rest of the coral head, killing the entire colony. Divers and snorkelers can be strong and effective advocates for coral reef conservation. Experienced divers know the best way to enjoy a reef is to slow down, relax, and watch, leaving the reefs undisturbed. Follow these guidelines developed by the **Coral Reef Alliance** (CORAL, www.coral.org) to be a coral-friendly diver.

PREPARING FOR YOUR DIVE TRIP

Choose coral-friendly dive operators that practice reef conservation by:

- Giving diver orientations and briefings.
- Holding buoyancy-control workshops.
- Actively supporting local marine protected areas.
- Using available moorings (anchors and chains destroy fragile corals and sea grass beds).
- Using available wastewater pump-out facilities.
- Making sure garbage is well stowed, especially light plastic items.
- Taking away everything brought on board, such as packaging and used batteries.

IN THE WATER

- Never touch corals; even slight contact can harm them, and some corals can sting or cut you.
- Carefully select points of entry and exit to avoid walking on corals.
- Make sure all of your equipment is well secured.

dolphins, and manatees are regular visitors. Rays, sharks, and tarpon hunt and mate here. During the wet season, the estuaries of Belize pump a tremendous amount of nutrients into the sea.

Mangroves

The doctor on Christopher Columbus's ship reported in 1494 that mangroves in the Caribbean were "so thick that a rabbit could scarcely walk through." Mangroves live on the edge between land and sea, forming dense thickets that act as a protective border against the forces of wind and waves. Four species grow along many low-lying coastal areas on the mainland and along island lagoons and fringes. Of these, the red mangrove and the black mangrove are most prolific. Red mangroves in excess of 30 feet tall are found in tidal areas, inland lagoons, and river mouths, but always close to the sea. Their signature is arching prop roots, which provide critical habitat and nursery grounds for many reef fish. The black mangrove grows to almost double that height. Its roots are slender upright projectiles that grow to about 12 inches, protruding all around the mother tree. Both types of roots provide air to the tree.

- Make sure you are neutrally buoyant at all times.

- Maintain a comfortable distance from the reef, so that you're certain to avoid contact.

- Learn to swim without using your arms.

- Move slowly and deliberately in the water

- Practice good finning and body control to avoid accidental contact with the reef or stirring up the sediment.

- Know where your fins are at all times, and don't kick up sand.

- Stay off the bottom, and never stand or rest on corals.

- Avoid using gloves and kneepads in coral environments.

- Take nothing living or dead out of the water, except recent garbage.

- Do not chase, harass, or try to ride marinelife.

- Do not touch or handle marinelife except under expert guidance and following established guidelines.

- Never feed marinelife.

- Use photographic and video equipment only if you are an advanced diver or snorkeler; cameras are cumbersome and affect a diver's buoyancy and mobility.

- Remember, look but don't touch.

BECOME AN ECOMAR VOLUNTEER

As a volunteer, you'll learn how to identify coral species, coral reef ecology, coral disease, and coral bleaching. After attending a training session, you will be equipped with the knowledge needed to help identify resilient reefs in Belize. Divers and snorkelers are asked to monitor sites and submit reports online. Look for a dive or snorkel center or resort that participates in "Adopt a Reef" with ECOMAR, and help it complete surveys. For more information, contact **ECOMAR** (www.ecomarbelize.org).

MANGROVE SUCCESSION

Red mangroves (*Rhizophora mangle*) specialize in creating land—the seedpods fall into the water and take root on the sandy bottom of a shallow shoal. The roots, which can survive in seawater, then collect sediments from the water and the tree's own dropping leaves to create soil. Once the red mangrove forest has created land, it makes way for the next mangrove in the succession process. The black mangrove (*Avicennia germinans*) can actually out-compete the red mangrove at this stage, because of its ability to live in anoxic soil (without oxygen). In this way, the red mangrove appears to do itself in by creating an anoxic environment. But while the black mangrove is taking over the upland of the community, the red mangrove continues to dominate the perimeter, as it continuously creates more land from the sea. One way to identify a black mangrove forest is by the thousands of dense pneumataphores (tiny air roots) covering the ground under the trees.

Soon, burrowing organisms such as insects and crabs begin to inhabit the floor of the black mangrove forest, and the first ground covers, *Salicornia* and saltwort (*Batis maritima*) take hold—thereby aerating the soil and enabling the third and fourth mangrove species in succession to move in: the white mangrove (*Laguncularia racemosa*) and the gray mangrove (*Conocarpus erectus*), also known locally as buttonwood.

DESALINIZERS

Each of the three primary mangrove species lives in a very salty environment, and each has its own special way of eliminating salt. The red mangrove concentrates the salt taken up with seawater into individual leaves, which turn bright yellow and fall into the prop roots, thereby adding organic matter to the system. The black mangrove eliminates salt from the underside of each leaf. If you pick a black mangrove leaf and lick the back, it will taste very salty. The white mangrove eliminates salt through two tiny salt pores located on the petiole (the stem that connects the leaf to the branch). If you sleep in a hammock under a white mangrove tree, you will feel drops of salty water as the tree "cries" on you. The buttonwood also has tiny salt pores on each petiole.

IMPORTANCE OF MANGROVES

Mangrove islands and coastal forests play an essential role in protecting Belize's coastline from destruction during natural events such as hurricanes and tropical storms. Along with the sea grass beds, they also protect the Belize Barrier Reef by filtering sediment from river runoff before it reaches and smothers the delicate coral polyps. However, dense mangrove forests are also home to mosquitoes and biting flies. The mud and peat beneath mangrove thickets is often malodorous with decaying plant matter and hydrogen sulfide-producing bacteria. Many developers would like nothing better than to eliminate mangroves and replace them with sandy beaches surrounded by seawalls. But such modification to the coastline causes accelerated erosion and destruction of seaside properties, especially during severe storms.

Birds of many species use the mangrove branches for roosting and nesting sites, including swallows, redstarts, warblers, grackles, herons, egrets, ospreys, kingfishers, pelicans, and roseate spoonbills. Along the seaside edge of red mangrove forests, prop roots extend into the water, creating tangled thickets unparalleled as nurseries of the sea. Juveniles of commercial species, such as snapper, hogfish, and lobster, find a safe haven here. The flats around mangrove islands are

Belize's waters are teeming with unique coral formations.

famous for recreational fisheries such as bonefish and tarpon.

The three-dimensional labyrinth created by expanding red mangroves, sea grass beds, and bogues (channels of seawater flowing through the mangroves) provides the home and nursery habitat for nurse sharks, American crocodiles, dolphins, and manatees.

Snorkeling among the red mangrove prop roots is a unique experience where you can witness the abundant marinelife that grow on prop roots and live between the roots. It is within the algae, plants, corals, and sponges that grow on the roots that juvenile spiny lobsters and seahorses can be found.

Destruction of mangroves is illegal in most of Belize; cutting and removal of mangroves requires a special permit and mitigation.

Sea Grass

Standing along the coast of Belize and looking seaward, many visitors are surprised to see something dark in the shallow water just offshore. They expect the sandy bottom typical of many Caribbean islands. However, it is this "dark stuff" that eventually will make their day's snorkeling, fishing, or dining experience more enjoyable. What they are noticing is sea grass, another of the ocean's great nurseries.

Sea grasses are plants with elongated ribbon-like leaves. Just like the land plants they evolved from, sea grasses flower and have extensive root systems. They live in sandy areas around estuaries, mangroves, reefs, and open coastal waters. Turtle grass has broader, tapelike leaves and is common down to about 60 feet. Manatee grass, found to depths of around 40 feet, has thinner, more cylindrical leaves. Both cover large areas of seafloor and intermix in some areas, harboring an amazing variety of marine plants and animals. Barnacles, conchs, crabs, and many other shellfish proliferate in the fields of sea grass. Anemones, seahorses, sponges, and starfish live here. Grunts, filefish, flounder, jacks, rays, and wrasses feed here. Sea turtles and manatees often graze in these lush marine pastures.

These beds and flats are being threatened in some areas by unscrupulous developers who are dredging sand for cement and landfill material (especially on Ambergris Caye).

CLIMATE

The climate in Belize is subtropical, with a mean annual temperature of 79°F, so you can expect a variance between 50°F and 95°F. The dry season generally lasts from December-ish through May, and the wet season June

mangroves on the Old Belize River

through November, although it has been known to rain sporadically all the way into February.

Rainfall varies widely between the north and south of Belize. Corozal in the north receives 40-60 inches a year, while Punta Gorda averages 160-190 inches, with an average humidity of 85 percent. Occasionally during the winter, "Joe North" (a cold front) sweeps down from North America across the Gulf of Mexico, bringing rainfall, strong winds, and cooling temperatures. Usually lasting only a couple of days, cold fronts often interrupt fishing and influence the activity of lobsters and other fish. Fishers invariably report increases in their catches several days before a norther.

The "mauger" season, when the air is still and the sea is calm, generally comes in August; it can last for a week or more. All activity halts while locals stay indoors as much as possible to avoid the onslaught of mosquitoes and other insects.

Hurricanes

Since record keeping began in 1787, scores of hurricanes have made landfall in Belize. In an unnamed storm in 1931, 2,000 people were killed and almost all of Belize City was destroyed. The water rose nine feet in some areas, even onto Belize City's Swing Bridge. Though forewarned by Pan American Airlines that the hurricane was heading their way, most of the townsfolk were unconcerned, believing that their protective reef would keep massive waves away from their shores. They were wrong.

The next devastation came with Hurricane Hattie in 1961. Winds reached a velocity of 150 mph, with gusts of 200 mph; 262 people drowned. It was after Hurricane Hattie that the capital of the country was moved from Belize City (just 18 inches above sea level) to Belmopan. Then, in 1978, Hurricane Greta took a heavy toll in dollar damage, although no lives were lost. More recent serious hurricanes affecting Belize include Mitch in 1998, Keith in 2000, Iris in 2001, and Dean in 2007. In 2010 Hurricane Richard did an unexpected

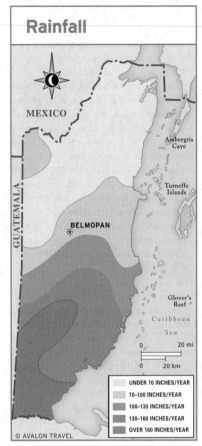

two-step into the Cayo District, destroying the Belize Zoo and a swath of forest canopy in the center of the country. There have also been less serious "northers." In the summer of 2008, Tropical Storm Arthur caused severe flooding throughout the country, and major bridges were washed out.

ENVIRONMENTAL ISSUES

Because of the country's impressive network of protected areas and relatively low population density, the widespread deforestation that occurs in other parts of Central America is not nearly as big a problem in Belize. However, Belize faces its own set of challenges. Perhaps the biggest problem is improper disposal of solid and liquid wastes, both municipal and industrial, particularly agro-wastes from the shrimp and citrus industries.

Mining of aggregates from rivers and streams has negative impacts on local watersheds and the coastal zones into which they empty, where sedimentation can be destructive to reef and other marine systems. Unchecked, unplanned development, especially in sensitive areas like barrier beaches, mangroves, islands, and riverbanks, where changes to the landscape often have wide and unanticipated effects, is another problem.

Energy—or lack thereof—is a major issue for Belize, which historically has had to buy expensive power from neighboring Mexico. The controversial construction of the Chalillo Dam on the upper Macal River brought all of Belize's energy and environmental issues to the forefront (the saga of Chalillo is told in *The Last Flight of the Scarlet Macaw* by Bruce Barcott).

The discovery of oil in 2005 near Spanish Lookout fueled a market of foreign prospectors hoping to tap into new petroleum resources. Oil exploration concessions have been granted for most of Belize's land and marine areas—including, recently, to US Capital Energy Limited to drill in the Toledo District on ancestral Mayan lands—which has caused much concern among environmental groups.

Meanwhile, the Belize Barrier Reef Reserve System was added to the list of World Heritage Sites in Danger in 2009 due to concerns over mangrove cutting and excessive development—and efforts to begin offshore oil drilling.

Plants and Animals

Belize's position at the biological crossroads between North and South America has given it an astonishingly broad assortment of wildlife. Belize's wide-ranging geography and habitat have also been a primary factor in the diversity and complexity of its ecosystems and their denizens.

PLANTS

Belize is a Garden of Eden. Four thousand species of native flowering plants include 250 species of orchids and approximately 700 species of trees. Most of the country's forests have been logged off and on for more than 300 years (2,000 years, if you count the widespread deforestation during the time of the ancient Maya). The areas closest to the rivers and coast were the hardest hit because boats could be docked and logs easily loaded to be taken farther out to sea to the large ships used to haul the precious timber.

Forests

Flying over the countryside gives you a view of the patchwork landscape of cleared areas and secondary growth. Belize consists of four distinct forest communities: **pine-oak, mixed broadleaf, cohune palm,** and **riverine** forests. Pine-oak forests are found in sandy dry soils. In the same areas, large numbers of mango, cashew, and coconut palm trees are grown near homes and villages. The mixed broadleaf forest is a transition area between the sandy pine soils and the clay soils found along the river. Often the mixed broadleaf forest is broken up here and there and doesn't reach great height; it's species-rich but not as diverse as the cohune forest. The cohune forest area is characterized by the cohune palm, which is found in fertile clay soil where a moderate amount of rain falls throughout the year. The cohune nut was an important part of the Mayan diet. Archaeologists say that where they see a cohune forest, they know they'll find evidence of the Maya.

The cohune forest gives way to the riverine forest along river shorelines, where vast amounts of water are found year-round from excessive rain and from the flooding rivers. About 50-60 tree varieties and hundreds of species of vines, epiphytes, and shrubs grow here. Logwood, mahogany, cedar, and pine are difficult to find along the easily accessible rivers because of extensive logging. The forest is in different stages of growth and age. To find virgin forest, it's necessary to go high into the mountains that divide Belize. Because of the rugged terrain and distance from the rivers, these areas were left almost untouched. Even today, few roads exist. If left undisturbed for many, many years, the forest will eventually regenerate itself.

Among the plantlife of Belize, look for **mangroves, bamboo,** and **swamp cypresses** as well as ferns, bromeliads, vines, and flowers creeping from tree to tree, creating dense growth. On the topmost limbs, orchids and air ferns reach for the sun. As you go farther south, you'll find the classic tropical rainforest, including tall mahoganies, *campeche, sapote,* and ceiba, thick with vines.

Orchids

In remote areas of Belize, one of the more exotic blooms, the orchid, is often found on the highest limbs of tall trees. Of all the orchid species reported in Belize, 20 percent are terrestrial (growing in the ground) and 80 percent are epiphytic (attached to a host plant—in this case trees—and deriving moisture and nutrients from the air and rain). Both types grow in many sizes and shapes: tiny buttons, spanning the length of a long branch; large-petaled blossoms with ruffled edges; or intense, tiger-striped miniatures. The lovely flowers come in a wide variety of colors, some subtle, some brilliant. The black orchid is Belize's national flower. All orchids are protected by strict laws, so look but don't pick.

ANIMALS

A walk through the jungle brings you close to myriad animal and bird species, many of which are critically endangered in other Central American countries—and the world. Bring your binoculars and a camera, and be vewy, vewy quiet.

Birds

If you're a serious birder, you know all about Belize. Scores of species can be seen while sitting on the deck of your jungle lodge: big and small, rare and common, resident and migratory—and with local guides aplenty to help find them in all the vegetation. The **keel-billed toucan** is the national bird of Belize

The national flower of Belize is the black orchid.

Keeping Wildlife Wild

You are guaranteed to see wildlife in Belize, whether in the wild or in captivity. However, in Belize some poached birds and wildlife are often sold on the international market, while others end up in Belizean homes or in businesses who want to add "color" to attract tourists. **Belize Bird Rescue** (www.belizebirdrescue.com), a nonprofit organization, reports that 65 percent of all wild-caught captive birds die before they reach sale. Of those that make it, most are sold to people who have no idea how to raise a baby bird.

This is particularly a big deal for the yellow-headed Amazon parrot (*Amazona oratrix*), a gorgeous species under serious threat of extinction in the world. Its numbers have plummeted from 70,000 to 7,000 in the last two decades. Human encroachment on their habitat fuels nest-robbing for the illegal pet trade.

In order to discourage the illegal trade in parrots and other animals:

- **Don't** have your photograph taken with captive indigenous wildlife. By encouraging the keepers of the wildlife, more will be taken from the wild.

- **Don't** patronize establishments with captive wildlife on display unless they are government sanctioned as a breeding or educational facility such as a zoo. There is no educational value to a single monkey or bird in a restaurant.

- **Don't** believe anyone who tells you that they "rescued" an orphan animal or bird, unless they run a licensed rescue facility. The vast majority of these animals were captured from the wild or bought from dealers. If people really want to rescue a bird or animal, they will turn it over to a proper rescue or rehab facility.

- **Don't** buy goods made from animal hides, skins, teeth or claws, or exoskeletons such as bugs and corals. Some leather goods are okay, but exotic ones (crocodile, snake, etc.) normally are not. Jewelry made from jaguar teeth has also appeared on the streets being offered to tourists. Buying them contributes to the decline of the remaining jaguar population. In Belize it is also prohibited to sell any products made out of sea turtles.

- **Do** contact the Belize Forest Department (tel. 501/822-2079, www.forestdepartment.gov.bz) if you observe any conditions where endangered terrestrial animals are being held in captivity or offered for sale. If you observe the sale of turtle meat or jewelry, report the location and date immediately to the Belize Fisheries Department (tel. 501/224-4552, www.agriculture.gov.bz).

and is often seen perched on a bare limb in the early morning.

Belize's hundred-plus cayes are teeming with sea birds, adding to the overall beauty of the scenery. According to the Belize Audubon Society, of the estimated 157 recorded species, 50 are residents, 42 of which breed in this off-shore area. Many more are migrant birds. The cayes are important breeding grounds. The most impressive sighting is the **red-footed booby** colony on Lighthouse Reef's Half Moon Caye—a protected breeding site—home to a bird population of approximately 4,000.

Man-O-War Caye, near the coast of Dangriga, is one of the largest nesting colonies in the Caribbean region for the **magnificent frigatebird** and is also the sole nesting site in Belize for **brown booby**. You can also spot these species in the deep south, around the numerous plots that make up the Port Honduras Marine Reserve and the Sapodilla Cayes Marine Reserve.

Pelicans and **royal terns** are a common sight, hovering around the southern cayes and coast, while **egrets** and **herons** can be spotted on the northern cayes.

Cats

Seven species of felines are found in North America, five of them in Belize. For years, rich adventurers came to Belize on safari to hunt the jaguar for its beautiful fur. Likewise, hunting margay, puma, ocelots, and jaguarundis was a popular sport in the rainforest. Today, hunting endangered cats (and other species) in Belize is illegal, and there are many protected areas to help protect their wide-ranging habitats.

The **jaguar** is heavy-chested with sturdy muscled forelegs, a relatively short tail, and small rounded ears. Its tawny coat is uniformly spotted, and the spots form rosettes: large circles with smaller spots in the center. The jaguar's belly is white with black spots. The male can weigh 145-255 pounds, females 125-165 pounds. Largest of the cats in Central America and the third-largest cat in the world, the jaguar is about the same size as a leopard. It is nocturnal, spending most daylight hours snoozing in the sun. The male marks an area of about 65 square miles and spends its nights stalking deer, peccaries, agoutis, tapirs, monkeys, and birds. If hunting is poor and times are tough, the jaguar will go into rivers and scoop fish with its large paws. The river is also a favorite spot for the jaguar to hunt the large tapir when it comes to drink. Females begin breeding at about three years old and generally produce twin cubs.

The smallest of the Belizean cats is the **margay,** weighing in at about 11 pounds and marked by a velvety coat with exotic designs in yellow and black and a tail that's half the length of its body. The bright eye-shine indicates it has exceptional night vision. A shy animal, it is seldom seen in open country, preferring the protection of the dense forest. The "tiger cat," as it is called by locals, hunts mainly in the trees, satisfied with birds, monkeys, and insects as well as lizards and figs.

Larger and not nearly as catlike as the margay, the black or brown **jaguarundi** has a small flattened head, rounded ears, short legs, and a long tail. It hunts by day for birds and small mammals in the rainforests of Central America. The **ocelot** has a striped and spotted coat and an average weight of about 35 pounds. A good climber, the cat hunts in trees as well as on the ground. Its prey include birds, monkeys, snakes, rabbits, young deer, and fish. Ocelots usually have litters of two kittens but can have as many as four. The **puma** is also known as the cougar or mountain lion. The adult male measures about six feet in length and weighs up to 198 pounds. It thrives in any environment that supports deer, porcupines, or rabbits. The puma hunts day or night.

Half Moon Caye is home to a nesting colony of red-footed boobies.

You're not likely to spot a cat on the cayes, although as recently as December 2013, a jaguar was spotted roaming loose on Ambergris Caye, as authorities spent weeks searching for it to ensure the safety of the animal and the population. Chances of spotting on the mainland are equally slim—but not impossible, particularly if in the lush area surrounding Chan Chich Lodge in northern Belize.

Primates

In Creole, the **black howler monkey** (*Alouatta caraya*) is referred to as a "baboon" (in Spanish, *saraguate*), though it is not closely related to the African species with that name. Because the howler prefers low-lying tropical rainforests (under 1,000 feet of elevation), Belize is a perfect habitat. The monkeys are commonly found near the riverine forests, especially on the Belize River and its major branches. The adult howler monkey is entirely black and weighs 15-25 pounds. Its most distinctive trait is a roar that can be heard up to a mile away. A bone in the throat acts as an amplifier; the cry sounds much like that of a jaguar. The howler's unforgettable bark is said by some to be used to warn other monkey troops away from its territory. Locals, on the other hand, say the howlers roar when it's about to rain, to greet the sun, to say good night, or when they're feeding. The **Community Baboon Sanctuary** is the best place to see howler monkeys in the wild in Belize, though they are very common in the forests around many jungle lodges throughout the country.

Spider monkeys (*Ateles geoffroyi*) are smaller than black howlers and live in troops of a dozen or more, feeding on leaves, fruits, and flowers high in the jungle canopy. Slender limbs and elongated prehensile tails assist them as they climb and swing from tree to tree. Though not as numerous in Belize as howler monkeys because of disease and habitat loss, they remain an important part of the country's natural legacy.

Rodents

A relative of the rabbit, the **agouti** or "Indian rabbit" has coarse gray-brown fur and a hopping gait. It is most often encountered scampering along a forest trail or clearing. Not the brightest of creatures, it makes up for this lack of wit with typical rodent libido and fecundity. Though it inhabits the same areas as the paca, these two seldom meet, as the agouti minds its business during the day and the paca prefers nighttime pursuits. The agouti is less delectable than the paca. Nonetheless, it is taken by animal and human hunters and is a staple food of jaguars.

The **paca,** or **gibnut,** is a quick, brownish rodent about the size of a small dog, with white spots along its back. Nocturnal by habit and highly prized as a food item by many Belizeans, the gibnut is more apt to be seen by the visitor on an occasional restaurant menu than in the wild.

A member of the raccoon family, the **coatimundi**—or "quash"—has a long, ringed tail, a masked face, and a lengthy snout. Sharp claws aid the coati in climbing trees and digging up insects and other small prey. Omnivorous, the quash also relishes rainforest fruits. Usually seen in small troops of females and young, coatis have an amusing, jaunty appearance as they cross a jungle path, tails at attention.

Tapirs

The national animal of Belize, the **Baird's tapir** (*Tapirus bairdii*) is found from the southern part of Mexico through northern Colombia. It is stout-bodied (91-136 pounds), with short legs, a short tail, small eyes, and rounded ears. Its nose and upper lip extend into a short but very mobile proboscis. Totally herbivorous, tapirs usually live near streams or rivers in the forest. They bathe daily and also use the water as an escape when hunted either by humans or by their prime predator, the jaguar. Shy, nonaggressive animals, they are nocturnal with a definite home range, wearing a path between the jungle and their feeding area.

Reptiles

IGUANAS

Found all over Central America, lizards of the family Iguanidae include various large plant-eaters, in many sizes and typically dark in color with slight variations. The young iguana is bright emerald green. The common lizard grows to three feet long and has a blunt head and long flat tail. Bands of black and gray circle its body, and a serrated column reaches down the middle of its back, almost to its tail. During mating season, it's common to see brilliant orange males on sunny branches near the river. This reptile is not aggressive, but if cornered it will bite and use its tail in self-defense.

Though hawks prey on young iguanas and their eggs, humans still remain its most dangerous predator. It is not unusual to see locals along dirt paths carrying sturdy specimens by the tail to put in the cook pot. Iguana stew is believed to cure or relieve various human ailments, such as impotence. Another reason for their popularity at the market is their delicate white flesh, which tastes so much like chicken that locals refer to iguana meat as "bamboo chicken."

CROCODILES

Though they're often referred to as alligators, Belize has only crocodiles, the **American** (*Crocodylus acutus,* up to 20 feet) and the **Morelet's** (*Crocodylus moreletii,* up to 8 feet). Crocodiles have a well-earned bad reputation in Africa, Australia, and New Guinea for feeding on humans, especially the larger saltwater varieties. Their American cousins are fussier about their cuisine, preferring fish, dogs, and other small mammals to people. But when humans feed crocs, either intentionally or by tossing food waste into the water, the animals can acquire a taste for pets, making them extremely dangerous. When apex predators become fearless of people, they are more prone to attack, especially small children.

The territories of both croc species overlap in estuaries and brackish coastal waters. They are most abundant in the rivers, swamps, and lagoons of Belize City and Orange Walk Districts. Able to filter excess salt from its system, only the American crocodile ventures to the more distant cayes, including Turneffe Islands. Endangered throughout their ranges, both crocs are protected by international law and should not be disturbed. Often seen floating near the edges of lagoons or canals during midday, they are best observed at night with the help of a flashlight. When caught in the beam, their eyes glow red (LED flashlights make white eye-shine).

SNAKES

Of the 59 species of snakes that have been identified in Belize, at least nine are venomous, notably the infamous **fer-de-lance** (locally called a "Tommy Goff"), the most poisonous snake in Central America, and the **coral snake.**

Marinelife

Belize is world-famous for the diversity of its rich underwater wildlife, primarily due to its unique geology, the barrier reef lagoon system, and a government that actively works to protect marine habitat. There is also a great deal of marine research in Belize, often with opportunities for visitors to get involved. While all the standard Caribbean species are found in Belizean waters, there are a few animals in particular worth noting.

MANATEES

These "gentle giants of the sea" are large and bulky—weighing 600-1,200 pounds. Manatees belong to the taxonomic order Sirenia, a group of four species that represents the only herbivorous marine mammals living today. There are three species of manatees: the **Amazonian** manatee (*Trichechus inunguis*), the **West African** manatee (*Trichechus senegalensis*), and the **West Indian** manatee (*Trichechus manatus*). The two subspecies of the West Indian manatee are the Florida manatee (*T. m. latirostris*) and the Antillean manatee (*T. m. manatus*). Belize has long been considered the last stronghold for West

Indian manatees in Central America and the Caribbean. West Indian manatees are also found year-round in Florida and are sparsely distributed throughout Central America and the Caribbean; they live as far south as Brazil. The **Antillean** subspecies (which excludes the Florida animals) is red-listed by the International Union for Conservation of Nature (IUCN) as endangered, in continuing decline, with severely fragmented populations.

With a relatively short coastline extending from the Gulf of Honduras in the south to Chetumal Bay in the north, Belize reports the greatest density of Antillean manatees in the Caribbean region, perhaps because of the extensive sea grass, mangrove, coastal, and riverine habitat within the Belize Barrier Reef Lagoon system, or perhaps because manatees have been protected by local laws since the 1930s and are currently listed as endangered under the Wildlife Protection Act of 1981.

Belize has designated several wildlife sanctuaries and protected areas for the benefit of manatees and other marinelife, including Swallow Caye Wildlife Sanctuary, Southern Lagoon Wildlife Sanctuary, Corozal Bay Wildlife Sanctuary, Bacalar Chico National Park and Marine Reserve, South Water Caye Marine Reserve, Burden Canal (part of the Belize River system), and Port Honduras Marine Reserve. Many foreign researchers and Belizean biologists have dedicated years of work to a countrywide research program, aerial surveys, and the stranding network through Coastal Zone Management Institute (www.coastalzonebelize.org): Caryn Self-Sullivan, PhD; James A. "Buddy" Powell, PhD; manatee researcher Nicole Auil of EcoHealth Alliance; Jamal Galves; and manatee tour guide and advocate Lionel "Chocolate" Heredia of Caye Caulker, who was instrumental in the creation of Swallow Caye Wildlife Sanctuary. Orphaned manatees in Belize are cared for by Wildtracks in Sarteneja, where volunteer positions are often available. For more information about manatees, visit www.sirenian.org.

SHARKS AND RAYS

There are at least 42 species of sharks and rays in the waters of Belize. Most people get a good close glimpse of nurse sharks and southern stingrays on their trip to Hol Chan, and divers occasionally spot other species as well, such as the Caribbean reef shark or the great hammerhead, especially on trips to the

a manatee in the north channel of the Belize Barrier Reef

The War Against Lionfish

The Caribbean region's coral reef has been battling an invasive, voracious, and predatory fish—destructive enough that it can devastate an entire reef system: the **red lionfish** (Pterois volitans). Belize is no exception.

Members of the scorpionfish (Scorpaenidae) family, lionfish were first spotted off the Belize Barrier Reef around 2001 but have appeared in greater numbers off the reef and atolls since 2008. Today, it's rare to go diving and not spot them. They hover above sponges and off walls, and they are easily identified by their long spines, considered venomous. Don't get too close!

Among several theories, it's generally believed that lionfish, native to Indian and Pacific Oceans, escaped and got into the Atlantic and Caribbean after a lionfish aquarium in Miami was destroyed by Hurricane Andrew in 1992.

Not only do lionfish have the potential to destroy reefs—which are already facing incredible stress—but they're able to do so at an incredibly frightening pace. They consume prey over half their size and can keep over a dozen victims in their stomachs at a time. They also spawn over 10,000 eggs every five days. The fear is that they will consume native species, like lobsters, snappers, and groupers.

Countrywide, the war against the spread of lionfish is ongoing, led by ECOMAR, a nongovernmental organization in Belize, in partnership with the Belize Fisheries Department. Their efforts have included awareness campaigns, to educate local fishers as well as dive leaders. In addition, lionfish tournaments are held, in collaboration with other organizations, including the Coral Reef Alliance, leading to the capture of thousands per round. Visitors can play their part in preserving the reef and combating this invasive species by signing up for tournaments or even asking for lionfish at restaurants—it is particularly tasty.

ECOMAR also launched an "Adopt A Reef" program, where specific dive and snorkel sites can be adopted by marine guides and dive operators and kept clean of lionfish.

If you're heading out on your dive with the goal of catching and handling lionfish, you can't do it solo—head out with a licensed dive shop, as permits are required from the Fisheries Department, and it must all be done legally and safely.

To learn more about the **Belize Lionfish Project** and how you can help, contact **ECOMAR Belize** (www.ecomarbelize.org).

---

farther atolls, particularly Lighthouse Reef. (The only recorded shark attacks in Belizean waters were due to sheer stupidity: a spear fisherman who refused to give up a fish to a curious shark, and a tour guide who pulled a nurse shark by the tail and wouldn't let go.) To learn more about sharks in Belize and how you can help them, check out www.belizesharks.org.

Although Belize is home to many species of sharks, the biggest and most notable is the **whale shark** (Rhincodon typus). Like all sharks it has a cartilaginous skeleton and visible gill slits, yet it feeds on zooplankton like a whale. It is the largest fish in the sea (up to 66 feet in length and weighing over 15 tons). Whale sharks bear live young (up to 300 have been found in one female), are believed to

be long-lived—living more than 60 years—and may require up to 30 years to mature. According to biologist Rachel Graham, PhD, who has been studying whale sharks since 1998, Belize hosts the only known aggregation of whale sharks that feeds on the eggs of large schools of reproducing snappers. Although this must occur elsewhere in the world, to date Belize is the only known site where it has been observed.

Rays are in abundance in Belize, home to the southern stingray, the manta ray and the spotted eagle ray. They inhabit the reef from north to south and are particularly in abundance in marine reserves. When entering the water from the beach, particularly off the cayes, be sure to do the "stingray shuffle"—slowly rub the sandy bottom as you enter, in order not to startle any rays that may be resting on the sea floor, where they usually sit when not swimming.

SEA TURTLES

Belize is home to five species of sea turtles, although only three are commonly spotted in its waters: the loggerhead, the green turtle, and the hawksbill. The leatherback turtle and the Olive Ridley turtle are an extremely rare sighting. Sea turtles have enjoyed protected status since 2002.

The loggerhead turtle (Caretta caretta) is the most endangered of the three species found in Belize. It can weigh up to 400 pounds, and the reddish-brown shell or carapace can reach four feet in length. They can live up to 150 years, and they roam in shallow, coastal waters, lagoons, and occasionally open seas. You'll see them gliding along in search of crustaceans, mollusks, jellyfish, and sea grass to feed on.

While endangered, green sea turtles (Chelonia mydas)—named after the color of their skin and not their shell—are the most commonly spotted species and the second largest. They can weigh up to 500 pounds. To identify them, note the single pair of pre-frontal scales—between the eyes—and note the white lines on their bodies or shells.

The hawksbill turtle (Eretmochelys imbricata) is my favorite. These gorgeous tortoise-shelled creatures have a beak resembling a hawk's and can weigh up to 200 pounds. Their shells were once valuable and used by European colonial powers to make eyeglass frames, hair combs, and even jewelry, leading to harvesting of the hawksbill and their inevitable decline. In 1993, Fisheries Regulations banned the capture of these turtles. Today, they are the highest in number of all sea turtles found in Belize—as confirmed by the Belize Sea Turtle Census. Hawksbill turtles love coral reefs, where they can feed on sponges.

You can help conserve turtles while you're out exploring—ECOMAR's Belize Turtle Watch Program (www.ecomarbelize.org) welcomes online submissions of your sightings and photos. Launched in 2011 by ECOMAR (www.ecomar.org), in partnership with the government's Fisheries Program and with support from various conservation organizations, the program provides training, monitoring, and in-water surveys, among other activities.

History

Early recorded comments following Columbus's fourth voyage to the New World led the Spaniards to hastily conclude that the swampy shoreline of what is now Belize was unfit for human habitation. Someone should have told that to the Maya, who had been enjoying the area for quite some time. The pre-Columbian history of Belize is closely associated with that of its nearby neighbors: Mexico, Guatemala, and Honduras. The Maya were the first people to inhabit the land. They planted milpas (cornfields), built ceremonial centers, and established villages with large numbers of people throughout the region.

ANCIENT CIVILIZATION

Around 1000 BC, the Olmec culture, believed to be the earliest in the area and the predecessors to the Maya, began to spread throughout Mesoamerica. Large-scale ceremonial centers grew along Gulf Coast lands, and much of Mesoamerica was influenced by the Olmec religion of worshipping jaguar-like gods. The Olmec also developed the New World's first calendar and an early system of writing.

The Classic Period

The Classic Period, beginning about AD 250, is now hailed as the peak of cultural development among the Maya. For the next 600

History in a Nutshell

The peaceful country of Belize is a sovereign democratic state of Central America located on the Caribbean. The government is patterned on the system of parliamentary democracy and experiences no more political turmoil than any other similar government, such as that of Great Britain or the United States.

IMPORTANT DATES

- 1798: Battle of St. George's Caye
- 1862: Became a British colony
- 1954: Attained universal adult suffrage
- 1964: Began self-government
- 1973: Name of the territory changed from British Honduras to Belize
- 1981: Attained full independence

years, until AD 900, the Maya made phenomenal progress in the development of artistic, architectural, and astronomical skills. They constructed impressive buildings during this period and wrote codices (folded bark books) filled with hieroglyphic symbols that detailed complicated mathematical calculations of days, months, and years. Only the priests and the privileged held this knowledge and continued to learn and develop it until, for some unexplained reason, the growth suddenly halted. A new militaristic society was born, built around a blend of ceremonialism, civic and social organization, and conquest.

Maya Society Collapses

All evidence points to an abrupt work stoppage. After about AD 900, no buildings were constructed, and no stelae, which carefully detailed names and dates to inform future generations of their roots, were erected. What happened to the priests and nobles, the guardians of religion, science, and the arts, who conducted their ritual ceremonies and studies in the large stone pyramids? Why were the centers abandoned? What happened to the knowledge of the intelligentsia? Theories abound. Some speculate about a social revolution—the people were tired of subservience and were no longer willing to farm the land to provide food, clothing, and support for the priests and nobles. Other theories include population pressure on local resources, that there just wasn't enough land to provide food and necessities for the large population. Others believe drought, famine, or epidemics were responsible.

Whatever happened, it's clear that the special knowledge concerning astronomy, hieroglyphics, and architecture was not passed on to Maya descendants. Why did the masses disperse, leaving once-sacred stone cities unused and ignored?

COLONIALISM

In 1530, the conquistador Francisco de Montejo y Álvarez attacked the Nachankan and Belize Maya, but his attempt to conquer them failed. This introduction of Spanish influence did not have the impact on Belize that it did in the northern part of the Caribbean coast until the Caste War.

Hernán Cortés

After Columbus's arrival in the New World, other adventurers traveling the same seas soon found the Yucatán Peninsula. Thirty-four-year-old Cortés sailed from Cuba in 1519 against the will of the Spanish governor. With 11 ships, 120 sailors, and 550 soldiers, he set out to search for slaves, a lucrative business with or without the approval of the government. His search began on the Yucatán coast and eventually encompassed most of Mexico. However, he hadn't counted on the resistance and cunning of the Maya. The fighting was destined to continue for many years—a time of bloodshed and death for many of his men and for the Maya. Anthropologists and historians estimate that as many as 90 percent of Maya were killed by diseases such as smallpox after the arrival of the Spaniards.

Roman Catholicism

Over the years, the majority of the Maya were baptized into the Roman Catholic faith. Most priests did their best to educate the people, teach them to read and write, and protect them from the growing number of Spanish settlers who used them as slaves. The Maya practiced Catholicism in their own manner, combining their ancient beliefs, handed down throughout the centuries, with Christian doctrine. These mystic yet Christian ceremonies are still performed in baptisms, courtship, marriages, illness, farming, house building, and fiestas.

Pirates and the Baymen

While all of Mesoamerica dealt with the problems of economic colonialism, the Yucatán Peninsula had an additional problem: harassment by vicious pirates who made life in the coastal areas unstable. In other parts of the Yucatán Peninsula, the passive indigenous people were ground down, their lands taken away, and their numbers greatly reduced by the European settlers' epidemics and mistreatment.

British buccaneers sailed the coast, attacking the Spanish fleet at every opportunity. These ships were known to carry unimaginable riches of gold and silver from the New World back to the king of Spain. The Belizean coast became a convenient place for pirates

to hole up during bad weather or for a good drinking bout. And although no one planned it as a permanent layover, by 1650 the coast had the beginnings of a British pirate lair and settlement. As pirating slacked off on the high seas, British buccaneers discovered they could use their ships to carry logwood back to a ready market in England (logwood is a low-growing tree that provided rich dyes for Europe's growing textile industry until artificial dyes were developed). These early settlers were nicknamed the Baymen.

For 300 years the Baymen of Belize cut the logwood, and then, when the demand for logwood ceased, they starting cutting down mahogany trees from the vast forests. For three centuries the local economy depended on exported logs and imported food.

Agreement with Spain

In the meantime, the Spanish desperately tried to maintain control of this vast New World across the ocean. But it was a difficult task, and brutal conflicts continually flared between the Spanish and either the British inhabitants or the Maya. The British Baymen were continually run out but always returned. Treaties were signed and then rescinded. The British meanwhile made inroads into the country, importing Africans into slavery (beginning in the 1720s) to cut and move the trees.

Politically, Belize (or, more to the point, its timber) was up for grabs, and a series of treaties did little to calm the Ping-Pong effect between the British and the Spanish over the years. One such agreement, the Treaty of Paris, did little to control the Baymen—or the Spanish.

In 1763, Spain "officially" agreed to let the British cut logwood. The decree allowed roads (along the then-designated frontiers) to be built in the future, though definite boundaries were to be agreed on later. For nearly 150 years the only "roads" built were narrow tracks to the rivers; the rivers became Belize's major highways. Boats were common transportation along the coast, and somehow road building was postponed, leaving boundaries vaguely defined and people on both sides of the border unsure. This was the important bit of history that later encouraged the Spanish-influenced Guatemalans to believe that Belize had failed to carry out the 1763 agreement by building roads, which meant the land reverted back to Spain. Even after Spain vacated Guatemala, Guatemala tried throughout the 20th century to claim its right to Belizean territory.

The Battle of St. George's Caye

The Baymen held on with only limited rights to the area until the final skirmish on St. George, a small caye just off Belize City. The Baymen, with the help of an armed sloop and three companies of a West Indian regiment, won the battle of St. George's Caye on September 10, 1798, ending the Spanish claim to Belize once and for all. After that battle, the British crown ruled Belize until independence was gained in 1981.

Land Rights

In 1807 slavery was *officially* abolished in Belize by England. This was not agreeable to the powerful British landowners, and in many quarters it continued to flourish. Changes were then made to accommodate the will of the powerful. The local government no longer "gave" land to settlers as it had for years (British law now permitted the formerly enslaved and other "coloureds" to hold title). The easiest way to keep them from possessing land was to charge for it—essentially barring the majority in the country from landownership. So, in essence, slavery continued.

Caste War

It was inevitable that the Maya would eventually revolt in a furious attack. This bloody uprising in the Yucatán Peninsula in the 1840s was called the Caste War. Although the Maya were farmers and for the most part not soldiers, in this savage war they took revenge on European men, women, and children by rape

and murder. When the winds of war reversed and the Maya were on the losing side, the vengeance wreaked on them was merciless. Some settlers immediately killed any Maya on sight, regardless of that person's beliefs. Some Maya were taken prisoner and sold to Cuba as slaves; others left their villages and hid in the rainforest, in some cases for decades. Between 1846 and 1850, the population of the Yucatán Peninsula was reduced from 500,000 to 300,000. Guerrilla warfare ensued, with the escaped Maya making repeated sneak attacks on the European settlers. Quintana Roo, adjacent to Belize along the Caribbean coast, was considered a dangerous no-man's-land for more than 100 years until, in 1974, with the promise of tourism, the territory was admitted to the United Mexican States. The "war" didn't really end on the peninsula until the Chan Santa Cruz people finally made peace with the Mexican federal government in 1935, more than 400 years after it had begun.

Restored Mayan Pride

Many of the Maya who escaped slaughter during the Caste War fled to the isolated rainforests of Quintana Roo and Belize. The Maya revived the religion of the "talking cross," a pre-Columbian oracle representing gods of the four cardinal directions. This was a religious-political fusion. Three determined survivors of the Caste War—a priest, a master spy, and a ventriloquist—all wise leaders, knew their people's desperate need for divine leadership. As a result of their leadership and advice from the talking cross, the shattered people came together in large numbers and began to organize. The community guarded the location of the cross, and its advice made the Maya strong once again.

They called themselves Chan Santa Cruz ("People of the Little Holy Cross"). As their confidence developed, so did the growth and power of their communities. Living very close to the Belize (then British Honduras) border, they found they had something their neighbors wanted. The Chan Santa Cruz Maya began selling timber to the British and in

What's in a Name?

No one knows for sure where the name Belize originated or what it means. The country was called Belize long before the British took the country over and renamed it British Honduras. In 1973 the locals changed it back to the original Belize as a first step on the road to independence. There are several well-known theories about its meaning. Some say it's a corruption of the name Wallis (wahl-EEZ), from the pirate (Peter Wallace) who roamed the high seas centuries ago and visited Belize. Others suggest that it's a distortion of the Mayan word *belix*, which means "muddy river." Still others say it could be a further distortion of the Maya word *belikin*, the modern name of the local beer.

return received arms, giving the Maya even more power. Between 1847 and 1850, in the years of strife during the Caste War in neighboring Yucatán, thousands of Mayan, mestizo, and Mexican refugees who were fleeing the Spaniards entered Belize. The Yucatecans introduced the Latin culture, the Roman Catholic religion, and agriculture. This was the beginning of the Mexican tradition in northern Belize, locally referred to as "Spanish tradition." The food is typically Mexican, with tortillas, black beans, tamales, squash, and plantains. For many years, these mestizos kept to themselves and were independent of Belize City.

They settled mostly in the northern sections of the country, which is apparent by the Spanish names of the cities: Corozal, San Estevan, San Pedro, and Punta Consejo. By 1857 the immigrants were growing enough sugar to supply Belize, with enough left over to export the surplus (along with rum) to Britain. After their success proved to the tree barons that sugarcane could be lucrative, the big landowners became involved. Even in today's world of low-priced sugar, the industry is still important to Belize's economy.

INDEPENDENCE

In 1862 the territory of British Honduras was officially created, even though it had been ruled by the British crown since 1798. The average Belizean had few rights and a very low living standard. Political unrest grew in a stifled atmosphere. Even when a contingent of Belizean soldiers traveled to Europe to fight for the British in World War I, the black men were scorned. But when these men returned from abroad, the pot of change began to boil. Over the next 50 years the country struggled through power plays, another world war, and economic crises, but always the seed was there—the desire to be independent. The colonial system had been falling apart around the world, and when India gained its freedom in 1947, the pattern was set. Many small undeveloped countries began to gain independence and started to rely on their own ingenuity to build an economy that would benefit their people.

Even though Belize was self-governing by 1964, it was still dominated by outside influences until September 1981, when it gained its independence from the British crown. In September 1981 the Belizean flag was raised for the first time—the birth of a new country. Belize joined the United Nations, the Commonwealth of Nations, and the Non-Aligned Movement. The infant country's first parliamentary elections were held in 1984. You can see that original Belizean flag at the George Price Centre in Belmopan.

Government and Economy

GOVERNMENT

The **Government of Belize** (www.belize.gov.bz), or "GOB," as you'll see it referred to in the newspapers, is directed by an elected prime minister. The bicameral legislature, or National Assembly, comprises an appointed senate and an elected house of representatives. Belize has two main political parties, PUP (People's United Party) and UDP (United Democratic Party). As in most democracies, the political rhetoric can get very animated, but political-based violence is unheard of.

The current prime minister, Dean Barrow of the UDP, took the post from longtime PUP front man Said Musa in 2008. Barrow's party had been gaining ground in recent years, especially as PUP rulers became increasingly implicated in various corruption scandals. The country's constitution, judicial code, and other legal documents are explained and can be downloaded from the **Ministry of the Attorney General** (www.belizelaw.org).

ECONOMY

The economy of Belize was traditionally based on the export of logwood, mahogany, and chicle (the base for chewing gum, from the chicle tree). Today, tourism, agriculture, fisheries, aquaculture (shrimp farming), and small manufactured goods give the country an important economic boost, but it is still dependent on imported goods to get by. The main exports are sugar, citrus, bananas, lobster, and timber. Overall, domestic industry is severely constrained by relatively high labor and energy costs, a very small domestic market, and the "brain drain" of Belize's most qualified managers, health professionals, and academics to the United States and Europe.

In general, and despite books by PUP economists declaring that all is well, Belize's economy is a mess, and the GOB has been on the verge of bankruptcy for years. In 2004, the government was rocked by a scandal over the use of millions of dollars of pension funds to pay the foreign debts of bankrupt companies controlled by government insiders. This led to the collapse of the overextended Development Finance Corporation (DFC), the effects of which are still being felt and evaluated today.

Thanks to tax concessions given to foreign investors, Belize has attracted new manufacturing industries, including plywood, veneer, matches, beer, rum, soft drinks, furniture, boat building, and battery assembly.

TOURISM

Belize is now a common destination for North American and European travelers. Tourism is one of the most critical economies in the country, responsible for about one in seven jobs and 22 percent of the country's GDP. The **Belize Tourism Board** (tel. 501/227-2420, www.travelbelize.org) has gotten the word "Belize" buzzing on the lips of millions of potential visitors who, only a few years ago, had never even heard of the tiny country. Today, roughly 250,000 overnight visitors come to Belize each year; the majority (about 150,000) are from the United States.

In 2011 there were 716 registered hotels providing jobs to nearly 5,000 Belizeans, and that's not counting restaurant employees, guides, transportation services, etc. Tourism has encouraged the preservation of vast tracts of forests and reefs; it has helped the Institute of Archaeology enhance and develop Belize's archaeological sites as destinations, making possible astounding excavations and discoveries at the Caracol, Xunantunich, Lamanai, Altun Ha, and Cahal Pech ruins.

Of course, tourism can be a double-edged sword, and Belize's founding father, George Price, warned against it; Price said tourism would make Belizeans indentured servants to rich foreigners.

George Price

George Price was Belize's first prime minister on independence in 1981, then served the position again 1989-1993. Born in 1919, Price entered politics in 1944 and never looked back. He did not step down from the leadership of the People's United Party, which he founded in 1950, until 1996 when he retired in Belize City. Price also served as the mayor of Belize City several times. He was the most respected and loved individual in Belize, and you'd be hard-pressed to find anyone who didn't admire him. George Price died on September 19, 2011, just two days shy of the country's 30th anniversary of independence. Belize held its very first state funeral that year, which I had the privilege of attending, and I witnessed the most spectacular display of love and unity all across the country. Belizeans were lined up for hours in the hot sun along the highways and streets of Belize City and Belmopan, waving flags, banners, and personal thank-you messages to their national hero. The **George Price Centre for Peace and Development** (www.gpcbelize.com) in Belmopan is a must-see to learn more about Price's central role in Belizean history.

Cruise Ships

The image of numerous hulking cruise ships on the watery eastern horizon of Belize City is striking. The arrival of the cruise industry to Belize's shores in the 1990s was both much hailed and a highly contentious event. It happened quickly, and Belize soon recorded the highest growth in cruise ship arrivals in the entire Caribbean region: Annual cruise visitor arrivals grew from 14,183 in 1998 to a peak of more than 851,000 in 2004. The year 2010 saw 767,000 cruise visits, according to the Belize Tourism Board, with a slight 3.7 percent drop in 2012.

The Belize Tourism Board officially promotes visits by cruise ships. There are approximately 2,000 people in Belize City who rely on cruise ships for their livelihoods, most of whom work in Tourism Village shops and restaurants. The board acknowledges the need to balance cruise ship tourism with overnight tourism, making sure that one does not take over the other.

In Belize City, cruise ship arrival days are boom days for taxi drivers, tour operators, and shopkeepers. But critics say that's not enough. Stewart Krohn, an esteemed Belizean journalist, writes that inviting cruise ship tourism is the equivalent of selling Belize cheaply. In one editorial, he wrote, "Tourism, at its heart, is a cultural encounter. Long, relaxed, unhurried stays by visitors who have time to meet, interact with, and understand Belizeans and Belize not only means more money in our pockets for beds, food, drinks, and tours; it produces the kind of relationships that small countries in a highly competitive world find increasingly necessary." Such meaningful encounters are impossible with hurried busloads of day-trippers, he argues. "Cruise tourism at best produces a few pennies for a few people; at worst a negative impression born of an impersonal encounter."

Other critics cite the impact on Belize's tiny, fragile infrastructure—damage to roads by cruise bus traffic, maxed-out septic systems, trash on the trails and in the caves. Passengers don't spend much onshore, and few of their dollars trickle very far from the pockets of those who own Tourism Village.

One thing is certain: Bring up cruise tourism at a Belizean barbecue, and you'll hear some fiery opinions (especially if you mention the expansion of cruise ships into Placencia and southern Belize). Despite resistance from Placencians, including many small business owners, the go-ahead was given, and it's a done deal. A brand new pier is currently under construction in Placencia Village. Many fear this upcoming cruise ship tourism will destroy the responsible tourism Placencia has worked so hard to build, as well as the natural resources surrounding the area.

BACKGROUND

GOVERNMENT AND ECONOMY

Keeping the "Eco" in Tourism

The word ecotourism was created in the 1980s with the best of intentions—ostensibly, to describe anything having to do with environmentally sound and culturally sustainable tourism. It was the "business" of preventing tourism from spoiling the environment and using tourism as an economic alternative to spoiling the environment for some other reason.

The success of the concept—and its marketing value—led to a worldwide surge in the usage of that prefix we know so well, even if its actual practice may sometimes fall short of original intentions. Indeed, eco has been used and abused all over the world, and Belize is no exception. Some word-savvy tourism marketers have tried to freshen things up by using "alternative" or "adventure" tourism; when trying to describe an operation that practices the original definition of ecotourism, better terms are "sustainable," "responsible," "ethical," or even "fair-trade" tourism.

Belize is generally acknowledged as one of the world's most successful models of ecotourism. In 2009 Belize hosted the **Third Annual World Conference for Responsible Tourism,** featuring experts from around the world speaking on local economic development through tourism, the impact of mass tourism on local communities, and climate change.

The **Belize Audubon Society** (BAS, www.belizeaudubon.org) is the main organization concerned with keeping the "eco" in tourism—and in keeping pressure on the government of Belize to do the same.

People and Culture

The extraordinary diversity of Belize's tiny population (about 320,000) allows Belizeans to be doubly proud of their heritage—once for their family's background (Maya, Creole, Garífuna, Mennonite, etc.) and again for their country. The mestizo (mixed Spanish and indigenous descent) population has risen to about 50 percent of the country's total, with Creoles making up about 21 percent, Maya 10 percent, Garífuna 4.5 percent, and others 9 percent (in the 2010 census). Here's a bit of background about Belize's diverse demography, but keep in mind that every one of these groups continues to mingle with the others, at least to some extent, ensuring continuing creolization.

CREOLES

Creoles are a mix of two distinctive ethnic backgrounds, African and European, and they use the local English-Creole dialect. Many Creoles are also descended from other groups of immigrants. The center of Creole territory and culture is Belize City. Half of

Belize's ethnic Creoles live here, and they make up more than three-quarters of the city's population. Rural Creoles live along the highway between Belmopan and San Ignacio, in isolated clusters in northern Belize District, and in a few coastal spots to the south—Gales Point, Mullins River, Mango Creek, Placencia, and Monkey River.

Cheap labor was needed to do the grueling timber work in thick, tall rainforests. The British failed to force it on the maverick Maya, so they brought Africans whom they enslaved, indentured laborers from India, and Caribs from distant Caribbean islands, as was common in the early 16th and 17th centuries. "Creolization" started when the first waves of British and Scottish began to intermingle with these imported enslaved and servants.

MESTIZOS

Also referred to as "Ladinos" or just "Spanish," mestizos make up the quickest-growing demographic group in Belize and encompass all Spanish-speaking Belizeans, descended from

a jankanu dancer in Dangriga

slaves. Many Mayan communities continue to live much as their ancestors did and are still the most politically marginalized people in Belize, although certain villages are becoming increasingly empowered and developed, thanks in part to tourism (although some would argue at a cultural cost). Most modern Maya practice some form of Christian religion integrated with ancient beliefs. But ancient Mayan ceremonies are still quietly practiced in secluded pockets of the country, especially in southern Belize.

THE GARÍFUNA

The Garífuna people, in plural Garinagu, came to exist on the Lesser Antillean island of San Vicente, which in the 1700s had become a refuge for escaped slaves from the sugar plantations of the Caribbean and Jamaica. These displaced Africans were accepted by the native Carib islanders, with whom they freely intermingled. The new island community members vehemently denied their African origins and proclaimed themselves Native Americans. As the French and English began to settle the island, the Garífuna (as they had become known) established a worldwide reputation as expert canoe navigators and fierce warriors, resisting European control. The English finally got the upper hand in the conflict after tricking and killing the Garífuna leader, and in 1797 they forcefully evacuated the population from San Vicente to the Honduran Bay Island of Roatan. From there, a large proportion of the Garífuna migrated to mainland Central America, all along the Mosquito Coast.

On November 19, 1823, so the story goes, the first Garífuna boats landed on the beaches of what is now Dangriga, one of the chief cultural capitals of the Garinagu. They landed in Belize under the leadership of Alejo Beni, and a small Garífuna settlement grew in Stann Creek, where they fished and farmed. They began bringing fresh produce to Belize City but were not welcome to stay for more than 48 hours without getting a special permit—the Baymen wanted the produce but feared

some mix of Maya and Europeans. These immigrants to Belize hail from the nearby countries of Guatemala, El Salvador, Honduras, and Mexico. Once the predominant population (after immigration from the Yucatecan Caste War), mestizos are now the second-most-populous ethnic group of Belize. They occupy the old "Mexican-mestizo corridor," which runs along New River between Corozal and Orange Walk. In west-central Belize—Benque Viejo and San Ignacio—indigenous people from Guatemala have recently joined the earlier Spanish-speaking immigrants from Yucatán.

THE MAYA

Small villages of Maya—Mopan, Yucatec, and Q'eqchi'—still practicing some form of their ancient culture dot the landscape and comprise roughly 10-12 percent of Belize's population. After the Europeans arrived and settled in Belize, many of the Maya moved away from the coast to escape hostile Spanish and British intruders who arrived by ship to search for

The Gulisi Primary School

The Garinagu in Belize have been struggling to keep their culture alive, particularly with the younger generation. English and Creole dominate the language scene, and with a diverse population, as well as a young population influenced by mainstream American pop culture and media, a significant number of Garífuna youth are not learning their native tongue, which isn't taught in most schools.

Enter the Gulisi Primary School. Established in 2007 and located adjacent to the Gulisi Garífuna Museum in Dangriga, it's unique in its genre: In addition to a regular primary school academic curriculum, it has a mandatory trilingual system, which requires students to take Garífuna language classes, along with English, the main language of instruction, and Spanish. The goal is to keep Garífuna children rooted in their culture and thus preserve their heritage, but not at the expense of a good education.

Teachers are required to speak fluent Garífuna (government-assisted funding covers their salaries), and the 185 students wear uniforms that have the colors of the Garífuna flag. The school accepts children up to the 8th grade, including those from other cultures who are willing to learn Garífuna alongside everyone else. So successful is the school that it now faces overcrowding. Occasionally, classes are held in part of the museum next door.

For more information, contact Phyllis Cayetano (pcayetano@gmail.com), the school's founder and general manager.

that these free blacks would help the enslaved escape, causing a loss of the Baymen's tight control.

The Garífuna language is a mixture of Amerindian, African, Arawak, and Carib, dating from the 1700s. The Garinagu continued to practice what was still familiar from their ancient West African traditions—cooking with a mortar and pestle, dancing, and especially music, which consisted of complex rhythms with a call-and-response pattern that was an important part of their social and religious celebrations. An eminent person in the village is still the drum maker, who continues the old traditions, along with making other instruments used in these singing and dancing ceremonies that often last all night.

Old dances and drum rhythms are still used for a variety of occasions, especially around Christmas and New Year's. If you are visiting Dangriga, Hopkins, Seine Bight, Punta Gorda, or Barranco during these times (or on Settlement Day, November 19), expect to see, and possibly partake in, some drumming. Feel free to taste the typical foods and drinks. If you consume too much "local dynamite" (rum and coconut milk) or bitters, have a cup of strong chicory coffee, said by

Garinagu to "mek we not have goma" (prevent a hangover).

EAST INDIANS

From 1844 to 1917, under British colonialism, 41,600 East Indians were brought to British colonies in the Caribbean as indentured workers. They agreed to work for a given length of time for one "master." Then they could either return to India or stay on and work freely. Unfortunately, the time spent in Belize was not as lucrative as they were led to believe it would be. In some cases, they owed so much money to the company store (where they received half their wages in trade and not nearly enough to live on) that they were forced to "reenlist" for a longer period. Most of them worked on sugar plantations in the Toledo and Corozal Districts, and many of the East Indian men were assigned to work as local police in Belize City. In a town aptly named Calcutta, south of Corozal Town, many of the population today are descendants of the original indentured East Indians. Forest Home near Punta Gorda also has a large settlement. About 47 percent of the ethnic group lives in these two locations. The East Indians usually have large families and live on small farms with orchards adjacent to their homes. A few trade in pigs and dry goods in mom-and-pop businesses. Descendants of earlier East Indian immigrants speak Creole and Spanish. A few communities of Hindi-speaking East Indian merchants live in Belize City, Belmopan, and Orange Walk.

MENNONITES

Making up more than 3 percent of the population of Belize, German-speaking Mennonites are the most recent group to enter Belize on a large scale. This group of Protestant settlers from the Swiss Alps wandered over the years to northern Germany, southern Russia, Pennsylvania, and Canada in the early 1800s, and to northern Mexico after World War I. The quiet, staid Mennonites and their isolated agrarian lifestyle conflicted with local governments in these countries, leading to a more nomadic existence.

Most of Belize's Mennonites first migrated from Mexico between 1958 and 1962. A few came from Peace River in Canada. In contrast to other areas where they lived, the Mennonites bought large blocks of land (about 148,000 acres) and began to farm. Shipyard (in Orange Walk District) was settled by a conservative wing; Spanish Lookout (in Cayo District) and Blue Creek (in Orange Walk District) were settled by more progressive members. In hopes of averting future problems with the government, Mennonites made agreements with Belize officials that guarantee them freedom to practice their religion, use their language in locally controlled schools, organize their own financial institutions, and be exempt from military service.

Over the 30-plus years that Mennonites have been in Belize, they have slowly merged into Belizean activities. Although they practice complete separation of church and state (and do not vote), their innovations in agricultural production and marketing have advanced the entire country. Mennonite farmers are probably the most productive in Belize; they commonly pool their resources to make large purchases such as equipment, machinery (in those communities that use machinery), and supplies. Their fine dairy industry is the best in the country, and they supply the domestic market with eggs, poultry, fresh milk, cheese, and vegetables.

LANGUAGE

More than eight languages are commonly spoken in Belize. English is the official language, although Belizean Creole (or "Kriol") serves as the main spoken tongue among and between groups. The number of Spanish speakers in Belize is increasing as Central American immigrants continue to arrive. Spanish is the primary language of many native Belizean families, especially among descendants of Yucatecan immigrants who inhabit the northern cayes, the Orange Walk District, and the Corozal District. There are only a few areas of Belize, mainly rural outposts in northern and western Belize, where knowing Spanish is essential to communicate. The Garinagu speak Garífuna, and the various Mennonite communities speak different dialects of Old German. Then there are Mopan, Yucatec, and Q'eqchi' Maya tongues. Still other immigrant groups, like Chinese and Lebanese, also often speak their own languages among themselves.

Sunday: A Day of Rest

Belize is serious about its Sundays. Expect businesses in most parts of the country (even restaurants and cafés) to close on Sunday. The streets are empty as well, giving a ghost-town feel to places like downtown Belize City. Usually, the only stores and eateries open are Chinese shops and maybe a few taco stands on the street.

The Arts

Belize has a fairly rich arts scene for such a small country. Several painters and visual artists from Belize have made a name for themselves internationally. Start your research by looking up the work of Gilvano Swasey, Pen Cayetano, Michael Gordon, Benjamin Nicholas, Carolyn Carr, Chris Emmanuel, and Yasser Musa, to name only a few. The government ministry responsible for the arts is the **National Institute for Culture and History** (NICH, www.nichbelize.org), which comprises four organizations: The Institute of Creative Arts (in Belize City), Museum of Belize and Houses of Culture (locations in Belize City, Orange Walk, Benque Viejo del Carmen, and San Ignacio), the Institute of Archaeology (in Belmopan), and the Institute for Social and Cultural Research (in Belmopan).

ARTS AND CRAFTS

You'll have a selection of Belizean and Guatemalan crafts to choose from when visiting any archaeological site, as vendors typically set up rows of stalls with similar gifts, crafts, textiles, and basketwork. You'll also see slate carvings, a recently resurrected skill of the Maya. Among the leading slate carvers are the **Garcia sisters, Lesley Glaspie,** and the **Magana family.** Their work can be found in several Cayo shops as well as elsewhere in the country. The Garcia sisters helped revive the slate craze, and their quality has always been high. **Mennonite furniture pieces** like hardwood chairs and small tables make possible take-home items.

MUSIC

The music of Belize is heavily influenced by the syncopated beats of Africa as they combine with modern sounds from throughout Latin America, the Caribbean, and North America. The most popular Belizean music is *punta,* a fusion of traditional Garífuna rhythms and modern electric instruments. The "Ambassador of Punta Rock" was Andy Palacio, a prolific musician from the southern village of Barranco, who died in 2008 and was honored as a national hero. While Andy Palacio revived interest in *paranda* and *punta,* the creator of the punta rock genre was actually Pen Cayetano, another renowned Garífuna musician, artist, and advocate. The newer form of *punta* is characterized by driving, repetitive dance rhythms and has its acoustic roots in a type of music called *paranda.* A recent PBS special described *paranda* as "nostalgic ballads coupling acoustic guitar with Latin melodies and raw, gritty vocals . . . which can feature traditional Garífuna percussion like wood blocks, turtle shells, forks, bottles, and nails." A few of the original *paranda* masters, like Paul Nabor in Punta Gorda, can still be found in their hometowns throughout Belize. Several excellent compilation albums of Belizean and Honduran *punta* and *paranda* music are available from Stonetree Records.

Brukdown (or "*bruckdong*") began in the timber camps of the 1800s, when the workers, isolated from civilization for months at a time, would let off steam by drinking a full bottle of rum and then beating on the empty bottle—or the jawbone of an ass, a coconut shell, or a wooden block—anything that made a sound. Add to that a harmonica, guitar, and banjo, and you've got the unique sound of *brukdown.* This is a traditional Creole rhythm kept alive by the legendary Mr. Peters and his **Boom and Chime** band until Mr. Peters passed away in 2010 at the age of 79.

Dub-poetry has emerged as an important format for musical expression in Belize. The most popular artist of this is **Leroy "The Grandmaster" Young,** whose album *Just Like That* is a wonderful listening experience and has been acclaimed by numerous international reviewers.

In the southern part of Belize, you'll likely hear the strains of ancient Mayan melodies played on homemade wooden instruments, including Q'eqchi' harps, violins, and guitars. In Cayo District in the west, listen for the resonant sounds of marimbas and wooden xylophones—from the Latin influence across the Guatemala border. In the Corozal and Orange Walk Districts in the north, Mexican *ranchera* and *romantica* music is extremely popular. Of course reggae is popular throughout the country, especially on the islands (Bob Marley is king in Belize).

Stonetree Records (www.stonetreerecords.com) has the most complete catalog of truly Belizean music, covering a wide range of musical genres and styles. This author's favorites include *Wátina,* a soulful album featuring traditional *paranda* music by the renowned Andy Palacio and the Garífuna Collective, and *Belize City Boil-Up,* a funky collection of remastered vintage Belizean soul tracks from the 1950s, 1960s, and 1970s, featuring The Lord Rhaburn Combo, Jesus Acosta and the Professionals, The Web, Harmonettes, Nadia Cattouse, and Soul Creations.

In addition to recording and marketing dozens of albums, Stonetree, based in the town of Benque Viejo in Cayo, western Belize, is also very active in encouraging new Belizean musicians to experiment and develop their individual sounds. Buy albums online, or pick up a couple of CDs at any gift shop or music store during your visit.

FESTIVALS AND EVENTS

When a public holiday falls on Sunday, it is celebrated on the following Monday. If you plan to visit during holiday time, make advance hotel reservations—especially if you plan to spend time in Dangriga during Settlement Day on November 19 (the area has limited accommodations). Note: On Sunday and a few holidays (Easter and Christmas), most businesses close for the day, and some close the day after Christmas (Boxing Day); on Good Friday most buses do not run. Check ahead of time.

National Heroes and Benefactors Day

On March 9, this holiday is celebrated with various activities, mostly water sports. English sportsman Baron Henry Edward Ernest Victor Bliss, who remembered Belize with a generous legacy when he died, designated a day of sailing and fishing in his will. A formal ceremony is held at his tomb below the lighthouse in the Belize Harbor, where he died on his boat. Fishing and sailing regattas begin after the ceremony.

Carnaval

Carnaval, one week before Lent, is a popular holiday in San Pedro on Ambergris Caye. The locals walk in a procession through the streets to the church, celebrating the last hurrah (for devout Catholics) before Easter. There are lots of good dance competitions.

Easter

Easter weekend in Belize is big: There are concerts, parties, and plenty of dancing and libation flowing all weekend from Belize City to the northern cayes and the south coast. The most popular events, including concerts and beach bashes, are in San Pedro and Caye Caulker, where most Belizean families head for a break by the sea. If you're not interested in being around large crowds, avoid the northern cayes on this long weekend.

Lobsterfest

Lobsterfest is now one of Belize's most popular festivals. The celebration of the lobster season is held the first two weeks of June in San Pedro, Caye Caulker, and Placencia. The celebration in San Pedro is the longest, with a week-long series of events including a bar crawl and a Saturday outdoor food feast with top restaurants serving the crustacean prepared in a myriad of ways.

San Pedro Day

If you're wandering around Belize near June 26-29, hop a boat or plane to San Pedro on Ambergris Caye and join the locals in a festival they have celebrated for decades, **El Día de San Pedro,** in honor of the town's namesake, Saint Peter. This is good fun; hotel reservations are suggested.

St. George's Caye Day

On September 10, 1798, at St. George's Caye off the coast of Belize, British buccaneers fought and defeated the Spaniards over the territory of Belize. The tradition of celebrating this victory is still carried on each year, followed by a weeklong calendar of events from religious services to carnivals. During this week, Belize City feels like a carnival with parties everywhere. On the morning of September 10, the whole city parades through the streets and enjoys local cooking, spirits, and music with an upbeat atmosphere that continues well into the beginning of Independence Day on September 21.

The city also celebrates its very own **Belize Carnival,** usually held in mid-September, following St. George's Caye Day. It consists of a full-blown Caribbean-style costume parade and dancing in the streets and along Central American Boulevard, with hundreds of themed floats blasting soca or *punta* music.

National Independence Day

On September 21, 1981, Belize gained independence from Great Britain. Each year, Belizeans celebrate with carnivals on the main streets of downtown Belize City and in all the district towns, as well as on Ambergris Caye and Caye Caulker. Like giant county fairs, they include displays of local arts, crafts, and cultural activities, while happy Belizeans dance to a variety of exotic *punta,* soca, and reggae rhythms. Again, don't miss the chance to sample local dishes from every ethnic group in the country. With this holiday back-to-back with the celebration of the Battle of St. George's Caye and Belize Carnival, Belize enjoys two weeks of riotous, cacophonous partying, known nationwide as the **September Celebrations.**

Garífuna Settlement Day

On November 19, Belize recognizes the 1823 arrival and settlement of the first Garífuna people in the southern districts of Belize. Belizeans from all over the country gather in Dangriga, Hopkins, Punta Gorda, and Belize City to celebrate with the Garinagu. The day

Belize Carnival takes place every September in Belize City.

begins with the **reenactment** of the arrival of the settlers and continues with all-night dancing to the local Garífuna drums and live *punta* bands. Traditional food—and copious amounts of rum, beer, and bitters—is available at street stands and local cafés. November 19 in Dangriga is one of the most memorable celebrations I've experienced in Belize, and anywhere in the Caribbean, for that matter.

Christmas and New Year's

Christmas is celebrated around the country, shops stay open late pre-Christmas Day, and there is a surge in visitors until just after Christmas, with hotels booked weeks ahead. Belizeans celebrate the eve, day of, and day after Christmas (Boxing Day). Prepare for two full days when stores are closed and everyone is home with family. New Year's is more festive, with various options for parties, concerts, and indoor parties across the country. San Pedro, Caye Caulker, and Placencia Village are known to have the liveliest New Year's bashes. In Belize City, the Radisson Fort George often puts on a New Year's Eve Gala with live music, food, and drinks.

Essentials

Transportation

GETTING THERE
Air

Dozens of daily international flights fly in and out of the country, served by a growing number of major carriers. In general, round-trip airfares to Belize range from $560 and up, although rates occasionally dip throughout the year.

Most travelers to Belize arrive at **Philip Goldson International Airport** (BZE, 501/225-2045, www.pgiabelize.com), 10 miles west of Belize City, outside the community of Ladyville. The airport is named after Philip Stanley Wilberforce Goldson (1923-2001), a respected newspaper editor, activist, and politician. The midsize airport offers gift shops, currency exchange, and two restaurants; Internet access is available in the Sun Garden Restaurant upstairs from the American terminal. Check out the "waving deck" upstairs by the other bar-restaurant for exciting farewell and hello energy. The airport's ongoing runway and apron expansion is in hopes of attracting new carriers from farther away, particularly from Europe.

When it's time to leave, don't forget to carry enough U.S. dollars for your US$18.75 departure tax (if it's not already included in your ticket).

FROM MEXICO

Because airfares to Belize are so high, a few travelers choose to fly into the Mexican state of Quintana Roo on the Yucatán Peninsula, especially to **Cancún**, where discounted airfares are common. Belize's **Tropic Air** (tel. 501/226-2012, U.S. tel. 800/422-3435, www.tropicair.com) now offers direct service (Mon.-Fri., US$155 each way) between Cancún and Belize City's international airport.

AIRPORT TRANSPORTATION

After clearing customs, you'll be besieged by taxi drivers offering rides into town for a fixed US$25; split the cost with fellow travelers if you can. If you are not being picked up by a resort or tour company and you choose to rent a car, look for the 11 rental car offices, all together on the same little strip, across the parking lot from the arrival area.

CONNECTIONS WITHIN BELIZE

To continue to the cayes, you can fly directly to Caye Caulker or San Pedro via the domestic airlines **Tropic Air** (tel. 501/226-2012, U.S. tel. 800/422-3435, www.tropicair.com) or **Maya Island Air** (tel. 501/223-1140 or 501/223-1362, www.mayaislandair.com). You can also take a taxi into town and catch a water taxi for about half the price and just a few hours longer. If it's your first time in Belize, flying is worth it—aside from saving time, you'll be treated to gorgeous aerial views of the water, surrounding cayes, and Belize Barrier Reef.

To reach your resort on a south caye, you can fly via Tropic Air or Maya Island Air to the nearest jump-off point—say, Dangriga, Placencia, or Punta Gorda—and from there catch a boat taxi or the resort's arranged pickup. If you're merely going on day trips to the south cayes, then the only connection you'll need is to your chosen mainland jump-off point by either bus or local flight.

Bus
FROM MEXICO

Getting to Belize by bus after flying into **Cancún** is a cinch; many daily buses travel from the main terminal in Chetumal, Mexico, all the way to Belize City and back. You'll have to get out to wait in various customs and immigration lines, and it's a longer journey, but just follow the crowd and you'll be fine. Several Mexican bus lines also run daily between Chetumal, Belize City, Cayo (Benque), and Guatemala.

After passing through customs at the Cancún airport, you will find service desks for shuttle transportation and the ADO bus ticket agent. You want to go **Playa del Carmen**, an hour south, where you will make a connection to Chetumal. It costs about US$23 for a shared shuttle to Playa del Carmen; private shuttle service is US$70-80, depending on group size. Visit the airport's website (www.cancun-airport.com) to search for rates and reserve shuttle transportation. The airport personnel are very helpful in directing you where you need to go and ensuring you have transportation from the airport; shuttle vans are immediately outside, and buses are to the right.

A bus to Playa del Carmen (about US$10) is the most economical route. Riviera buses are comfortable and air-conditioned; if you're the type of person who packs a sweater for your tropical vacation, it may be useful in this instance. After arriving at the station, a few blocks from an amazing beach, you have two options: continue immediately to **Chetumal** near the Belize border, or overnight in Playa del Carmen. Playa del Carmen has two bus stations: Terminal Alterna on Calle 20 and Terminal Turística (a.k.a. Terminal Riviera, 5th Ave. and Ave. Juárez); you can buy tickets for any destination at either station, so always double-check where your bus departs from when you buy a ticket.

If you continue directly to Chetumal, check the bus schedule; you may need to take a taxi (US$2.50) to Terminal Turística. Buses to Chetumal (US$13.50-20) depart every hour until 5:15pm; the trip takes 5-6 hours and has a few stops in between if you need to grab a snack or use the restroom. Chances are you'll arrive in Chetumal later in the evening, and public transportation options to Belize may not be available.

If you'd rather linger in Playa del Carmen,

you won't be sorry; find a hotel, head to the beach, or stroll along 5th Avenue (Avenida 5). You can book a morning bus to Chetumal, and most likely, it will be departing from Terminal Turística.

The main ADO bus terminal in Chetumal is not too far from the Nuevo Mercado Lázaro Cárdenas, where local buses to Belize depart. Outside the station you can find a taxi or continue walking across the plaza to Avenida Insurgentes. Continue left toward the Pemex gas station on the corner and turn right onto Avenida de los Héroes. Continue two blocks to Calle Segundo Circuito Periférico and turn left. You'll see the repainted school buses waiting at Nuevo Mercado, in a parking lot on the right side of the street.

Car
FROM THE UNITED STATES

The road from Brownsville, Texas, to the border of Belize is just under 1,400 miles. If you don't stop to smell the cacti, you can make the drive in three days, especially now that there is a toll-road bypass around Veracruz and the Tuxtla mountains. The all-weather roads are paved, and the shortest route through Mexico is by way of Tampico, Veracruz, Villahermosa, Escárcega, and Chetumal. There is often construction on Mexican Highways 180 and 186. Lodging is available throughout the drive, although it is most concentrated in the cities and on the Costa Esmeralda, a beautiful strip of mostly deserted beach near Nautla (prices start at around US$20 for a very simple double). If attempting this trip, be sure you have a valid credit card, Mexican liability insurance, a passport, and a driver's license—all original documents and one set of photocopies.

One very important detail when entering Mexico from the United States is to request a *"doble entrada"* on your passport to avoid steep fees. This should only cost about US$10, if it's available. Returning to Mexico from Belize, you'll pay a US$19 per person Belizean exit tax.

FROM MEXICO

It is possible to rent a car in Cancún and continue south on a Belizean adventure, but it'll cost you both money and patience. Still, with the money you save with the cheaper airfare into Cancún, the mobility may be worth it. Cancún is 229 miles from the border at Santa Elena, roughly 4.5 hours in a car on Highway 307. Corporate international rental companies will not let you take their vehicles across the border, so you'll have to find a more accommodating Mexican company, like **J. L. Vegas,** with one office near the Cancún airport and another in the Crystal Hotel. Next, you'll need to "make the papers," as the car guy will surely remind you. Another company that says they'll let you drive into Belize is **Caribbean Rent A Car** (U.S. tel. 866/577-1342, Mexico tel. 800/212-0750, www.cancunrentacar.com).

The most crucial part of driving into Belize from Mexico is having a letter of permission from the car's owner; customs will scrutinize this document. Next, to avoid being turned back at the border, be sure to get the vehicle sprayed with insecticide (US$5) from one of the roadside sprayers near the border—it's tough to pick them out, but look for a little white shack past the bridge after leaving Mexico, and keep your receipt for when you reach customs and immigration. After passing through Mexican immigration (have your passport stamped and hand in your tourist card), you will cross a bridge welcoming you to Belize. On the right-hand side, you will see two unsigned buildings where you must purchase insurance. The tire fumigation is near the fork in the road before the free zone. You will likely be greeted when you first pull over by men offering to help you through the stations, but their services are unnecessary. Still, it can be wise to befriend these touts, as many of them are related to the officers at the border. Give a small tip and ask them to clean your windows while you are getting insurance at the Atlantic house (you must have insurance before you enter immigration).

Although in Mexico proof of registration suffices as proof of ownership, in Belize you may be asked to show a title. You will not need a Temporary Vehicle Importation permit if entering for one month or less; for more time, you may need to post a bond on your vehicle (in greenbacks, to be refunded in Belizean dollars later).

Boat

Boats travel to Punta Gorda back and forth daily from Puerto Barrios, Guatemala. There are two boat services to Puerto Cortés, Honduras (one leaves from Placencia, the other from Dangriga). Vessels traveling to the area must have permission from the Belize Embassy in Washington, D.C.

GETTING AROUND
Air

It is very reasonable and common to get around the country in puddle-jumper planes. Some Belizean airstrips are paved and somewhat official looking (Belize City and San Pedro, for example); the rest are more like short abandoned roadways or strips of mowed grass, but they work just fine. Because such small planes are used, you not only watch the pilot handling the craft, you may also get to sit next to him or her if the flight is full (which is easy in a 12-seater). Best of all, flying low and slow in these aircraft allows you to get a panoramic view of the Belize Barrier Reef, cayes, coast, and rainforest (keep your camera handy).

Two airlines offer regularly scheduled flights to all districts in Belize, from both the international and municipal airports: **Tropic Air** (tel. 501/226-2012, U.S. tel. 800/422-3435, www.tropicair.com) and **Maya Island Air** (tel. 501/223-1140, www.mayaislandair. com). Daily flights are available from Belize City to Caye Caulker, San Pedro, Dangriga, Placencia, Punta Gorda, and a handful of other tiny strips around the country. Flights also link San Pedro to the Cayo District. The Maya Island Air and Tropic Air flights usually combine several destinations in one route, so if you're traveling to Punta Gorda, you may have to land and take off in Dangriga and Placencia first. Ditto for Caulker and San Pedro, which are linked together. There are also regular flights to Flores, Guatemala, and you can fly between Corozal and San Pedro. If your scheduled flight is full, another will taxi up shortly and off you go.

Several charter flight companies will arrange trips to upscale caye resorts like The Phoenix. **Javier's Flying Service** (municipal airport, tel. 501/824-0460 or cell 501/610-0446, www.javiersflyingservice.com) is one such charter, offering local and international flights, air ambulance, and day tours. **Astrum Helicopters** (Mile 3½, Western Hwy., near Belize City, tel. 501/222-5100, www.astrum-helicopters.com) also takes guests to Azul, Isla Marisol Resort, and Cayo Espanto, among others.

HELICOPTER

Charter a chopper for a transfer, adventure tour, filming or photography assignment, aerial property survey, search and rescue mission, or medical evacuation with **Astrum Helicopters** (Mile 3½, Western Hwy., near Belize City, tel. 501/222-5100, www.astrumhelicopters.com); expect to pay around US$1,000 per hour (US$250 pp for most sightseeing tours). Astrum is a modern, professional outfit with new aircraft and a very skilled father-son pilot team.

Bus

Save money, meet Belizeans, and see the countryside on an unrushed trip between towns. The motley buses that serve the entire country range from your typical run-down recycled yellow school bus to plush, air-conditioned luxury affairs. Belize buses are relatively reliable, on time, and less chaotic than the chicken-bus experience in other parts of Central America and Mexico. Even so, buses make many extra stops, including a requisite break in Belmopan for anywhere from 5 to 30 minutes for all buses traveling between Belize City and points west and south; it's a good restroom and taco break.

Your best up-to-date resource for all Belize bus schedules and information is www.belize-bus.wordpress.com, an independent website that pays impressive attention to travel details. Another website with bus schedules is www.guidetobelize.info. Travel time from Belize City to Corozal or San Ignacio is about two hours, to Dangriga 2-3 hours, and to Punta Gorda 5-6 hours. Fares average US$2-4 to

Buses in Belize cover the entire country and fares are cheap.

Distances from Belize City

Belmopan	55 miles
Benque Viejo	81 miles
Corozal Town	96 miles
Dangriga	105 miles
Orange Walk Town	58 miles
Punta Gorda	210 miles
San Ignacio	72 miles

most destinations, US$7-12 for the longer routes.

In Belize City, nearly all buses still begin and end at the **Novelo's Terminal** (W. Collett Canal St., tel. 501/207-4924, 501/207-3929, or 501/227-7146); it's still called that even though the company no longer exists. Reach it by walking west on King Street, across Collett Canal, and into the terminal. Definitely use a taxi when departing or arriving at night. Another walking route from the downtown area and the water taxi is to go west along Orange Street, a busy shopping area, cross over the canal, then turn left and continue a short distance to the terminal.

James Bus runs the most reliable daily Punta Gorda service, using the block in front of the Shell station on Vernon Street (two blocks north of Novelo's) as its terminal.

There are at least a dozen booths for buying a ticket on the various international express bus services **to Guatemala and Mexico.** All are inside or in front of the Caye Caulker Water Taxi Terminal and Swing Bridge. Boat-bus connections are convenient and easy to make, but it all happens in the middle of one of Belize's busiest intersections.

Car

Driving Belize's handful of highways gives you the most independence when traveling throughout the country, but it is also the most expensive. Rental fees were running US$75-125 per day and gasoline was approaching US$6 per gallon at press time. You'll also

have to be adept at avoiding careless dri and obstacles like pedestrians, farm animals, cyclists, iguanas, and the occasional moped-riding cruise ship passengers.

RENTAL CARS

One of the first things you'll see on walking out of the arrival lounge at the international airport is a strip of about a dozen car rental offices offering small, midsize, and 4WD vehicles. Vans and passenger cars are also available, some with air-conditioning. Insurance is mandatory but (like taxes) not always included in the quoted rates. If you know exactly when you want the car, it's helpful and often cheaper to make reservations. Note the hour you pick up the car and try to return it before that time: A few minutes over could cost you another full day's rental fee. Also take the vehicle inspection seriously to make sure you don't get charged for someone else's dings. And don't forget to fill the tank up before giving it back.

Crystal Auto Rental (Goldson International Airport as well as Mile 5, Northern Hwy., tel. 501/223-1600, www.crystal-belize.com) has the largest, newest, most reliable fleet of cars in Belize. It is also the only company that will allow you to drive across the border into Guatemala or Mexico, but you won't be insured. **Jabiru Auto Rental** (tel. 501/224-4680, www.jabiruautorental.bz) is also reliable and has low Internet rates. **Budget Rent a Car** (tel. 501/223-2435, www.budget-belize.com) offers new cars that are well maintained. You'll find a few other international brands with local Belizean branches, including **Avis.**

Travel Specialists and Tour Companies

BELIZE TRAVEL SPECIALISTS

More than travel agents, not quite tour operators, Belize country specialists are small, independent operations that work directly with their clients to arrange all kinds of niche, group, and solo travel within Belize. There is usually no charge for their services, so you

Drive defensively! Expect everyone out there to make sudden passes and unexpected turns—it's your job to stay out of their way.

- Valid U.S. or other foreign driver's licenses and international driving permits are accepted in Belize for a period of three months after entering the country.

- Try not to drive at night if you can avoid it. Besides the additional hazards of night driving in general, some Belizean drivers overuse their high beams, and many vehicles have no taillights.

- Watch out for unmarked speed bumps. No matter how slow you drive, on some you may bottom out.

- Driving rules are U.S.-style with one very strange exception: Sometimes a vehicle making a left-hand turn is expected to pull over to the right, let traffic behind pass, and then execute the turn.

Speed bumps in Belize are called "sleeping policemen."

- If you're going to the cayes and leaving a vehicle on the mainland, be sure to seek out a secure pay parking lot in your city of departure, especially if it's Belize City (the municipal airport is probably the best choice).

- Tires frequently pop, so make sure you have a good spare to get you to the nearest used-tire dealer. New tires may be hard to come by, but Belizeans are geniuses with a patch kit. A decent used spare can be had for around US$30, a patch job about US$5.

- If you plan on traveling during the rainy season or without a 4WD vehicle, make sure you are prepared in the event you get stuck in the mud.

- In general, road conditions may dictate where you can and cannot go, and it is always best to ask around town if you plan to go off the beaten path. Watch out for speed bumps, even on the highways.

- Expect police checkpoints anywhere around the country: They'll check your seat belt, car papers, and driver's license, and dogs will sniff the vehicle for any drugs (courtesy of the U.S. Drug Enforcement Agency).

really can't go wrong by letting them handle some of the planning and booking.

Belize Trips (tel. 501/610-1923, U.S. tel. 561/210-7015, www.belize-trips.com) helps you arrange active itineraries, weddings, and honeymoons and can book you at the best mid- to upscale accommodations in the country. Owner Katie Valk finds out exactly what kind of experience her clients want and then, through her vast network of friends and colleagues across the country, makes that experience happen. Katie is a self-described "music business refugee from New York City" who

has lived full time in Belize for 20-odd years, and you'll often find her swinging a machete through the bush or paddling her kayak as she seeks out and test-drives every adventure she promotes.

Barb's Belize (U.S. tel. 888/321-2272, www.barbsbelize.com) is another small operation that offers custom itineraries for any budget, from backpacker to decadent. Barb's specializes in unique interests, such as traditional herbal medicine, jungle survival, and extreme adventure expeditions. She charges US$50 for her planning services and advice, which she credits to your invoice if you book through her.

ADVENTURE TRAVEL

Dangriga- and Vancouver-based Island Expeditions (U.S. tel. 800/667-1630, www. islandexpeditions.com) has been leading exciting sea kayaking, rafting, ruins, nature, and snorkeling adventures in Belize since 1987. It's a very experienced and professional outfit, and it has stunning island camps in Glover's Reef and Lighthouse Reef Atolls with canvas-wall platform tents. It also offers popular lodge-to-lodge sea kayaking trips and inland river adventures and can help you outfit your own kayak expedition.

Slickrock Adventures (U.S. tel. 800/390-5715, www.slickrock.com), based on its primitively plush camp on a private island in Glover's Reef Atoll, offers paddling trips of various lengths and specializes in sea kayaking, windsurfing, and inland activities like mountain biking.

With decades of experience as a premier land operator in Belize, International Expeditions (U.S. tel. 800/633-4734, www. ietravel.com) has a full-time office in Belize City. It offers group and independent nature travel in sturdy, comfortable vehicles and is staffed by travel and airline specialists, naturalists, and an archaeologist. Trips run 7-14 days with two- and three-day add-ons available.

You'll also find an interesting menu of tours offered by Intrepid Travel (tel. 800/970-7299, http://intrepidtravel.com), an Australian company that runs trips around the world and has a dozen trips that include Belize, some Maya-themed.

Tour Operators

For those interested in letting someone else do the driving (and planning, booking, etc.), various tour operators are reliable. In Belize City, Sarita and Lascelle Tillet of S & L Travel and Tours (91 N. Front St., tel. 501/227-7593 or 501/227-5145, www.sltravelbelize.com) operate as a husband-wife team. They drive late-model air-conditioned sedans or vans and travel throughout the country, with airport pickup available. The Tillets have designed several great special-interest vacations and will custom-design to your interests, whether they be the Mayan archaeological zones (including Tikal), the cayes, or the caves and the countryside.

InnerQuest Adventures (U.S. tel. 800/990-4376, www.innerquest.com) has over 14 years of experience leading wildlife-viewing trips with local guides around the country. It's been featured in dozens of magazines. Minnesota-based Magnum Belize Tours (U.S. tel. 800/447-2931, www.magnumbelize. com) is one of the biggest, longest-standing tour operators, with an extensive network of resorts across the country; the staff is very experienced and can customize every aspect of your trip.

Sea & Explore Belize (U.S. tel. 800/345-9786, www.seaexplore.com) is run by owners Sue and Tony Castillo, native Belizeans who take pleasure and pride in sharing their country with visitors by means of customized trips. They know every out-of-the-way destination and make every effort to match clients with the right areas of the country to suit their interests. Susan worked with the Belize Tourism Board before coming to the United States.

Mary Dell Lucas of Far Horizons Archaeological and Cultural Trips (U.S. tel. 800/552-4575 or 415/482-8400, www.farhorizons.com) is known throughout the Maya world for her excellent archaeological knowledge and insight. Her company provides trips into the most fascinating Mayan sites, regardless of location. Although Mary is an archaeologist herself, she often brings specialists along with her groups.

Also check Jaguar Adventures Tours and Travel (4 Fort St., tel. 501/223-6025, www.jaguarbelize.com), located in Belize City and offering night walks at the Belize Zoo, cave tubing trips, visits to Mayan ruins, snorkeling the reef, and diving the atolls, to name a few adventures.

Belize Travel Representatives (U.S. tel. 800/451-8017, www.belizetravelrepresentatives.com) specializes in tour packages to the cayes, Placencia, and most of the mainland resorts and lodges. It has some of the most extensive archaeologically themed tours in Belize. Contact The Mayan Traveler (U.S. tel. 888/843-6292 or 281/367-3386, www.themayantraveler.com); this company can satisfy even the most serious temple junkie, going to some of the most spectacular sites in the region.

Accommodations and Food

HOTELS AND HOMESTAYS

Of the 700-plus licensed hotels in Belize, the vast majority are very small boutiques. Large foreign-owned hotel chains are rare in Belize.

The Belize Hotel Association (BHA, 13 Cork St., Belize City, tel. 501/223-0669, www.belizehotels.org) is a nonprofit industry organization of some of the country's most respected resorts and lodges. It works with the Belize Tourism Board and handles much of the global marketing for Belize; it also has a helpful listing of accommodations on its website.

Budget accommodations are ample in Belize, with nightly rates under US$25. In Belize, US$10-15 is the bottom line for low-cost lodging. Guesthouses and budget hotels sometimes offer a shared dormitory or bunkroom, often with shared baths and cold water.

Some villages around the country try to emulate the guesthouse and homestay networks available in the southern Toledo villages. Such options are usually primitive accommodations, often lacking electricity, running water, and flush toilets.

Hotel Rates

Exact hotel rates are an elusive thing in Belize; seasonal pricing fluctuations are compounded by various hotel taxes and service charges, sometimes as much as 25-30 percent above the quoted rate. Using a credit card can add another 3-5 percent. Universal standards for presenting prices are absent in Belize's hotel industry. Always make sure the rate you are quoted is actually the same amount you will be asked to pay.

High season is loosely considered to be mid-December through the end of April and is marked by a rise in both the number of visitors and the price of most accommodations. Some places kick their rates up even higher during Christmas, New Year's, and Easter, calling these "holiday" or "peak" rates. A few hotels keep their rates the same year-round, but it's rarely that simple.

Great deals are abundant in the low season (May-Nov.), when room rates plummet across the board, and walk-in specials can save you as much as 50 percent off normal winter (high-season) rates.

FOOD

Throughout this book (and throughout Belize), you will find references to "Belizean" food, often preceded by words like "simple" and "cheap." It should be noted that the very idea of a national cuisine is as new as every other part of Belizean identity. Since the times of the Baymen, Belize has been an import economy, surviving mostly on canned meats like "bully beef" and imported grains and packaged goods. With independence, however, came renewed national pride, and with the arrival of travelers seeking "local" food, the word "Belizean" was increasingly applied to the varied diet of so many cultures. Anthropologist Richard Wilk wrote about the process in his book, *Home Cooking in the Global Village: Caribbean Food from Buccaneers to Ecotourists*.

The common denominator of Belizean

food is **rice and beans,** a starchy staple pronounced as one word with a heavy accent on the first syllable: *"RICE-'n'-beans!"* Belizeans speak of the dish with pride, as if they invented the combination, and you can expect a massive mound of it with most midday meals. Actually, Belizean rice and beans *is* closer to the Caribbean version than the Latin: They use red beans, black pepper, and grated coconut, instead of the black beans and cilantro common in neighboring Latin countries. The rest of your plate will be occupied by something like **stew beef, fry chicken,** or a piece of fish, plus a small mound of either potato or cabbage salad. Be sure to take advantage of so much fresh fruit: oranges, watermelon, star fruit, soursop, mangoes, and papaya, to name a few.

For breakfast, you should try some **fry jacks** (fluffy fried-dough crescents) or **johnnycakes** (flattened biscuits) with your eggs, beans, and bacon.

One of the cheapest and quickest meal options, found nearly everywhere in Belize, is Mexican "fast-food" snacks, especially **taco stands,** which are everywhere you look, serving as many as five or six soft-shell chicken tacos for US$1. Also widely available are *salbutes,* a kind of hot, soggy taco dripping in oil; *panades,* little meat pies; and *garnaches,* which are crispy tortillas under a small mound of tomato, cabbage, cheese, and hot sauce.

Speaking of hot sauce, you'll definitely want to try to take home **Marie Sharp's** famous habanero sauces, jams, and other creative products. Marie Sharp is an independent Belizean success story, and many travelers visit her factory and store just outside Dangriga. (Her products are available on every single restaurant table and in every gift shop in the country.) Her sauce is good on pretty much everything.

Then, of course, there's the international cuisine, in the form of many excellent foreign-themed restaurants. San Pedro and Placencia, in particular, have burgeoning fine-dining scenes.

Many restaurants in Belize have flexible hours of operation and often close for a few hours between lunch and dinner. The omnipresent Chinese restaurants provide authentic Chinese cuisine of varying quality. Most Chinese places sell cheap "fry chicken" takeout and are often your only meal options on Sunday and holidays.

Markets are in every district and have the best local eateries on site.

Responsible Seafood

Many ocean waters are overfished, due in large part to increasing demand from tourists. These helpful tips will ensure you eat seafood responsibly.

- Don't order seafood out of season. The once-prolific lobster (season closed Feb. 15-June 15) is becoming scarce in Belizean waters, and conch (season closed July 1-Sept. 30) is not nearly as easy to find as it once was. Most reputable restaurateurs follow the law and don't buy undersize or out-of-season seafood; however, a few have no scruples.

- Small snappers are great fish to eat. Not only are they delicious, but they are one of the most sustainably caught fish in Belize (often caught locally with a hook and line).

- When dining out, don't patronize any restaurant offering shark fin soup or *panades* (meat pies) made with shark meat. Not only are sharks critical to a functional marine ecosystem, but the meat is high in methyl mercury, so it's bad for you too.

- Avoid any restaurant that displays endangered reef fish, like the Nassau grouper or goliath grouper, in tanks as meal choices. In fact, stay away from grouper in general, especially goliath grouper (*Epinephelus itajara*, locally known as jewfish), a critically endangered species that is also high in methyl mercury.

- Lastly, don't buy marine curios such as shark teeth or jaws, starfish, or coral.

Seafood

One of the favorite Belize specialties is fresh fish, especially along the coast and on the islands, but even inland Belize is never more than 60 miles from the ocean. There's lobster, shrimp, red snapper, sea bass, halibut, barracuda, conch, and lots more prepared in a variety of ways.

Conch has been a staple in the diet of the Mayan and Central American communities along the Caribbean coast for centuries. There are conch fritters, conch steak, and conch stew; it's also often used in ceviche—uncooked seafood marinated in lime juice with onions, peppers, tomatoes, and a host of spices. In another favorite, conch is pounded, dipped in egg and cracker crumbs, and sautéed quickly (like abalone steak in California) with a squirt of fresh lime. Caution: If it's cooked too long, it becomes tough and rubbery. Conch fritters are minced pieces of conch mixed into a flour batter and fried—delicious. On many boat trips, the crew will catch a fish and some conch and prepare them for lunch, as ceviche; cooked over an open beach fire; or in a "boil-up," seasoned with onions, peppers, and *achiote*, a fragrant red spice grown locally since the time of the early Maya.

DRINKS
Beer

Perhaps the most important legacy left by nearly three centuries of British imperialism is a national affinity for dark beer. Nowhere else in Central America will you find ale as hearty and dark as you do in any bar, restaurant, or corner store in Belize, where beer is often advertised separately from stout, a good sign indeed for those who prefer more bite and body to their brew.

At the top of the heap are the slender, undersize 280-milliliter (9.5-ounce) bottles of **Guinness Foreign Extra Stout,** known affectionately by Belizeans as "short, dark, and lovelies." Yes, Guinness—brewed in Belize under license from behind the famous St. James's Gate in Dublin, Ireland, and packing a pleasant 7.5 percent punch of alcohol. No, this is not the same sweet nectar you'll find flowing from your favorite Irish pub's draft handle at home, but c'mon, you're in Central America. Enjoy.

Asking for a "beer" will get you a basic **Belikin**, which, when served cold, is no better or worse than any other regional draft. Brewed in Belize since 1971 by Bowen & Bowen Limited, it's the only beer in the Caribbean and Central America that uses a high percentage of malt, very close to Germany's 100 percent. **Belikin Stout** weighs in with a slightly larger 342-milliliter (11.5-ounce) bottle distinguishable from a regular beer bottle by its blue bottle cap. Stouts run 6.5 percent alcohol and are a bit less bitter than Guinness, but it's still a delicious, meaty meal that goes down much quicker than its caloric equivalent of a loaf of bread. **Belikin Premium** (4.8 percent alcohol) boasts a well-balanced body and is brewed with four different types of foreign hops; demand often exceeds supply in many establishments, so order early.

Lastly, the tiny green bottles belong to **Lighthouse Lager,** a healthy alternative to the heavies but packing a lot less bang for the buck with only 4.2 percent alcohol and several fewer ounces of beer (often for the same price).

All beer is brewed and distributed by the same company, Bowen & Bowen, in Ladyville, just north of Belize City; it also has the soft-drink market cornered. Most Belizeans vigorously wipe the open bottle mouths with the napkin that comes wrapped around top—you'd be smart to do the same. Beers Belize cost US$1.50-3 a bottle, depending on where you are.

Rum

Of all the national rums, **One Barrel** stands proudly above the rest. Smooth enough to enjoy on the rocks (add a bit of Coca-Cola for coloring if you need to), One Barrel has a sweet, butterscotchy aftertaste and costs about US$8 for a one-liter bottle, or US$3 per shot (or rum drink). The cheaper option is **Caribbean Rum,** which is fine if you're mixing it with punch, cola, or better yet, coconut water in the coconut. Everything else is standard white-rum gut rot.

The **panty ripper** is Belize's national cocktail—a perfect blend of coconut rum and a splash of pineapple juice. Don't underestimate it as a girly drink; a couple of well-made panty rippas can get you well tipsy.

Bitters

Bitters are made by soaking herbs like *palo del hombre* (man-root) and jackass bitters in 80-proof white rum or gin. They are available under the counter of many a bar and corner store, known in Garífuna as *gífit.*

Belikin beer is the "beer of Belize."

a cure-all used to treat everything ...mmon cold to cancer, sometimes ...daily shot to keep your system

Garífuna expats used to bring
...to the United States by the gal-
...ne most famous bitters maker in the country was Doctor Mac (also known as "Big Mac"), a formidable man who used to make a "fertility" version of bitters for women, with the bottles labeled either "boy" or "gal." The latest bitters-making wonder is "Kid B," a spry senior from Silk Grass Village who spent 36 years as a welterweight prize fighter in Chicago. Find him at **Kid B's Cool Spot** (in Silk Grass, north of

ESSENTIALS
TRAVEL TIPS

the Hopkins turnoff), just off the Southern Highway.

In addition to curing what ails you, however, bitters can get you quite wasted. Be careful with any usage—both for your liver's sake and because some say the ingredients carry trace amounts of arsenic. Talk about a hangover.

Nonalcoholic Beverages
There are wonderful natural fruit drinks to be had throughout Belize. Take advantage of fresh lime, papaya, watermelon, orange, and other healthy juices during your travels—they are usually made with purified water, at least in most tourist destinations.

Travel Tips

VISAS AND OFFICIALDOM
Passports
U.S. citizens must have a passport valid for the duration of their visit to Belize; U.S. citizens, British Commonwealth subjects, and citizens of Belgium, Denmark, Finland, Greece, Iceland, Italy, Liechtenstein, Luxembourg, Mexico, Spain, Switzerland, Tunisia, Turkey, and Uruguay do not need a visa. They are automatically granted a 30-day tourist pass and technically must have onward or return air tickets and proof of sufficient money (though I've never heard of anyone checking this). Visitors for purposes other than tourism, or who want to stay longer than 30 days, need to visit an immigration office of the Government of Belize.

If you are planning on staying more than 30 days, you can ask for a new stamp at any immigration office in the country—there's one in every district, including in San Pedro, Belize City and Dangriga—or you can cross the border and return, but this technique is no guarantee of readmission, particularly if you're gone only for a few days. The fee to extend for a month is US$25.

Make a photocopy of the pages in your passport that have your photo and information. When you get the passport stamped at the airport, it's a good idea to make a photocopy of that page as well, and store the copies somewhere other than with your passport. This will facilitate things if your passport ever gets lost or stolen. Also consider taking a small address book, credit cards, a travel insurance policy, and an international phone card for calling home. A separate passport pouch can be used for documents, but make sure it's waterproof so it won't get soggy when you sweat.

Foreign Embassies
Only a handful of countries have embassies in Belize. The **United States Embassy** (Floral Park Rd., Belmopan, tel. 501/822-4011, fax 501/822-4012, http://belize.usembassy.gov) is open for U.S. citizen services 8am-noon and 1pm-5pm Monday-Friday. The after-hours emergency number for American citizens is 501/610-5030. For inquiries pertaining to American citizens, email ACSBelize@state.gov.

U.S. citizens are strongly encouraged by the

State Department (www.travel.state.gov) to register their trip online, no matter how short, so that the local embassy has emergency contact information on file.

The **British High Commission** (Embassy Square, P.O. Box 91, Belmopan, tel. 501/822-2146, www.ukinbelize.fco.gov.uk/en) is open 8am-noon and 1pm-4pm Monday-Thursday and 8am-2pm Friday. El Salvador and India also have embassies in Belmopan.

Countries with embassies in Belize City include China, Cuba, Mexico, Colombia, Holland, Sweden, and Taiwan.

CONDUCT AND CUSTOMS

Cameras can be a help or hindrance when trying to get to know the locals. When traveling on the mainland or on the islands, you'll run into folks who don't want their pictures taken. Keep your camera put away until the right moment. *Always* ask permission first, and if someone doesn't want his or her picture taken, accept the refusal with a gracious smile and move on. Especially sensitive to this are Mennonites and Maya, who often specifically request that you not take their photos. Many Internet cafés have readers for your digital camera card, so you can make backups as you go. To be safe, travel with extra cards, readers, and cables, as well as a dry bag for those often-wet boat trips.

WHAT TO TAKE

Pack for hot weather (80-95°F, both humid and dry), as well as the occasional cool front (60-80°F). Nights on the islands can get breezy. At least one pair of pants and a light shell or rain jacket are recommended, as rainy season can push all the way into February, and it's guaranteed to be damp June through November. Long sleeves are helpful for avoiding mosquito or sandfly bites and sunburn on the cayes. Bring a small first-aid kit, a flashlight or headlamp, and waterproof plastic bags for protection during rain or boat travel.

ACCESS FOR TRAVELERS WIT DISABILITIES

There are probably about a chair ramps in all of Belize as lights (three); disabled travele: be treated with respect, but ex be challenging on the mainlan tent in the cayes.

TRAVELING WITH CHILDREN

Children love Belize, and Belizeans love children: It's very much a family-oriented society. While a select few romantic resorts do not allow children, most do. Any place offering a special "family package" is a place to start your research. Always check in advance and tell the staff the ages of your children. You'll find most resorts are quite experienced at dealing with all ages.

For babies, be prepared with your own travel kit, but don't stress too much if you forget something. There is a modern selection of jarred food, diapers, bottles, formula, and the like at Brodie's supermarkets in Belize City. If you're short on jars, or if baby wants more than breast milk, you'll find enough fresh fruit and fish to keep your baby growing the whole time you're in Belize. A few resorts can provide a crib in your room if you want one, but make sure you verify this in advance; otherwise bring your own fold-up contraption, which can be great for the beach too, especially since you can easily drape a mosquito net over the top.

Once in Belize, a side visit to the zoo before you hop on to the cayes is worthwhile. There are a few kid-friendly cave trips inland, and, of course, scrambling on the pyramids at any of the archaeological sites is heaven for young explorers. All these can be done from an island base, if a tad more distance and expense. Just be extra careful about covering the kids up with loose, long clothing against the sun and mosquitoes, and make sure they stay hydrated while they rage through the rainforest.

Belize's reputation for romance is growing, and an increasing number of resorts cater to exotic weddings and honeymoon packages, including ceremonies conducted underwater, atop Mayan pyramids, or in caves. (Actually, I don't think anyone's been married in a cave yet, but someone's bound to do it.) Most couples, however, are quite content with a barefoot beach ceremony.

For a US$50 marriage license, the couple must arrive in Belize three business days before submitting marriage paperwork to the Registrar General's office on the fourth business day. A rush job costs US$250 and allows you to obtain your marriage license before arriving in Belize, in which case you can get married on your first day in country, if you so wish. For this service, you'll need a travel agent or wedding planner to act on your behalf in Belize.

The **Registrar General of Belize** (tel. 501/227-2053, www.belizelaw.org) handles marriage licenses. You'll need to show proof of citizenship (i.e., a valid passport), proof that you're over 18, and, where applicable, a certified copy of a divorce certificate or death decree to annul a previous marriage. Forms can be obtained at two locations: the General Registry, Supreme Court Building, Belize City, and the Solicitor General's Office, East Block Building, Belmopan. No blood test is required.

A few select Belize wedding specialists can help you facilitate the paperwork, find ministers, and handle your party's flowers, accommodations, receptions, and everything else. Contact **Iraida Gonzales** (www.belizeweddings.com) in San Pedro or **Lee Nyhus** (www.secretgardenplacencia.com) in Placencia.

Also, during the rainy season, it's best to steer clear of river activities like cave tubing, since rivers can be unpredictable when they swell with rain.

WOMEN TRAVELING ALONE

For the independent woman, Belize is a great place for group or solo travel. Its size makes it easy to get around, English is spoken everywhere, and if you so desire, you won't be lacking for a temporary travel partner in any part of the country. You'll meet many fellow travelers at the small inexpensive inns and guesthouses. Belizeans are used to seeing all combinations of travelers; solo women are no exception.

That said, sexual harassment of females traveling alone or in small groups can be a problem, although most incidents are limited to no more than a few catcalls. Just keep on walking; I've found that usually, some minor acknowledgment that you have heard them will shut harassers up more quickly than totally ignoring them. If they persist and follow to talk to you, tell them you're "on a mission"; i.e., rushing to your next stop—don't feel obligated to stop and respond. Although violent sexual assault is not a common occurrence, it does happen (as it does anywhere in the world). Several American travelers were the victims of sexual assaults in recent years. At least one of these rapes occurred after the victim accepted a ride from a new acquaintance, while another occurred during an armed robbery at an isolated resort. Never give the name of your hotel or your room number to someone you don't know.

Wearing revealing clothes *will* attract lots of gawking attention, possibly more than you want. Most of the small towns, villages, and islands are safe even at night, with the exception of Belize City—don't walk anywhere there at night, even with friends.

A few international tour companies specialize in trips for independent, active women. For "uncommon advice for the independent woman traveler," pick up a copy of Thalia Zepatos's *A Journey of One's Own* (Eighth Mountain Press), a highly acclaimed women's travel resource.

SENIOR TRAVELERS

Active seniors enjoy Belize. Some like the tranquility of the cayes, others the bird-watching and the Maya ruins. Many come to learn about the jungle and its creatures or about archaeology. **Road Scholar** (formerly Elderhostel, U.S. tel. 800/454-5768, www.roadscholar.org) has tours to Belize, including dolphin and reef ecology projects.

GAY AND LESBIAN TRAVELERS

Although there are plenty of out-and-about gay Belizean men (in Kriol, "batty-men"), particularly in San Pedro, there is no established community and no gay clubs per se. The foreign gay travelers I've seen are accepted by both their fellow lodge guests and Belizean hosts. Still, the act of "sodomy" (between men) is officially illegal in Belize, so discretion is advised.

Health and Safety

For up-to-date health recommendations and advice, consult the Belize "Mexico and Central America" page of the **U.S. Centers for Disease Control and Prevention** (CDC, wwnc.cdc.gov/travel/regions/central-america.htm) or call their International Travelers Hotline (877/394-8747). Another excellent resource is the Belize page of **www.mdtravelhealth.com.** You can also call the Belizean embassy in your country for up-to-date information about outbreaks or other health problems.

STAYING HEALTHY

Ultimately, your health is dependent on the choices you make, and chief among these is what you decide to put in your mouth. Expect your digestive system to take some time getting accustomed to the new food and micro-organisms in the Belizean diet. During this time (and after), use common sense: Wash your hands with soap often; alcohol-based hand sanitizers are less effective at removing germs from your hands. Eat food that is well cooked and still hot when served. Be wary of uncooked foods, including shellfish and salads. Most importantly, be aware of flies, the single worst transmitter of food-borne illnesses. Prevent flies from landing on your food, glass, or table setting. You'll notice Belizeans are meticulous about this, and you

should be too. If you have to leave the table, cover your food with a napkin or have someone else wave a hand over it slowly.

Drinking the Water

Even though most municipal water systems are well treated and probably safe, there is not much reason to take the chance, especially when purified bottled water is so widely available and relatively cheap. Canned and bottled drinks, including beer, are usually safe, but should never be used as a substitute for water when trying to stay hydrated, especially during a bout of traveler's diarrhea or when out in the sun.

If you plan on staying awhile in a rural area of Belize, check out camping catalogs for water filters that remove chemical as well as biological contamination. Alternatively, six drops of liquid iodine (or three of bleach) will kill everything that needs to be killed in a liter of water—good in a pinch (or on a backcountry camping trip) but not something you'll find yourself practicing on a daily basis. Also, bringing any water to a full boil is 100 percent effective in killing bacteria.

Oral Rehydration Salts

Probably the single most effective preventative and curative medicine you can carry is packets of powdered salt and sugar, which, when mixed with a liter of water (drink in small sips), is the best immediate treatment for dehydration due to diarrhea, sun exposure, fever, infection, or hangover. Particularly in the case of diarrhea, rehydration salts are essential to your recovery. They replace the salts and minerals your body has lost due to liquid evacuation (be it from sweating, vomiting, or urinating), and they're essential to your body's most basic cellular transfer functions. Whether or not you like the taste (odds are you won't), consuming enough rehydration packets and water is very often the difference between being just a little sick and feeling really, really awful.

Sports drinks like Gatorade are super-concentrated mixtures and should be diluted with water to make the most of the active ingredients. If you don't, you'll pee out the majority of the electrolytes. Rehydration packets are available from any drugstore or health clinic. They can also be improvised, according to the following recipe: mix a half teaspoon of salt, a half teaspoon baking soda, and four tablespoons of sugar in one quart of boiled or carbonated water. Drink a full glass of the stuff after each time you use the bathroom. Add a few drops of lemon juice to make it more palatable.

Sun Exposure

Belize is located a scant 13-18 degrees of latitude from the equator, so the sun's rays strike the earth's surface at a more direct angle than in northern countries. The result is that you will burn faster and sweat up to twice as much as you are used to. Did we mention that you should drink lots of water?

Ideally, do like the majority of the locals do, and stay out of the sun between 10am and 2pm. It's a great time to take a nap anyway. Use sunscreen of at least SPF 30, and wear a hat and pants. Should you overdo it in the sun, make sure to drink lots of fluids—that means water, not beer (or at least water and beer). Treat sunburns with aloe gel or, better yet, find a fresh aloe plant to break open and rub over your skin.

DISEASES AND COMMON AILMENTS

There is moderate incidence of hepatitis B in Belize. Avoid contact with bodily fluids or bodily waste. Get vaccinated if you anticipate close contact with nature or plan to reside in Central America for an extended period of time. Get a rabies vaccination if you intend to spend a long time in Belize. Should you be bitten by an infected dog, rodent, or bat, immediately cleanse the wound with lots of soap and get prompt medical attention.

Tuberculosis is spread by sneezing or coughing, and the infected person may not know he or she is a carrier. If you are planning to spend more than four weeks in Belize (or plan on spending time in the Belize jail), consider having a tuberculin skin test performed before and after visiting. Tuberculosis is a serious and possibly fatal disease but can be treated with several medications. No cases of cholera have been reported in Belize since 2000.

Ciguatera

This is a toxin occasionally found in large reef fish. It is not a common circumstance, but it is possible for groupers, snappers, and barracuda to carry this toxin. If, after eating these fish, you experience diarrhea, nausea, numbness, or heart arrhythmia, see a doctor immediately. The toxin is found in certain algae on reefs in all the tropical areas of the world. Fish do nibble on the coral, and if they happen to find this algae, over a period of time the toxin accumulates in their systems. The longer they live and the larger they get, the more probable it is they will carry the toxin, which is not destroyed when cooked.

Dengue Fever

Dengue, or "bone-breaking fever," is a flulike, mosquito-carried illness that will put a stop to your fun in Central America like a baseball bat to the head. Dengue's occurrence is extremely low in Belize, but a few dozen cases are still reported each year. There is no vaccine, but dengue's effects can be successfully minimized with plenty of rest, acetaminophen (for the fever and aches), and as much water and hydration salts as you can manage. Dengue itself is undetectable in a blood test, but a low platelet count indicates its presence. If you believe you have dengue, you should get a blood test as soon as possible, to make sure it's not the hemorrhagic variety, which can be fatal if untreated.

Diarrhea and Dysentery

Generally, simple cases of diarrhea in the absence of other symptoms are nothing more serious than "traveler's diarrhea." If you do get a good case, your best bet is to let it pass naturally. Diarrhea is your body's way of flushing out the bad stuff, so constipating medicines like Imodium A-D are not recommended, as they keep the bacteria (or whatever is causing your intestinal distress) within your system. Save the Imodium (or any other liquid glue) for emergency situations like long bus rides or a hot date. Most importantly, drink lots of water! Not replacing the fluids and electrolytes you are losing will make you feel much worse than you need to. If the diarrhea persists for more than 48 hours, is bloody, or is accompanied by a fever, see a health professional immediately. That said, know that all bodies react differently to the changes in diet, schedule, and stress that go along with traveling, and many visitors to Belize stay entirely regular and solid throughout their trips.

Pay attention to your symptoms: Diarrhea can also be a sign of amoebic (parasitic) or bacillary (bacterial) dysentery, both caused by some form of fecal-oral contamination. Often accompanied by nausea, vomiting, and a mild fever, dysentery is easily confused with other diseases, so don't try to self-diagnose. Stool-sample examinations are cheap, can be performed at most clinics and hospitals, and are your first step to getting better. Bacillary dysentery is treatable with antibiotics; amoebic dysentery is treated with one of a variety of drugs that kill off all the flora in your intestinal tract. Of these, Flagyl is the best known, but other non-FDA-approved treatments like tinidazole are commonly available, cheap, and effective. Do not drink alcohol with these drugs, and eat something like yogurt or acidophilus pills to repopulate your tummy.

Malaria

By all official accounts, malaria is present in Belize, although you'll be hard-pressed to find anybody—Belizean or expat—who has actually experienced or even heard of a case of it. Still, many travelers choose to take a weekly prophylaxis of chloroquine or its equivalent. The CDC specifically recommends travelers to Belize use brand-name Aralen pills (500 mg for adults), although you should ask your doctor for the latest drug on the market. A small percentage of people have negative reactions to chloroquine, including nightmares, rashes, or hair loss. Alternative treatments are available, but the best method of all is to not get bitten by mosquitoes, which transmit the disease.

BITES AND STINGS

Thousands of people dive in Belize's Caribbean and hike its forests every day of the year without incident. The information on possible bites and stings is only to let you know what's out there, not to scare you into remaining in your resort. Know what you're getting into and be sure your guide does as well, and then get into it.

Botfly

Also known as *torsalo,* screw-worm, or *Dermatobia hominis,* this insect looks like the common household fly. The big difference is that the botfly deposits its eggs on mosquitoes, which then implant them in an unsuspecting warm-blooded host. Burrowing quickly under the skin, the maggot sets up housekeeping. To breathe, it sticks a tiny tube through the skin, and there it stays until one of two things happen: You kill it, or it graduates and leaves home (to witness this, Google "botfly removal" and get ready for an eyeful).

A botfly bite starts out looking like a mosquito bite, but if the bite gets red and tender instead of healing, get it checked out. Though uncomfortable and distasteful, it's not a serious health problem if it doesn't get infected. A tiny glob of petroleum jelly or tobacco over the air hole often works to draw out or suffocate the creature; just make sure you squeeze all of it out.

Mosquitoes and Sand Flies

Mosquitoes are most active during the rainy season (June-Nov.) and in areas with stagnant water, like marshes, puddles, and rice fields. They are more common in the lower, flatter regions of Belize than they are in the hills, though even in the highlands, old tires, cans, and roadside puddles can provide the habitat necessary to produce swarms of mosquitoes. The mosquito that carries malaria is active during the evening and at night, while the dengue fever courier is active during the day, from dawn to dusk. They are both relatively simple to combat, and ensuring you don't get bitten is the best prophylaxis for preventing the diseases.

First and foremost, limit the amount of skin you expose—long sleeves, pants, and socks will do more to prevent bites than the strongest chemical repellent. Choose accommodations with good screens, and if this is not possible, use a fan to blow airborne insects away from your body as you sleep. Avoid being outside or unprotected in the hour before sunset, when mosquito activity is heaviest, and use a mosquito net tucked underneath your mattress when you sleep. Consider purchasing a lightweight backpackers' net, either freestanding or to hang from the ceiling, before you come south—mosquito nets are more expensive in Belize than at home. Some accommodations provide nets; others are truly free of biting bugs and don't need them. If you know where you're staying, ask before you arrive whether you'll need a net. Once in Belize, you can purchase mosquito coils, which burn slowly, releasing a mosquito-repelling smoke; they're cheap and convenient, but try to place them so you're not breathing the toxic smoke yourself.

Sand flies don't carry any diseases that we know about, but, man, do they *suck!* Actually, these tiny midges, or no-see-ums, bite. Hard. They breed in wet, sandy areas and are only fought by the wind (or a well-screened room). Don't scratch those bites! If you do, you'll not only have massive red bumps on your skin, but they will itch for days, even in the middle of the night, and you risk infection. For prevention, any thick oil is usually enough of a barrier—most people like baby oil or hempseed oil, and some swear that a hint of lavender scent in the oil keeps sand flies away too.

Scorpions, Spiders, and Snakes

Scorpions are common in Belize, especially in dark corners, at beaches, and in piles of wood. Belizean scorpions look nasty—black and big—but their stings are no more harmful than that of a bee and are described by some as what a cigarette burn feels like. Your lips and tongue may feel a little numb, but the venom is nothing compared to that of their smaller, translucent cousins in Mexico. Needless to say, to people who are prone to anaphylactic shock, it can be a more serious or life-threatening experience. Everyone has heard that when in a rainforest, never put on your shoes without checking the insides—good advice—and always give your clothes a good visual going-over and a vigorous shake before putting them on. Scorpions occasionally drop out of thatched ceilings.

Don't worry; despite the prevalence of all kinds of arachnids, including big, hairy tarantulas, spiders do not aggressively seek out people to bite and do way more good than harm by eating things like Chagas bugs. If you'd rather the spiders didn't share your personal space, shake out your bedclothes before going to sleep and check your shoes before putting your feet in them.

Of the 59 species of snakes that have been identified in Belize, at least nine are venomous, most notably the fer-de-lance (locally called a "Tommy Goff"), considered the most dangerous snake in Central America, and the coral snake. The chances of the average visitor being bitten are slim. Reportedly, most snakebite victims are children. However, if you plan on extensive jungle exploration, check with your doctor before you leave home. Antivenin is available, doesn't require refrigeration, and keeps indefinitely. It's also wise to be prepared for an allergic reaction to the antivenin—bring an antihistamine and epinephrine. The most important thing to remember if bitten: *Don't panic and don't run.* Physical exertion and panic cause the venom to travel through your body much faster. Lie down and stay calm; have someone carry you to a doctor. Do not cut the wound, use a tourniquet, or ingest alcoholic beverages.

Marine Hazards

Anemones and sea urchins live in Belize waters. Some can be dangerous if touched or stepped on. The long-spined black sea urchin can inflict great pain, and its poison can cause an uncomfortable infection. Don't think that you're safe in a wetsuit, booties, and gloves. The spines easily slip through the rubber, and the urchin is encountered at all depths. If you should run into one of the spines, remove it quickly and carefully, disinfect the wound, and apply antibiotic cream. If you have difficulty removing the spine, or if it breaks, see a doctor—pronto! Local remedies include urinating on the wound if nothing else is available.

Tiny brown gel-encased globules called *pica-pica* produce a horrible rash; look for clouds of these guys around any coral patch before getting in. Avoid the bottom side of a moon jellyfish, as well as the Portuguese man-of-war (usually only in March). Sea wasps are tiny four-tentacled menaces that deliver a sting. Many varieties of fire coral will make you wish you hadn't come so close. Their transparent hair-like spines are hard to spot in the water and divers tend to get too close without realizing it. Wearing a full wetsuit is your best bet to prevent cuts.

Cuts from coral, even if just a scratch, will often become infected. If you should get a deep cut, or if bits of coral are left in the wound, see a doctor.

MEDICAL CARE

Although there are hospitals and health clinics in most urban areas and towns, care is extremely limited compared with more developed countries. Serious injuries or illness may require evacuation to another country, and you should consider picking up cheap travel insurance that covers such a need—otherwise, you're looking at US$12,000 just for the medevac transportation.

Many Belizean doctors and hospitals require immediate cash payment for health services, sometimes prior to providing treatment. Uninsured travelers or travelers whose insurance does not provide coverage in Belize may face extreme difficulties if serious medical treatment is needed. **International Medical Group** (www.imglobal.com) is one reliable provider that offers short-term insurance specifically for overseas travelers and expats for very reasonable rates.

Belize Medical Associates (5791 St. Thomas St., tel. 501/223-0302, 501/223-0302, www.belizemedical.com) is the only private hospital in Belize City. They provide 24-hour assistance and a wide range of specialties. Look under "Hospitals" in the yellow pages for an updated listing of other options. In Santa Elena, **La Loma Luz Hospital** (tel. 501/824-2087 or 501/804-2985, www.lalomaluz.org) offers primary care as well as 24-hour emergency services and is one of the best private hospitals in the country.

First-Aid Kit

At the very minimum, consider the following items for your first-aid kit: rehydration salts, sterile bandages or gauze, moleskin for blister prevention, antiseptic cream, strong sunblock (SPF 30), aloe gel, some kind of general antibiotic for intestinal trouble, acetaminophen (Tylenol) for pain and fevers, eye drops (for dust), and antifungal cream (clotrimazole).

Medications and Prescriptions

Many medications are available in pharmacies in Belize. Definitely plan on the conservative side: Bring adequate supplies of all your prescribed medications in their original containers, clearly labeled and in date; in addition, carry a signed, dated letter from your physician describing all medical conditions and listing your medications, including their generic names. If carrying syringes or needles, carry a physician's letter documenting their medical necessity. Pack all medications in your carry-on bag and, if possible, put a duplicate supply in the checked luggage. If you wear glasses or contacts, bring an extra pair. If you have significant allergies or chronic medical problems, wear a medical alert bracelet.

Female travelers taking contraceptives should know the generic name for the drug they use. Condoms are cheap and easy to find. Any corner pharmacy will have them, even in small towns of just a few thousand people.

CRIME

Most of the crime in Belize (besides drug possession and trafficking) is petty theft and burglary, although gang-related violence in Belize City and parts of Ambergris Caye is a worsening problem. It's best not to wear expensive jewelry when traveling. And don't carry large amounts of money, your passport, or your plane tickets if not necessary; if you must carry these things, wear a money belt under your clothes. Most hotels have safe-deposit boxes. Don't flaunt cameras and video equipment or leave them in sight in cars when sightseeing, especially in some parts of Belize City. This is a poor country and petty theft is its number-one crime.

It is not wise to wander around alone on foot late at night in Belize City or anywhere. Go out with others if possible, and take a taxi. Most Belizeans are friendly, decent people; however, as in every community, there are a small percentage of unscrupulous thieves who will steal anything given the opportunity. To many Belizeans, foreigners come off as "rich," whether they are or not. Local hustlers are quite creative when it comes to conning you out of some cash. Keep your wits about you, pull out of conversations that appear headed in that direction, don't give out your hotel name or room number or mention them where they can be overheard by strangers. If you're riding a bike late at night, don't put your purse or valuables in the bike's basket. Instead, conceal any cash, credit cards, or phones on your person. There have been incidents where riders were thrown off of their bikes to get access to their valuables. Better yet, try not to carry anything valuable (credit cards, passport, or too much cash) on you at all while out and about, whether during the day or night.

In emergencies, dial **911** or **90** for police assistance. The number for fire and ambulance is also 90.

Police

If you are the victim of a crime while overseas, in addition to reporting it to local police, contact your embassy or consulate as soon as possible. The embassy or consulate staff can assist you in finding appropriate medical care and contacting family members or friends, and will explain how funds can be transferred to you. Although the investigation and prosecution of the crime is solely the responsibility of local authorities, consular officers can help you to understand the local criminal justice process and to find an attorney if needed. Belize police detectives and tourism police respond quickly and take these matters—even near misses—seriously.

Belizean police can hold somebody for 48 hours with no charges (one U.S. embassy warden called prison conditions in Belize "medieval," though this situation is improving). Some police officers have been arrested for rape and routinely beat and torture detainees (usually Belizeans). On the whole, though, most officers are good folks, making the best of a poorly paid job with very few resources. Don't try to bribe them if you're in trouble—you'll only contribute to a more corrupt system that does not need any encouragement.

Drugs

Belize's modern history began with law-breaking pirates hiding out among the hundreds of cayes, lagoons, and uninhabited coastlines of the territory. The same natural features have made Belize a fueling stopover for Colombian cocaine traffickers. The drug runners' practice of paying off their Belizean helpers with product (in addition to sums of cash) has created a national market for cocaine and crack with devastating effects, especially in Orange Walk Town and numerous coastal communities.

The U.S. Drug Enforcement Agency (DEA) is active in Belize—as it is throughout Central America—to battle the flow of cocaine and other illegal drugs; the agency provides boat patrols, overflights, drug war technology and herbicides, and sniffing dogs at roadside checkpoints.

Cannabis sativa grows naturally in the soils and climate of Belize, although the country is no longer the major producer it once was. In the early 1980s, the DEA put an end to that with chemical-spraying programs, seizing and destroying 800 tons of marijuana in one year. Today, small-scale production continues, primarily for the domestic market. Some argue that the job vacuum created by marijuana suppression led directly to Belize's role in the trafficking of cocaine and the subsequent entrance of crack into Belizean communities.

Foreign travelers will most likely be offered pot at some point during a visit. Legally, marijuana prohibition is alive and well in Belize, despite widespread use throughout the population. The policy allows harsh penalties for possession of even tiny quantities for both nationals and visitors alike.

Information and Services

MONEY

The currency unit is the Belize dollar (BZD), which has been steady at BZD$2 to US$1 for some years. While prices are given in U.S. dollars in this book, travelers should be prepared to pay in Belizean currency on the street, aboard boats, in cafés, and at other smaller establishments. Everyone else accepts U.S. dollars.

When you buy or sell currency at a bank, be sure to retain proof of sale. The following places are authorized to buy or sell foreign currency: Atlantic Bank Ltd., Scotiabank, Barclays Bank, Belize Bank of Commerce and Industry, and Belize Global Travel Services Ltd. All are close together near the plaza in Belize City and in other cities. Most banks are open until 1pm Monday-Friday and until 11am Saturday. You can also change money, sometimes at a rate a bit better than 2:1, at Casas de Cambio. But because Casas de Cambio must charge the official rate, many people still go to the black market, which gives a better rate.

At the Mexico-Belize border, you'll be approached by money changers (and you can bet they don't represent the banks). Many travelers buy just enough Belizean dollars to get themselves into the city and to the banks. Depending on your mode of transportation and destination, these money changers can be helpful. Strictly speaking, though, this is illegal—so suit yourself. The exchange rate is the same, but you'll have no receipt of sale. If selling a large quantity of Belizean dollars back to the bank, you might be asked for that proof.

Banks

Many banks are only open until 1pm or 2pm Monday-Thursday (staying open a bit later on

Friday) and are often closed for lunch. Banks are always closed Saturday afternoon and Sunday. Automated teller machines (ATMs) are available in nearly all major Belizean towns, but they may operate on different card networks (Plus, Cirrus, etc.). You may have to try a few to get your card to work; it's best to check before traveling. They're also often out of cash, particularly close to the weekends or major holidays.

Costs

Make no mistake: Belize vies with Costa Rica for being the most expensive country in Central America, and backpackers entering Belize from Mexico, Guatemala, and Honduras can expect some serious sticker shock after crossing the border. This was true even before the advent of tourism because of the import-reliant economy and whatever other invisible market hands guide such things. Shoestring travelers squeaking by on US$25-50 per person per day in Belize are most likely stone sober and eating street tacos three times a day; they are not paying for tours or taxis, and they are surely not diving in the Blue Hole. They can still have a grand old time, though, camped out in the bush (or in a US$10 room), doing lots of self-guided hiking, paddling, and cultural exploring. It's possible to travel on this little—but it depends on your comfort zone and definition of a good time.

If you've only got a seven-day vacation, you won't have to stretch your dollars over as many weeks or months as Jimmie Backpacker and his dog, Dreddie, and can thus spend more on lodging and activities. Figure at least US$100 pp per day if you want to pay for day trips and don't want to share a bath; serious divers or anglers should add a bit more. Weeklong packages at many dive and jungle resorts run US$1,000-1,600 and go up from there.

There are usually low-budget, decent quality exceptions to the rule across Belize, and I've tried to point all of those out in each region. In general, though, prices are high and getting higher. Many mid- and upscale accommodations have raised their rates by as much as 20 percent—and not all have increased the quality of their service to match. Alcohol is always a good indicator: A bottle of One Barrel Rum is peaking at US$12 in most stores; a six-pack of Belikin beer can go for US$10.

Be prepared for some additional taxes and service charges on your bill, which sometimes are and sometimes are not included in quoted rates:

- General sales tax (GST): 10 percent
- Hotel tax: 9 percent
- Service charge (often placed on bill): 10-15 percent
- Airport departure tax: US$18.75

If you use your credit card, it will cost you a little more at most businesses, sometimes an extra 3-5 percent of the bill.

Tipping

Most restaurants and hotels include a 10-15 percent service charge on the bill; if they don't, you should pay this amount yourself. It is not customary to tip taxi drivers unless they help you with your luggage. Always tip your tour guide 10-15 percent if he or she has made your trip an enjoyable one.

MEDIA AND COMMUNICATIONS
Mail

Posting a letter or postcard is easy and cheap, costing well under US$1, and the stamps are gorgeous. If you visit the outlying cities or cayes, bring your mail to Belize City to post—it's more apt to get to its destination quickly. Post offices are located in the center of (or nearby) all villages and cities in Belize, although they usually don't look too post-officey from the outside. You can receive mail in any town without getting a P.O. box—just have the mail addressed to your name, care of "General Delivery," followed by the town, district, and "Belize."

FedEx, DHL, and other international couriers are widely available, and the Mailboxes, Etc. in Belize City (on Front St., just up from the Water Taxi Terminal) can take care of most of your mailing and package needs. Sending mail within Belize, you can either use the post office system or hand your package to a bus driver or go through the bus station office.

Cell Phones
Some car rental companies offer a free cell phone; always ask. If not, they'll rent you one. Otherwise, **DigiCell** (www.digicell.bz) offers prepaid temporary service to travelers. Get it at BTL's Airport Service Center, or bring your own GSM 1900 MHz handset and purchase a SIM pack from any DigiCell distributor nationwide. There are several local cellular services, both analog and digital, and coverage along roadways and in major towns is decent but still improving. You'll need your passport or ID with you when visiting a BTL (Belize Telecommunications Limited) store to purchase a SIM card—by law all cell numbers must now be registered.

Smart Phones (Mile 2½, Northern Hwy., Belize City, tel. 501/678-1010, www.smart-bz. com) is more user-friendly and cheaper than BTL and the rest, offering roaming service on your CDMA 800 MHz phone from home (including Verizon and Sprint). Activation fee is US$20, and then you use prepaid cards available throughout the country.

Local Calls
To make a call within Belize, there's no need to dial the 501 country code. Simply punch in the seven digit number you wish to reach. There are no additional city codes to worry about.

International Calls
To call out of Belize, find a phone with international direct dialing service, then dial the international access code **00,** followed by your country code, and then the city or area code and the number. The country code for Canada and the United States is 1, Britain is 44, and Australia is 61. BTL's telephone directory has a complete listing of country codes. An (often cheaper) alternative is to dial 10-10-199 instead of 00, followed by the country code, etc. Although they are not toll-free from Belize, 800 numbers are dialed as they are written, preceded by the 00.

Belize's country code is **501.** To receive a call in Belize from the United States, for example, tell the caller to dial 011 to tap into the international network, followed by 501 and your seven-digit number. To call collect to

There's a local post office in every district.

Belize from other countries, dial the MCI operator at 800/265-5328.

Public Telephones

Buy a prepaid phone card from **Belize Telecommunications Limited** (BTL, www. btl.net) and punch in the card's numbers every time you borrow a phone or use a pay phone. All towns also have a local BTL office, usually identified by a giant red and white radio tower somewhere very nearby; they can place calls anywhere in the country or the world for you and will assign you to a semiprivate booth after they've dialed the number. They can also connect you to your homeland phone carrier. Note: According to one BTL employee, credit-card calls made through hotel phones are expensive because the touch-tone "international operator" charges US$16 per minute.

VoIP Services

Skype and VoIP (voice over Internet protocol) are finally available in Belize, unrestricted and—believe it or not—only a recent development. Free VoIP services (like Skype) offer dirt-cheap rates on international calls and are getting better to use by the day. Prior to April 2013, BTL blocked full and open access to VoIP-based services and applications. You can now use Skype freely wherever you get free Wi-Fi access, thus saving on international calls.

Internet Access

Web access is widely available throughout the country and is improving all the time. Crappy dial-up connections are now the exception rather than the norm, and broadband (DSL, cable, and satellite) is springing up everywhere. If you're in town for a while, many Internet businesses have monthly memberships that include unlimited access. You are welcome to sign up for a BTL account if you don't have your own ISP (Internet service provider), but that may lead to more headaches then you need, and there are many other options.

Wireless Internet (Wi-Fi) access is increasingly available in Belize's accommodations, bars, and restaurants. I won't go so far as to tell you to *expect* wireless access yet—particularly on the cayes, where service can be sporadic at best—but if it's a concern of yours, definitely inquire whether your hotel has it or not. Most of these connections are free, with the exception of BTL Hotspots, which are US$16 per 24-hour period (plus tax!), and it's your only option at a handful of upscale hotels, including the Radisson and the Inn at Robert's Grove. Note that there is no network or cell service on some of the more remote deep southern cayes, like the Sapodilla Cayes, but isn't that the idea of an island escape?

Newspapers and Magazines

Four weekly, highly politicized Belizean newspapers come out on Friday, with occasional midweek editions, and you'll find many a Belizean conducting the weekly ritual of reading his or her favorite over a cup of instant coffee and then going to happy hour to yap away about the latest scandal. *Amandala* and the *Reporter* seem to be the most objective and respected of these rags. The other two are *The Belize Times* and *The Guardian*. There are also publications in San Pedro and Placencia.

The Image Factory in Belize City is a good place for books and periodicals, and there are only a couple of other bookshops in the country. In most hotel gift shops, you'll find at least a few colorful Belizean history and picture books put out by Cubola Productions, a local publisher specializing in all things Belize, including maps, atlases, short stories, novels, and poems written by Belizeans. Cubola's publications give great insight into the country.

You will not find the *International Herald Tribune* on every newsstand like in other destinations. In fact, you probably won't find it at all. Check with the Radisson Hotel or Fort Street Guest House in Belize City, where you can sometimes find the *Miami Herald*,

Useful Numbers

- Police, fire, ambulance: 90 or 911

- San Pedro Hyperbaric Chamber: 501/226-2851 or 501/604-7591

- Diver's Alert Network: 001-919/648-8111

- Directory assistance: 113 or 115

- To report crimes: 0800/922-8477

- To report child abuse: 0800/776-8328

- Operator assistance: 114 or 115

- Date, time, and temperature: 121

- Belize Coast Guard: 501/222-5262

- Belize Port Authority: 501/232-9440

- Belize Tourism Police Unit: 501/227-1440

a relatively recent *Newsweek,* or if you're lucky, the *New York Times* or the *Times* of London. Brodie's (Albert St.) and the Book Center (North Front St.) also carry American magazines.

MAPS AND TOURIST INFORMATION
Maps
The most readily available and up-to-date map of Belize is published by International Travel Maps, whose 1:250,000 map of Belize makes a useful addition to any guidebook (or wall). The best, biggest country map to hang on your wall at home, or in your classroom (it's way too big to use as a travel guide) is a physical-political 1:265,000 scale, distributed by Cubola Productions and available at Angelus Press in Belize City for US$40. All of Belize's most heavily touristed areas create updated town maps, found most often at visitor information booths and car (or golf cart) rental places.

The **Government of Belize Land Department** in Belmopan has detailed topographic maps for the entire country—spendy at US$40 per quad, but vital if you're doing

any serious backcountry travel. The British Army and United Kingdom Ordinance Survey have created a number of map series of various scales, but tracking them down will be a challenge.

Tourist Information
The **Belize Tourism Board** (BTB, 64 Regent St., tel. 501/227-2420, U.S. tel. 800/624-0686, info@travelbelize.org, www.travelbelize.org) has a central office in Belize City, near the Mopan Hotel. The **Belize Tourism Industry Association** (10 N. Park St., tel. 501/227-1144, www.btia.org) can also answer many of your questions and give you lodging suggestions. **The Belize Hotel Association** (BHA, 13 Cork St., Belize City, tel. 501/223-0669, www.belizehotels.org) is a nonprofit industry organization of some of the country's most respected resorts and lodges. The BHA can help you decide where to stay.

You'll find more information at the **Embassy of Belize** in the United States (2535 Massachusetts Ave. NW, Washington, DC 20008, U.S. tel. 202/332-9636, www.embassyofbelize.org) and also the **Caribbean Tourism Association** (80 Broad St., Suite

3302, New York, NY 10004, U.S. tel. 212/635-9530, www.onecaribbean.org).

WEIGHTS AND MEASURES

The local time is Greenwich mean time minus six hours year-round, the same as U.S. central standard time; Belize does not use daylight saving time. Electricity is the U.S. standard 110 volts, 60 cycles, and uses U.S. two-prong plugs. Most distances are measured in inches, feet, yards, and miles, although there is some limited use of the metric system.

Time

As in many other Central American and Caribbean cultures, the Belizean clock is not as rigidly precise as it is in other parts of the world. "Nine o'clock am" is not necessarily a moment in time that occurs once a morning, as it is a general guideline that could extend an hour or two in either direction (usually later). As Creoles say, "Time longa den da roop, mon" ("time is longer than the rope").

A great deal of patience is required of the traveler who wishes to adapt to this looser concept of time. Buses generally leave when they are scheduled, but they may stop for frustratingly long breaks during the journey. Don't use Belize Time as an excuse to be late for your tour bus pickup, and don't get angry when your taxi driver stops to briefly chat and laugh with a friend.

Resources

Phrasebook

KRIOL

I was once told that you're only a true Belizean if you speak Kriol. It's the first thing you'll hear when you arrive in Belize—the accent, the intonation, and the sentences that chop away at articles and verbs. Creole, or Kriol, is the lingua franca here. Like most patois tongues in the Caribbean, it has its roots in the days of slavery, when the workers in mahogany camps were exposed to English and mixed it with their own West African dialects, hence the choppy grammar and the borrowed English words. Over time, efforts were made to ensure that Kriol was properly studied, written, and recorded as a language, thanks to the National Kriol Council, created in 1995 to promote all aspects of the Creole culture. Keeping this language going has been their goal, as a way of instilling a sense of identity and cultural pride in its people. It's now spoken and understood by almost all Belizeans, even non-Creoles, and knowing a couple of phrases is a great way to immerse and break the ice.

Basic Phrases

Gud maanin! Good morning!
Weh gaan an? What's up?
Aarite. All right.
Cho! What on earth!
Weh yuh naym? What's your name?
You da Belize? Are you from Belize?
Gyal. Girl.
Da weh time? What time is it?
Mi naym da ... My name is ...
Lata. See you later.

Ah tayad/mi tayad. I'm tired.
Weh/weh-paat ... Where is ... ?
Evryting gud/aarite. Everything's fine.
Haul your rass! Get the hell out of here!
Fu chroo? Really? (Is that right?)
Mi love Bileez! I love Belize!

Sayings

Wahnti wahnti kyah geti an geti geti nuh wahnti. You always want what you can't have.
Dah no so, dah naily so. Where there's smoke, there's fire.
Wait bruk down bridge. Don't make me wait too long.
Sleep wit' yo' own eye. Only rely on what you know, not what others tell you.
One one craboo fill barrel. Every little bit counts (craboo is a Belizean fruit).
Ah wah know who seh Kriol noh gat no kulcha? Who said the Creole don't have any culture? (A phrase coined by renowned Belizean Creole artist and performer, Leela Vernon.)

GARÍFUNA

A mix of Arawak, Carib, traces of West African dialects, French, and Spanish, the Garífuna language is being spoken less and less by the younger generation and isn't taught in Belize's school system. But it's hard to believe that this is a dying tongue after spending time in the south and hearing Garinagu addressing each other in their language every day. When I took the bus from Hopkins to Dangriga, and even walking around the village and town, there was no Creole and no English exchanged, just Garífuna. If you're feeling brave, you too can practice and use these phrases to break the ice.

Basic Phrases
Mabuiga! Welcome!
Buiti binafi. Good morning.
Buiti rabounweyu. Good afternoon.

Buiti guñoun. Good night.
Ida bian? How are you?
Magadientina. I'm fine.
Seremein. Thank you.
Ka biri? What is your name?
... niri bai My name is ....
Uwati megeiti. You are welcome.
Ka fidu ínwirúbei? What's up?

Suggested Reading

Start with Belizean writers, particularly the novels of Zee Edgell, and then continue with the catalog of **Cubola Productions** (www. cubola.com), a publishing company whose Belizean writers series includes six anthologies of short stories, poetry, drama, folk tales, and works by women writers. Cubola also publishes sociology, anthropology, and education texts; seek them out at any bookstore or gift shop in Belize, or order a few titles before your trip. **Angelus Press** is the other main publisher of Belizean writers. There is a large Angelus Press store in Belize City, as well as in other districts. You'll also want to read a book—or six—by **Emory King;** King arrived in Belize in 1953 when his yacht crashed on the reef at English Caye and has been talking and writing about his adopted country ever since.

ARCHAEOLOGY AND MAYA CULTURE
Coe, Michael D. *The Maya,* 8th ed. New York: Thames and Hudson, 2011. This updated classic, which has been in print for nearly 50 years, attempts to understand the "most intellectually sophisticated and aesthetically refined pre-Columbian culture." This edition has information on new discoveries, including the polychrome murals of Calakmul and evidence of pre-Classic sophistication. Coe, an archaeologist,

anthropologist, epigrapher, and author, is a forefather of Mayan studies. This book is mandatory reading for both amateur Mayanists and pros.

De Landa, Friar Diego. *Yucatán: Before and After the Conquest.* New York: Dover Publications, 1978 (translation of original manuscript written in 1566). The same man who provided some of the best, most lasting descriptions of ancient Maya also singlehandedly destroyed the most Mayan artifacts and writings of anyone in history.

González, Gaspar Pedro. *13 B'aktun: Mayan Visions of 2012 and Beyond.* Berkeley, CA: North Atlantic Books, 2010. González is a Q'anjobal Mayan novelist, philosopher, and scholar from Guatemala. This book, translated to English by Dr. Robert Sitler, is unlike any other you'll read on the subject. It is written as a deep, lyrical dialogue—not just about 2012, but about all of creation, blending "past and present thought into a persuasive plan for moving into the new era."

Jenkins, John Major. *The 2012 Story: The Myths, Fallacies, and Truth Behind the Most Intriguing Date in History.* New York: Jeremy P. Tarcher, 2009. Jenkins is one of the most prolific, passionate 2012-ologists out there. *The 2012 Story* is his most all-encompassing book yet, covering the entire story—from the ancients' forward-reaching stone inscriptions to the modern-day 2012 meme and a summary of his and others' work on the subject.

FICTION

Edgell, Zee. *Beka Lamb*. Portsmouth, NH: Heinemann, 1982. The first internationally recognized Belizean novel, this story of a girl named Beka who is growing up with her country is required reading for all Belizean high schoolers and offers an excellent view of Belizean family life, history, and politics.

Lukowiak, Ken. *Marijuana Time*. London: Orion, 2000. Follow the author's experiences on a six-month "hardship posting" to Belize in 1983 with the British military: "The long days are palliated by a constant and increasingly compulsive supply of drugs and japes, until he starts using his position in the army post-room to send improbably large bundles of the stuff home—to his army flat in Aldershot."

Miller, Carlos Ledson. *Belize: A Novel*. Bloomington, IN: Xlibris, 1999. This history-laden piece of fiction offers an impressively thorough snapshot of Belize over the last four decades of the 20th century.

HEALTH

Arvigo, Rosita. *Sastun: One Woman's Apprenticeship with a Maya Healer and Their Efforts to Save the Vani*. San Francisco: Harper, 1995. One of the better-known books about Belize, this tells the story of the American-born author's training with Elijio Panti, the best-known Mayan medicine man in Central America. It takes place in the remote, roadless expanse of the Cayo District in western Belize.

Bezruchka, Stephen. *The Pocket Doctor: A Passport to Healthy Travel*. Seattle: Mountaineers Books, 1999.

Schroeder, Dirk. *Staying Healthy in Asia, Africa, and Latin America*. Emeryville, CA: Avalon Travel, 2000. An excellent resource that fits in your pocket for easy reference.

Werner, David. *Where There Is No Doctor*. Berkeley, CA: Hesperian Foundation, 1992. A standard in the field.

HISTORY

Shoman, Assad. *Thirteen Chapters of a History of Belize*. Belize City: Angelus Press, 1994. A no-nonsense history of Belize from a Belizean perspective.

Sutherland, Anne. *The Making of Belize: Globalization in the Margins*. London: Bergin & Garvey, 1998. This book deserves to be read by any visitor to Belize, whether arriving as a tourist or as a volunteer with one of the many international conservation organizations now operating there.

Wilk, Richard. *Home Cooking in the Global Village: Caribbean Food from Buccaneers to Ecotourists*. New York: Palgrave Macmillan, 2006. Using food to describe Belize's longtime struggle within "the great paradox of globalization," Wilk raises questions like "How can you stay local and relish your own home cooking, while tasting the delights of the global marketplace?" Includes menus, recipes, and "bad colonial poetry."

NATURE AND FIELD GUIDES

As Belize is one of the most exhaustively studied tropical countries in the world, there are innumerable references that span every conceivable niche of flora, fauna, and geology. They come in massive coffee-table sizes with color plates as well as in pocket-size field guides: *Tarantulas of Belize, Hummingbirds of Belize, Orchids of Belize,* and so on. Following are a few titles that make up the tip of the iceberg for this category.

Arvigo, Rosita, and Michael Balick (foreword by Mickey Hart). *Rainforest Remedies: 100 Healing Herbs of Belize.* Twin Lakes, WI: Lotus Press, 1998. A reliable and respected guide to medicinal plants found in Belize and herbal remedies of Maya healers.

Beletsky, Les. *Belize and Northern Guatemala: The Ecotravellers' Wildlife Guide.* San Diego, CA: Academic Press, 1999. One of the best reasonably sized general nature guides to the area, with abundant color plates for all types of fauna.

Chalif, Edward L., and Roger Tory Peterson. *Peterson Field Guide to Mexican Birds.* New York: Houghton Mifflin Harcourt, 1999. This is one of the best birder bibles for this region.

Dunn, Jon L., and Jonathan Alderfer. *National Geographic Field Guide to the Birds of North America.* Washington, DC: National Geographic, 2006. A gorgeous field guide worth lugging into the jungle.

Jones, H. Lee, and Dana Gardner, illustrator. *Birds of Belize.* Austin, TX: University of Texas Press, 2003. This is the long-awaited, much-acclaimed bible of Belize birding (say *that* three times fast); it's a big book (445 pages, 56 color plates, 28 figures, 234 maps), prompting some birders I met to cut out all the plates and travel with those only.

Sayers, Brendan, and Brett Adams. *Guide to the Orchids of Belize.* Benque Viejo del Carmen, Belize: Cubola Productions, 2009. This is an excellent field guide to the many orchids found throughout Belize.

Stevens, Katie. *Jungle Walk: Birds and Beasts of Belize, Central America.* Belize City: Angelus Press, 1991. Order through International Expeditions, tel. 800/633-4734.

PHOTOGRAPHY

Jovaisa, Marius. *Heavenly Belize.* Lithuania: Unseen Pictures, 2009 (www.heavenlybelize.com). This is a magnificent coffee-table tome of aerial photography. The Lithuanian author is an ultralight aircraft pilot who wanted to share the extraordinary vistas he had discovered. If you don't pick it up in Belize, download the iPad version from iTunes, with more multimedia features than just the book.

TRAVEL AND MEMOIR

Barcott, Bruce. *The Last Flight of the Scarlet Macaw: One Woman's Fight to Save the World's Most Beautiful Bird.* New York: Random House, 2008. Fantastic nonfiction narrative about the Chalillo Dam in western Belize, a highly contentious construction project on the upper Macal River in Cayo. The author skillfully lays out the story and characters around the dam business, while providing a sweeping panoramic snapshot of a unique country as it makes its debut in the new global economy.

Bolland, O. Nigel. *Belize: A New Nation in Central America.* Boulder, CO:

Westview, 1986. This book is one of many sociopolitical analyses by this prolific author.

Duffy, Rosaleen. *A Trip Too Far: Ecotourism, Politics and Exploitation.* Sterling, VA: Earthscan, 2002. A critical look at the impacts of ecotourism, using Belize as a case study.

Pattullo, Polly. *Last Resorts: The Cost of Tourism in the Caribbean,* 2nd edition. London: Latin America Bureau, 2005. Pattullo provides an interesting breakdown of how the Caribbean tourism industry is structured, as well

as a hard-hitting commentary on who benefits and how, providing numerous examples from Belize.

Rabinowitz, Alan. *Jaguar: One Man's Struggle to Establish the World's First Jaguar Preserve.* Washington, DC: Island Press/Shearwater Books, 2000 (originally 1986). If you've only got time to read one book on Belize, I recommend this excellent eco-memoir. In addition to telling the true story of his jaguar work in Belize, Rabinowitz gives an alluring glance at Belize's wild postindependence, pre-tourism phase.

Suggested Films

There are many excellent short films on Belize, on both the natural world and cultural issues. Look up Richard and Carol Foster's *Path of the Rain Gods* and Channel 5's *The Sea of Belize* and *The Land of Belize.* Then tune in to www.trphoto.blip.tv, which has some gorgeous educational shorts on Belize; these would be excellent for families to watch together before or after their trip to Belize.

Curse of the Xtabai, by Make-Belize Films (www.makebelizefilms.com). If you're into drama and fiction, check out U.S. producer Matthew Klinck's first feature film. The story revolves around an evil spirit, Xtabai, unleashed onto the population of a Mayan village after an oil company blows open a sealed Mayan cave in San Antonio. What ensues is an attempt to save the villagers from an epidemic of deadly fevers, through sacred tasks as dictated by a Mayan elder.

Punta Soul, produced and directed by Nyasha Laing (www.parandamedia.com). This 2008 documentary film by a Belizean tells the story of Garífuna music as it evolved with the Garífuna people's journey from the Caribbean islands to Central America. Laing addresses how the rhythms continue to influence the cultural revival of the ethnic communities in Belize. Buy the DVD at the Image Factory in Belize City.

Three Kings of Belize, by Katia Paradis. This 2007 film is a beautiful, poignant tribute to Belizean musicians Paul Nabor, Wilfred Peters, and Florencio Mess, who represent Garífuna, Creole, and Mayan music traditions, respectively. Though their music is internationally recognized, they live humble lives in Belizean villages. The film moves at the slow, relaxed pace of Belize itself. To find a copy, go to the Image Factory in Belize City or contact Stonetree Records (www.stonetreerecords.com).

Internet Resources

Ambergris Today
www.ambergristoday.com
Ambergris Caye's top online news and travel publication, run by a dynamic Belizean team, with excellent reviews on the latest and greatest hotels, restaurants, activities and more across the island and other parts of the country.

Belize Audubon Society
www.belizeaudubon.org
Belize Audubon manages national parks and protected areas throughout the country and is the place to go for basic info on visiting them. It also has background information on birding and checklists.

The Belize Forums
www.belizeforum.com/belize
This is one of the more popular forums, inhabited by many prolific and colorful Belize-aholics.

Belize Search
www.belizesearch.com
The premier search engine for all things Belize, with access to 250,000 Belizean web pages and documents (and growing).

Belize Tourism Board
www.travelbelize.org
The official BTB website is helpful for quick background information for anyone planning a trip.

Caye Caulker Vacation
www.cayecaulkervacation.com
The official site of the Belize Tourism Industry Association's Caye Caulker chapter is filled with information on where to stay and how to best spend your time on the island with the best sunsets in Belize, just a 20-minute boat ride from San Pedro.

Destination Belize
www.destinationbelize.com
The online version of the print magazine *Destination Belize* provides a summary on each main tourist destination in the country and a shortlist of things to do and see.

Government of Belize
www.belize.gov.bz
The official page of the federal government, an informative portal to the country.

Naturalight
www.belizenet.com
This is the main portal to the vast Naturalight network, which hosts a variety of sites and forums.

San Pedro Sun
www.sanpedrosun.com
Belizean news and links from this island newspaper.

United States Embassy in Belize
www.belize.usembassy.gov
Official site of the U.S. Embassy in Belize.

List of Maps

Acknowledgments

I want to express my sincere gratitude to all the wonderful friends and contacts in Belize who offered and continue to offer their support and assistance with my numerous inquiries and visits. Your willingness to share expert insights on Belize, whether in tourism, fishing, diving, culture, or wildlife and conservation, among other topics, is beyond appreciated. It has made me a better Belize writer, traveler, and person.

These wonderful folks include my Caye Caulker and Ambergris Caye friends, who are brilliant, selfless Belize advocates: Joanna Arellano, Heidy and Haywood Curry, Stacy Badillo, Gina Badillo, Ernesto Marin, and Dorian Nunez. Your support during my grueling months of guidebook writing and research, two years in a row, kept me sane.

An immense thanks goes to Patricia Ramirez and Ralph Capeling of Splash Dive Center in Placencia, for sharing their in-depth knowledge of the reef and all the diving and snorkeling opportunities along the southern cayes.

Thanks to Tony and Therese Rath, for sharing their love of Dangriga and the Stann Creek District with me, for their hospitality and help in coordinating my crazy schedule. Special thanks to Tony Rath for my author photo—the best one I have of myself after years of travel—and for the gorgeous underwater photos in Belize Cayes. Additional thanks to Roy and Phyllis Cayetano, who kindly welcomed me into their home to answer all my questions on their fascinating Garífuna culture, and to all the residents of Dangriga who shared a slice of their lives with me, including Austin Rodriguez, Marie Sharpe, and the Sabal family.

Thanks to the hard-working business owners, guides, and conservationists who make Belize's tourism industry what it is, and are ready and willing to assist me at any time: Bruno Kuppinger, Leisa Caceres-Carr, Francoise Lays, Dennis Garbutt, Denver Willson-Rymer, and Lee Mcloughlin, among many others. Your passion and dedication are inspiring.

Last but not least, a huge thanks to my wonderful team at Avalon Travel, who worked with me on my editions of *Moon Belize* and *Moon Belize Cayes*: Grace Fujimoto, for believing in my work and Belize expertise; Elizabeth Hansen; Sabrina Young; Erin Raber; Darren Alessi; Lucie Ericksen; Kat Bennett; and the rest of the team.